CW00689875

∾ *worlds in the mirror*

editorial

Wain Farrants
Christopher Kidman
Maureen Ramsay
Robert Clay
Brian Rée
Henning Hansmann

illustrations

Allmut ffrench
Günther Lehr

publishing & design

Nicholas Poole

~ *worlds in the mirror*

Peter Roth

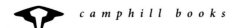

camphill books

edition
1st Edition 2007

publisher
TWT Publications Ltd.,
on behalf of
The Camphill Movement

copyright
© 2007 TWT Publications Ltd.

british library CIP data
A catalogue record of this book is available from the British Library

ISBN
978 1 897839 21 8

acknowledgement
This publication has been assisted by the
Camphill Foundation in the British Isles

~ CONTENTS

~ FIRST YEAR

~ CHRISTMAS & THE HOLY NIGHTS

~ EPIPHANY

~ TOWARD LENT

~ LENT & PASSIONTIDE

publisher's note

Nicholas Poole

A glance at the front matter, and even a brief look at the acknowledgements, reveals just how many hands have been involved in bringing this volume to fruition: a truly enormous collaborative effort. One cannot escape the thought that Peter would have approved of such communal involvement!

In an undertaking of this breadth it is inevitable that some omissions will be forced upon editor and publisher alike in trying to keep the project within reasonable bounds. A first casualty was some of the illustrative material (both drawn and photographic) which, although not part of the articles when they first appeared, might have served to lighten the text. Unfortunately, there simply was not enough room. A second restriction was to limit supplementary material to brief footnotes or endnotes. In a work of this nature, drawing on articles spanning more than three decades, the original readers would gradually have become familiar with many of the concepts discussed, or have direct experience of the events described. Although perhaps less readily accessible to a wider audience, on balance it seemed better to leave the reader to ponder the unfamiliar rather than burden the text with so much extra weight.

Our primary consideration throughout has been to make transparent the essential thoughts and insight which poured out of Peter in an almost unbroken weekly flow as a gift to the community he helped to guide over the years. But his wonderfully idiosyncratic use of English posed a considerable challenge to interpretation by the editors — as sometimes also to his readers — with the obvious risk of different 'voices' speaking through the text. We trust the reader will forgive the occasional infelicity.

This book is published to commemorate the tenth anniversary of Peter's death in 1997, and with it the hope that his practical spiritual wisdom may kindle vigorous — and socially courageous — resolves in the coming generations to meet the challenges of our 21st century world.

*When showing visitors around Botton Village, one of them asked Peter if
it was a 'Christian' community. He replied, characteristically: "Not yet!"*

preface

Vivian Griffiths

Within these pages lies an unfolding history, almost a biography — steps in evolution from Paradise to materialism — taken from the life story of Botton Village, the first Camphill community with adults with special needs founded in 1955. In that village, nestling in a dale of the North York Moors, a Christian social environment emerged that marks one of the quieter chapters of the social history of the latter half of the 19th century. The Camphill communities with adults, pioneered in the 1950s and 60s, were part of the movement that called into question the hospitalisation of people with mental disabilities. The fledgling village community with its working, social and cultural life provided a new kind of integration into society, convincing many who came for longer or shorter visits that the development of the person with learning difficulties holds very real potential. Such people can become active, participating, working citizens, producing fine crafts, performing plays (which demands a high degree of skill), expressing themselves fully in religious devotion and, like all human beings, engaging in every aspect of social life.

Many people attracted to a social vocation could come to Botton and work in a manner they had found no opportunity for in other, more traditional staff-patient settings. The importance of this mutual relationship forged a bond between co-worker and the so-called 'villager' such that *together* they could achieve many things in life that a conventional salaried job and career path denied. An alternative career structure emerged, springing from the interplay between community and individual. In this crucial respect Botton has 'never knowingly undersold' itself, always offering its members co-responsibility in the evolving areas of its life, each initiative finding its proper place in the community at a particular time. This happens as and when an individual is given the opportunity to develop a particular project within the community, and when he or she is willing to give up certain freedoms for the greater good of the community well-being.

From a biographical perspective these writings accompanied Botton's childhood as a protected, nurtured group of pioneers in the Yorkshire countryside, its stormy adolescence in the early 1970s with accidents and mistakes, the constant working at 'community', growing slowly from its experiences, and more recently entering the maturity of adulthood with its efficient working, busy social and rich cultural life — with of course the inevitable doubts and struggles that every adult encounters. Community is a very strong concept, demanding much, yet giving much, and the chemistry of a family-based way of life — secure yet creative in its complexity — makes for an active, interesting life on whichever level you care to look at it; culturally, socially, or in the realm of economic work.

The articles gathered here accompanied this unfolding biography and gain significance when seen against the background from which they sprang. Botton — and in a sense the articles themselves — was born of a similar spirit: a living being. Working with the tension between community and individual gave life to these writings which appeared over the years in the *Botton Village News* and *Botton Mirror*. It was Rev. Peter Roth's idea that a news-sheet should appear each week which would tell people not only who was on such and such a rota, but would also provide a measure of inspiration, a challenge to start the week or to think about some aspect of the Christian social life that the community aspired towards. The first newsletter appeared in 1959, and has appeared weekly ever since. As the reader will discover, these articles cover many aspects of life far beyond the confines of a little village community tucked away in the North York Moors. There are visits to foreign countries, comments on world events and observations on fashions and people's actions, from the death of Marilyn Monroe to deeper questions of the social life.

Peter's articles in Botton's newsletters, hand-delivered as they were from its busy post office to the households, farms and workshops, offer an illuminating insight into the stark contrasts of community life. Lies, for example, are real daggers with very sharp blades; the celebration of a Christian festival is a tangible deed which, if achieved, rises to the stars and unites earth and heaven in an age when the spiritual world is largely unrecognised by human beings.

Many topics may appear new or strange to the reader on first meeting. For example the idea of reincarnation and karma, long ago shelved by western peoples as an eastern notion, now appears as a central, complementing motif in Christianity, opening areas of conviction and faith previously closed to our understanding. The consideration of evil in its twofold manifestation is also present. In addition there is much to ponder, much to understand, and perhaps also something with which to disagree.

These articles are a selection — with all the attendant dangers of selection. Some have become dated since they were written, and some lost, unfortunately. There is no complete record of the Botton news-sheets from their inception and many have had to be omitted through lack of space. Nevertheless, we have tried to include the full spectrum of Peter's thought, and hope that the selection is a fair one.

Peter never 'led' Botton Village in the conventional sense. He was always there as a presence, a helping hand, allowing the freedom to make mistakes, yet faithful always to the ideal that everyday life be Christianised.

Rev. Peter Roth OBE

biographical sketch

Christof-Andreas Lindenberg

Peter Roth was born in Vienna on 12th March 1914 of Jewish parents. In 1937 he and Thomas Weihs were both medical students when they discovered Dr Karl König's group of young people studying the works of Rudolf Steiner. The group met for the last time on 11th March 1938 when the Nazi annexation of Austria took effect. From that meeting they carried with them a pledge to meet again somewhere in the world, filled with a determination to do so under the guidance of Michael, the Time-Spirit. With his first wife, Anke, Peter went to Switzerland and then emigrated to London where they translated medical papers, and Peter was engaged as a chauffeur.

Eventually they found their way to Kirkton House in north-east Scotland where work with children in need of special care began in April 1939. On Whit Sunday 1940 the men from Austria were interned on the Isle of Man as enemy aliens and the women moved alone to Camphill House on an estate near Aberdeen. Peter was released from the camp in the early spring of 1941.

In 1942 Peter began his study for the priesthood and was ordained in the Christian Community on 1st October 1944. After almost two years in London with Dr Heidenreich and others he returned to begin his pastoral work in the newly acquired estate of Newton Dee.

On 16th February 1947 he contracted polio, the consequences of which he bore throughout the remaining fifty years of his life. His marriage had also come to an end.

In October 1952 he moved to the Sheiling Schools near Ringwood as a curative teacher, during which time he married Kate Elderton whom he had met in London and in Camphill. In 1955, together with Kate and others, he founded Botton Village, the archetypal village community with adults with special needs, which many later 'villages' took as their exemplar, both within

This article first appeared in the memorial issue of *Camphill Correspondence*, January/February 1998.

and beyond the Camphill Movement.

Many people knew Peter from the thirty-seven years he lived at Botton because hundreds of villagers and co-workers passed through the village, and thousands visited each year. Peter was undoubtedly the heart of the community. He knew everyone by name and, although officially titled Reverend Peter Roth OBE, his social wisdom and humble personality meant that he was known by everyone simply as 'Peter' — not only in the village and the wider community of Camphill, but also to authorities in the field of social integration.

People flocked to Botton just to have a consultation with Peter who seemed to many to be the best representative of what is often referred to as the 'Middle European Impulse'. Widely read, he knew the latest developments in the world of literature, and his deep love for the giants of Europe's literary heritage kindled a quest for that knowledge out of which anthroposophy had also sprung — the realm of Goethe's 'Fairy Tale of the Green Snake' which bridges our troubled world with that of the Spirit. Peter's life of selfless devotion built many a pathway to the reality of social-spiritual life in the future.

He died on 14th October 1997 in St Albans.

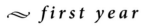 *first year*

∿ christmas & the holy nights

christmas eve

The pageant composed by Richard and Mary Poole was impressive, moving and convincing for all who saw it. The march of all past ages appeared in the beams of stage light, with Mary and Joseph as the beginning of Christian history. In the glow of all the candles one actually *saw* the path of evolution — the sinking out of star-guided heights into earthly darkness and the starry light reappearing out of the goodness of humanity. Perhaps because it was Christmas Eve one could also imagine that the Apocalyptic seals of the Book of Revelation were opening. Something of the inner Logos of the story of humanity became visible.

BOTTON VILLAGE NEWS, 27 XII 1968

the holy nights

The time between 24th December and 6th January is called the Holy Nights, but the intervening days are part of it too. We look with our consciousness into the darkness of the nights, and they seem to be filled with abundant and shining gold. Out of the nights are woven hidden threads which shine into our days and frame their greyness with gold. It is that time in the year when Christ, the Lord of the Earth, blossoms unhindered by the summer comfort of the senses, by outer warmth and light. Growth and green are near the soul and we can look at the earth in its greys and browns and contemplate the words of Isaiah: "For he [the Lord] shall grow up before him as a tender plant, and as a root out of a dry ground: he hath no form nor comeliness; and when we shall see him, there is no beauty that we should desire him." (Isaiah 53: 2)

The golden signs on the Christmas fir tree are symbols of this. From the fir-like darkness of our minds we look through bright, golden, differently-shaped keyholes from the outer darkness of earth into the palace of heaven; from the day into the night. Yet we should not think that we are dark and the golden

brightness is outside us, for 'Behold, the Kingdom of God is within you.'
(Luke 17:21) Our minds may be dark and our experiences narrow and warped,
but the golden-lit Holy Nights are within us.

BOTTON VILLAGE NEWS, 29 XII 1967

meditation & the service — christmas thoughts

If held regularly, the Act of Consecration of Man can become the most
powerful element in the life of a social organism. It forms people into a
congregation on the basis of the awakening, deeper self. This power flows into
our homes and work places through hidden channels, and into our destiny.
Every time we sit in front of the altar our deeper self becomes present through
the presence of Christ in whose arms this deeper self is held. The more we are
able to engage our activity in the progress of the Service, the more we become
educated towards our deeper self.

The first part of the Service (Gospel Reading) is like the green calyx of
the flower. Although still at the stage of leaves and greenness, the vegetative
growth of the plant comes to a stop here, and out of the calyx rises the
blossom. In the Service this is represented by the three parts following the
uncovering of the cup: the Offering, Transubstantiation and Communion. The
taking of communion is like the seed in the blossom; something is planted in
our soul and from it grows the higher human being. The fundamental element
in which all this takes place is the spoken word.

Conversely, the element in which meditation takes place is the *un*spoken,
silent word within the solitude of the individual, although in regard to the
stages of calyx, blossom and seed the process is similar to the Service. That
which is achieved in the Service through the Gospel Reading (the forming
of the green cup in which the blossom can arise), is reached in meditation
through the dimming down of sense impressions and the stilling of all bodily
movement. Meditation itself can be likened to the evolving and appearance
of the blossom. The more the praying will is directed towards it, the more the
blossom can expand and fill the soul with its grace. For this span of time the
soul — otherwise bound to senses, muscles and brain: indeed to the whole
body — is filled consciously, half-consciously or unconsciously with a quite
different world. The seed of communion is also planted within the human
soul in meditation.

That which is warmth, light and life in the flowering plant is, in both

Service and meditation, the Sun of Christ. It is the appearance of the sun of love within the winter of our earthly existence which we especially revere at Christmas.

BOTTON VILLAGE NEWS, 22 XII 1961

Summary of the foregoing thoughts

Plant	Act of Consecration of Man	Meditation
Calyx	Gospel Reading & Creed	Dimming sense impressions & stilling bodily movements
Flower	Offering	Meditation — the Sun of Christ
Fruit	Transubstantiation	The praying will
Seed	Communion	Planting the Communion's seed

the sun at midnight

In our time the human being is a day-orientated being. Our wakefulness needs to be filled with earthly objects which can only appear in the light. We try to help ourselves overcome the blindness into which the darkness plunges us by illuminated rooms and lit-up streets. But the country is dark even on a moonlit night, trees, rocks and houses appearing only as silhouettes. Humanity's wakefulness remains in the darkness, always hungry, as it were.

In a deeper sense, humanity in our time can only take the world-content into consciousness in daylight; the world has to sink into souls, and souls must transform it and bring it to birth anew. With man-made things this is obvious: houses have to be lived in, machines must serve our activities, music has to be heard — it all makes sense only in relation to human beings. But with nature it is perhaps mainly through art that it becomes human-centred: trees and mountains, clouds and stars have to be beheld and then recreated in human souls in order to achieve their goal. Only then do we do justice to what surrounds us as creation, not just by using it for material purposes. Animals and plants, even landscapes, seem to look at us dumbly, questioningly. Many artists (Rilke especially), understood their task as being to *answer*, and their answer is really another step in the world's becoming. The great task of our time is that not only do the gods no longer create, but that creation is now vested in human beings. This urges upon us the insight that art is a necessary step on the road towards a renewed understanding, a 'knowing' science.

Our present understanding of objects is based on physical light: the objects of our knowing must appear in the light in order to be understood. No wonder we call the physical sun the 'Prince of this World'. In the past, perceiving the Sun at Midnight was restricted to one moment in the cycle of the year — in the Holy Nights at the turn of the new year. But today the sun can shine through the darkness and density of the earth at any time when seen with inner, spiritual sight. Understanding enhanced by the Sun at Midnight will allow us to perceive the questions posed by creation. The responses of poets, musicians and painters will stir in us; we will feel love and tenderness towards creation and will be overwhelmed by the conviction that our life is worthwhile. Thus, it will also shine in our daylight and make daylight an adjunct to and not a condition of our waking 'I am' consciousness.

Only this midnight-light will help us to see that we take in the world not only through our senses, our consciousness, but also through eating, through metabolism. Apart from chewing and tasting consciously, our food disappears into the dark, unconscious powers of the will. These powers move not only our arms and legs but also our thoughts; we use our unknown will to relate one thought to the other, to think. Meditating is a higher, hallowed thinking. We bear the night, and also the stars, in our will, in our moving, in our metabolism. The Christmas dinner is an appropriate custom because night is lifted up into day.

The Prince of this World enables us to think, but only when the powers and beings of the night enter the realm of this world can we move, act and think in the element of reality. Anthroposophy is not only the knowledge of sense-darkness in agriculture, education, medicine — in all plant-animal-human-astronomical science — it raises and transforms what seems to have its existence only in the light of day. The Communion in the Service, the taking of bread and wine, is the perfect blending of night and day.

BOTTON VILLAGE NEWS, 1 1 1977

holidays

Strange as it may seem, it is very fitting to think about holidays during the holy days of the Holy Nights. Our need to go on holiday is a complicated matter. As a mass phenomenon, it only emerged about 150 years ago and is therefore something that belongs very much to our time. A small part of this need is understandable and reaches our consciousness; the larger part loses itself in our unconscious. We will try to understand a little more about it.

Three main factors help to build our need for holidays. The first is connected with our own, very personal biography; the second with our understanding of the seasons; the third with our thirst for a higher existence.

Firstly, our need for and experience of 'holidays' is a historic phenomenon. It arose in the course of mankind's evolution, his social conditions and his world-conception. A century or more ago people went to a spa for medical reasons or, if they had the money, they took the 'Grand Tour' for the sake of learning — and later for business reasons. Destiny led them to change, albeit temporarily, the place on earth where life had anchored them for somewhere else; their knowledge of the earth's different landscapes and climates was dependent on the dictates of personal biography.

Today we are all cosmopolitan and therefore at home not only where we live, but potentially also on the canals of Venice, among the mosques of Isfahan, on the slopes of the Himalayas or the sand dunes of the Gobi Desert. In our time the travel possibilities and the mass media (newspapers, periodicals, radio and television, etc.), have widened our awareness of the earth immeasurably. Today, journeys have a totally different value than they had in the days of our forefathers. But journeys to far-off lands, insofar as they are just holiday journeys, leave us in a strange vacuum. The ordinary building of destiny in the place where we live — our house, our locality, our friends, our profession and the people we are connected with through it — all this is absent during the holiday. Perhaps only the presence of our family, which we may have taken with us, helps to keep out the winds of change blowing around us from this vacuum. We can learn much regarding the burdens as well as the grace of our destiny through its sudden absence. 'Needing a holiday' is partly our longing for the weeks-long non-existence of our destiny.

Secondly, our image of 'holidays' is very much influenced by summer, by the yearning for outer warmth and light, for the comfort of friendly elements. In autumn the country fills us with sadness; its desolation in December (if there is no snow), strikes us as bare and ugly. Hence for us holidays have become *summer* holidays. Our hesitant understanding of the seasons and the land constitutes one of our holiday drives. Mixed with this wish for the comfort of the elements is the fact that we have become town dwellers and that 'country' is now only really bearable in its summer state. We try to look away from the disintegration of life in autumn, which is so much more apparent in the country than in town; life in summer seems to us more complete. But during autumn and winter life has not gone away; only its visibility has disappeared.

One of the great mysteries of our time is to learn to equate spring and summer with falling asleep and sleeping; autumn and winter with waking up and full consciousness.[1] We are meant to learn to experience this, as Rudolf Steiner pointed out. In the morning we wake refreshed, but by what? Through restoring sleep, through unconsciousness, as anyone who suffers from sleeplessness can confirm. Consciousness makes us tired, and not only bodily exertion but also sitting in a chair can do it.

Spring and summer are not to be likened to an awakening, to a rising of consciousness — consciousness is a blight, a burden on life. Life starts to be restored when we fall asleep, when we lose consciousness. In the night, our bodies go through spring and summer. When we behold the beauty of visible life on a part of the earth's surface where growth and flowering occur, we are faced with sleep; when beholding the bareness of autumn and winter we are faced with consciousness. This is, of course, the falling asleep and waking up of the earth, but one of the tasks of spiritual science is to teach us that in the distant past humanity and earth were one, and in the far future will again become one.

Thirdly, we are in search of a new paradise, an enhanced or higher existence. As part of the annual holiday army, whether we visit a theme park, a sun-drenched Italian village beside blue waters, or an alpine chalet, each year we try to find this higher life and return, always a little disappointed, to the valleys of our ordinary, workaday life.

At some time in the future, holidays will become retreats once again, and thereby Holy Days, as they once were in ancient times. These retreats will be founts of rejuvenation and wellsprings of new life. Through them we will be able to embrace our destiny with enthusiasm and zeal; we will look upon the earth's formations with more and more interest. With ever deeper understanding we will divine, increasingly, that through the Mystery of Golgotha, Christ united Himself with the earth, and we will understand the part summer and winter play in this.

JOURNAL OF THE CHRISTIAN COMMUNITY, VII-VIII 1970

the word, courage and love

At the beginning of the Apocalypse (Rev 1: 12–16), Christ is described as standing before seven candlesticks clothed in a white garment with a golden girdle, His eyes as a flame of fire and a sharp, two-edged sword issuing from His mouth. We tend to connect this picture instinctively with judgement and punishment, but in fact His sword is the sword of the Word because this image of Christ is the continuation, the transformation of the beginning of St John's Gospel, 'In the beginning was the Word and the Word was with God.' (John 1: 1)

With the Fall of Humanity came a split in the unity of word and sword: the sword became a weapon and the word diminished to the level of human language which is now little more than a means of communication. But something else began to glow amid all the misery, imperfection and guilt of earthly life, and that was human love! Through the power of Christ this love will become articulate, and human love and human word will grow nearer to each other. Love and the divine Word are one; they are like substance and form. Christ, who descended into human destiny, melts the sword into courage within the human heart and fills our words with creative power. More and more will human beings wield the courageous, creating Word.

Christmas marks the beginning of the Light shining in the darkness. From 24th December throughout the Twelve Holy Nights until 6th January, we celebrate the festival of the human soul — the human soul that shines into the earthly and cosmic spaces, full of strength and comfort, for it knows it is lying on the breast of Christ.

BOTTON VILLAGE NEWS, 22 XII 1967

∿ epiphany

three kings: the light of prayer

It is an indescribable experience to see the mauve backcloth and altar on
Three Kings Day after the white and gold of the Holy Nights. It is as if the
essence of what time and space really is reveals itself especially in this
transition from white-gold to mauve: 'Time becomes Space.' The copper signs
and symbols, the roses, the apples, the candles on the Christmas tree, the
morning lectures, the whole mood and colour of the time between the 24th
of December to the 6th of January — it is as if divine space were entering the
stream of time. Of course, the stream of time flowed on during these twelve
days, but within this on-flowing stream of earthly time, the divine — not
subject to earthly becoming and decaying — was unchangingly present and
gazed upon us.

What remains of this divine space, inserted into earthly time after the
6th of January, is the 'light of prayer' to meet and behold the Star of Grace.
We ourselves, the human soul, bear the Three Kings hidden within us. The
image of the Kings and their gifts release us into the year with its seasons, its
changing weathers in all spheres of life, its achievements and failures.

One of the Kings' gifts — incense, which is the physical expression of
prayer — comes to the surface openly whenever the Service is celebrated. The
light of prayer is the divine soul space within which we were graced to move
during the Holy Nights.

BOTTON MIRROR, 10 I 1964

self-righteousness

Human relationships would be infinitely simpler if the question of right
and wrong played no part in them. Being right condemns one's soul to a
considerable degree, for two reasons. Firstly, we all suffer from the illusion
that if we were right more often, we would be better, stronger, a more shining

example, more admired, etc. We cover up our frustrations, weaknesses and aggressions by hurling self-evident truths at our adversary. He or she feels only the wound of the attack and is thus unable to contemplate these self-evident truths with equanimity. Secondly, we must find scapegoats — the husband blames his wife, the office worker blames his colleague or boss, Hitler blames the Jews, the capitalist countries blame the communist states, the third world blames the developed world.

Being right makes little or no difference in a social tableau (even one as small as Botton), but being interested in the other person makes an enormous difference to every individual in society. Interest makes us stronger, and in the light of our interest in the other, finding a scapegoat dwindles into insignificance because the question of who is right and who is wrong becomes unimportant — the wrongdoer is also interesting! The question of right and wrong becomes one of alleviating suffering. We all suffer but we can all help, perhaps by just listening with interest.

We all suffer under what in theological terms is called original sin. Whether we know it or not, we all feel (although differently according to our world conceptions), that we have fallen from some previous light-filled, majestic state of grace, and so we suffer from a feeling of existential guilt, of being wrong. We therefore take the question of being right seriously, as if the salvation of society and ourselves depended on it.

By being genuinely interested in the other person we enter the stream of Christianity. The Christianity of today is not a church-Christianity. It is only by entering this stream that our existence turns towards its majestic light-filled goal and our feelings of guilt diminish.

Social life — not the general kind with authorities and parliaments, but the I-to-You kind — is a mysterious thing. Self-knowledge is not a matter of delving into oneself alone in one's lonely room, it is very much a question of unbiased observation, of how we behave towards each other in our being and talking together.

BOTTON MIRROR, 8 I 1977

togetherness

We live in a time when millions of words concerning facts or imagined facts are available to us, and when most decisions are taken by voting and by majority rule. But we all know that there can be something deeper among human beings — the power of harmony, the strength of togetherness. Facts are still facts, opinions are opinions and words are words, but our awareness and affirmation of each other is more valuable than these, and we can gain a feeling that although our own strength may be small it is infinitely enhanced by the presence of others. Part of the mystery of marriage lies in this. My relationship to my partner does not depend merely on communicated facts or opinions. Our togetherness *resounds* because we share our ideas and ideals and are moved by the same questions and events.

One of the great errors of our time is to think that we can argue things out, come to an agreement and all will be well. But if it is only an agreement, all is definitely *not* well — it is an illusion, a temporary truce, as we can see all too often in the case of industrial disputes. If an agreement does not rise to the level of insight, the 'resounding together in silent harmony' cannot be reached. Arguments are pale and weak, their 'truth' is of a theoretical (and therefore temporary) nature, and even insights on their own do not achieve enough in the world. If the builders of the pyramids in ancient Egypt had merely had insight alone, those miraculous structures would never have been erected. It was the resounding harmony of their togetherness, of their community, which unleashed the necessary power.

As you can see, there are varying degrees of opinion, argument, insight and resounding harmony. We all know that insight arises through listening with selfless interest in a genuine attempt to understand what the other person is saying, and being similarly heard in return. And resounding harmony? In olden times it may have come through rhythm, dancing and choirs. Today when our consciousness is very much wider and clearer it need not be anything outer. But if those who do achieve insight put their hearts together and really *will* it, mountains will move because the power resounding through silent harmony will move them.

This is usually overlooked, partly because it is strenuous but mainly because the characteristic expression of the human being in our time is to be a person with a definite name, bounded by birth and death and in possession of opinions. Opinions arise when we are comparatively isolated from our surroundings. Indeed, none of us could really be a person if we did not have opinions — *my* opinion, *my* point of view.

We *all* have our opinions. But groups who come together for a specific purpose must take a further step and let opinion become *will*: it must be each person's individual will; an active yet selfless will, not merely a passive member of a group. These silent harmonies of will are the building stones of our social life.

BOTTON MIRROR, 8 IV 1988

meetings

At our meetings in Botton we can see that social life is not just a question of arrangements. It is also a question of how the various problems are handled; not so much their content (for example, whether someone sticks to the point or digresses, etc.), but more in the way we behave, and especially how we listen to one another. We do try to listen to the other person, of course, but in doing so we lose the freedom of our own thinking. Our emotional life, reacting from below as it were, barks opinions and spouts all manner of selfish emotions which accompany them. Meetings should build us up and nourish us, but on the whole they are tiring, not because they take too long but because of this loss of freedom in our thinking — we could also call it a slight de-personalisation — as we become 'fixed' in our listening to each other. What can be done about this?

Many things play into this de-personalisation, into this slight loss of our 'I am' consciousness, and I do not know what all of them are. But nothing is more mysterious in our time, foreshadowing our Christian future, than what takes place when a small group of people sit down together. Whatever the composition of the group, when they assemble something of the therapeutic community is always present. But one of the hindering aspects of our meetings is the presence of any kind of hidden agenda, and therefore sending out an agenda beforehand is very important. Other things are less easy to define. For us every meeting has an element of a social occasion, and this more than anything else determines the quality of our listening.

However, it is only a sham social occasion. What makes us unfree in meetings? We react to what the others say, but we only react, and therefore only a part of our humanity is brought into play. We get involved by reacting to whatever the other person expresses with our own counter-opinions, with our sympathy or antipathy. How can we be involved without reacting?

There are two kinds of listening. In one, our own answer is ready as soon as the other person speaks — as in a game of tennis bat follows ball, or in a boxing match; an eye for an eye, a tooth for a tooth — we listen only for the sake of answering back. In the other kind, we listen but suppress the answer that arises from our usual reactions, even though the answer may be a considerate, thoughtful or important one. In the act of suppressing an immediate answer, creative listening becomes possible in which the listener becomes a 'non-I', a negative. We normally feel our 'I' as something positive — I walk, I have opinions, I do this or that — but while this sense of being empowered by the 'I' is, of course, a necessary part of our development, it gains its real power through blotting itself out, through becoming a negative among positives. The annihilation of the positive ego is a Christian process. Rudolf Steiner described the sun as a negative space, and thereby it shines.[2] In a similar way our 'I' is meant, through Christ, to become a sun.

Listening so that we try to become a hollow among hills makes us free; meetings release us if we no longer think that our own thoughts are the only important ones. We are discouraged by history from the desire to become a dictator. In our thinking, however, we still want others to think as we do.

BOTTON VILLAGE NEWS, 11 II 1972

e x a m p l e & p r o j e c t i o n

It is one of the hopes of the Christian soul that contact and relationship among human beings will become so strong, so intense and direct, that our present human dealings will seem comparatively shadowy. As a kind of *ersatz* mutual compensation, two soul attitudes, one 'good' the other 'bad', played a great part in the past but are less effective, or happen less, in our time.

One of these is the *example* — hero-worship in all its guises — in which one admires a person, or admires a certain quality or gift in him or her, and tries to live up to or imitate it. This kind of thing led to the righteousness of the Victorian matron, the earnestness of a teacher, the charm of a man-about-town, the courage of Napoleon.

The second soul attitude is what Nietzsche, and later the psychoanalysts, called *projection* — you see in the other person sides of yourself which you dislike (the beam and mote in the gospels). (Matt. 7: 4, Luke 6: 42)

The first, the example, does not work now because most people in our time are not enthused to imitate anything. They understand the world less in shades of virtues and faults and more in each individual being looked upon as a phenomenon in him- or herself. The second, the projection, happens far less now, not because the relation between people has become more real and brotherly, but because the walls surrounding each person, and thereby separating them from one another, have become much more solid.

There is a certain longing in us that the 'sun of righteousness' will continue to shine on us from outside, that the source of all virtue is a kind of Mosaic law: 'If we are good we walk in its light, if we are bad we walk in its shadow.' (cf. John 11: 9–10.) Both example and projection are phenomena of the moral light shining from outside.

At the moment the moral light, the sun of righteousness, is within each one of us. Virtue is not something which can be imitated, nor are faults things which can be projected. There are only individuals who are like this or like that. The world of moral categories will melt in the spring sun of a new individualism — good, bad, Christian, Hindu, atheist, magnanimous or miserly people — and there will remain a certain number of individuals who have a connection to each other. To a great extent the walls between us consist of prejudices, their bricks are our abstract moral categories. We, the human beings of our time, really walk in the night. There are innumerable stars lighting the night sky, but it is our own heart and soul which, more and more, will have to become luminous and shine upon the paths of life and upon each other.

BOTTON VILLAGE NEWS, 17 II 1967

Botton Village News

~ toward lent

the parable of the labourers in the vineyard

The key to this mysterious parable (Matt. 20: 1–16) is the householder's question, 'Is your eye evil because I am good?' It remains mysterious as long as the work in the vineyard is looked upon simply as one of several work situations or necessities of the world, for which the usual payment is given. But if the work in the vineyard is considered as a grace, as something we love doing which is worthy of our enthusiasm, the question of remuneration at a penny a day or a penny an hour becomes quite different.

There are many interpretations of this parable, and a narrow, purely economic one would not be appropriate. The parable was given just before Christ's entry into Jerusalem, in the last days before the crucifixion and resurrection — the event that counterbalances the Fall, the expulsion from paradise, when God said, 'In the sweat of thy face shalt thou eat bread.' (Genesis 3: 19) The Fall had, and still has, many consequences which have but one common denominator, namely that in the course of time all sense impressions, thoughts, feelings, joys, pain and sorrow, converged on the Self, their subject being the 'I' — in other words, they became selfish — and to the same extent human beings become responsible for them. The incarnation of Christ means making the self we have achieved, unselfish.

It is the same with our work. Out of the dusk of the past came the work of the slaves, work that made life possible yet could hardly be called 'work' because the slaves were barely conscious of it as such; rather they were cogs in the process of life. Then in the Middle Ages, castes seem to have divided work into artisan, farmer, hunter, clerk or judge. Finally, in the Industrial Revolution, work became work, but still under the guise of earning a living.

The deeper underlying cause of the social problems of the last 150 years has been the dawning wish to work not only to earn a living, but for the sake of others who need the outcome of my work, as I need the outcome of theirs. We thereby feel the warmth and enthusiasm of unselfishness firing our work. This change — from work as chore to work as blessing — is seen in the attitude of old people. If others no longer need them, their life begins to lose its value. Many illnesses of old age are caused by not being needed any more. Machines not only further this process but are invested in so as to save wages. A lot of work is done not in order to fulfil the needs of others but to earn wages, to satisfy trade unions or to gratify the temptations of advertisements.

The curse of labour is connected with the Fall: the grace of labour with its Christianising. The Fall made work selfish; it became part of the cursed ground, cursed because of us human beings. But if we become more intertwined with each other through work then the grace of work will become apparent and the Fall will reveal its hidden gifts. It is only when work is *not* done purely for a living that it loses its curse and reveals its glory. When others must fulfil our needs and we theirs, then work cannot be paid for. However, the penny a day or an hour is only unjustified as remuneration, as a salary for work — its rôle in meeting the needs of the worker is a quite different question. The penny has nothing to do with the amount of work done, but everything to do with the way and the degree to which we are intertwined with the needs of others, and how much we thereby fulfil the task we have on earth.

DATE UNKNOWN

social integration

Sweeping through the western world — mainly in Britain and America, but originating in Denmark and Sweden, the most 'westernised' Scandinavian countries — there is a wave, an ever-increasing outcry, demanding social integration for the handicapped person.* There has been a recent White Paper calling for better services, pamphlets from the Campaign for the Mentally Handicapped, the 1973 Convention of the American Association on Mental Deficiency in Atlanta, and so on. Underlying all these is the experience of the intrinsic equality of *all* human beings, and a conviction that the handicapped person cannot be deemed a patient (except when in a shorter or longer spell of illness), and that imprinted in each one of them is what is called in traditional religious parlance, 'created in the image of God', which is now thought of as the dignity of the human being. We no longer view them as a

---

* The word 'handicapped' and related terminology has been retained here since it was accepted usage when the article was written. It provides a balance to that equally difficult term 'normal'.

minority group needing special provision, but as individual human beings who are meant to use existing provisions in the hope that thereby their right to participate in the general life of our time will be safeguarded. This process of taking them out of hospitals, from the status of being branded as 'patient' in a group existence towards entering ordinary life as singular individuals, is called 'normalisation'.

This 'normalisation' presumes that social life in the western world (whether it be in family, culture, leisure, work or politics), is itself 'normal', and that we are doing justice to each person's individuality by letting him or her take part in it. This normality seems infinitely desirable because it is part of our present time, and hence by participating in social life we become a member of our time. But it is obvious that what is deemed normal today is only one aspect of our time because, demonstrably, this 'normality' is inextricably permeated by inhumanity — like the habit of the Pharisees and Levites of 'looking the other way' (Matt. 23) — and by loneliness.

Two examples may stand for many. In our efforts to help some of our handicapped adults into the 'open community', we found a family which was willing to take some who were on the waiting list of our community at Delrow. That family life was turbulent, but thanks to an atmosphere of tolerance and mutual acceptance it was a valuable expression of society today. But then the family broke up, husband and wife were unable to deal with each other and their children, and the local doctor proved unequal to the task of caring for the epileptics and psychotics in their household. On another occasion one of our villagers went to a communal house and got a job in the local park. He exposed himself in front of an open bathroom window, obviously because of a difficult situation in the house which he could not cope with. The woman opposite, in her fright, informed the police and a court case followed.

These two examples show that 'integration' is not a concept complete in itself but it has another side, which is community involvement. If, in the first example, the neighbours had bothered about the problematic family which was augmented by those who until then had been labelled as handicapped, the process of integration could have proceeded. Similarly, in the second example, if the woman living nearby had been more aware of the situation, things might have been different. The responsibility for emptying sub-normality hospitals no doubt lies with the recipient of these 'immigrants' — with the community! How does one bring about its involvement?

The term 'community involvement' stems from the Seebohm Report of

1968,[3] which we should never forget was one of the major documents of the 20th century. At its heart is the chapter on community which had unavoidable consequences in the subsequent organisation of social services departments. 'The development of citizen participation should reduce the rigid distinction between the givers and the takers of social services and the stigma which being a client has often involved...' The levelling out of this rigid distinction is the task of the social worker. Without it, hostels or halfway houses of whatever kind cannot be other than humane replicas of hospitals, i.e. it will not be possible for the *group* of handicapped persons to integrate as *individuals* into society. Without this social work, society will not allow integration to come about. But it is a kind of social work which cannot be taught. Social workers themselves should increase in human value, in human stature, in order to convince others.

But even if this were to happen, integration and community involvement will only descend from the somewhat theoretical sphere of moralistic feeling into practical life if actual *work* is accessible to the so-called handicapped person in, for instance, places such as coffee houses, restaurants or shops in town, or farming, gardening and forestry in the country. As long as integration and community involvement do not reach into the economic sphere of everyday life this whole question of 'handicap' will remain a medical one. Social organisms are bound together by mutual needs. The mere construction by society of more and more humane 'provisions' merely subscribes to the 'I'm all right, Jack' mentality. The handicapped need, individually, to enter with us into the realm of mutual needs.

BOTTON, AUTUMN 1973/CAMPHILL CORRESPONDENCE, SEPTEMBER 1975

integration as a gateway to adult education

It is understandable that the concept of adult education should undergo a re-evaluation in our time. In the 150 years or so since the Industrial Revolution gathered momentum, manual work for men and women, whether skilled or unskilled, on the shop floor or in park and garden departments, in cleaning, cooking or child-minding has assumed the character of being only for those not bright enough for something 'higher'. The consequences of this are that people shun it because they feel that their human dignity is less upheld in manual work and they do not want to be numbered among the 'less bright'. Unlike in the past, strikes are not called only for economic reasons, they are also a cry for human dignity. It is for this reason that so many students fill the universities of western-inspired countries.

Those who do manual work do it mostly as a means of earning money. But it is only the restricted thinking of our time that makes it seem as if earning money is the reason for work; the true reason being that its fruits are needed and consumed by others. These fruits can be as varied as a table made in a workshop or factory, potatoes grown on a farm, or the outcome of medical therapy or research.

Since the inception of democracy there is an increasing trend towards equality, but this longing for equality can never be assuaged by mere economic solutions, or by voting. Equality is realised through the creative, cultural energy of each human being, and adult education is at least as strong an incentive towards equality as is the question of wages. The one without the other is of no use. An adult education that is not only specialised but also comprises a general knowledge that is relevant to human existence as such, whatever the curriculum or particular subject, can begin to lead every human being towards personal dignity — no matter what education he or she had as a child, and independent of work or status.

The effort to integrate mentally handicapped and mentally ill people into society stems from the 'democratic' feeling that equality belongs to the real experience of our human self. Adult education is therefore a necessity for the integration of the mentally handicapped person into society. It is not just aimed at evoking intellectual skills. Adult education is an attempt to open windows both to our cultural and historical heritage, as well as to the wonders of zoology, botany, mineralogy, geography and so on. And who is to say that adult education of this kind makes any distinction between handicapped and non-handicapped people who are becoming citizens of the world? The equality of all of us consists in this: we are inhabitants of the Earth; we are born and we die.

BOTTON, AUTUMN 1973

integration: responsibility

Payment for work, the selling of a human being's labour, is the last vestige of slavery. But today the individual's very existence depends on this selling; without 'earning his livelihood' he and his dependants are only kept from starving by the welfare state.

Many of our people in Botton, having achieved a certain maturity, strength and independence through village life, want to leave and get a pay packet for their work. Like all of us they were not paid for their work in the village during their time of maturing. Their work was divorced from money or wages because the available money here covers our needs.

There is no doubt that in Camphill villages the caring, the responsibility for one another, is considerably increased through not having wages. Precisely this increase in responsibility and caring for one another is one of the main factors in the maturing rôle of the villages. The more this mutual caring for one another is achieved in the community, the more valuable will be the social standing of such a person in ordinary life.

The concept of 'responsibility' is not easy to define, partly because it is an attitude of caring and has little to do with the part of the day we devote to work. It is mainly in the non-working part of the day that we find the caring and responsibility of mother for child, of wife for husband, husband for wife, lover for beloved. But this attitude is not always directed to a person. Rather it is an attitude, and can be directed to a machine, a household, an institution, a company, etc. — an attitude, in short, which is not determined by office or working hours, but is part of our existence. It does not last only from 9 am to 5 pm but helps to make up our moral weight throughout the full twenty-four hours of the day. We might even say that the degree to which our day (which includes our private *and* our personal life), contains this element of caring and responsibility, to that same degree do we gain in moral weight, while as much as we do out of *duty* (whether in our private life or in work), our moral weight remains static. Our conscience is lulled by sheer duty but roused by responsibility.

The question therefore arises: in a village with and for handicapped people, can this element of responsibility be augmented? The difficulty lies in our confusing intelligence with responsibility. Because the handicapped person can appear to lack intelligence (which is mostly just intellect), we leave his or her powers of responsibility untapped. We, the co-workers, manage the affairs of workshops, houses, farms, etc., and so there is always the danger that the villagers become, if I may exaggerate, the 'cheap labour' which helps us fulfil our aims. But the co-workers should guide the villagers to help each other so that responsibility can grow. Somewhere we are convinced that only we, the so-called 'normal' ones, can be responsible, but in this conviction we mix up intellect and responsibility. Intellect is, necessarily, related to oneself;

it cannot *care*. But if a house could be run by the group of those inhabiting it, handicapped *and* non-handicapped alike; if a workshop could be run by a group of similar nature, but smaller, and the 'normal' ones could silence their intellect, then the question of mental handicap would look very different. It would make the handicapped workers members of humanity — instead of treating them ever so humanely but still as a group (hostel, family-home, etc.) — because we accept the division of the world into disabled *and* non-disabled people.

The equality of human beings is a question of participating in at least a little responsibility and care. In the sight of Christ, human beings are equal whether they know it or not. The integration of disabled people into society is not meant to happen because our society is glorious; rather it ought to happen because through their integration society will slowly progress to more human standards.

BOTTON, AUTUMN 1973

～ *lent & passiontide*

anthroposophical professions

Work in the past was of two kinds. The first was necessary in order to maintain life, from cooking to diplomacy; the second was more connected with inclination and gifts; the artist, the doctor, etc. Today *any* work is clouded by a grey veil — the wage, the salary, the payment for it. A large amount of the work done in the world today is done because one has to earn a living. It is one of the merits of Camphill that it tries to separate work from money. The grey veil covering work is thus removed to a large extent, and work as a task of human beings can therefore reveal itself in all its clarity. But what is this clarity?

The veil proves to be something like a cocoon, hiding the transformation of the caterpillar within; lift the veil and work reveals itself as a beautiful human activity, quite independent of inclination, gifts or necessities, dictated only by the need of others for its fruits. Anything can be done and learnt by anybody. Of course, what someone actually does depends on many inner and outer factors.

With the French Revolution, the *equality* of human beings began to dawn. The kinds of work, varying according to gifts or social class (playing the violin, painting, mathematics or street cleaning), are not really dependent on ability any more. As Fichte said, 'If a man says he cannot, he does not want to.'[4]

We see this in Camphill where to a certain extent people do what is needed regardless of what they might like to do. Enthusiasm for a certain kind of work is no longer dependent on gift or ability alone; the incentive for doing it is neither money (because we do not get paid for what we do), nor status. This enthusiasm is engendered solely by becoming aware of the background of the work that is needed, not just the social network out of which the need arises, but the esoteric or cosmic background of the work itself. With the teacher, the doctor, the farmer, we can see it easily. In education, for example, the etheric body, astral body and ego organisation unfold with a curriculum that fits the child. In medicine, the patient is healed with medicines containing parts of the infinite variety of the world. The cosmic knowledge of the farmer changes growing and ripening into food. These people have the power to transform child or patient, earth and plant through meditation, and in doing so they become aware of the spirit reality in the world. It gives them an existential joy to discover that their own observing, searching, willing-spirit-reality mirrors the spirit reality of the world. What could be more delightful than to discover new, unknown landscapes and features which depend on human activity? Of course, in other professions this background is more difficult to see. It is, however, necessary for all professions to become aware that there exists an interchange, socially, between 'consumer' and 'producer', and spiritually between the person and the work he is meant to do, whether a plumbing repair, electrical work, or whatever it might be.

This love, interest and enthusiasm for the background of our profession or occupation is very important; as important for the world as it is for ourselves. Only through this interest and enthusiasm can the active person — teacher, cook or plumber — develop the creative zeal through which tradition and conventions will be overcome, new realms researched, new methods invented, thus rekindling the inner flame. Without such creative zeal earthly life stops moving, becomes sedentary and boring: creative zeal makes life worthwhile.

To do our daily duty is not enough in itself. Any profession, any work we do with creative zeal, will uplift us.

BOTTON MIRROR, 9 IV 1983

saving

Whether it applies to spending in one of our households or to lending or donating to other causes or endeavours, saving always has one underlying concept, *money* — money as a heavy bag of coins or a lighter bundle of paper notes. This is quite true, although not the end of the story, even though for most people it is the end.

We can look upon money as a noun, so to speak, when it is a fixed sum (£2 or £500), or more akin to a verb when it enables an activity that yields fruits needed by others. In the first case (the noun) it is equated with possession, and if you lend it, it even takes on the sheen of activity as it increases through dividends. Ever since Roman times the fact of *possessing* money has chained humanity in a dreadful fashion. The possession of money has been the source of many of the evils that human beings are capable of. It has warped human relationships, invented salary scales, produced armaments. The underlying aim of business was, and is, to earn money. Money became the motive for many crimes — the rôles played by bribery and corruption in contemporary life is enormous. People betray their own beliefs and therefore change the course of their own and others' karma. Without the specific rôle money plays in our time, the morality of the individual would be very different.

Human society would be quite different if work and money could be separated, which was the underlying idea at the inception of socialism. Equality was its ultimate aim, but for many reasons this did not succeed.

Why is the possession of money such a powerful incentive? With it you can dress better, buy bigger and better cars, you can travel and frequent luxury hotels. With the carelessness which the possession of money brings you buy a certain superiority of your ego — in a quite inhuman, impersonal way you are buying the respect of others.

Before applying these insights to Botton and Camphill, let us insert a general consideration. When tempted to turn stones into bread, Christ could not answer the temptation fully, but said: 'Man does not live by bread alone.' (Matt. 4: 4, Luke 4: 4). Rudolf Steiner explains that in this context 'stone' means mineral, metal, money, and that because this temptation was only partly refuted, the devil could enter Judas and betray Him for thirty pieces of silver.[5] The betrayal was followed by the Crucifixion, but Christ's death was followed by the Resurrection — the third temptation was bought for the price of both betrayal and of death overcome. We understand that because we must pay for our bread (and here bread means everything we pay for), the many paths of human karma are possible. All the consequences of the Fall are balanced, again and again, because we must pay for everything; money has become our teacher, corrector and scourge. So it is understandable that the one who 'has' money is looked up to by others as a better or higher person; he seems beyond reproach and incapable of error. On the other hand, when someone spends money he feels a kind of self-assurance and does not reckon with death or accountability.

Now back to Camphill and Botton. We do not receive salaries and therefore do not have fixed incomes according to which we must adjust our requirements. We spend money according to our needs, not according to the amount of money we have. Hence we fall less under the spell of the third temptation. We tend to expect that a much greater opportunity for individual freedom will be gained thereby, and no doubt there is a greater space for realism, for personal goodness and individual creativity. But are we, in fact, able to fill it? We all have a certain tendency to live and work and be consumers of modern day goods, but without the scourge of the second anxiety: Will the money we have (or will get) suffice for our needs? We want to keep up with the Joneses without sharing their burdens.

We do not succumb to the third temptation only as long as money facilitates our activity instead of ruling it — as long as money is not accumulated and therefore cannot turn into the thirty pieces of silver. There is nothing wrong in giving money to a greengrocer for a head of cabbage so that he can live — as long as he does not save it. You may say: 'How can we know what the greengrocer needs, or what he intends to do with it?' Local associations, meetings between producer and consumer, are necessary. Perhaps Botton's money structure is too monolithic, too centralised. Perhaps there is too little discussion between people at a decentralised level. Of course, the arrangements of the 'outer world' create a need for something like the Stewards (our Finance Group) to administer our accounts, but should the neighbourhoods play a part in it too? In a way, the vast number of lectures and knowledge contained in anthroposophy is only the background for social and economic renewal through spiritual science today. Our time is the time of Judas. The new Christianity arises not through theological sentimentalities but through economic disasters and their overcoming. Our time is also the time of brotherhood, but brotherhood on a large, not a small, scale.

BOTTON VILLAGE NEWS, 3 III 1984

The Temptations in the Gospels

Temptation	St Matthew	St Luke	Fifth Gospel
"Worship me"	3rd Temptation	2nd Temptation	1st Temptation
"Throw yourself from the parapet of the Temple"	2nd Temptation	3rd Temptation	2nd Temptation
"Turn these stones into bread"	1st Temptation	1st Temptation	3rd Temptation

normality

Normality is the curse of our time — normality which turns a man or woman into a bourgeois Philistine, makes any kind of idealism difficult and allows only for eccentric aberrations like the beatniks of the 1950s, or the flower-children of the 60s. The concept of normality is an unhappy composite made up of democratic patriotism, keeping-up-with-the-Joneses, belief in the wisdom and authority of science and the lure of swinging London or New York — a composite in which the United Nations and the Welfare State ultimately shape the image of the human being. All this submerges the human being in the grey, murky water of *phrases*. Phraseology rules, and 'normality' has become a phrase, one in which lies a multitude of cobwebs, spinning a vast cocoon that imprisons and suffocates the realities of our life.

The many images, events and words of the gospels open their being and their manifest secrets to the on-flowing river of time in ever new ways. They are never museum-like, relics of the past or of ancient history, but always direct the beam of their sound and light to the new and the present in ever-changing colours.

The Transfiguration of Christ (Matt. 17) seems to have a special link with our time. Raphael's picture of the Transfiguration shows within a small space what is narrated in the gospels in the sequence of time. On the mountain surrounded by the light of transfiguration are Christ, Moses, Elias and the three disciples. Below, within ordinary earthly light, are the sick boy, his family and the remaining disciples who cannot heal him.

But the ill, contorted, misshapen boy looks up to the transfigured heights of Christ. The radiance and reality of the Spirit shines upon the ill, the lame, and the crippled; it shines into our pain and laments unbearable conditions. In us there is always a twofoldness: the shining Kingdom of Heaven and our dark, malformed and seemingly incurable conditions. Only in this twofoldness does the human being, created in the image of God, appear, and only above the suffering and malformation in our time does the light of transfiguration appear. 'Normality' obscures this twofoldness and reduces the interplay of light and darkness to grey; the disappearance of phrases which accept 'normality' would allow the manifold colours of this interplay to appear.

BOTTON VILLAGE NEWS, 8 III 1968

work & time

The film we saw the other day showed the way of life in a Slovakian village, and as it was about a village it was very moving to compare it with our own village. As it was a very small village in the eastern part of Europe it was hardly touched by any of the technical achievements of our time. To all outward appearances it was hardly touched even by the 'Iron Curtain' and all its unreal political divisions. Our village is built on very different lines, as it is very much part of the present age, and is situated in the West.

But the main difference lay in the position of work — harvesting, threshing, spinning, weaving, cooking, washing, etc. — which constituted almost the whole of life for the people. This made it seem a natural way of existence and utterly humanised it; work was *not* a means of earning money but a way of life. It was, therefore, permeated not only by *human* dignity and *human* splendour but also by a religious glory — the spiritual hierarchies wove in the threshing, scything, stooking and all the other activities.

It is far more difficult for us in the West to live in such a dignified way. What today is a divine urge for the Slovakian peasant — and probably for all people in the past — is a huge effort of will for us because of our freedom. For us, work is something very different because *beside* it are so many other things — evening activities, the various organising groups, the services, etc. The Slovakian peasants pour their whole being into their work, which is therefore enlivened and perfected by divine grace. Our life is filled with effort and, consequently, also with laziness, blunders, and general imperfections. We exist in a hollow space of freedom where everything we do depends only on ourselves. But just because of this that hollow space can sometimes be graced by a new light, and it is this light which will enliven us divinely as human beings of the present and not of the past.

Why has such enormous technical progress occurred since the beginning of the 19th century? The number of technical achievements, the discovery of natural forces and laws, the invention of so many different types of machine, seems staggering. Possible answers to this question are many, and as yet we do not have all of them. An attempt to come to one such answer arises from the description of the Slovakian village.

Rudolf Steiner often pointed out that through the use of machines many more 'people' are actually working than the population of the earth.[6] Each machine does the work of a number of people, and this hidden labour force in each machine is in fact a real presence, as of many unseen beings. Many incomprehensible problems — spiritual, social and human — are a result of this unseen 'over-population' that is present in addition to our physical one.

The increased production of goods and their resulting worldwide distribution, the circulation of money and the emerging of a world economy are some of the reasons for the invention of machines. The global economy is one of the main Christian forces of our time.

But beside this we must consider the fact that, because they are labour-saving, machines are therefore time-saving. This does seem logically true. But every cook using a blender or potato-peeling machine achieves this only partly, for the machine could justifiably ask: 'What will you do with the time I have saved you?' It is one of the hallmarks of our age that we have too much to do, that we are over-worked, that we have *no* time. In the Slovakian village this was clearly not the case.

The time saved by machines (including all electrically powered implements, even electric lights) is not of the same order as our everyday time — which is why it is so difficult for us to have an ordered timetable. The time saved by machines belongs to the world in which Christ reappears. The etheric world is a time world and the etheric powers are time powers. It is very difficult for our space-bound mind to imagine a time world. Our 'ordinary' time is actually time as it appears in space.

However, nowadays *there is no more ordinary time* because all our time is mixed with time saved through the use of machinery. That is why 'having time' is a Christian problem — not that one can ever 'have' time! One can be enthusiastically interested in something, one can so *love* something that time is miraculously created for it; a quarter of an hour here, ten minutes there. If this happens every day, it can add up to quite a lot. It is as if the wedge of love had widened the time-space into which time streams.

BOTTON VILLAGE NEWS, 11/18 X 1963

on suffering

Three kinds of suffering help to build future worlds. One is the unconscious suffering in our time; another is a spiritual-social suffering, while the third is individual suffering.

We could call the first kind of suffering the more or less unconscious suffering that arises from the conditions of our time. (The husband must go every morning to earn money for his family and himself; the wife has to look after the children, the house and the meals.) The prevailing world conception with its threatening climate of electronics and moon landings is recognised even by the most illiterate. And the churches, now empty, forsaken relics among a mass of skyscrapers, re-echo the mumbled phrases about eternal life after death.

Concerning the second suffering, we who are anthroposophists and recipients of the Sacrament know of karma, reincarnation and Christianity. But if a certain balance is not created through our tiredness, our daily duties of cooking, mending, entertaining guests and so on, we would only be victims of Lucifer. In Paradise our eyes were opened by Lucifer and we knew good and evil, but anthroposophy is the regaining of Paradise in the name of Christ. We are allowed to enter Paradise in thought, provided that we do not throw away the burdens and sufferings which we have to endure. If we discard these burdens not only will we be imprisoned by Lucifer, but our spiritual knowledge will no longer benefit the world; it will be held in Lucifer's kingdom. If we take into account our night-existence as well as our day-existence, it may dawn upon us that our life is really very complicated. Our conscience urges us on into realms which seem to satisfy our abilities. However, we should be neither foolhardy nor heartless but rather we should recognise that through such endurance undertaken for the sake of others we extricate anthroposophy from Lucifer's kingdom.

The second and third kinds of suffering overlap. We are born to certain parents in a certain place and spend our formative years in particular circumstances. We are therefore biased, prejudiced and conditioned in many ways which we cannot easily ignore or overcome. These carry others in their wake. The second and third sufferings overlap because Christ has become the Lord of Karma.[7] The paying or balancing of individual debts is used in the web of progress and the needs of man and humanity. And who suffers? — it is we human souls who suffer. But we must come to see that we are not just victims of suffering in our time; such an attitude of self-pity sentimentalises, it blurs with selfishness what is really a shining glory.

It is nothing but a reactionary tendency in us to try to remove the causes of suffering, to pull out the thorn embedded in our flesh, so to speak. This is as unimportant as the urge to drink when we are thirsty. It is far more important to recognise that happiness has to do with the past, suffering with the future. This is because happiness needs no effort — the sun shines on us just as we are

— but we can never come nearer to Christ in our time simply through being as we are. Only through Christ can we become human beings, and this effort is necessary even if it involves suffering. The opposite of happiness is effort, not suffering. The solution and harmony of suffering can only lie in the future, just as a pearl is the future resulting from the pain caused by the grain of sand in the oyster. Without grains of sand there would be no pearls; without our suffering there will be no shining future for the human being and the earth.

BOTTON VILLAGE NEWS, 29 I 1970

the earth as the body of christ

There was once a time when the sun was within the earth. At that time not only was the surface of the earth illumined from within rather than from outside as it is today, but it was transparent just as, when standing on a bridge, we can see through the sunlit surface of a pool into its depths. Hardness only came with interior darkness. When Christ eventually descended from the sun to the earth it was actually a return, and from His death on Golgotha onwards the earth has begun to shine out again into the cosmos. But what was physical light when the sun was still within is now, in our time, a spiritual, moral light.

Every deed, every situation in life, has to be balanced by a counter-deed or counter-situation in a following life. Before Christ came, the web of karma was nothing but our own deeds and wishes and the reactions set up through them. Since Christ replaced Moses as the Lord of Karma,[8] this web of our karmic necessities is used for the building up, the coherence, the becoming of the concept *mankind*. If I need to suffer as a consequence of a former deed it may not necessarily mean that I have to become ill myself; I may be required to nurse someone else who is ill. In this way my suffering is used for nursing; it is put to the service of mankind. Because using our karmic propensities in the service of mankind is only possible on the basis of our individual decisions, we have to take that decision to nurse. Something which would otherwise be only a self-centred weakness is tempered by the will to nurse. We have to actively decide to go in for this or that otherwise our karma cannot unfold in a Christian, selfless way but remains stuck in the round of cause and effect. It is our decision-making that lights it up.

The sign for Moses as Lord of Karma was the head (not the countenance), but the sign for Christ as Lord of Karma is the feet. Our head is the transformed result of our previous incarnation, our former life shaped into form, while our feet carry us where our decisions lead us. Among the zodiacal stars it is the powers of Aries the Ram (which looks back) that form the head, while Pisces relates to the feet. The fish depicted in the catacombs in many variations denotes Christ. The feet are the expression of karma serving mankind. The Washing of the Feet (John 13: 4–17) during the Last Supper is like the promise of a new morning, which is why it is one of the experiences which the Christian pupil must undergo.

When we say the earth is the body of Christ we should not be tempted to think of something fixed: His being is not static. In our time it is the new karma, the karma our wandering feet fulfil, which will make the earth contain the Sun again. Love is the ever-renewed Washing of the Feet. The water heralds the new light issuing not from an outer sun but from the earth. Washing the feet of others signifies serving mankind.

In the story of the adulteress in St John's Gospel (John 8: 3–11), Christ writes in the dust with His finger. In doing so He makes her karma a karma of the Fishes, the zodiac sign that rules the feet (and hands), which will place her suffering in the service of mankind. In writing on the ground in this way, He prepares the earth to contain the sun. Hence Christ says immediately afterwards: 'I am the Light of the World' (John 8: 12). The stones, which would have condemned her under the Law of Moses, would have made the earth harder and darker.

Against the sunlit flood of the water of the Washing of the Feet rises the darkness of Judas (symbolised by the black vestments in the Good Friday service of the Christian Community). Judas went out into the night after he had dipped bread in the dish with Christ at the Last Supper (Matt. 25: 23).

BOTTON VILLAGE NEWS, 20 III 1969

christ as the lord of karma

One tends to think of the law of karma somewhat on the lines of 'an eye for an eye, a tooth for a tooth' (Exod. 21: 24, Lev. 24: 20, Deut. 19: 21, Matt. 5: 38), such that if I box someone's ears in this life, they must do the same to me in the next life. Thoughts like this take causality into realms where it was never valid; it is simply upholding a kind of Judaic morality which says that the better you behave now the luckier you will be in your next life, i.e. if you never harm anyone (in whatever form), nobody will injure you in return. Christianity, unfortunately, absorbed something of this ascetic-cum-selfish character and as a result the fact that karma and reincarnation are actually *inherent* within it became blurred. Why inherent? Because it calls up the deepest and most exacting responsibility a human being can encompass, and makes us aware of this responsibility in regard to each single life. We will discover that all responsibilities, both fulfilled and missed, have their reverberations, and the more aware we are, the more we will become masters of our own karma.

This growing awareness will go hand in hand with an enhanced capacity for experience, and will contain different motives for acting (if you see a lion, you run; if you do not see it, you have no reason to run). Gradually, over the course of many years, this 'seeing' will grow into 'vision' — perceiving far more in people, in nature, in buildings and in institutions than we did before — and these experiences will be apocalyptic, they will show us the inherent and the ideal, the future *purpose* of our experiences rather than their *origin*. In this way we will come to a very clear perception of the Ahrimanic and the Luciferic power and being in the world, as opposed to what is purely human, that is, Christian. Destiny is composed of balancing out the Luciferic and Ahrimanic aberrations in our past.

Through Christ, the Lord of Karma,[9] our freedom is infinitely greater because on the hard-beaten ground of necessity we are enabled to stand and move freely according to our insights and experiences. As Lord of Karma, Christ does not alter the moral law of balances; rather, He enhances our experience so that more, new nuances of balance are introduced into society. The more we can act out of empathy the more karma will alter, not because empathy is something good (although it is), but because through it something new is introduced into the body social of mankind.

Up to now, karma consisted mainly of the influence of one human being on another. By way of the selfless intuition of empathy, there is an evolution from experiencing the inmost self of our fellow human being to an actual alteration of the social organism — for example, curative education in one life will lead to social regeneration in the next. A human being will be moved, if someone steals his coat, to give the thief his jacket as well (which will be the end of all burglary). However, the motive for giving the jacket is not so as to prevent burglary, but rather it stems from empathy. Because empathy is beyond sympathy and antipathy, the words and deeds resulting from it will be woven into the social life of humanity; words and deeds will spring up which are not confined to the two people between whom the empathetic encounter takes place. Christ as Lord of Karma means this: that objective relationships will begin to exist between human beings and will gradually permeate and transform social organisms. The social implications of Christianity will dawn.

BOTTON VILLAGE NEWS, 9 II 1973

Botton Village News

EASTER

~ *holy week & easter*

good friday & easter sunday

The joy of Easter Sunday is easier to bear than the grief of Good Friday. On Easter Sunday, that which is beyond human measure merges into the rising life of a new spring. In every spring there is something eternal, something immortal and therefore Easter-like.

The grief of Good Friday is much harder. Christ experiences agony in Gethsemane because He is in danger of dying before He has completely spiritualised His earthly body.[10] Christ stands more and more alone, the disciples failing to understand His cosmic element, until He is seized by the soldiers, at which moment the Christ impulse in the form of a youth with a fine linen garment flees from Jesus. (Mark 14: 51–52)[11] The Mother of Jesus and the disciple whom Jesus loved stand beneath the black cross amidst the growing warmth and light. The supreme divine being undergoes physical death. Love and death, the divine and the human, enmesh and intertwine in an unfathomable way.

The four accounts in the gospels from the Last Supper to the Crucifixion and Entombment are *all* true because *one* gospel alone could not encompass an event of such width and magnitude. We are impressed by the sequence of the events taking place on this human level. How ignominious that a god is subjected, or subjects himself, to Pilate's doubts, to the hatred of the Jews, to the cruelty of the soldiers, and so on! We are then tempted to suffer all this in an all too human way, until we realise that although it is all real and human, it is set against the shining background of Easter.

The black altar and vestments of Lent are black as the background of the shining red of Easter. All that we human beings suffer and enjoy on earth becomes real only when they come together, as with the red of Easter and the black of Lent. Our experiences, joyful or painful, become *whole* only if the red is added in the sequence of time to what at first is only black, the symbol and colour of turmoil, chaos and death. But through the red, death turns from a material end to the gate of the Resurrection. Our human feelings, even the smallest and least significant, are meant to hammer the metal of our soul into the arched bridge leading from Good Friday to Easter Sunday, from our mortal soul to our immortal youth.

BOTTON VILLAGE NEWS, 11 IV 1969

the empty grave

In his lectures *The Fifth Gospel*, Rudolf Steiner's account of the empty grave brought about two things. It restored the four synoptic gospels to more than simply realistic narrations or reports of what took place at the time of the Mystery of Golgotha, and it destroyed the old concept of miracles. Rudolf Steiner described how an earthquake (Matt. 28: 1–6), tore open a cleft in the earth at the site of the grave and Christ's body fell into the chasm. Another earthquake then closed the chasm, throwing the gravestone aside so that on coming to the tomb the women and disciples found it empty (Mark 16: 1–4, Luke 24: 1–3, John 20: 1–2). Thus Steiner removes the Resurrection from the realm of miracles and places it within the evolution of the world.[12] The fabric of nature remains intact.

Regarding Christianity, nothing is more problematic for the modern mind than miracles, especially the miracle of the Resurrection. Christianity has become a religion tied to the understanding and acceptance of miracles. However, belief in natural laws is by no means as authoritative today as it was in the second half of the 19th century, and what was then the very antithesis of natural law, namely miracles, has also lost some of its significance — quite apart from the fact that it was through the flood of materialism that natural laws created the modern attitude to 'miracles'.

Miracles have always had an aura of magic. Natural events like thunderstorms or floods became endowed with a moral character, or the moral seemed so strong that it broke through into the world of nature and became the cause of these events. We can say that miracles thereby replaced the power of transubstantiation (Matt. 26: 26–28, Mark 14: 22–24, Luke 22: 17–19); the sudden shattering of the thread, and evolution of nature replaced alchemical transformation. Christians could no longer grasp that transubstantiation was the only miracle; that it was the very essence of the Mystery of Golgotha. The reality of the Resurrection showed itself in Christ's appearance to Mary Magdalene and the disciples in the forty days after Easter, and has continued to do so in innumerable experiences which human beings have had, then and now. The power of the Resurrection has gone into the power of transubstantiation, of transformation, of metamorphosis.

When we eat the bread and drink the wine at the end of the Communion Service, we are not only consuming the body and blood of Christ as the earth once did; rather it is that we — our eternal future — become as wide as the whole earth. 'Christ in us' means the earth becomes human again. The New Jerusalem has begun, invisibly.

BOTTON VILLAGE NEWS, 2 V 1969

israel

The first and indeed persistent impression of Israel is of many Mediterranean layers held together by the Jewish religion and its youthful nationalism — and by something else which will be described in the course of this article. Compressed together in the southeastern corner of the Mediterranean, these layers are as follows: Roman and Hellenistic ruins, amphitheatres, harbour buildings and quays, statues, pillars and arches; Crusader castles with their halls, moats and ramparts; old Jewish houses and synagogues; Arab and Turkish peoples, eating places, bazaars and mosques. These can all be found within the biblical landscape of the Old and New Testaments, from the snows of Mount Hermon in the north to the Dead Sea in the south, along the sunken course of the river Jordan from the Lake of Galilee and onwards below sea level flanked by Mount Carmel towards Lebanon in the north and the high desert mountains of Judea and Jerusalem in the south.

One can only admire the groves of orange, avocado and grapefruit trees and the fruitfulness of the fields and gardens amidst this desert soil — a visible result of the tremendous Israeli will, zeal and perseverance. No doubt this will is a phenomenon of modern times. It sprang consciously from the desire of Jews all over the world, although mainly from Germany, Austria, Czechoslovakia, Poland, Hungary and Russia, to have a geographical home. This will is personified in Herzl, for example, and in people like Martin Buber and Marc Chagall, who were members of an older generation partly assimilated into European culture. These do not really represent the will which permeates a generation either born in what now exists on the map as Israel, or who left Europe as babies.

This younger generation is untainted by the socio-cultural values of its chequered European heritage, which also contained all that anti-Semitism, but is thoroughly imbued with a will that derives its strength from a pioneering and very determined nationalism which could not avoid arms and aggression but which also garnered impressive skills in building, technology, cultivation of the land, etc. It is also a will that is permeated by an old Mosaic spirituality, although the religion has faded into mere morality as well as, amazingly, a Christian courage. It is this Christian courage which renders the human atmosphere in this strongly nationalistic land of Israel not only tolerable but, indeed, attractive, and it has, perhaps, to do with the landscape which bears the imprint of so many events in the Old and New Testaments. The Bible is the best known book in the world and makes the landscape within which all this happened a landscape *par excellence*, the archetype of all landscapes, home to us all as citizens of the earth. That the landscape is in some way expressive of the very home of humanity makes Israel's nationalism somewhat understandable and excusable. One's love for this home is a love of a more general, human kind, pre-Tower of Babel as it were, and not strictly nationalistic because it is not one home among many, but *the* home.

But there is something else. Rudolf Steiner tells us that every year at Easter,[13] Jesus of Nazareth revisits the places where Jesus Christ performed the Mystery of Golgotha. This is the fulfilment of the landscape in which the Old and New Testaments took place, for the Mystery of Golgotha is the sense, purpose and centre of the Bible. The landscape of Jerusalem, of Judea and then up into Galilee (because they are not paradisal), possess this deeply human gift which Jesus, the Son of Man — Jesus who bears the imprint of the Christ — brings when he visits the landscape each year in the Easter light. Many strands of history seem to converge there and He may carry, every year, the achievements and the failures of humankind into that light.

BOTTON VILLAGE NEWS, 29 V 1982

about the course of the act of consecration of man

Once the candles are lit on the altar it is as if a different element surrounds us: our space is no longer just ordinary space. What surrounds this space contains more silence and stillness than usual. If this stillness is interrupted by some distraction (the barking of a dog, the shout of a child, the noise of a car), we are shocked and slightly wounded.

This lit-up space surrounded by a dense stillness stretches to the moment the candles are extinguished. Between the lighting and extinguishing of the candles is a time-space which has four levels: the Gospel Reading, Offertory, Transubstantiation and Communion. But unlike a tower in ordinary space, we descend the levels: we go down the inverted tower, Transubstantiation being the deepest, darkest and narrowest level; Communion being the highest, embracing all the others. The Word, which makes us whole when we take bread and wine, is the word from the gospels, coming from the first (but highest) level of the Gospel Reading now filled out, made real. The word which is spoken and heard in the first level of the gospel will become the Word that is eaten in the fourth.

We can imagine the time-space of the Act of Consecration in many colours but it is difficult to describe them. Being more than feelings, they evoke in us the rainbow colours themselves. We can imagine the first part of the service, the Gospel Reading, as a bluish-green peach-blossom light, like the colours at Michaelmas. The Offering is darker, a night-blue but lit up by many bright stars, while the third part, the Transubstantiation, is entirely dark, like a deep purple valley or gorge. In it is the erected cross and the re-enacted death of Christ. It is the physical death of the god. We can imagine the death of human beings perhaps, but we should not think that we can imagine divine death. Gradually we learn to take the first steps in understanding it. Therefore we cannot really imagine the gathering purple darkness of the Transubstantiation. It is the midnight hour of all existence. Then, at the end of the Transubstantiation comes the Lord's Prayer, the words which Christ speaks in each one of us, sounding out of the folds of the darkest valley of heaven and earth.

As the words of the Lord's Prayer ascend, the triumphant bright red of the Resurrection rises, lightens and widens, not only rising but also embracing the three far-reaching, descending, narrowing, darkening levels. The fourth part of the service fills the cup to the brim with the red of Easter.

BOTTON VILLAGE NEWS, 5 IX 1969

interference

The mantle of morality surrounding the earth is many-layered. The layer which brings disorder into many others is that of politics. Voting is inhuman simply because instead of an issue being decided by a shared insight common to all, the numerical majority overwhelms the minority. Foreign policy is even more unreasonable because it is determined to a large extent by the principle of non-intervention — the business of another state is sacrosanct, while within our own boundaries we can do whatever we like. The boundaries themselves are absolute: we are subject to the laws of the country we enter. The globe and humanity is divided into nations, every atlas showing political as well as physical maps.

Non-intervention and the State are two mutually supportive concepts and would be valid if the country were a person — another person is an individual and we should be tolerant; we can interfere in his or her life only out of interest and love — but a state is *not* another person. It is a multitude of individuals, sometimes governed by an archangel who has quite different relationships from those between individuals; sometimes it is simply a product of historical events. Humanity is under the illusion that different states are as independent and circumscribed as are single human beings, and that they act and react in the same way. But foreign politics is very different from personal relationships. The concept of non-interference, taken from personal relationships, confuses international and personal morality.

There is also a huge gap between governments and the people they govern — and not just in the case of the minority which, in the name of democracy, is overwhelmed by the majority. The whole idea of government in our time is based on the notion that elected representatives will represent my views on traffic, education, money, etc. Their commitment to party and electorate may be unquestioning, yet they cannot avoid being individuals as well, entering into relationships with other individuals in parliament, ministry or cabinet: they cannot just be puppets. (I feel sure the Camphill custom of interlocking working groups of experts in education, money, production, etc. is far better.)

Different governments relate to one another. The unreality of this relationship is again multi-layered. In the foreground is the single citizen and his relation to morality. How many acts of horror have been perpetrated, and still are, all over the world in the name of the law and the state! But it is always an individual who perpetrates them. Morality should be the outcome of an individual's conscience. A nation, party or sect can have a common belief or mission but it cannot have a conscience, and only moral intuition can be the wellspring of morality.

In the background looms the paradox of the law. With only slight exaggeration we could say, 'Each state has its own laws.' With no reference to conscience (a glaring example of which was revealed in the Nürnberg Trials), these laws command and forbid. What is looked upon in one country or one set of circumstances as sinful, is criminal in another. St Paul's saying that sin came with the law has, two thousand years later, gained a dreadful reality.

We could imagine a future society in which laws might be of the same nature as traffic regulations, and criminal law be replaced by individual conscience. Courts would have to transform into places of soul care, and social conditions would have to be different. But in the light of the ideals of a threefold social organism all this is not as utopian as one might think. The truth or validity of the law lies only in its being enforced by police, army or officers of the State, but if the State disappears many anti-social, selfish, chauvinistic conditions will vanish with it. The natural goodness of men and women will appear, mutual care for one another will warm the frozen soil of social life, and self-determination of people circumscribed by states will be consigned to the museum of history. Michael will become the true Spirit of our time.

BOTTON VILLAGE NEWS, 31 VII 1981

democracy & materialism

Our evolutionary age, which began about four hundred years ago, contains many riddles regarding the connections between the various phenomena that arose with it. Printing was invented, new continents discovered, astronomy was revolutionised, Protestantism emerged, natural science was expanded, and, later on, machines were invented. All this reached a culmination in the second half of the 19th century. We still live on the receding slope of that peak, although something entirely different has already begun, namely the ending of the Dark Age, or Kali Yuga,[14] in 1899 and the beginning of the Light Age. Two things keep all these half-truths together as if bound by iron shackles: democracy and materialism. These emerged together and in connection with everything else over the last four centuries. Materialism developed mainly in conjunction with natural science. Democracy emerged in the Dark Age with humanity's growing conviction in the equality of all, leading to parliaments, the party system, voting, trades unions, etc., all forms that were humane and liberal in the second half of the 19th century, but which today can obstruct true development.

The equality of human beings is an experience which has its origin in the gospels: 'Blessed are the poor in spirit: for theirs is the kingdom of heaven'

(Matt. 5: 3) and 'What you have done unto the least of one of my brothers you have done unto me' (Matt. 25: 40). The divinity of every human being is quite different from the divinity of priests and hierophants in the ancient mysteries, or the divine right of kings, or even the apparently superhuman status of the gentry in the past, accompanied as it was by the less than human condition of slaves and downtrodden serfs. The presence of the spirit in the bearers of these past theocratic systems founded on priest-kings was a common conviction, an unquestioned experience. In later times the light of the spirit in such specially initiated and anointed men and women began to fade and, starting perhaps with Wycliffe, men began to question it. Nevertheless, as in the theocratic past, the presence of spirit still continued to be an unquestioned experience, although only in regard to comparatively few individuals, and was therefore unchristian, even in Christian times. But the divinity of *each* human being is Christian, and because it can be doubted its insight needs the will and decision of the individual.

Democracy is, in itself, Christian, and therefore confirms the reality of the spiritual world. But as long as democracy is fettered by materialistic science not only will the priest-kings cease to rule but, due to a sham equality, the devil of institutions will take hold of us instead. The gulf between the single individual and the institutions he serves is widening considerably, as we see in universities, political parties, denominations, trade unions and in the all-powerful welfare state. The power of the institution has more and more enmeshed the immortal individual.

We can vividly imagine the rising, irresistible tide of equality sweeping away the old theocratic caste system, but also sweeping away the experience of spiritualised individuals and thereby suffocating their realisation of the spiritual world. Brotherhood, however, arises with equality while also recognising the inequality of human beings, and brotherhood will become the teacher of immortality and reincarnation.

BOTTON VILLAGE NEWS, 24 V 1968

death

No topic is more shunned today than death. All scientific and technological inventions apply only to life between birth and death and so leave the ultimate question of life before birth and after death unanswered. Death is something that cannot be mentioned, a new taboo, so that our earthly life seems to be like a brightly-lit island surrounded by black, mysterious oceans. But the island of earthly life can only make sense if we have some possibility of reaching into the black oceans. Like a heritage of the Dark Age, a blanket of fear covers the question of death, stemming from the conviction that our thinking cannot understand anything pertaining to the dark oceans.

This question of death is closely connected with ritual and meditation. If we accept that death is a threshold beyond which quite different forms, beings and events pertain, then we can also accept ritual and meditation as being unlike anything we can find in our earthly existence. In this way, the more we experience the words and events of a ritual; the more we learn to dwell inwardly on a meditation, and the more we experience the reality beyond the threshold, we thereby experience something of the immortality of our being.

It is not simply the case that we are born, grow up, and that our body becomes increasingly worn out and brittle until, finally, we die. Many death processes already permeate our body during life but they are hidden from us because we owe our consciousness to these very same processes.[15] As our eye cannot see itself but is a sense organ for anything visible, so our consciousness does not become aware of these death processes, which originate in the nervous system. But, over the course of seven years, everything in us that dies — bone, blood, tissues, etc. — is balanced by our growing, healing, rejuvenating powers until these become so weakened, or excarnated, that balance is no longer possible, and then we die.

But where death is, there Christ is also. Ritual, as well as meditation, could make us aware of these powers of death because Christ is stronger than they are. Through ritual and meditation we could experience death more as a transformation into a different existence, and not as an end, a drowning in the dark floods.

The Light Age expresses itself overwhelmingly in human relationships. In it dawn mutual respect, tolerance and recognition, quite independent of nationality, race, creed, sex or official position, particularly among the young. This recognition of the person is no doubt a recognition of the immortal individual, but we have as yet no world-conception (except through anthroposophy) of what makes this concept of the immortal individual possible.

Recognising the *person* is the main driving-force in all social work. The many young people studying social work are undoubtedly enthused by the hope of drinking at these wells of existence. Their efforts — and the effort of all social work — is deeply Christian, but without recognising the death processes in those for whom they care (and thereby also recognising them in themselves) their Christianity will remain unconscious. Social work will be throttled by the claws of the state.

Ritual and meditation are natural consequences of social work. As a deepening of feeling takes place within it, so an immeasurable quickening of efficiency coupled with practical ideas and presence of mind would result if ritual and meditation became the wellsprings of social work. But without the recognition of death and the death-processes, the inherent fact of its permeation by Christianity cannot arise.

BOTTON VILLAGE NEWS, 5 V 1972

c u l t u r e

For years now the question of cultural activities, undertaken mainly in the evenings, has vexed our minds in Botton. There is no doubt that spending a major part of one's waking day in work is a tremendous boost to morale and helps one feel oneself a necessary member of humanity — especially if it is not work done for the sake of earning one's own livelihood but because its outcome is really needed. That is why unemployment in the world is such a problem because one's morale is necessarily low. But to create the hygienic-economic day in which work and cultural activities complement each other humanly, is no doubt the task of any social organism today, not only ours. Nor is it merely a question of quantity. Too much work does not call on all the abilities of a human being, while too many cultural activities diminish their quality to that of leisure activities, or simply turn human beings into consumers.

One could look upon human life in a trinitarian way. Work is not an individual thing but something we all share; its morality has to do with what is common to us all. Where and how we fit in so as to implement the needs of the world is of secondary importance.

Culture, in the spiritual-religious sphere, is the pole of the Holy Spirit that complements the pole of the Father Ground of the common platform of work. Individual freedom (both to advise and to choose) pertains in this realm. If people object that too many things are happening — various entertainments such as lectures, performances, musical treats, as well as groups of an enlightening or administrative nature — one could ask why they attend so many things? The variety is laid on for the different tastes of different people, rather than everything for the whole population. Neither advice nor freedom of choice is practised enough. The temptation to attend what others attend is great because the social, the communal life, has a persuasion of its own.

Cultural life in itself makes an impact in two directions: on its producer and on its consumer. The more the audience (the 'consumers') participate, the less they are merely passive recipients, and the more they feel their creative faculties touched and enhanced. The more that cultural activities have a chance to enter this process to enhance the creative potential of the 'consumer', the more they will achieve that magic hygiene and balance out our working life. And nothing slipshod from the producer's side will do: proper preparation is of the utmost importance.

Every human being has a cultural as well as a working nature. Division of labour is a blessing that has arisen just in order to give every one of us the opportunity to take part in all three spheres of the social organism — although how it is practised elsewhere, for example in China, where the university professor has to spend a part of his life working manually, is probably able to prove its reality only in a social organism such as we have in Camphill. What takes place as division of labour on the factory floors of our time is but the shadow of the reality to come: the threefold activity of every human being.

BOTTON VILLAGE NEWS, 25 IV 1980

~ *a s c e n s i o n & w h i t s u n*

a r t c a n r e v e a l t h e a s c e n s i o n

Like all the Christian festivals, Ascension is an historic event. Forty days after the first Easter Sunday, Christ disappeared from the disciples' sight. But the Ascension is also inscribed into every human being and into our time so that we must imagine it not as a one-off occurrence, but as one of the continuing conditions under which we live. How are we to understand this?

Ascension is the promise that earthly life and death are not all there is, but that beyond our earthly senses and thinking lie the glorious roots and causes of our own and the earth's being. And just as Christ's Ascension was not really a departure, so our death is only an apparent end. Christ 'ascended' to the Father, but the Father is not beyond the being of the earth; He is *within* it. Christ vanished into the depths of the earthly world just as we do not disappear completely when we die but permeate earthly nature, even man-made creation, in a different way from before death. The picture of the Ascension is of the opening of a gate, the Great Way Out of mere physical existence. If Christ had stayed with the apostles, the Heavenly Sun would still have warmed and enlightened earthly existence, but that gate would have remained shut and we would have been caught within earthly life as in a prison.

It is the task of *art* to make earthly things and bodies translucent, to make them shine from within; it is to kindle the fire of Ascension under all our earthly heaviness and darkness so that in the upward movement the earthly rigidity of our form is changed and transformed. As a result of this fire, 'upward' ceases to be confined in space: it becomes a movement from space into time and the time-nature of earthly bodies and conditions reveals itself.

Of each stone, each plant, each new state of the weather or climate, we only ever see its shape, the 'space-form' it has at any given moment, even if that 'moment' is thousands of years long. Growth and decay, past and future, are hidden from us — in the seed and fruit in a plant, in the origin of a mountain, in a stone or in a metal. Their future existence as the stream of time evolves is concealed in *space*. Art can make the idea, the ideal, transfigure spatial form. The frantic 'contortions' of art throughout the 20th century have actually been a continuing effort to overcome space-shapes in order to behold and enter the stream of time. It has been a constant effort to Christianise art.

Christianity and vanishing are related, which is why death and Christianity are related: *in Christo morimur* — in Christ we are in the process of dying. It is also why the disciples who met the Christ on the road to Emmaus realised Who it was only after He had vanished.

BOTTON VILLAGE NEWS, 23 V 1965

the apostles & paul

The Christianity of the apostles grew through their being present, physically, with Christ until His capture in the Garden of Gethsemane when they all fled, except for John the Evangelist (probably not one of the twelve), who stayed with Christ until the Crucifixion. Then they were with Him again, spiritually, between Easter Sunday and His disappearance at Ascension. During the ten days between Ascension and Whitsun the disciples experienced (according to Rudolf Steiner), a pain incomparable with any earthly pain, which slowly woke them up.[16] Then at Whitsun, as if in a kind of blind, super-consciousness, the light of the Holy Spirit granted them awareness of what they had experienced in the past. Only then did ego-consciousness, individualisation in the ordinary sense of the word, begin to develop. Before that they had been part of the twelvehood, each serving one aspect of it. Every human being carries the cosmic twelvehood within himself. What had been the twelvehood of the zodiac in the past was formed out, inscribed in us in order that we could become human. The twelve world directions flowed in towards the centre, and where they met stood a human being. Christ was the *Son of Man* and the apostles were the new twelvehood, standing around the *new* creation; the renewed human being.

Over against all this is Paul, not serving a part of the new twelvehood, not an apostle, not belonging to the physical manifestation of the Son of God, not meeting Christ or the apostles in the flesh, but a Christian merely through individual, inner experience. What is described of Paul's experience before Damascus (Acts 9: 1–22) is an objective event. It is a repeatable event, the consciousness of which, however, can vary enormously. Many people in our time may have an experience similar to Paul's, and yet their consciousness is unable to embrace it. Rudolf Steiner predicted that it would happen more and more from the year 1933 on. In fact it was, and is, the experience of the etheric coming of the Christ.[17] How much of the experience we perceive is dependent on our consciousness, which can be limited by preconceived ideas, blinded by the effects of our surroundings, education, newspapers, etc. Only a few are as yet able to take hold of such an experience — and in some it may appear clothed in different garments — but it is really *the* Christian experience of our time.

Paul is human in the sense that we all are. The apostles, with Christ, were the new humanity, but it was only after Whitsun that they gradually became like Paul: individual human beings. At first the apostles thought that we must become Jewish in order to go on to become Christian. Paul had begun life as Saul, persecuting the Christians, but after the experience at Damascus he became convinced that, outwardly, the way to Christianity could go either through Judaism or paganism, namely through the common human being. Inwardly we are all Jews, but we make the first steps in Christ's kingdom in so far as we shed the shell of Judaism. Surrounded by the twelvehood of the disciples, Christ is like the new sun with its rays. We are like Paul, in whose heart this new sunrise dawns.

BOTTON VILLAGE NEWS, 10 II 1967

smell

Between Easter and Whitsun there is always a distinct threshold. During winter the cold air is empty. The growing, greening, warming world of spring starts to fill the air not only with various distinct scents like apple blossom and lilac, but also with an unspecified scent which streams into the far spaces. The air beyond the threshold is filled with a tender, warm scent, which makes the air wider and fuller.

The whole realm of smell is mysterious because our consciousness is not able to probe very deeply into it. Whenever we try to focus our attention on smell — a particular smell — we have an experience similar to trying to focus on objects in twilight: they vanish as we look directly at them; we see them only when we look away from them.

Our consciousness is centripetal; it surges from a vague circumference to a clear centre. If the onrush of consciousness reaches the centre, the smell becomes unclear, but if the onrush stops short of the centre, the scent then evokes a flood of emotions.

A strange connection exists between the sense of smell and memory: it is impossible to remember a smell clearly. However, nothing loosens memories more, frees them from enchantment as it were, than the sense of smell.

We could describe the connection of the twelve senses[18] to the ego on the one hand and to ego-consciousness on the other. The sense of smell serves our consciousness as a kind of conceptual confirmation. Our sense of sight tells us, 'This is a rose,' and its scent confirms that it is. Or, if we smell the fragrance of a rose, our consciousness says there must be a rose nearby. But as superficial as the connection is between smell and ego-consciousness, so deep is it between smell and ego. Love *always* has its source in the ego.

The scents of spring fan our love towards the earth. Permeated with thankfulness and bliss, our love lightens the weight of our body through which we contact earthly form and substance as well as other earthly beings. The sense of smell binds our existence to our body.

The warm spring scents belong to the ten days between Ascension and Whitsun. The non-physical side of this is the darkness and despair of the disciples over the vanished Christ.

The scent of incense also evokes our love, but it is a praying love, a love in whose light emerge divine, majestic spiritual beings like snow-covered mountain peaks rising in clarity out of the darkness of earthly valleys. At the same time as the clouds of incense rise, we can feel that through its scent the gods can gaze down at us and behold us. We are not less connected with our body, but it seems as if the grace descending through the rising clouds of incense wish to make this connection innocent.

The gazing, divine snowy peaks appearing in the scent of incense are Whitsun.

BOTTON VILLAGE NEWS, 7 VI 1963

whitsun & equality

The white of altar and vestments at Whitsuntide has something of a blossom-like quality, and with it the sense of innocence and truth. Petals, flowers, whatever their colour, become the physical expression of the flaming tongues of the Holy Spirit, the Spirit of Truth.

The blossom-like Spirit of Whitsun, this touching of earthly souls by the burning white of the Spirit, the flower-like opening, the gazing upward and flaming upward of our earthly souls — all this makes us brothers and sisters. Through our common response we become equal.

This equality of human beings arising from the hidden stream of Whitsun — from the Spirit which Christ promised to send after his disappearance — expresses itself in many aspects of history. Since the end of the Middle Ages, the most powerful aspect has been democracy: parliaments, local councils, federations and trade unions emerged to replace the rulership of kings and dukes. In all these, truth is sought by voting as the means to decide who shall be elected to such bodies, and how various problems are to be solved. But voting has something warlike about it and the blossom-like quality of truth withdraws before this attitude of fighting. If sixty vote *for* something and forty vote *against* it, then what the sixty propose wins and the forty are overpowered: the sixty become dictators and the forty are silenced. Tuesday, the day of the war-like planet Mars, is followed by Wednesday, the day of healing Mercury. The truth will be found if a group of people who are responsible for a problem do not vote, but talk with one another until the solution is reached. One can only seek the truth through voting if one is blind to the Whitsun flame within every human being. In the Act of Consecration of Man the Holy Spirit, the Spirit of Truth, is the Healing Spirit.

BOTTON VILLAGE NEWS, 8 VI 1962

printing

The Renaissance of the 15th and 16th centuries evinced a profound change in the human constitution and consciousness. The words of the Bible, 'Your eyes shall be opened' (Genesis 3: 7), seemed to acquire a new dimension. Great vistas opened up in science, art and religion. Science leapt forward through the influence of Sir Francis Bacon; realism and perspective appeared in art, while religion burgeoned in the great efforts of men like Martin Luther and John Calvin. Universities sprang up, medicine was grounded on a true anatomical foundation, and voyages of discovery led to the conviction that the earth is round. All this was crowned by the invention of the printing press in the middle of the 15th century, in England by Caxton and in Germany by Gutenberg. Printing was the yeast in the dough.

It is only in our time, with the help of anthroposophy, that we have begun to see that the Renaissance was not just a glorious new beginning, but that it also marked the beginning of materialism and the end of the spiritual world as a self-evident reality. The human being would only gain entry to the world of spirit again after all efforts of re-conquest had been made, and even then as a different creature from the one he had been when he was forced to leave it.

The invention of printing had two momentous consequences which are difficult for us to appreciate fully today. First the Bible was printed, followed soon after by newspapers and, later, by history and travel books. Then the mass media took over, leading to the assumption that human beings know everything, but this 'everything' was in reality an illusion. 'Everything' was reduced to a thin layer and despite illustrations in black and white, grey or colour, on paper and later on television, it had all the immediacy removed from it.

Common sense resulting from direct experience was increasingly lamed by indirect 'news', whether in print or on radio or television. Subjective intellectual opinions grew like weeds, obliterating our ability to think for ourselves. Today we have gone so far down this road that we readily believe what is in print rather than the evidence of our own eyes and ears.

Before the invention of printing we were dependent for news on hand-written letters or verbal accounts by people who had been present at the event. The *directness* of our experiences was infinitely greater then. Whether a person's speech comes via loudspeaker, dictaphone or broadcasting studio does not seem to make much difference.

A second consequence of printing has been that our sensitivity to voices and their individual nuances has become much decreased. News reporters are becoming increasingly 'objective' with speech conveying nothing more than information. They do not tell us about another's experiences, events or about his or her own soul-life.

But there is something else in language which played an important rôle in the past and (although in a different way), will play a great rôle again in our future, and that is its healing and creative power. Nowadays, power is the last thing one would connect with speech. However, some of us have watched the Chladny experiment in school in which a heavy substance such as iron or sand is ground to a powder and spread thinly on a plate. As a violin bow is drawn across its edge the plate vibrates and the amorphous layer of powder orders itself into forms: i.e. sound creates form.

It is perhaps a long way from this to the Word which in the course of Earth evolution created all that surrounds us in the world, as indicated at the beginning of St John's Gospel (John 1: 1–5). Yet the Chladny experiment is an image in microcosm of what took place in those huge, cosmic events in which, over the course of the aeons of world evolution, the Word became the Son God. We are not talking here only of the Cosmic Word. *We* can speak, too. Human beings are the only creatures in the kingdom of nature that can *speak*. Our sounds alone, never mind our words, are different from the songs of birds and the noises of animals. In the past our human words also had creative power — we need only think of the magic words of the African medicine man or the battle cry of the northern Germanic tribes against the Roman legions. A faint afterglow of this power still lies in the words of a mother to her baby.

Whitsun is the festival of the future of speech. On that first Whit Sunday everyone understood Peter, and they all understood one another, even though they came from different countries. This was because on each head burned the same sacred flame. The words of the gods, the Word of the Son God, created the world. We, the friends of the Son God, are each endowed with speech, with language, with words. In each one of us the power of the gods will ripen and the individual sound of our speech will kindle the flame of the 'We' (our collective 'I ams') on our heads. The printed word, the informing word, will be no more than a help to the word that is spoken and the word that is heard, which will contain a new human being and a new world; a world of life.

BOTTON VILLAGE NEWS, 29 XI 1991

h o p e

Our psychology — the contents and configuration of our soul life — is like an iceberg of which only 10% reaches up into the light of consciousness, 90% being submerged in the ocean of unknowing. This simile is not quite accurate because the part of the iceberg which reaches into the light is different from the part beneath the surface. Hope is one example of such an iceberg.

The only thing we know of hope is 'wishful thinking' — 'I hope the weather will be fine tomorrow'; 'I hope the girl I have fallen in love with likes me'; 'I hope the illness that afflicts me will heal'. We always hope that the unknown future will hold some light. But in each earthly event some unknown future is contained — hope not as a feeling, but hope as a solid ingredient; the nine-tenths of the iceberg.

When Christ speaks with the Woman of Samaria (John 4: 4–26) at the well, we become aware that many decisive events in the history of the Israelites took place at wells, and that these past events were already permeated by the meeting between Christ and the Samaritan woman. Out of the future into the past, they glowed prophetically with the light in which this meeting shone.

Hope lies in the seed. We hope the plant will sprout from the seed in which 'hope' is the light of the still unborn leaves, blossom and fruit, shining from the future towards the seed. We hope the illness may mend; in the illness 'hope' is the light of future health and healing permeating the dark illness. All earthly events are meeting points between a past which the gods arranged and which bears an iron necessity, and the future and the freedom of hope. That we fear the future and that we hope are merely the shadows of the reality of hope.

But what is this reality? It is the apocalyptic future inherent in each created thing. One could also say it is the moral content of everything, and that this moral content depends on us. The physical sense-presence of each thing is the outcome of creating powers in the past; the future can only be a realm of freedom. Where else can this freedom be other than within our own souls? In a microcosmic psychology our souls contain the future, and thereby the Apocalypse, the content of the Book of Revelation. Our souls, therefore, let hope shine from the future into the present.

The Father God was once the root and cause; the Son God loves and therefore transfigures all the present; the Spirit God enlightens the world with Hope and eternal future. Faith, Love and Hope are the weavers and the web.

BOTTON VILLAGE NEWS, 20 VI 1969

groups & esoteric work

We try not to regulate our life hierarchically, vertically, but through groups, horizontally. Each group has its own sphere of responsibility and all have equal validity, each next to the other. Ideally — and it often works — our life is well regulated because of the balance between groups. Yet, coldly observed, these groups can often be painful: people are convinced of their own opinions and do not *answer* one another, each giving a little monologue without noticing that, in doing so, they are hopping from one topic to another and breaking the objective line of thought. As a result people offend one another without realising it.

No outer measures can change this; only an inner discipline can do so; the discipline of strengthening one's thinking. This can be helped by following the composition of a lecture by Rudolf Steiner, or through meditation and concentration exercises — efforts repeated over a long time to hold in one's consciousness some content (a verse or sentences from St John's Gospel, for example), uninterrupted by inner or outer disturbances. When we practice this, understanding of what the other person says is increasingly illumined; the enhanced power of our own thinking enables us to enter into the thinking process of the person listened to. We also become alert to the breaking of the thread of thought when someone gallops away on their own track.

In both an inner and an outer sense, keeping to an agenda results in the creation of a common space, whether the group is discussing money, buildings, co-workers or anything else. A unity is created through the effort of the participants, a space in which something like a Whitsun light is kindled — a Whitsun light which is really lit by the flames above one another's heads. The flames arise because each one is truly listened to by everyone else; thus everyone has a flame above his own being yet is aware only of the enlightenment of the others.

Spiritual beings can use this enlightened space so long as the unanimity of thought persists, a unanimity of thought which is *not* a unanimity of *opinions* but a unanimity of effort; the effort of listening to one another with the strengthened thinking described above. Once this space is created it is only a question of remaining faithful to the spiritual being who has incarnated in it, or to each other's flame — which is the same thing.

This *strengthened thinking* is the basis upon which our groups, already a mighty attempt at social renewal, could become better. If we do not continually make such efforts nothing ever happens except decay, the running down of an organism, or fruitless resolutions.

BOTTON MIRROR, 13 II 1987

communication & reporting

Along with the growth of democracy in our time grew the need, the longing, to *know* things in a physical, earthly sense, both the latest satellite news from around the world reporting wars and natural disasters, as well as petty political intrigues and other scandals. Or, nearer home, we want to hear about the content of the latest cultural life meeting or the New Year Assembly, and so on. It is understandable that democracy — or what today we call democracy — carries with it a duty to inform. However, it is a duty that leads to a kind of impotence because it only feeds people's curiosity and does not stimulate their sense of co-responsibility or engage their power of will. But how can our will be stimulated through a news report? It is an enormous question and one that concerns us in the Camphill centres with our problems of communication and responsibility. But first, we should look at the democracy of today.

Over recent centuries humanity has made a great effort to achieve *equality*, to develop beyond the 'divine right of kings', only it seems to have stopped halfway, thinking that equality is achieved by voting. But equality ('the divine right of every man') will never be reached by voting because voting does not take the minority into consideration. Voting is a kind of refined but ultimately brutal fight in which the stronger side (the one with the most voices), wins. It is obvious, therefore, that the only way voting can be superseded and social life renewed is by looking upon *everyone* with respect, devotion and interest. Interest alone saves us from looking down on others with contempt, or up to them in fear. Interest alone saves us from looking at the differences between people with disdain, and prevents us from thinking that everybody should really be like me! For us to be 'our brother's keeper' is far greater than voting. As long as there are differing opinions, voting seems necessary, but it is eternal *insight* which unites human beings with dignity and makes voting an outdated and antisocial tool. Coming to a shared insight, however, usually takes time, and has turned the forming and structuring of groups for finance, production, etc., into one of the main tasks of our time. But what about those who are not in the group, to whom what happened in it should be reported?

One of the salient features of the growing wave of democracy over the past centuries has been its accompaniment by a kind of paralysis. The spectator-consciousness of the consciousness soul spread out from Europe, then from the whole of the West, until finally it embraced the entire globe. Although concealed behind an outer show of demonstrations, riots and revolutions, democracy was essentially paralysed by its own impotence — whether it was the French Revolution followed by Napoleon, or the Russian Revolution by the dictators in the Kremlin. This paralysis is due entirely to the majority-minority principle, and to the absence of a willingness to be 'my brother's keeper'. In Camphill centres voting is not practised and so the gap between government and governed — which is its consequence — does not occur. Instead, the problem of communication arises. Why is this so?

Along with the democratisation of public life and people's feeling of responsibility for it, came also the need to have enough information which, with the growth of delegation, was simply not possible. In a society based on voting or parties, information plays a very different rôle from a non-voting social organism. The partly correct, partly insufficient half-truths of the mass media complement each other to a certain extent.

Why do we in Camphill communities, Waldorf schools and other anthroposophical institutions not vote? Because we think that everyone's word is of equal importance and value, and that voting would not do it justice. To report on a meeting in which shared insight was the aim is almost impossible because the process leading to a common insight is usually alive and real, while a report is in danger of following mere outlines shaped by a life and reality that has long since vanished. Therefore listening to reports (and especially reading them), is tedious.

How can the subject of a group, or its insights and decisions, reach the 'consumer'? Only by the consumer not staying as passive as when reading the newspaper or listening to the radio — by asking, for example, what the meeting achieved — thereby assuring the participant of the questioner's interest. Nothing is worse than speaking to unresponsive ears. Something of the personal involvement of the participant will be revealed in his report through the interest of the questioner. In other words, a report can not — and cannot ever be — a repetition: if so it will be no more than the corpse remaining after all the life has vanished. It must carry a new, enlivening sense between participant and questioner. Through the questioner asking expectantly how it was, the participant understands the meeting's subject in a renewed way, and the subject itself attains its relevant social dimension. As long as the topic stays in the hands of the group it remains at an embryonic stage: the purpose of the group is to understand it and make it grow. But the group does this on behalf of all those who are not present. If the right channel is not found between the group and the many, the group has wasted petrol, money and time, or it has just become another form of dictatorship.

The burden of the group lies with the many: the groups are the preparers; the many are the harvesters. One side of the problem of communication is quantitative ('we have too many things to think about'); the other side is qualitative (our social conscience, which really gives these groups their justification, is not wide enough). We, the many, drive these groups into anti-social isolation. We think that sending minutes to people will do the trick, but the spoken word alone will solve the problem of communication. 'In the beginning was the Word', but words become a museum piece if they are not renewed in the flames of an everlasting Whitsun.

CAMPHILL CORRESPONDENCE, IV 1986

thomas weihs

Thomas Weihs (b 30.4.1914, Vienna; d 19.6.1983, Aberdeen) was one of the significant servants of Michael in our time. On the one hand his intelligence was his own in quite a modest way. On the other hand it was a world-intelligence, not hemmed in by personal limitations. There was nothing cold in his intelligence: light and love, expressed most clearly in his profession as child-psychiatrist, were in perfect balance. Through being a co-founder of Camphill and imbued by its ideals, this profession was able to radiate more widely into a healing social order.

Thomas Weihs was the second of three children born into a well-to-do Viennese family. He studied medicine and, being clever in a special way with his hands, wanted to become a surgeon. During this time he met anthroposophy. In March 1938 Hitler occupied Austria; anthroposophy was forbidden and so all of us who wanted to live a common life out of anthroposophy emigrated. He went to Switzerland where he obtained his medical degree and in August 1939 joined Dr König and his friends in Scotland.

He became one of the main inner and outer pillars of Camphill which, after the war, broadened into Europe, America and Africa. As the medical officer and adviser, especially after Dr. König's death, he interviewed almost all the children and adults who were to be admitted into our schools and adult communities in Great Britain.

His activity widened considerably in the course of time, partly within the confines of Camphill communities (which included much travelling for seminars, lectures and clinics), partly in other anthroposophical areas, and later in non-anthroposophical circles. His book *Children in Need of Special Care*[19] entered the list of titles that social workers were required to read, and was translated into German and many other languages.

It will be some time yet before a biographer is able simultaneously to see, understand and interrelate both the inner and outer aspects of his life. A biographer will have to perceive what Camphill meant for Thomas and what he meant for Camphill; what the world meant for him (especially in his later years, when again and again he became depressed by spiritless non-understanding), and what he meant for the world. Undoubtedly, this is not something which, by today's standards of fame and renown, can be adequately measured.

Two things must be added. His marriage was a remarkable and paradigmatic phenomenon comparable, in a mythological way perhaps, with Odysseus and Penelope. He was the embodiment of fearlessness. I have never met anyone else whose connection to the world was never tainted by fear. This was not because he felt himself superior to the world, but because fear, even in his own body and soul, did not prejudice his understanding or actions. He therefore spread objectivity around him which, for anyone who came into contact with him, was a great comfort.

Thomas Weihs died at 8.30 a.m. on 19th June, a radiant Sunday morning. Throughout all the events of those days, the arrival of the many friends from America, Africa and Europe, the funeral on the following Wednesday and the service early on Thursday morning, there was a continual communion between earth and heavens in the abundant light of the summer sun. His widening soul entered the embrace of the heavens, as if dying into this summer union were the high point and climax of his earthly life.

BOTTON MIRROR, 9 VII 1983

✺ *s t   j o h n ' s*

s t   j o h n   &   c a t h a r s i s

> I indeed baptise you with water unto repentance; but He that cometh after me is mightier than I, whose shoes I am not worthy to bear; He shall baptise you with the Holy Ghost and with fire. (Matt. 3: 11)

Thus speaks John the Baptist who was the living image of baptism by water, of what in olden times was called catharsis or purification. Through submersion in water the disciple experienced a sudden widening of self-knowledge or, to be more precise, of self-beholding; a beholding not of the superficial self, but of the significance of the particular epoch on the self, and the latter's connection to the stars and to higher beings. With the shock of the water the strong ties between soul and body were loosened, and as a result of this new freedom the soul was cleansed, as if after death.[20]

But on the occasion of Christ's incarnation into Jesus of Nazareth at the Baptism in the river Jordan, John the Baptist also said, 'And I knew Him not.' (John 1: 31, 33) The baptism with 'water unto repentance' did not serve knowledge of the coming of Christ, nor of the fulfilment of the human being in the baptism of the Holy Ghost by spiritual fire. This knowledge, this recognition of Christ, came only after John's beheading when he became the group spirit of the disciples and Peter (in the name of all of them), said, 'Thou art the Christ, the Son of the living God.' (Matt. 16: 16, John 6: 69) Catharsis, sinlessness, widened consciousness — all these had to die in one earthly body in order to resurrect as knowledge and recognition in another, in the twelvefoldness of the disciples.

One could also say that knowledge is the higher metamorphosis of catharsis, as in plants the blossom is the higher metamorphosis of the leaves. The many-coloured flowers of summer with their full, green foliage — one thinks especially of the roses — are living parables of the Spirit-Sun knowledge of the disciples growing out of John the Baptist's catharsis in repentance. We, in our time, take part in the baptism both by water and by fire. We are disciples of both John the Baptist and Christ. Through the sacrifice of John and the grace of Christ we can partake of knowledge even before our souls are wholly cleansed.

BOTTON VILLAGE NEWS, 6 VII 1962

voice & inner work

John said of himself, 'I am the voice of one crying in the wilderness.' (Mark 1: 3) Christ is the creating World-Word of the Father, the Word actually become human. For us human beings, who become *truly* human only through Christ's coming to the earth, the Word is words and language for communicating thoughts, information and so on. Animals have a voice but no words, only sounds — singing, barking, roaring, etc. Our voice speaks mainly in words and is therefore very different from an animal voice which seems entirely chained to the whole organisation of its being. The human voice does not simply translate appearance and configuration into sound: it seems to have a certain individual freedom. Animal voices also have their individual timbre, but not to the same extent as the human voice.

That the Gospel of St John opens with 'In the beginning was the Word' is completely beyond our understanding. But if our words or sounds, vowels and consonants, had kept their original creative power we too would have a magic tool in our speaking. We had to forgo that power lest in attaining individual freedom we would have wreaked havoc in the world. But through the reduction of words to powerless shadows used only for communication, our voices have become overpowering — by which I do not mean their loudness; rather that they are too much in the foreground. As soon as we speak we help to kill the Word, being left only with its silhouette. Meditation, in which words are spoken silently — intoned without voice, so to speak — slowly revives the Word, and is therefore (with the guidance of Rudolf Steiner), an entirely Christian activity. It imbues the word with new life. 'I (the voice) must decrease. He (*the Word*) must increase' is true in this sense also.

SOURCE UNKNOWN

IDRIART

Many people attended the Scandinavian Festival in Vidaråsen (Norway) from 27th June to 5th July. There were people from our Norwegian, Swedish and Finnish Camphill communities, plus some guests. The first three days contained lectures, contributions, discussions and artistic groups on the theme of 'Conscience — Compassion — Awe'. The next three days were mainly dedicated to music. Among other pieces, Miha Pogačnik (violin) accompanied by Einar Steen-Nöckelberg (piano) played Beethoven and Bartók. Miha not only played but he also taught us to listen to Bartók's music which seemed at first wild and chaotic. The two musicians played together with a perfection in which technique — which has something of the overcoming of matter and gravity — melted away so that the sun of tones and music shone through unhindered, brilliant, cloudless. Miha Pogačnik plays loudly and softly, quickly and slowly, with great feeling but never gives the impression of rubato; it is always objective.

Through his descriptions he educated us into a completely new way of hearing. For me, the world of music has always been the world of Bach to Mahler, or Britten to Prokofiev; a world built on major and minor harmonies, a world in which the atonal is like waves of sound beating without power against the solid background of the tonal. But now imagine a musical experience in which the solid major-minor tonality transforms into a passing phase, an island in the oceanscape of music. Beethoven sounded like a well-clipped garden whose forms, harmonies and composition under Miha Pogačnik's guidance unfolded and opened in a breathtaking way into the musical compositions of our time and the future — the same with Mozart, Haydn and Bach.

Miha Pogačnik's playing, his words and his stormy personality convinces us that art (music especially), inspired by anthroposophy, the knowledge of our time, could help to build the foundations on which human beings can relate to one another independent of politics. The festivals in Chartres in the past years, in Bled, Slovenia this year, and next year planned for Trondheim, Norway, are held with this idea in mind. IDRIART (Institute for the Development of Intercultural Relations through the Arts) with its headquarters in Geneva was created by him for this purpose. It is hoped that IDRIART will spread (and spread behind the Iron Curtain as well), but this will depend, of course, on our support.

There is no doubt that the so-called planetary scales were a powerful step away from the bondage of tonality. IDRIART is fighting for the next step. Let us hope that the unfolding of the realm of music, which Miha Pogačnik stands for, spreads to other arts and also into other realms of humanity. The Christianising power of the unfolding of music shows the earnestness of the consciousness soul, and the promise of its width and grandeur.

BOTTON MIRROR, 14 VII 1984

thoughts during the summer arcs of the sun

We modern human beings are fettered by our senses, most consciously by our sense of sight, although also by the senses of hearing, smell and taste, and less consciously or unconsciously by our other senses. We are fettered somewhat like Gulliver by the Lilliputians, or the King of Ireland's son by the dwarfs' net and strings.[21] We take our sense-experiences for granted, thus forgetting what we have seen. We are surrounded by a flux, an ocean of sense-impressions, and if we direct our attention to *what* we see or hear we can only stare at it and the thing turns into a dead object — a butterfly impaled on a needle in a showcase; an insect caught in a piece of amber; a block of ice in a fridge.

All natural science stares. There is no movement between the single snapshots. As in a film, the sequence of many, many stills creates the illusion of movement. The value within the totality of these stills can never be determined by our staring-perceiving. But ever since Goethe (and even more so since Rudolf Steiner), we can acquire the ability to 'see' — to 'see' in a root not only the root but also the basis for stem and leaf; to 'see' in the stem and leaf the basis for the flower, and in the flower the basis for the seed. We can acquire the ability to see beyond stills to metamorphosis.[22]

The past course of the summer arc of the sun is its course in spring; its future will be its path in autumn. We must learn to 'see' the past and future of natural phenomena. Normally, meaning lazily, we fail in this because of the rather stupid, dull staring of our senses and the clever, intellectual, wisp-like nature of our modern thinking which builds innumerable bridges to cover the cracks and abysses between the stills. However, if our senses became clever, if we trained them, they would be redeemed from their dull staring, and our thinking would be released from the thin, abstract clutches of intellectualism.

This enlivening of the senses — whereby we become their masters rather than their victims and can guide them rather than remain caught and fixed by them — is the main way in our time to heed the warning call of St John. The Greek word is *metanoia*. It means, 'change'; in other words, 'change your hearts and minds.' (Matt. 3: 3).[23]

st john's-tide of the earth

St John's time is the period when immature fruit begins to swell. As the seeds ripen later (apple pips and poppy seeds become black, the ears of corn turn golden-brown, etc.), their capsules either become ripe fruits such as apples, rosehips, gooseberries and so on, or they shrivel up and turn hard and papery like a wasp's nest. But during St John's time seed and capsule are still one and green; both are still growing and not yet ripe.

We can compare the ripening of seed and fruit, and the seed capsule, with cooking. As the raw meat turns brown, the white dough rises and becomes golden bread, so the seed becomes dark and hard, the capsule becomes ripe and edible or just a dead enclosure. The raw state of our food is like the bitter green fruit. The light and heat of the sun are the stove and the cook.

The priest at the altar feels himself, as priest, to be like a fruit; first green and without flavour, then gradually ripening. Christ is the Word, and as the priest speaks the words of the service, the more the food for the congregation is warmed and cooked, becoming ripe and edible, and is then shared out as bread and wine. The words of the service become the Word, which goes into the Earth as seed for the creation of a new world, the New Jerusalem.

However, the warming and cooking of bread and wine is not a natural process like the ripening of the fruits of the earth, but a sacred one. Christ, who was once the Sun-Spirit, has entered the souls of human beings: the new world creation starts in the soul-space of human beings.

The service always embodies a whole year: Gospel Reading — Christmas and winter; Offering — Easter and spring; Transubstantiation — St John's and summer; Communion — Michaelmas and autumn. The entrance into the temple of the service is coloured and the sounds accord with the season and festival in which we live. *Inside*, we always find the whole year, and the manifoldness of the year is nothing but our higher self.

meditation: hollowing out the soul

The taking up of esoteric exercises (described in so many ways by Rudolf Steiner), as well as attending the Act of Consecration of Man, affects each individual differently because each person inserts his or her will into these things in a different way. But there is one factor common to both: the souls of those who turn towards the Sun power of the spirit become more and more hollowed out. It is as if the spirit beings would burn or melt an ever-widening cave in them.

From the time of waking to the moment of falling asleep the soul is tied to sense perceptions. The soul, or our consciousness, is filled with the sympathy or antipathy engendered by these sense impressions, as well as the memories and thoughts derived from past or present impressions. We could be forgiven for thinking that our consciousness consists of nothing *but* sense impressions or their derivatives were it not for the 'cave', the hollowed-out place in the soul, which is free of sense impressions.

Indeed, when concentrating, meditating or in the Service, Rudolf Steiner's oft-repeated precept is to ignore all sense impressions — of sight, sound or touch; the sensation of sitting, the various pressures on the skin and so on, and also warmth and cold. (There are stories of saints who meditated while sitting in the snow and whose souls began to glow with an inner fire so strong it began to melt the snow around them.) One can imagine how, in the morning, the space one is attempting to carve out through spiritual effort is relatively clean and empty because sense impressions are few as yet and have hardly begun to invade that 'cave' in the soul. This is also the reason for taking Communion on an empty stomach. In the evening, on the other hand, the colours and sounds of the day have filled the soul, and the cave has been completely flooded with their abundance, so that much more effort is needed to find its hollow spaces. Through earnest perseverance, however, this cave widens and becomes, so to speak, a feature in one's soul landscape — not so much a cave as an inner chapel into which one can withdraw.

In one respect esoteric effort and attending the Service are like sleep in that here, too, all sense impressions as well as our thinking and feeling, our doing and remembering, are entirely shut out. But we are rather the victims of sleep, and perhaps of dreams, while in esoteric work we try to induce sleep as far as body and general soul-life are concerned, yet still maintain consciousness in the cave, in the chapel which contains the words of meditation and exercise, or the content and sequence of the Service.

This element of the 'night' in the spiritual efforts of our time brings them into connection with the Feeding of the Five Thousand and the Beheading of John the Baptist (Mark 6: 17–44). Because we depend on our head to sense the outer, visible world, spiritual efforts seek to achieve a headless or 'beheaded' consciousness. The image of the beheading of St John is inherent in the efforts of our time to reach a higher humanity. Contrary to the 'day' with which the world confronts our head and thereby our 'normality', the spirituality of the world (signified by the stars which appear when the daylight is gone), can only dawn when our 'day' consciousness has dissolved and 'night' consciousness — not sleep, but true night consciousness — awakes.

BOTTON VILLAGE NEWS, 4 IX 1970

⁓ toward michaelmas

machines & will

What is the nature of the subtle pleasure we experience when handling a machine such as driving a car or using a power saw or planer? Through the engine of the car, the power saw and so on, our will is extended. All the machines invented for our use, including computers, atomic fission and fusion, extend our will enormously. We are thus enabled to do things that we would otherwise be quite unable to do. The more the particular machine conquers an aspect of earthly life, the more we become 'lords of the Earth': just think of a well-lit room or road, the speed of a train, a car, a plane, and so on. But this is only one side of the coin. (We cannot compare the rôle that the invention of machinery has played in history since the end of the 18th century with 'machines' existing before that time.) On the one hand there is that which chains us to the machines, but on the other hand much more is achieved through them than in the past, and it is done far more quickly. Through increased automation, work time is considerably reduced. It follows therefore (and Rudolf Steiner often pointed this out[24]), that there will be an excess of unused human will because machines not only do more, they also take over what human beings had to do for themselves in earlier times.

There is no doubt that some of the things which machines do are evil — atomic warheads, for instance — but a great deal is beneficial. We can see this immediately by looking at the workshops in the Camphill villages. Without machines, much of the work done in them would be impossible, and the moral value of work (not to mention its economic aspect), and its power to integrate the workers into the community could not then be realised. But what happens to the human will that is saved through the use of machines? It is unused. Football hooliganism, vandalism, hijacking and terrorism are the result of unused will. But unused will is a resource that each one of us possesses, and it represents the richness of our time. The richness of our time lies neither in material values nor in the gifts or genius of single individuals or cultures; it lies in that multitude of individuals who offer up their will to the ideas, aims and realities of the spiritual world. To start a Waldorf school, however small; to establish an unorthodox hospital or sanatorium; to create a bio-dynamic farm or a science laboratory, however modest, all these require will, human will, which is put at the disposal of the spiritual world and is available for the future of our world, thanks to machines. Any Waldorf teacher working with the curriculum who has tried to assist the incarnation process of the children in his or her care will know what it means to use the will to shape the earthly and the physical so that they become an expression and vessel of the spiritual.

This is perhaps the greatest difference between Buddhism and Christianity. In the Christian-anthroposophical understanding of the world, everything rests on the Resurrection. The physical dies, but when the spiritual meets and permeates the physical, new life arises through the power of resurrection. Whenever we make use of our will to bring about something spiritual on earth, this process always occurs. The renewal of education, medicine, agriculture, etc., is a direct consequence of this transmuting power. Therefore this renewal is fundamentally Christian. In Buddhism, the physical and the spiritual co-exist, side by side, but unless the physical and spiritual coalesce through the Resurrection, new earthly life cannot arise. The creative Word, as an earthly human being, had to die in order to bring about the Resurrection of the old Adam. In human will made superfluous through machines lies the future of the western world, and therefore of the whole of humanity.

BOTTON VILLAGE NEWS, 28 VII 1979

justice

Roman justice has warped our sense of social life. Even the concept 'social life' is unreal, because any human life on earth between birth and death is social, even if one is alone in one's private chamber. Roman justice saw life in polarities: bad and good, punishment and reward, cause and effect, and, therefore, inner and outer life. Time was envisaged as a thin line, along which the story of our life proceeds. The place where we are on this line is the *now*, the length of the line behind us is the *past*; what lies before us on the line is dark and *future*. Thus the former became the cause of the latter; past events the cause of future ones; the father the cause for the son. To explain why our causal and logical thinking is dominated by a juridical background, let us take the following example. Money is lying about; in a moment when nobody is looking I am tempted to steal it; I come under suspicion of being the culprit; I am taken go to court and found to be the culprit; I receive my punishment. Long ago, wrong-doing was viewed as a disturbance of the world-organism or world-order which the gods healed through our repeated earth-lives, but because of human freedom, wrongdoing became increasingly easy. This divine restoring, this healing of disturbed cosmic unity, sank into the world of human beings and was called justice. Restoration became punishment; disturbance of the cosmic order became disturbance of the secular (earthly) social order of the particular time and nation, and thus became a cause for punishment. This took place in the course of the fourth post-Atlantean epoch. Because human beings are continually balancing their freedom, and in so doing are violating the divine order with inner and outer deeds, thinking had to accompany the descent of this restoration into earthly justice. Judgement was increasingly placed in the hands of the human being, and judging and judgement became more and more an earthly tool. In the word 'judging' we can see the connection between thinking and jurisdiction.

This juridical thinking spread into our understanding of Nature as well as the human realm. The human being himself and his motives (in our example: whether he stole the money because of hunger, or because he was a kleptomaniac, or simply because he wanted to), became unimportant. The sequence and interlocking of events, their lawful or unlawful character, now became all-important. No wonder cause and effect became the sole relationship that made facts and events understandable in an earthly sense. Nature was once the expression of divine beings, permeated by divine powers and divine moods. Mythology is full of divine stories beneath the still surface of Nature: Europe is the immovable, external shape of the virgin Europa riding on, and seduced by, Zeus disguised as a bull. Laurel is the material expression of Apollo's pursuit of Daphne. The Decalogue and the laws of Moses are the outside and outcome of the thunderstorm on Mount Sinai. Superhuman morality once expressed itself in Nature's surface. Today, we have only the amoral natural laws. Morality has retreated from its world-widths into the nexus of earthly events caused by the human being, but measured only by the law. Humanity's being is immeasurably richer than that which is contained in law books, and will eventually find its expression in social life. The human being contains the morality of the worlds, but if he were aware of it now he would lose his freedom, the freedom to err and to learn. All his inner and outer actions are moral or immoral, but the law grasps only a small, external part of them. The concept of a 'decent, law-abiding citizen' stems from this incomplete understanding of the human being by the law.

The concept of 'citizen' arose in Rome and, because of its incompleteness, has falsified the image and self-understanding of the human being for two thousand years. This has been particularly disastrous for Christianity. The Sermon on the Mount, the proclamation of Christianity, which seeks to overcome the limitations of Jewish morality and Roman law, was bound to be misunderstood.

BOTTON VILLAGE NEWS, 31 VIII 1979

computers & the like

We will only do justice to our humanity if we try to meet the growing automation of our life (electric light, washing machines, computers, cars, trains, etc.), with *thinking*, by which I do not mean thinking that leads to understanding these various technical appliances, but thinking as an activity of the human soul. I mean thinking which does not have an object from the sense world as its content, but which moves in relation to a gospel passage, a verse; any thought content of a non-sensual nature which unfolds an activity of its own, not guided by sense-data.

This independent activity of thinking has two qualities which make us immediately aware of our humanity. The first is the understanding of one's 'I', one's person, and that this person is really the bearer of the responsibility for one's biography. The second (related) quality, is the experience that this 'I' is distinct from the body and so is perhaps independent of the limits of our bodily life, of birth and death. This I-permeated thinking has one overriding quality: the quality of creativity. This applies over its whole spectrum, from the ordinary to the sublime, from how to alter one's business methods or have ideas about fund-raising, to composing music and writing novels — indeed, any action which depends on our ability to have ideas.

Once this has been recognised, we become aware of the true rôle of machines in human life, which is to help us by executing our intentions. (The train was invented to get us from A to B more quickly. The car does the same, but independently of timetables and fixed routes, and so on.) With each mechanised process, from washing machines and typewriters to computers and iron foundries, we can describe what each achieves that is quicker, more precise or more detailed than human labour.

Through the enormous growth of what is mechanically possible, over the last hundred or hundred and fifty years technology has become the governing force in our life. Meanwhile, the study and knowledge of our intentions has become increasingly vague. Thinking has become vague not only regarding possible short term achievements, but also how the purpose of our intentions fits into the social organism in which we live. I do not mean that people take car rides or plane journeys for the fun of it. But there is the whole question of *why* I produce what I do simply because I am enabled to do so by machines. What do I do with the time saved by machines? What human consequences does the use of machinery have (e.g. mechanical teaching aids and the outpouring of detailed information which doesn't actually educate the receiver, not to mention its relation to workers in factories, etc.)? Machines exert a fascination which tends to blur what I called our intentions (with a little self-observation, anyone who drives a car will acknowledge this).

It is quite understandable that some people's feelings will turn against machines, at least against some. (In Camphill, it has been against computers.) But it is senseless to do so; one might as well be opposed to rocks or bones. It is futile to be angry with a stone on the road because it makes us trip up; we can only strengthen our attention and uprightness. The increase in invention and use of machines alone will never do justice to the failings and greatness of our humanity. Nor can we turn the clock back to horse-drawn transport, the abacus and candle light. We are cowards regarding the human potential in the 'You' and miss the opportunities that are given us by social and community life, just as we are weaklings in the power of our uprightness if we think we will walk better because the stone has been removed from our path.

Today we can no longer exist without machines. Our way of life, from electric light to computers and silicon chips (including the production of our food, furniture or clothing), is irrevocably polluted with the machinery that has become so inextricably part of our physical existence. With or without computers, if we wish to rescue our humanity we have no choice but to balance our machinery-possessed life by exercising the thinking described above. Rudolf Steiner outlined this often enough in his books and lectures. Without thinking, the spiritual power of machines will be stronger than we are, and will suck us down like quicksand. In our time, interest in the other person is the royal gate to both this uprightness and this thinking.

BOTTON MIRROR, 12 VII 1980

c o r n

When we walk along the drive to Botton Hall and see the oats ripening on the left and the wheat on the right, we experience a truth which Rudolf Steiner first pointed out, saying that if children learn to recognise the various kinds of corn their morality will be built up.[25]

This ripening corn expresses the unity of goodness and beauty. For the Greeks these *were* a unity, and they had one word for both — *Kaloskagathos* — but in the subsequent history of mankind the two have become separated to the extent that today beauty is *entirely* divorced from any moral quality, as exemplified in the film star. The suicide of Marilyn Monroe moved the world as much as it did because it seemed to show that beauty, if separated from goodness, has to die. Why does this unity of beauty and goodness appear in the varieties of corn; less so in maize, rice and millet, but clearly in wheat, oats, barley and rye?

Consider these four. Wheat is the most perfect and compact, while rye, barley and oats are more like variations on a theme in colour and form. In all fruit either the power of the seed or its value as food is the outcome of fire, of cooking: of the warmth processes. Ripening is the giving up of blossom, the giving up of youth, for the sake of fruiting. It is the giving up of light — for no blossoming is possible without light — for the sake of warmth. In the corn (and to a large extent in the grasses as a whole), the blossom is very minute, and a large amount of light has gone into the developing of the fruit, as can be seen from the high silica content of the ears.

But warmth has two sides, a physical and a soul side. *Every* feeling of love (from compassion to the simple love for a certain picture), creates warmth in the soul. The highest love is the love of the good, the enthusiasm for the divine in each human being. Morality is love in which selfishness is sacrificed so far that it can become food for others. The most direct impact of morality is the Communion in its various forms; eating the body and drinking the blood of Christ. Christ sacrificed Himself to become food and the highest good.

Fruit, being the outcome of warmth, always bears the shadow image or light image of this soul warmth. In corn, the beauty of the blossom has been sacrificed to a high degree for the perfection of the fruit. The ear of corn is therefore not only the outcome of physical warmth, but has already something of soul warmth, of nourishing goodness, of morality. In the past (and even

today in remote areas of the continent), loaves of bread were marked with the
sign of the Cross, the symbol of the ever-present Christ.

BOTTON VILLAGE NEWS, 24 VIII 1962

drama & the social question

Address dedicated to Anke Weihs (b 30.6.1914, Melbourne, d 27.8.1987, Aberdeen)
who had died that morning after a long illness borne with patience. She had even
attended part of the IDRIART Festival in Bled, Slovenia earlier in the summer.

Although Anke's death has been expected for weeks, it is different when it
happens. Our own life sheds different lights on such an event because we live
in both a bad and a good way. The light which death affords us is yet another
kind of light, for which we feel our own lives are a kind of prologue. What the
light and dark will make out of our own lives cannot be foreseen.

I will try to say briefly what I want to say. I want to start with Larchfield [a
Camphill community]. Here we can see the social question really as a kind
of image. We look over the fields towards the town; the houses, factories,
chimneys, the squalor, and finally the promise, of Middlesbrough. This is the
kernel of the social question.

It was the tragedy of the 19th century that although the working class
played an enormous rôle in the Industrial Revolution, thousands were
condemned to work in factories. Karl Marx said that if wages and salaries
were handled better, i.e. put into the hands of the proletariat, then all would
be well. For Marx, the soul was merely the outcome of material conditions;
the doors to the spiritual worlds remained closed.

When men and women worked in factories they were no longer part of
a whole process as in earlier times when they had to see a job through from
beginning to end, making decisions at each stage of the process. There was no
longer an opportunity to cultivate their 'I' or to become an 'ego'.

A solution was sought for in art, especially in theatre. It was both a
materialistic and a naturalistic time — the horrors of contemporary life
could be shown in drama. One dramatist who was concerned with the social
question was Henrik Ibsen. Living in the second half of the 19th century in
Norway, he was a familiar sight with his fork-shaped beard, frequenting the
best coffee-house in Oslo. He wrote many thrilling plays which make exciting
watching (or reading) because he described social conditions, and also the

strengths and weaknesses of the human soul.

In *Pillars of Society* (1877),[26] a wealthy shipbuilder becomes a 'pillar of society' but the inner, moral issue plays little part in the process. A perfect family becomes possible and he could give many public amenities to his town. However, he realises that it is all built on a lie so he persuades his *younger brother* to go to America and admit that *he* had embezzled the money for the amenities, thus removing the guilt from himself. In the end he confesses and in that moment of 'death', that moment of untying the knot, the play itself ends and the audience experiences a great relief, for he had been moved by outer circumstances.

Hedda Gabbler (1890)[27] married a man who earned very little, while she had had an aristocratic upbringing. Then this strange woman is driven to suicide. Another man, a friend from her youth, comes back into her life. He is a kind of higher being for her, a mentor. Bacchanalian statues are depicted with vine leaves around their heads, hinting that this play harks back to the Dionysian cult, as all of Ibsen's plays link to the ancient Mysteries.

Like a shadow of the Mysteries, the Greek stage had a kind of altar, centre stage. In Rudolf Steiner's 'The Portal of Initiation',[28] in a prologue and interlude, a dialogue takes place between two friends, one of whom is going to Rudolf Steiner's play, the other to a play entitled *Disinherited of Body and Soul*. It had the same outer content as the Mystery play but without the inner consequences and events, which lead to the threshold.*

The reason why the chimneys grew and the industrialists became slave drivers, masters of the people who worked in the factories, is that we see life in too materialistic a way. Each one of us is guilty and morally responsible. The inner side of the social question will by no means be solved until a path is found by human beings to equality.

BOTTON SUMMER SCHOOL LECTURE, 27 VIII 1987

folk dancing

Every year the core of the Billingham Folk Festival is folk dancing from many places around the world, mostly from behind the Iron Curtain — Russia, Romania, Korea, Hungary, China, etc.

---

*On a visit to Larchfield, Peter once said, "It's wonderful to stand in Larchfield. With its background of factories it reminds me of a scene in Rudolf Steiner's third mystery play"[29] (which is set in a pleasant country landscape beyond which is an industrial city with many factories).

This year we saw groups from Malawi, Hungary, Korea and Israel. Apart from Korea (and other groups from the East where the expression 'folk dancing' does not really apply), the forming principle underlying it is rhythm, rhythm executed by the legs, the rest of the body following or enhancing it. This dominance of rhythm has a huge preponderance of will, but will containing within it — albeit to a pale, as yet undifferentiated degree — the rest of the world content and the future rôle of the human being. Even in the African dances, where the footwork is negligible, the whole body seemed to express will and rhythm, and also in singing.

However, this will is very different from the kind of will we bear in our constitution today. In this dancing there is something huge and divine, world-like, a past where humanity was still close to *Ex Deo Nascimur*, to its birth out of the divine. Our will today seems to be limited to our person while we have added our senses and our 'I am' consciousness to the instinctive will nature of an old humanity.

Today's folk dancing is but a meagre remnant of what was once a widespread wealth. In earlier times the dancing of people with accompanying music and singing was part of all festive days, and guided by the priests any lifting up to the gods was always expressed by sounding movement, by the colours and forms of the swirling clothes and head-dresses.

Music plays an interesting part in all this, having grown out of beat and rhythm. The African piece showed that well, the whole moving body becoming rhythm. A music historian could describe the development from rhythmical beat into harmony and melody, and no doubt the latter made beat subservient to music only after Bach when harmony and melody emerged in our sense and understanding. For the Indian and Eastern peoples it was, and still is, something quite different. A strange branch on the tree of music, a derivative of Negro spirituals, is what in the widest sense we could call jazz with its one-sided, or misguided, connection between rhythm, melody and harmony. One could describe at length the Russian ballet and the Fred Astaire-Ginger Rogers variety of dancing.

Eurythmy as the most modern — and also the crown — of the moving human body is still hamstrung by a limitation of suitable music or poetry, by the inability of modern music to incorporate rhythm into it. Through the development of art in our time, eurythmy will reveal its unfolding glory.

BOTTON VILLAGE NEWS, 30 VIII 1986

the good samaritan

Every year, towards the end of August or the beginning of September, we read and hear the parable of the Good Samaritan from St Luke's Gospel (Luke 10: 30–37) in the Act of Consecration of Man. It is as if in this parable the first trumpets of Michaelmas start to sound ever more loudly and brightly, accompanying the dying lushness of summer, until at Michaelmas they find their shining and resounding solution.

As in all parables, the characters are the personified soul qualities of each human being; we ourselves bear within us the wounded man, the thief, the priest, the Levite, the Samaritan.

The wounded is mankind. Instead of 'wounds' we could also say 'needs'; the tempter wounds mankind, so it is only since the Fall that mankind has needs. The complement to wounds or needs is sympathies, antipathies, urges, wishes, all *rising out of* the human soul and dictating our actions from within, while the needs of others call forth our actions from outside. The Fall resulted in human souls becoming full of wishes and so obscured their seeing the needs of their surroundings. The subjective wishes from within were sometimes far louder than the calls from outside. Our eyes were opened and thereby the possibility — even necessity — of continual temptation and continual 'Fall' arose.

The difference between the thief and the Jewish priest is that the thief is clearly a criminal, while the priest and the Levite, wounding others through their blindness and hardheartedness, are hidden criminals, their essential crime being self-righteousness. Their sin, their blindness, is the other side of the coin of lawlessness of the thief. They adhere to the law; we adhere to logic, and feel ourselves superior to others who have a lower intelligence than ours. The thief does not abide by the law while we, in spite of our evil, cruel, greedy thoughts, keep within the law in our actions.

The Samaritan does neither; he sees and feels the other as a 'neighbour', while the thief and priests are blind to this quality. In olden times when the Jewish religion was still alive, other people were not yet 'neighbours', brothers or sisters. They came to have this quality (which is beyond language, nation or creed), only through Christianity because it was through Christianity that self-consciousness, i.e. consciousness of the Self, had to develop. But self-righteousness is a sinful by-product of self-consciousness.

Work is meant to fulfil needs and is therefore something whose regularity has to be relied on. If, for instance, Ferdi goes milking, not because there is a real need but simply because he is occasionally compelled by a liking for it, the nature of his work is distorted. In the past, the great innovators and benefactors of humanity created needs, but in our time and toward the future it will be increasingly important to be aware of needs and try to satisfy them, not to create them artificially. The Buddha and St Francis taught and instilled compassion, and in compassion we have a virtue which, in our time, will be increasingly connected with Michael because compassion makes one aware, makes one willing to answer the call of wounds and needs. Michaelmas is the festival of selfless self-consciousness.[30] The Samaritan (both in the parable and in us), is able to act out of compassion because he saw other human beings as neighbours.

DATE UNKNOWN

positivity:
the fourth fundamental spiritual exercise

The fourth fundamental spiritual exercise described by Rudolf Steiner[31] directs our attention, firstly, to that which is beautiful and perfect in the phenomena of the world, and secondly, draws our attention away from what is bad and evokes criticism towards that which shines and is special. Every criminal has a good side.

Our own time is, necessarily, overloaded with criticism. We simply have to learn to judge, otherwise the consciousness soul would never learn to observe. But in learning to observe as well as to judge, one seems to exclude the other. Today, our criticism of the bad far outweighs our rejoicing in the good, and usually we do not bother to even look for it. To discover the good in the other person is an enormous relief: we become aware of what a burden criticism is, however necessary.

With a degree of self-observation, we notice that criticism, negativity and doubt work on us like sleepless nights, making us tired, listless and nervous; hollowing us out. Positivity, on the other hand, or delight in the aims and deeds of others, overcomes all tiredness. To find the bad or crooked to be good and praiseworthy would be simply dishonest, of course, because it is only honesty that leads to this health-giving delight; only honesty can turn delight from a shallow or sentimental opinion into a conviction which permeates the whole human being. Should we therefore ignore or look away from the bad and look only at what delights us? It all depends on the context. A good example is the story of Christ praising the teeth in the decaying corpse of the dog while the disciples are so spellbound by the decay that they do not even notice the teeth.

Our attentive gaze should be drawn to the praiseworthy while at the same time noticing the bad. If we praise somebody and then say: 'but regarding… you did wrongly', everyone will understand. But if we tell them only what they did wrong we just wound them and they learn nothing.

The positive and its relationship to the negative or bad is valid not only in personal dialogue, but also among people and groups. The most idiotic statements (or what seem to me the most idiotic) may be made, but if the conversation degenerates into a tit-for-tat of opinions (however correct they may be) in the end everyone becomes exhausted and the meeting is barren. But if what is said is listened to with appreciation and interest, and one's own opinion suppressed, then the objective sun of goodwill rises above such a meeting. Positivity is an objective power, not merely an absence of criticism nor a purely personal effect, but a quite definite event drawn towards a situation through personal effort. It is not a question of compromise or of saying 'yes' to something that is wrong, but a question of listening with honest appreciation. Therefore the preparation of every one of us before a meeting is extremely important; it is like the breathing in of common sense and goodwill towards the thoughts of others so that this sun may rise. Its power not only helps to order tasks in the life of any social organism, but it also has a health-giving strength. We will be amazed at how the power of this sun melts away tiredness like the snows of winter.

Groups also bear the promise of something else as well, which is that not only will each person be heard, but in being listened to he will be recreated, and in listening to others he will also recreate them. In living together we become too used to one another; the other person acquires a veneer of ordinariness for us, just as we do for them. But by listening to one another in an unbiased way the other person assumes the light of the unexpected. To expect the unexpected from each other, to sit opposite each other as if for the first time, is tremendously important. It is the main reason for community living. Groups should really be institutions for the renewal of their members.

All this has another side, too. Of all the hundred and one jobs we do in the world — keeping house, cooking, working in a workshop, managing finance, playing music — nothing is worse than being unnoticed and being neither praised nor criticised. In Camphill, we live together in order to bear the fruit of having neighbours. To be oneself, alone, is one of the conditions of our time, but only with effort do we become neighbours. To become a neighbour requires interest in the other person, especially in what he or she does. If other people are neither praised for what they do nor criticised and shown how to do better, they lose self-respect.

We prove ourselves to ourselves in what we do; we invest our doing in ourselves. For that reason the value of what we do is bound up with our self-respect. If our neighbours take notice, it affirms that we are of value to the world. We must learn the art of praising our neighbour, or of giving constructive criticism, which helps him to do better. We must separate his actions from his Self and recognise that he is worth our interest and devotion quite apart from what he does.

In Botton we eat bread made in the bakery and sleep on beds produced in the wood workshop, and we take for granted the various activities which keep the village going — Stewards Group, College of Learning, Land Group, and so on. But we do an injustice to those who produce all this if we merely accept it silently. How radiant our neighbours become when we react! We liberate them from their loneliness.

All this seems to me important for our village life. The 'rift' in Botton would disappear if we knew a little more about what our neighbour does, and thereby discovered his 'beautiful teeth'. He would become transparent, and we would discover his higher Self. When we are admitted to the Inner Community, and thereby pledge ourselves to its ideals, we become aware that everyone is, in reality, a divine being. And everyone can recognise that reality although it takes hard and persistent effort, but persistent effort in a climate of compassion and trust.

There have to be people today who commit themselves, continually, to this awareness otherwise the approaching times will be far more plagued by polarising rifts than Botton is at present. The rift among people who share the same commitment must become illusion; it can only be the testing onslaught of the threats of our time.

BOTTON VILLAGE NEWS, 30 V 1980 & 25 VIII 1989

tilla könig

Tilla König [b 9.3.1902, Gnadenfrei, Silesia] died during the night of 16th/17th September in Camphill Village [Alpha] in South Africa, following a fall and hip operation on 21st June. She was 81½ years old.

Children, friends and those who simply met and knew her could not fail to recognise in her a higher, enhanced humanity. Toward everyday objects she was full of spirituality and Christianity, as if they were all plants or children needing to be cared for. Those who came to live with her in the years when she lived in Tourmaline here in Botton were surrounded by order, cleanliness, beauty and by a nourishing light. She cooked like a priestess of the everyday: a meal with her was a joyous festival.

This nobility towards the world — a nobility permeated by the devotion of a Franciscan nun — was complemented by a kind of 'knighthood for truth'. It was a knighthood which had not been acquired gradually by stages but an instant knighthood, so to speak, arising from an inborn courage, effortless and entirely natural, like a clear spring emerging miraculously from the rocks.

Because of her Michaelic purity the whole Camphill Movement was coloured by her influence from its beginning. Quoting Adalbert Stifter, she taught us what Rudolf Steiner called 'devotion to the small things'. Nothing was more intolerable to her than unmade beds, disorder, flower beds full of weeds, and dirt. She taught us to become aware of and listen to the laments of neglected, maltreated, disregarded objects and creation. We laughed with her about the anthroposophical hermit who meditated amidst piles of dust. Her humanity was warm and light enough for her to become our teacher of what is called in the journeys of Goethe's *Wilhelm Meister*[32] the third reverence, the reverence towards what is beneath us. In this, both pupils and teachers alike are taught that underlying all education are three reverences: one for what is above (for the divine); one for what is equal, is brother to us; and one toward what is hateful, evil, unformed and dark. Her radiance made us aware that the lowly, the weak and the dark are qualities which are in everything and everyone, and are raised up through our service to them.

She really was a priestess of the earth for the new Christianity, a Joan of Arc who was allowed to become a mother, a mother not only of four children, but a Mother of the Good on earth.

BOTTON MIRROR, 24 IX 1983

the christian nature of the seasons

We can gain a certain idea of the Christian nature of the seasons if we consider the following. History, ideas, human aims and destiny march through nature in their changing development. Nature, in its slow evolution, seems stationary compared to this march. Nature seems not only static but also guiltless and innocent compared to human effort. In human beings one life requires many more lives for its fulfilment and balance and history has periods, an ever-changing course. Nature is always perfect and contained, while morality pertains only to human beings.

But is this entirely true? If we recall the time of spring and early summer — the infinite variety of young, rising green, the manifold shapes and colours of leaves and blossoms, the vigorous purity of air and scent, the perfect and tender growth in the expanding light and warmth — we feel delighted and humbled, amazed that we, whose innocence depends on morality, can experience this vast and perfect innocence. But what if we go for a walk now, in late summer? The leaves have become almost fleshy; colour and form have succumbed to a certain extent to darkness and heaviness. This darkness, especially of the green, increases towards the end of August and September, and in autumn we are relieved by the decay and disappearing matter; its windswept, empty spaces are glorious after the suffocation of late summer.

Something of the guilt of humanity seems to have crept into nature. Though we breathe in freedom in autumn, having escaped the throttle of matter, nature dies. By the end of November or the beginning of December the trees are bare, the fields and gardens empty, visible life and scented colour has vanished, and from deep feelings we connect winter and death with guilt and its consequence.

Christmas and the Holy Nights are the darkest time of the year. But every year, winter is followed by a new spring, a new life, a new innocence: the waters of winter and the Holy Nights have washed and baptised the New Year. The Land of the Blessed, the New Jerusalem, knows no winter. In it there is a natural innocence and there is a human, an adult, a fought-for innocence. Despite the onslaught of human guilt to which nature succumbs in autumn and winter, this natural innocence asserts itself in spring and early summer.

The human being can be a victim of the seasons, tossed upward in spring and summer, downward in autumn and winter, as if by waves on the ocean of world-being. But through the grace of the festivals he can also become an immovable island among these waves. Only humanity can celebrate festivals.

In uniting Himself with the earth Christ entered human time, but He also remained the One Who overcame and Who overcomes time. He became the serving Brother as well as the *Kyrios*, the Lord. He suffered and overcame suffering. As the seasons follow each other in time, He unites Himself with the course and waves of the seasons, but in the festivals He overcomes the seasons. As Christ is always the Brother as well as the Lord, Christmas is not chained to winter, or Easter to spring. He is the Lord of the Earth and in the southern hemisphere the seasons are more or less reversed, therefore Christmas can be in summer, and Michaelmas in spring. Christ is indeed the Lord of the Earth.

BOTTON VILLAGE NEWS, 16 VIII 1968

MICHAELMAS 1995

∾ *m i c h a e l m a s*

m i c h a e l m a s :   f e s t i v a l   o f   o u r   i m m o r t a l   b e i n g

As we watch the leaves, the plants and the fields lose their green to glorious yellows, oranges and browns, and as we feel the fullness of summer changing into the bounty of autumn, and later into winter, we can only feel a certain hopelessness, a tiredness and a wish to sleep until, with its rising warmth and light, spring wakes us up again. The festival of Michaelmas was instituted and renewed to free our consciousness and soul from this sadness and make us aware that our real being is immortal.

In daily life we are completely devoted to the tasks of the day, poured out into the impressions of our senses, at one with ephemeral feelings of sympathy and antipathy and glued to the up and down progress of the year. Of course, we can sit in our chair in comparative stillness and read books such as the gospels, the Bhagavad Gita, or other books containing world-wisdom and truth. Yet while reading we are, to a certain extent, tied to the sense-impressions of the letters, words and sentences. But if we start to *think* with fervour the thoughts which the sentences express, we slowly become aware that our existence does not arise merely from the existence of our body, and therefore is not bound to it alone. We also grow aware that sleeping is not merely a resting of the physical body but that during sleep our soul-spirit being lifts itself out of the body, freeing itself from the senses into spaceless unconsciousness, into many soul and spirit experiences of which we are not conscious. From spiritual science it becomes clear that while asleep we are among gods, but to understand this we must first go through the autumn experience of our twofold nature.

It is our bodies which isolate us from one another. Although the soul-spirit effort to become aware of our unborn and undying existence is based on our own individual effort, nevertheless a true social life — not just of rules or laws, but based on what can be experienced as the brotherhood of mankind — is possible only if our mutual interest kindles acknowledgement of every human being's immortal and unique nature. Michaelmas is the festival of social life, the strength of the Spirit of Humanity. Michael helped fashion the Creation, and hence also our physical body, but in our greed our spirit became imprisoned in our flesh. Michael is not interested in our greed, however refined it may be. The future is built out of our love, our determination and our understanding for the Word.

BOTTON VILLAGE NEWS, 1 X 1983

the flash of future light

There were many factors on many different levels that led to the founding of Camphill. There were political events such as Hitler's rise to power in central Europe and the impending war, and there were more intimate moments; moments of personal destiny, or the meeting of destinies, under the guidance of Dr. König, and a study of the personality and teachings of Rudolf Steiner. Eventually, those of us who wanted to live and work together were enabled to make a start because an old manse on the estate of friends, near Aberdeen in Scotland, was put at our disposal.

That early beginning was fraught with difficulty. We were refugees whose situation in the world was very uncertain and who had as yet little to give and everything to learn, and the house we lived in was primitive and the conditions rough. But in all these difficulties — and there were inner ones as well — there was often a flash of that bright light which in the future we would recognise as Camphill. This always left us filled with hope and gratitude, and with a sense of having been called to an important task.

I can remember one of those sudden flashes. The scope of the farm work on the estate where our old manse stood was such that often we were all required to join in and help. During the harvest of 1939, a few weeks after the war began, we were stooking sheaves of oats and loading cart after cart with dried corn. September 28th arrived, the day before Michaelmas when we were going to celebrate our first festival. (The celebrating of the Christian festivals of the year, which would later play so great a part in the life of Camphill, was then only at its dawning.) We were full of trepidation as to how we would live up to it — as often happens, even now — but also full of anticipation of the holy morrow. We had begun to learn that only in preparing everything with great care and exactitude would the real significance of the festival be made manifest in our celebration.

The afternoon of that day before Michaelmas drew on and the first long shadows that come before dusk lay over the stubble-field. My friend and I had to finish stooking that last, vast field. It was a sloping field and along its upper ridge stood a dark wood; on one side there was a steep valley, almost a gorge, which led up towards the plains of Huntly and Elgin, and down behind us lay the little manse where all the others were busily preparing for the evening ahead. This was to be a solemn opening of the Michaelmas festival with a reading of Rudolf Steiner's *Last Address*,[33] in which he speaks with great earnestness of the future understanding of the festival of St Michael. Up there in the field we two could play no part in all the preparations, the tidying up and the arrangements; we had to complete our work before dark.

The late afternoon was warm, yet lowering and thundery. Later, towards evening, it became lighter and cooler. In our urge to finish what we had been asked to do, we worked with ever-increasing pressure and speed. Suddenly, into this mounting pressure, a light shone which permeated the work with a new element. It was as if the effort, the tense will to achieve, had transformed the work into a kind of sheath, an outer shell inside which our deeper, more real selves glowed in selfless warmth. And it felt as if the outer shell would melt away in the rays of this new sun, this sun from within.

We were able to complete our task in the field and be in time to take part in the celebration with our other friends in the evening. It was a small experience and yet it proved to be an archetypal one. Variations of it have accompanied the development of Camphill ever since — an effort, the intense will to achieve something (compressed work, physical or otherwise), and then the light of grace filling and completing what was begun.

We can exert the full might of our will with all the strength of our ordinary self-consciousness, but if our work does not become a dissolving, *selfless* outer sheath from which the sunlight of grace can shine, lighting up our truer selves, then any achievement will remain shallow. This sunlight of grace is nothing else than the Being of Christ Himself, and any kind of work can become the husk, the shell which contains this sunrise. If the true nature of work is not to be lost in our age, more and more groups of human beings will have to learn to experience it too, not as an end in itself, but as a selfless means to a higher end. I believe that Camphill is one of the pioneers in this field.

THE CRESSET, SUMMER 1961

the bible evening

The inception and development of the Bible Evening, its branching out and changing forms, are part of the inner wellsprings of Camphill, and have accompanied the various phases and aspects of our work. As the Camphill Movement spread, the Saturday Bible Evening was held in different places, in different countries, and finally on different continents. It required the development of different forms; for the schools, in which we care for handicapped children, or for the villages, which are working communities with handicapped adults. And it is envisaged that the Bible Evening will also become the cornerstone of our various training centres.

In the early days, only those few who had pledged themselves to Camphill took part in the Bible Evening, but now all who wish to do so may attend. Yet throughout all the changes, the same basic form has remained. After a period of quiet waiting, one of the participants (all of whom wear their Sunday clothes), lights a candle on the table, which is simply but festively laid. Then the first part of the evening begins when grace has been said. In the schools, (the children having been put to bed after their usual, earlier supper), the co-workers share a token meal; bread or home-baked buns and fruit juice. In the villages, the meeting takes place around the simple, Saturday supper table. During the meal a conversation takes place, reflecting on matters of the past and present, of the world at large or the small world at home, about great personalities or earthly concerns, about the human soul or about the heavens.

When the table is cleared, the second part begins with a reading from the Bible. The passage chosen is the same that will be heard at the Sunday service and which has been studied and pondered during the week. Some or all who participate may speak about the passage and a dialogue may ensue but never a discussion or a study. A verse or a song will conclude the evening.

As a kind of spiritual essence of Camphill life, the Bible Evening has become like a sign which distinguishes us from various other communities striving towards human ideals in our time, such as the Kibbutzim, the International Voluntary Service, or the Bruderhof. The Bible Evening is not celebrated once a year like other festivals, but is a recurring weekly event. It is not only a preparation for the Sunday but also the ending of the work and life of the past week, and is its confirmation. It has taken on the meaning of a festival of human equality. Our life and work with handicapped children and adults, as well as with each other, is a daily-renewed attempt to recognise the divine spark in all who bear a human countenance. This in turn may give us the possibility of directing our feeling and will from the divine spark within ourselves. These two attitudes are like positive and negative electricity.

In the course of time, it became natural for us to invite everyone under our roof to Bible Evening. This arose from our feeling that we ourselves are also only guests at the table of the Bible Evening, invited to share a meal which is really a heavenly meal and for which the physical conditions stand only as a token. As can be seen in the parable of the kingly wedding (Matt. 22: 1–13), we learn to feel ourselves invited, as everyone else is, to the banquet which the king prepares for the marriage of his son. Finally the angels, his messengers, are sent out to invite those from the highways and byways.

This does not mean to say that the Bible Evening *is* the earthly reflection of this marriage banquet, but it could be said that the Bible Evening is *one* of the earthly facets, or mirror pictures, of this archetypal heavenly meal. If we do not put on the wedding garment (to remain within the parable of the kingly wedding), we have not prepared our soul — even if it be only the awareness that such an invitation, to a far more spiritual meal, is constantly extended to us — and in such moments we may feel ourselves inwardly cast out. In a Bible Evening, the words that are read or spoken can become food for all who take part. Here, food is not meant in a metaphorical sense, but in the sense of another gospel story, the feeding of the five thousand (Matt. 14: 15–21), in which the many are fed with the consecrated bread that has been multiplied. Ever and again it is a moving experience to meet together in this recurring weekly festival of human equality. At the table sit those who cook or dig the gardens, who farm or teach, who are craft masters or workshop workers, or who care for the needs of the house. All sit together around the lighted candle and listen reverently to the words of the Bible; all are warmed and awed by these words, and their existence can feel enlightened by the understanding and widening horizons given to the words by Anthroposophia.

Everyone who takes part feels called on to be active, at least in his listening, because the opening up of the realm from which the powers of the heavenly banquet descend depends on this activity. A cult or a rite takes place if the priest is there to speak and act, but at a Bible Evening there is no priest, unless it be the priesthood of all believers. As the evening proceeds, the innate relationship of every human being to the divine becomes apparent, as does Christ's readiness to be both guide and lover of each individual soul.

When the step was taken from holding the Bible Evening with those who worked with handicapped children to being held together with handicapped adults, it was like stepping from holy secrecy into open daylight. It was a step into humanity at large; a step by which, in the ordinary human existence of those gathered around the supper table each Saturday, a holy presence could be made real. It was a step requiring great inner effort, but one which also made those who attempted it feel more humble.

All man-made events that recur rhythmically are in danger of becoming stale. Similarly, the Bible Evening was in danger of becoming a kind of duty, and many continued to attend simply because they had done so for many years. Thus the inner activity, which alone can safeguard the colour, scent and heavenly dew of the Bible Evening, was beginning to disappear. This activity is composed of two parts. First, the acknowledgement that the deeds of the past week shrink to their proper proportions, a residue to which an objective distance can be gained. (One of us had a dream that he threw his sword onto an altar on which many others had already cast their own swords, and he understood that the altar was the Bible Evening and the sword from which he parted was his immediate past and his accumulated destiny.) The second requirement is the recognition that the words 'stagnation' and 'inner complacency' have no place in a Movement which has dedicated itself to a task, the fulfilment of which asks for a tireless, ceaseless self-schooling.

I am sure that there are many of Karl König's pupils who, like myself, are willing to admit that it is through him that they have learned to face themselves, to overcome themselves — at least at times — and tread the path toward their true higher natures. To be able to say this in an age which makes it increasingly difficult for people to face and overcome themselves is itself a grace. This grace of which we are conscious will always remain connected with the great living being of Dr König, who acted as its mediator and to whose life work we dedicate our own life and work in gratitude.

THE CRESSET, MICHAELMAS 1961

assisi

When I was a young man in Vienna it was the custom for students who had just matriculated to go on a long journey to see something of the world. Matriculation was more than a scholastic landmark, it was also a human one since before it the adolescent was subject to his family (which was responsible for him), whereas after matriculation the adolescent gradually changed into a young adult who began to take the reins of his life into his own hands.

After my own matriculation I decided to study medicine because I was deeply interested in psychotherapy and psychiatry. I thought that if I mastered these sciences the hidden realms of the human soul would appear to me; that they could be explored, and that a far-reaching therapy of psychoses and neuroses would be the result.

My 'matric' journey took me to Italy where I visited Florence, Perugia, Sienna and Assisi. One of the greatest impressions I received was from the paintings of the pre-Giotto masters such as Cimabue and Duccio who painted their stern and regular subjects on a background of gold. This gold seemed to speak of a spiritual life of which the old masters still retained a kind of memory, and the transition from the gold background to the more naturalistic backdrops of those who came after seemed to indicate the transition of the consciousness of human beings from a spiritual state to an earthbound one.

With these deep impressions I then went on to Assisi where I spent the most outstanding days of my whole journey in Italy. The peculiar layout of the town on the rocky, arid slopes of the Appennines with its wonderfully rich view down into the fertile Umbrian plain, and the Church of St Francis at one end of the town, traversing the slopes like the prow of a ship — all this filled me with wonder and joy.

The Church of St Francis is on two levels: a sober, light-filled upper part at ground-level where the famous frescoes of Giotto can be seen, and a dark, crypt-like lower part beneath ground-level, lit dimly by flickering candles, decorated with paintings that pre-date Giotto, and still pervaded by the sacred atmosphere of Franciscan devotion. While I was there, Mass was being sung in the lower church, and when it was finished I came out onto the hot, sunlit piazza in front of the upper church.

I stood there for some time, moved by what I had just witnessed. It seemed strange that here were these two churches, an upper and a lower, which in a sense seemed to symbolise the twofoldness of religion and psychotherapy which at that time was so often in my mind. It was as if the upper church, with its clear, day-lit atmosphere and colourful frescoes, represented for me the more conscious scientific approach to the hidden depths of the human soul. The dim, candle-lit lower church with its paintings still on a background of gold where I had heard mass being sung in its crypt-like hollows, seemed in an inward way to represent the religious approach. And it came to me that upper and lower should become one; that psychotherapy and religion would have to unite in order that the profoundest depths of the human soul could become manifest. But it should not be a union between one of the established religions and the analytical psychology of Jung (at that time the most advanced, in-depth psychology), but a union in which the known, not just the believed, reality of the Being and the deeds of Christ would be the basis for both.

After some blissful days in Assisi, and visits to a few other towns, I returned home again. The ideas that had connected themselves with the two churches in Assisi, against the golden background of the early, pre-Giotto masters, remained the outstanding essence of that journey.

Four years later, in Vienna, a circle of young medical students, teachers and painters formed a group with Dr König as its mentor. Through him, spiritual science and its initiator Rudolf Steiner became the ideal to which we dedicated our lives. Now the candle-lit darkness of the lower church in Assisi rose to the surface in full daylight and became one with the upper church because, at least for me, the division between faith and knowledge, between religion and psychotherapy, was overcome through the new understanding received from Rudolf Steiner's great work.

In the world-view opened up by Steiner the human soul is permeated by the beings and powers of the spiritual world; the golden background of old is transfigured in the daylight of human understanding.

THE CRESSET, EASTER 1961

camphill's relevance for our time

When Camphill began amid the windy hills of Scotland we were convinced that we were not just doing what we had to do, nor were we trying to prove, as such, that anthroposophy worked in a human-social way. We were simply filled with the enthusiastic certainty that this particular way of life was the way forward for a humanity which would gradually follow more and more. We were merely the torch-bearers in whose light people would become more truly human. There was nothing megalomaniac about it; we were filled with the conviction that we were doing it in the service of Anthroposophia, the new Christianity.

This ethos, which belonged to our beginnings, has since waned, not so much because we no longer believe it, but because the surrounding world increasingly looks upon us as saints, as oddities, as 'those people from

Camphill'. Through what was intended as a pioneering example of a better social organism, of a living together of free human beings based on spirit-insights, we have come to be seen as a sect, and often as a group of people fleeing the outer world and living in a fool's paradise.

I do not think that living in a community is necessarily a good thing. But as an education in mutual interest, in tolerance, in responsibility for and idealism towards each other, it is indispensable, at least for a time. The basis for social life today is the gradual overcoming of sympathy and antipathy. For most of us, a modicum of this is achieved in our professional lives (we should, of course, get along with our superiors and our equals). But how much more is it achieved in a community, where one cannot avoid the other, where many of the others are our neighbours, and where any real discord mars the harmony of the whole! To interest oneself in someone whom we like (in one's children, for example), is really a matter of course. But to interest oneself in someone we dislike or who we think despicable or ridiculous — we discover that our antipathy towards him melts in the sun of our interest. Where before he was seen (in our eyes) to be lying in the mud, his person rises in our growing understanding and experience of him.

In the future, responsibility for one another will have to become one of the strongest Christian emotions. We should learn to educate one another because only by so doing will we fulfil the responsibility incurred through having met. In this responsibility lies one of the strongest arguments for reincarnation and for Christ's being the Lord of Karma.[34] We cannot possibly fulfil this responsibility in one life, but already to experience it brings about a very different social order.

Concerning idealism, in living together we learn to look upon the other person with a certain awe, as when looking from a plain up to a mountain peak — not a peak of the 'here and now', however, but one rising in the course of time — as if the landscape were incomplete without the mountain. Without being responsible for and therefore dependent on each other, we could never approach our own star; the other one has to see our star. The development of each one of us is, therefore, a social phenomenon and it can more easily be learnt in a community.

Many people today have experiences very like those described above, but outer circumstances prevent the experiences from rising to the surface of social life and so they remain bottled up as individual, subjective feelings when in reality they are the voice of the Michaelic spirit of our time. We in

Camphill had the great advantage of arranging outer circumstances ourselves; we were our own state, mass media and public opinion. We did not have to fight against that which shapes the lives of most of our contemporaries, the linking of work to money, wage-differentials, career structures, etc. We could develop our own way of separating work from wages and in our undertakings we saw that enough money was earned to fulfil the needs of our estates and all who lived on them. The work we did personally, on the other hand, was independent of the money thus earned and we learned to love the work. It had its own needs and shape and we adapted to it out of our insights, not according to the time paid for it.

I am sure that the deeper reason for mass unemployment in Great Britain is that the spirit of our time urges circumstances towards recognising the dignity of the human being. This dignity can be upheld only if a person learns to work for the sake of work, that is, for those who need the work, and not because he has to earn a living. There is a vast number of people who work because they have to earn money, while a very small number of people earn enough so that they can work and live according to their liking. Through the close interlinking of earning money and work, human activity loses its value. At present, work seems increasingly to have an economic value only, but we must come to an economy where human work has a moral value.

The economic valuing of work gives it an automatic, superficial countenance. If work were directed with earnestness not to earning one's living but rather towards its intended objective — to teach for the sake of children and the joy of teaching; to lay bricks for the sake of building a house — then the famous 'nine to five' situation in which work is related solely to demarcated hours would not occur.

It seems to me that from these twin pillars of Camphill life (the idealistic and the educating; the respect for the other person and the place of work in human life), everything else flows. These two pillars seem to emerge in the morning of the Light Age and make it possible for Anthroposophia to descend into the social life.

Falling on Camphill ears, these words seem to sound through open doors. But something like a missionary zeal also belongs to the Camphill impulse, and only by kindling this zeal within us again and again will its hidden apostleship be evoked. With tact and empathy we should try to persuade other people to share the ideals of our life.

CAMPHILL CORRESPONDENCE, IX 1982

rhodes

Kate and I went for a week in mid-October to Rhodes, one of the most southerly Greek islands very close to the Turkish coast. The sun shone almost continually. The plants grew in Mediterranean abundance — the palms, the deciduous and coniferous trees, bougainvillaea and, Rhodes' symbol, the ubiquitous hibiscus. In still greater abundance hordes of English and Dutch tourists wandered or lay about, in shades of brown to red. All this was suffused with the elements of the incomparable light of the Mediterranean and the gentle autumn air, equally warm by day and night. Physically, it is a tremendously satisfying place, especially at this time of the year. We also became aware that it is so satisfying because it makes one content — perhaps more with some things, less with others — but in such a way that the reactivity of one's soul is not roused.

This soul calm belongs to the fourth post-Atlantean cultural epoch (748 BC to 1413 AD). The fourth post-Atlantean epoch was a culture that developed mainly around the Mediterranean and then later permeated the European continent. It was a time full of productive creativity — Aristotelian philosophy, classical Greek sculpture and architecture, Alexander's expeditions and foundations, Hellenic astronomy and libraries, Roman law, Christian monasteries, and also the gradual changing of Christianity into a religion and a Church. Although its productivity was based on this soul calm, the activity was not a reaction to other conditions. Its accomplishments were waves on this balance between the heavens and the earth, the soul calm resulting from living in this light, a light which makes understandable the Greek saying: 'Better a beggar on earth than a king in the realm of shades.'

The fifth post-Atlantean cultural epoch dawned in 1413 AD, and we are still only at its beginning for it will last until 3573 AD. It is based mainly north of the Alps and has its geographical roots in that region. What corresponds to the Mediterranean calmness and light are the seasons. The human being in the north must develop a greater flexibility within the seasons than in the mainly summer-like calm of the Mediterranean, as the warmth only rises in our summer and sinks in the winter.

Many specific events in recent centuries have increasingly enclosed us in an earthly prison of heavenly cosmic sensations and archetypes, debasing religion. These events include: the invention of printing; the discoveries of new continents; the earth and the stars being seen as merely physical bodies;

matter becoming the basis for scientific observations, and physical causation being relied upon instead of heavenly beliefs, thus laying the ground for the beginnings of technology. Religion has been reduced to superstition and empty phrases, and Christianity has splintered into Catholicism, Protestantism and other churches. Reactions to our polluted, and apparently non-spiritual, environment will develop even further. In response to the seeming barrenness of our intellectual technical achievements, human-spiritual answers will become the content of our fifth period and Christianity will no longer be a question of church or churches.

The peak of the fourth period was, in one sense, the earthly beauty of the classical time of Greece. The peak of our fifth period will be the width and majesty of heavenly-inspired morality and goodness.

This great reminiscence was brought about by our beautiful autumnal visit to the warmth and the light of the splendid Greek island of Rhodes, making it into a truly memorable holiday!

BOTTON VILLAGE NEWS, 31 X 1986

dilettante & expert

If there were a Spitzweg* in our time, he would paint the 'expert' as someone bent in concentration over a microscope, oblivious to what is going on in the room around him (perhaps his children playing), because in looking through the microscope he excludes all else from his attention. And if he did look about him, or out of the window, his vision and thoughts would be blurred by what he had seen and thought while peering down the microscope.

The dilettante, much rarer in our day, does nothing for any length of time. In the course of his life he may dabble in acting, play chamber music, paint, write or study, but intermittently.

By the intrinsic nature of these two types, the expert inclines more to the scientific, the dilettante more to the artistic (as we understand science and art today). Life is becoming so full of detailed knowledge that experts can master only their own field, especially in physics, chemistry and technology.

Every human being carries both types within himself, and these two are therefore not only a psychological but also a social phenomenon. In olden times the gentry, the experts, the artisans and craftsmen were all dilettantes.

---

*A 19th century German genre painter.

Young princes and princesses, even the higher bourgeoisie, learned to paint, sing, act or play an instrument, but it remained dilettantish — their existence did not depend on it — whereas a smith, a gardener, a builder or cobbler was a type filled with individual earnestness borne of necessity.

Through the economic, democratic and technical developments of the last hundred years, evolution has mainly gone the way of craftsmanship, but in two directions — the employee and the scientific expert — while the gentry have faded. The experts, each in their own sphere of knowledge, are the authorities of our time because they dominate our world view, and 'popular science' has swamped, or paralysed, our thinking and judging consciousness.

One sees why education in our time has quite a different task from even a hundred years ago. No doubt children are also different today. The Waldorf method of education is the appropriate way to support the growing school child during its soul development. Instead of educating the child into an adulthood surrounded by many microscopic pictures of the world, the content of Waldorf education endows the child with a capacity for judgement. The ability to judge can only arise from experience — of people, landscapes or situations — which is world content of a natural, aesthetic, physiological or religious kind. It is this tremendous variety of world content which has to find access to the child's soul and should make adult education more interesting than television or other diversions.

The capacity for judgement is weak in our time and paralysed by the power of expert knowledge. On the one hand, judgement or common sense in the eyes of expert opinion is like the child in Hans Christian Andersen's fairy tale *The Emperor's New Clothes*,[35] who declares, 'But the Emperor has nothing on.' On the other hand, judgement is the ability to understand the findings of spiritual science without having to prove them through clairvoyance or surrendering to faith, leaving proof to the experts. In believing our own individual viewpoint, we also feel, vaguely, that our understanding is objective. Rudolf Steiner often said that the findings of spiritual science are understandable by the healthy human mind. The paralysed mind is not healthy, and a lack of common sense is the greatest hindrance to an understanding of spiritual science.

The three spheres of the social organism will only be able to emerge if expert knowledge is enhanced by the human ability to judge. Common sense and judgement can be far from personal viewpoints; they can be as objective as sense perceptions, but they always have to be individual: they cannot repeat someone else's conviction.

Enthusiasm for the world-content, in the school teacher as well as in adult education, is the only means of kindling judgement and common sense, and of holding the wrong generalisations of experts at bay. In the future stream of time the old-fashioned dilettante will resurrect, but only when the expert is overcome. However, it will be more and more difficult for him to overcome the expert because the power of computers will overload his brain.

BOTTON VILLAGE NEWS, 13 XI 1964

all saints

In Roman Catholic countries, the first of November is a high holiday commemorating those who have died. In Protestant countries, too, the dead are especially remembered during November. There are various reasons for this. One is that the colourful abundance of the weeks of Michaelmas is fading and to a large extent only the bare skeleton of the landscape appears in the misty light. Only life's afterglow seems to linger — the light of Advent has not yet begun to shine — and therefore it is as if during November the bare earth becomes transparent for the existence of those who went beyond the threshold of the visible.

This existence has three tiers. The lowest tier gave rise to Hallowe'en (31st October), when the uncanny activity of witch-like beings call the dead up, under dusky moonlight, into their dances and haunts.

The second tier is connected with the fact that November is opposite to May and the festival of Whitsun. In the life of nature the parable for the Holy Spirit is the flower. Thousands, millions of spiral lines connect the heavens, the vault of the stars, with the earth. The plants grow not only because the earth pushes them upwards, but also because the star powers pull them upwards along these spiral ladders. In November these spiral lines are empty of plant growth, but human souls in the heavenly world communicate with each other along them.

The third tier is alluded to in the old expression for dying: 'to go to the eternal East'. The human soul on earth feels that the soul dies into the light of an everlasting morning and sunrise. The soul after death expands as far as the sphere of the Moon. It then rises along the spiral ladders, expanding into the spheres of Mercury and Venus, until it reaches and expands into the huge realm of the Sun.[36]

The substance of this realm is beyond earthly words and thoughts. But nearest to it is what we call tolerance — a tolerance which includes the loving recognition of the other one, and also the recognition that we can fulfil our humanity only through Christ Who is on earth. It includes the recognition that all religions are ways to the being of Christ.

BOTTON VILLAGE NEWS, 2 XI 1962

the birth of the son of man
in the act of consecration of man

The words and events of the four parts of The Act of Consecration of Man are so all-embracing that to follow and interpret them with our ordinary intellect is quite futile. It is like trying to scoop up the ocean with a beaker. We can say that it is the birth of the new Creation — new due to the indwelling of Christ within each human soul, rather than a Divine power from outside; new as against the old Creation which encompassed Paradise, the Fall and the whole of human history until the dawn of the new era at the time of the Mystery of Golgotha. Since then, humanity has entered a stage of transition from being a creature of the old creation to becoming a creator — from that of Man to the Son of Man as described in the Apocalypse, lying between the heavenly throne surrounded by the four beasts, and the altar on which stands the Mystic Lamb (see Revelation, chapter 4 onwards). In this transition, Creation becomes increasingly hollow and husk-like, yet within it lies the development of something new which is meant to survive beyond the Earth's evolution.

We can imagine the development of this new, Christian world-human-being through the four stages of the Act of Consecration as follows. In the first stage, after the preparatory prayers, the gospel is read. We should imagine that this new creation will arise from the Word. The Word is the seed of the new creation and although the inspired words of the gospels are read by human voices, they are nevertheless seeds.

In the second stage, the Offertory, the human soul, which has derived its being from the old creation, is offered up and, in the second part of the Offering, the words spoken are prayer-like, surrounded by incense. Christ comes near to the human being and thereby enables him, through His flame of love, to follow Him by his own will into the third part, the Transubstantiation. Christ should not be seen in the sense of an outer guide or shepherd, however, because through the Offering we have taken Christ into ourselves. In the third stage, our 'I' and Christ have become one. Our differences have vanished — it was for this purpose that Christ was crucified — and He rises in each one of us through the transformation of bread and wine. Our differences are the last outcome of the old creation, of our created soul.

All this has taken place outside us, although it calls on our presence, and it needs the ordained priest to bring it about. In the last stage, the Communion, we take into ourselves what has been achieved. The eternal life of the Son of Man permeates our mortal, created human being. In taking bread and wine we can feel, at least for a moment, like a husk.

It is necessary that we feel the monumental composition of The Act of Consecration of Man and do not merely try to accompany it with our all too human understanding. In having an upright feeling and view of its composition, The Act of Consecration of Man does not merely last for an hour; it is beyond time. It rises, comes wholly into view, and we are allowed to partake of it. Finally, this 'space within time' dissolves, and the ordinary time of our finite existence takes us once more into its stride.

BOTTON VILLAGE NEWS, 22 X 1971

the word from the trenches

In my childhood and youth in Vienna people lived very much under the impact of the recent past, of the First World War — although of course seen and experienced from the other side of the Channel, from the point of view of the vanquished. The overt tragedy of the First World War (about whose occult beginnings Rudolf Steiner[37] spoke often and at length), was that millions of young soldiers from many countries, glowing with patriotism, marched to their deaths. The highest, most spiritual qualities of the human soul were misused by Lucifer for nationalistic ends; all the apparent enthusiasm for god and country was a mockery, imprisoned in the illusion that there was an English, a German or an Italian god because patriotism was holy. The power of their sacrifice seemed to be offered at the altar of their respective countries only. But in the night, or after their death, the souls of those soldiers were connected in love with the people and nations they had hated most during the day or in life.

The heritage of nationalism from those years has remained an unresolved question right up to the present. Moreover, because of an ineffective international socialism, a nationalistic communism and the legacy of Hitler and the Second World War, it has changed from Luciferic enthusiasm into an Ahrimanic divisiveness of nations which has crept up on us almost unawares. The race for better armaments will rush on unabated; the problems of inflation and unemployment will remain unsolved, and science and technology will not reach their highest expression as long as there are separate nations. Although many of the younger generation do not accept this viewpoint, they do still acknowledge customs barriers, passports, currencies, and the various national governments with their parliaments, or if not quite accepting them they do not have thoughts strong enough to know how these things should be overcome.

The night existence and after-death existence of those who found themselves in the trenches made an enormous contribution to the beginnings of the Camphill Movement. In the youth group in Vienna* in the 1930s, where the idea of a common life and work was born, we spoke about the life and aims of some of those young men killed in the First World War. There were the two painters, Franz Marc and August Macke, the student writer Otto Braun, the poet Georg Trakl, the Hölderlin editor, Hollingrath. (Because we were on the other side of the Channel it was those on the German side that we knew about, but I could just as easily speak about the composer George Butterworth and the poet Wilfred Owen. Their sentiments were similar.) Those of us in Vienna felt that we had taken over where they left off with their death, that we carried forward their aims and ideals. Because we were lucky enough to be alive and, in addition, had met Anthroposophia, we took their ideals into earthly life. Their deaths were not in vain.

BOTTON VILLAGE NEWS, 3 1 1976

autumn — the human season

The radiance of spring always contains the promise of summer, the leaves striving towards substance, the tender growth and green spreading into colours and scents, upwards and outwards. The sap, the powers of growth and the elemental beings all work centrifugally from the centre in springtime. We

---

*As Barbara Lipsker recalled, the Vienna youth group included Trude Amann (née Blau), Willi Amann, Alex Baum, Hanna Förster, Karl König, Barbara Lipsker (née Sali Gerstler), Rudi Lissau, Carlo Pietzner, Alix Roth, Peter Roth, Hans Schauder, Lisl Schwalb, Thomas Weihs and Eduard Weinberg. It did not include Marie Korach, a childhood friend of Alix and Peter, who joined later.

could say that in autumn it is the other way around; the same processes take place, but centripetally. While there is some truth in this, it is only one side of the story.

The relation between the human being and the seasons differs from one season to another, and in autumn it is fundamentally different from the other three. In winter, there is hope for the warmth and light of spring when we become citizens of the whole world once more and leave our winter prison of darkness and cold. Then spring rushes towards summer's complacency, its fullness and majesty. These three seasons tend to take human beings along with them: we suffer the constricting embrace of winter, we delight in the scented melodies of spring, and sit in the world-glory of summer as in a warm bath.

The difference in autumn is that the human being *transcends* the season. The colours cannot assail and tempt him in the same way for the air is cooler and has a sobering effect on life. He is alone and must centre his being in himself, yet without selfishness for he is surrounded by a beautiful world. It is in autumn that the human being becomes aware that his constitution makes him an observer of nature. What tempts him in other seasons is now meant to strengthen that part of his being which is separate from nature. And in this special autumn loneliness he can grow aware that his essential being reaches *through* this particular earthly life, in which he bears a certain name, to beyond his present birth and death. In truth he is simply an 'I' who in other earth lives will bear other names.

As the spirit of autumn, Michael belongs to the seasonal Archangels along with Gabriel, Raphael and Uriel[38] But he evokes our understanding, our idealism and our delight in existence to a greater degree because he is also the Spirit of our Time, and in no other season of the year is the completeness of the world so much a part of our experience. In autumn our existence acquires a clarity, reaches a luminosity, against which its darker and heavier sides become unimportant. At no other season does the human being rejoice: 'How wonderful to be human!' Spring becoming summer is part of our nature, but autumn turning to winter belongs to that in us which *triumphs over* our nature, and over cold and dark. Autumn is, essentially, the human season, when life and consciousness are in perfect balance.

Of course, in our time we try not to be dominated by *any* of the seasons — we have air-conditioning in summer, heating in winter, etc. But this balance in autumn seems to be an unforced one, as if the temperature of our blood were equal to the temperature outside and around us. It is as if this outer balance in the world of nature frees an inner, human balance which has a strength beyond nature and seasons, one which is released through autumn's balance and is not simply a *result* of these natural forces. It is a strength which is meant to bear the human being through — indeed, above — that which in other seasons engulfs him.

The mysterious place of autumn among the seasons in relation to human existence is also due to the emergence of new elemental beings at this time. In autumn they arise — although whether, and how, they join in the breathing in and out of the other elemental beings is still unclear. But they do seem to belong to this special potency of autumn, this balance which for a few weeks reconciles nature and consciousness and which allows a creative stillness to arise. In this stillness the human being can observe out of love, and the old opposition between the human being and nature can be overcome.

To be able to raise oneself above nature is the ideal. As with any ideal, it should first be experienced, and then tried out according to that experience. Europe is the perfect place for this. In the southern hemisphere, for instance, autumn is more rare so the educating strength of the northern autumn is missing and the chance to experience the ideal mentioned above is considerably less. In places like eastern America, on the other hand, autumn is so magnificent it is outwardly overpowering. But here in Europe autumn has a balance which makes possible that special stillness out of which the monumental strength of the human being can arise, and this year was a quite special opportunity to experience it. Autumn this year was incomparably peaceful and radiant. It was as if the earth wanted to turn golden from a sea of green leaves against the blue of the sky. One could experience that autumn was not just a transition from motherly summer to black and contracted winter, but a season in its own right.

BOTTON VILLAGE NEWS, 25 XI 1988

illustration & composition

A new dimension in painting is required of us today. In the past, except with the beginnings of Expressionism, all pictures were illustrations. There is a great difference between a picture having a theme, or being an illustration of a theme. The Renaissance paintings of the Madonna or, much later, Constable's very realistic landscapes, are illustrations — even the Sistine Madonna is a pictorial description of the Madonna. Before Giotto, and ending with Duccio and Cimabue, pictures were, in fact, simply part of the religious ritual, a continuation of the icon. After Giotto, pictorial description began; first of scenes and themes from the gospels, legends and miracles, and later more secular themes emerged such as landscapes, the human body, etc. But by the end of Impressionism and around the beginning of the Light Age in 1899, painters had moved away from painting impressions: they wanted to paint the thing itself. When compared to Leonardo's 'Last Supper', the one by Nolde is crude, even a little contrived: Leonardo's is infinitely truer. On the other hand, Nolde's 'Last Supper' does try to express something, whilst Leonardo's picture is a holy description.

With illustration the picture can describe events in a book — illustration in the narrow sense — but it can also describe forms and events in the outer world. Expressionism went two ways: one was towards so-called abstract art — pictures expressing their theme in all kinds of colours and geometric forms, but not depicting the subject realistically — while the other was through the impulses and inspiration which Rudolf Steiner gave to art.

This second stage of Expressionism was to paint out of the colour itself and, from a truer knowledge and experience of colour, express a mood or theme in colours which would, of themselves, then demand their appropriate forms and composition. But if one tries to paint (or draw with coloured crayons) forms arising out of colours, one comes to the end of illustration, to the end of describing or depicting a theme, and thus also to the end of all realism. We may also come to despise colours and forms as such; we want a theme, we want to express a certain part of reality through colours and their arising forms. And just as one needs a theme to set this special act of creation into motion, so one wants to fit the picture into a certain place in the house (whether on a staircase or over a bed), so that it may enhance the daily reality which is always somewhat utilitarian.

In trying to paint out of colours, composition assumes a new importance. In the centuries of realism (from Giotto to Monet), composition could be nothing more than reality forced into some balance, whereas before Giotto the various forms had something magical about them, like Eastern mandalas. By the time of Cézanne, the magic of composition arose again because realistic depiction no longer hindered the artist. Meditations also have something magical in them, in so far as the consonance of their sounds, words and thoughts has a power quite apart from their comprehensible meaning. But it is a power that one can turn to or not; a power which leaves one free. In a similar way this is also the case (and is meant to be so), with Expressionist art, with Cézanne, or with Rudolf Steiner-inspired painting.

Regarding the forms arising out of colour, formerly colour could only be hemmed in by form. The artist had to colour in the form, so to speak (of the mantle, the tree, or whatever it was), and these forms depicted outer, perceptible objects. In our time, we are hindered in this effort of creative activity because we imagine the theme in forms and figures as if it were already a pictorial description of the subject (just as our ability to read is similarly a hindrance to meditation). But we should labour — in actual attempts on paper — to let the forms arise out of the colours. Trying to do it is much less difficult than describing it. When we do this (and only when we do it), we feel that through the effort something spiritual is brought into human habitation, and only then do the colours have a certain urge to arrange themselves rainbow-wise: red wanting to change into orange, orange into yellow, and so on. But we should not take this rainbow colour sequence as a law; we must take it rather as an aim, a longed-for aim. It is true only so long as one can say 'I' to it; so long as I would have done it myself in the way the colours follow each other in the rainbow. Something of this effort, bordering on despair, has to precede each finished picture: grace can come only after effort.

To make the effort is our duty as human beings. If it is too easy, we can be sure that our morality has not been sufficiently engaged and that the picture was only a selfish expression.

All our civilisation — our buildings, paintings, music (indeed all our art), as well as all forms of knowledge, of life and traditional religion and esotericism — is a product of the Kali Yuga,[39] the Dark Age, in which human beings, gradually cut off from the world of divine Beings, had to build their own world. This second step of Expressionism is meant to be an activity of the human being in the Light Age. Its social significance, its importance for the world, cannot yet be gauged, and it certainly cannot be compared with what painting was in the past, for painting then was something of a decoration to life — although sometimes deeper than life itself. The occupation of the soul with the colours, and the forms arising out of them, are building-stones for the new life itself, something which the world needs. This is by no means a hobby or private affair, but world-deeds of humanity.

BOTTON VILLAGE NEWS, 3 IX 1971

~ advent

the dawning of new advent values

In my childhood and adolescence I found myself listening to jazz again and again, I suppose because it can lead into such a pleasurable world — an artificially-lit world beyond earthly burdens and worries; a kind of magical sweetness which asks for abandon yet defies it, where perhaps one can abandon oneself only after death. From a certain point of view there is really very little difference between what jazz was then (for example, the music of Duke Ellington), and a song of the present day by, for instance, the Beatles. Both lead us into the same territory. The difference is that today the influence of this territory has grown enormously and permeates human life in an all-embracing way. Why is this?

In the last four hundred years our thinking, and with it our consciousness, has become amoral. While our feelings for beauty and ugliness can be moral (and morality can of course rise up into thinking), thinking itself is judged to be true thinking only when it is unclouded, observing and uninvolved — and therefore amoral. In the earlier years of the 20th century we possessed remnants of a bygone morality which, to a certain extent, still determined our feelings and our will or actions. As the century progressed those remnants gradually melted away like last year's snow, and were it not for the habits and customs of the world which hold together a kind of sham morality from without, this crumbling destruction would be far more evident.

Jazz and popular music lead into an amoral sphere (please note, I do not mean *im*-moral, but *a*-moral), one where values do not exist; a place between feeling and willing, between the astrality and the ego-organisation of the human being. But values do not exist in our thinking, our consciousness, and through this disappearance of values (I'm talking here about present, not past, values), our human existence threatens to dissolve. If our thinking were able to progress beyond the merely observant and learn to perceive — or we might say 'touch' — that which it lights upon, it would step out of its uninvolved isolation and begin to comprehend the world. Such new perception could not be other than permeated by values and true morality.

We still know only the outer courtyards and antechambers of the human soul of which Advent — that new Advent which prepares us for the Second Coming — is the festival. In the gospels, we read, 'For as the lightning that lighteneth out of the one part under heaven shineth unto the other part under heaven, so shall also the Son of Man be in His day.' (Luke 17: 24) This is an Advent sentence, but at the same time a Michael sentence in the sense explained by Rudolf Steiner in his lecture cycle, *Michaelmas and the Soul Forces of Man*.[40] The human soul can only appear in its full reality in the light of the Second Coming of Christ (Matt. 24: 29–35, Mark 13: 24–31, Luke 22: 25–33), because only then will our consciousness be pervaded by bright-hued and harmoniously ringing thoughts.

Popular music can seem to satisfy that longing which arises in our soul as a result of our consciousness becoming observant and amoral, grey and cool as the weather in November. Yet as soon as the first dawn of this 'touching' perception lifts our consciousness towards the Second Coming, *values* will again become visible, like stars in a dark and cloudless night. Only *values* evoke the powers of the human soul to the full, and to a morality that is beyond tradition. The great danger of that magic sweetness of the world of jazz and popular music is that it lulls our will to sleep. The Prince of our Advent-thinking will awaken this enchanted 'Sleeping Beauty'.

BOTTON VILLAGE NEWS, 13 XII 1963

rainbow truths

One of the dangers in discovering the enormous width of that world which Rudolf Steiner made available to us is that we reduce truth, knowledge and the interpretation of experience to mere abstractions. His books themselves can easily hoodwink us, written as they are in a cool and abstract style. But the concepts they contain, those thought sequences, have been distilled from very concrete, substantial imaginations. We have no business using them just as we receive them, because when *we* utter them they are then quite differently derived (although of course we *must* use them, otherwise we would understand nothing of the world and would not be pupils of spiritual science). The danger is compounded by the fact that on the one hand we live, experience and perceive things relatively inaccurately and vaguely, and on the other, because we have been granted more knowledge than others through the revelations of Rudolf Steiner, we can easily be lead to intellectual pride. This is a danger we can overcome only very slowly, over the course of many years.

Our relation to truth is Newtonian. We think all colours are hidden within white light, and that white light belongs to our sense world. We think that truth, including anthroposophical truth, is like 2+2=4; valid at all times and in all places. But in reality the white light is something supersensible and on Earth we can only perceive colours, lighter or darker. Abstract truths are like the illusory white light; concrete truths are like colours. Whenever we reconcile our thoughts with actual perceptions, the hidden rainbow emerges between the human being and the Earth, the rainbow of the covenant after the Great Flood (Genesis 9: 13–14), the rainbow of which the Advent prayer speaks, 'a bow of colour spanning the universe'.

BOTTON VILLAGE NEWS, 22 XI 1963

'o u t e r   s i g n s'

Festivals are times when we renew and strengthen our consciousness of creation, and this is especially true of Advent. The way one lays the table at the Bible Evening and then decorates it with the Advent wreath, red candles and ribbon against the dark green of the fir; the hanging of transparencies in the windows; stars and scenes from the birth of Christ; angels bearing candles, and so on — all this raises the question: Why these outer signs? The answer is that without such 'outer signs' we risk the danger of looking for the divine only within, while outside us poverty, dirt, and ugliness could all exist without our trying to transform it.

This is at the heart of the drug problem, too. It is not so much the drugs themselves, but rather that smokers of hashish, opium or marijuana create private pipe-dreams, mystical anti-social castles, which leave the earth un-ordered, unadorned, and therefore un-transfigured. When we make 'outer signs' we do it out of our individual fantasy and conviction. We work actively from inside to outside: we commit ourselves to redeeming the earth.

BOTTON VILLAGE NEWS, 29 XI 1968

the new gods

One aspect of Advent and the Second Coming of Christ is that in pre-Christian antiquity two groups of people existed in the then known 'civilised' world who had no interest in being missionaries or converting each other. There were the Jews, the chosen people, who were *monotheistic*, looking towards a Messianic future, and the Gentiles, consisting of everyone else — Greeks, Babylonians, Phoenicians, Indians, Romans, Teutonic tribes, etc. — who were *polytheistic*, worshipping an enormous number of gods and goddesses which were cross-culturally identical only to a limited extent. For instance, the Babylonian goddess Ishtar can be compared with the Egyptian Isis and the Greek Artemis, but only partly. Thor, Indra and Ares also overlap, but again, not completely. Yet this vast pantheon of gods and goddesses who related to one another only to a certain extent did nevertheless have *one* thing in common. They were all locally, geographically determined, as if the view into the spiritual world in the time before Christ was slightly different if seen from Greece or from Egypt, and different again from a Babylonian viewpoint. It is as if what rises out of a certain place on earth determines and colours the heavenly configuration, so they were all *spatial* gods. Even Jahwe (Jehovah) and His laws started off being bound to a certain earthly locality, namely Palestine. *His* power, however, was inserted into the blood of the Jewish generations and hence they felt they were the 'chosen' people and that the future of humanity, not just of the Jews, depended on Him. Jahwe was the forerunner of the Messiah, the Christ, and so in a certain sense His Father.

Not surprisingly, therefore, when it came Christianity wore the Jewish garment of monotheism, the Trinity being simply the threefold aspect of it. But in our time, with the Second Coming, the new Advent, a second phase of Christianity is beginning, and with it a new Christian polytheism arises. The Trinity is the highest Divine Being but between that sphere and the sphere of humanity are many other higher beings. 'Hereafter shall you see heaven open and the angels of God ascending and descending...' (John 1: 51) Nothing furthers the irreligious attitude of our time more effectively than the mistaken idea that the Trinity and the sphere of humanity border on each other without the infinity of higher beings in between. If anything, it was the *Church* that stood between. The coming of Protestantism was a foreshadowing of spiritual science and *individual* access to the heavens, and it also developed more of a Jewish direction to Christianity than Roman Catholicism had done.

As the old pagan gods were bound to certain lands and peoples, the new Christian gods and their mythology will be bound to time and to mankind. We can imagine that this new mythology will be connected to the seasons, to the geology and geography of the *whole* earth, and to the movements and relationships among the stars. The Christian core of spiritual science reveals the seasons as the countenance of the new presence of Christ. The four seasonal archangels — Gabriel, Raphael, Uriel and Michael — manifest the dominance of the cycle of the year over everything that is purely historical. The changing altar colours and words of the seasonal prayers in the Act of Consecration of Man are all different doorways to the presence of Christ. The star constellation in which the sun stands in any month is invisible only to the physical eye, not to our image making. There are twelve star constellations as there were twelve apostles. The seasons, their archangels, the course of the sun, the position of the zodiac and the other stars, all have one centre — the Earth, which has become the body of Christ.

The old gods were rooted in the heavens, their appearances on Earth were like passing images. The new gods and their mythology will be rooted in the Earth, an Earth that is not only dark and material but is beginning to be transfigured by the dawn of the new Advent.

BOTTON VILLAGE NEWS, 9 XII 1976

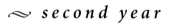 *second year*

~ *christmas & the holy nights*

human existence

The radiance of the Christmas season can make us aware that, as children of our time, we are divided beings. We look at the altar and at the Christmas tree and can feel at least something of the quality of our nights and of sleep and recognise that although modest in our uprightness among the exalted, shining beings we also can take part — rather like Cinderella, as it were — in the heavenly banquet. But we are also earthbound, 'day' beings and when in the Service we hear that we should be able to behold the Divine with our eyes, we become aware of just how earthbound we really are. We seem to see only the outer shell of matter and we suppose that if we could see better we would see atoms, electrons, etc. Our thinking gives way to our muddied senses otherwise we would behold the divine, creating powers in the forms and evolution of nature. We stare at the fabric instead of following the gestures and expressions extending in space or developing in time.

What makes us divided beings is *not* because something in us is good and something else evil, while in the background a kind of Moses judges us. And nor is our consciousness able to judge, because our consciousness is necessarily biased: judgement between good and evil is, in fact, a red herring.

Much more pertinent for us is the polarity of active and passive. For nine-tenths of our life we are *forced* to do things. If I am a farmer I must plough; as a parent I have to care for my children, etc. The circumstances need us and we obey them. But obeying — even if we love what we do, or because we have resolved to do it — is in every case passive. It is only with that last tenth of our existence that we are active or creative. Hobbies (painting or eurythmy, for instance), lead us in that direction, but only in a slight or hazy way because, again, we end up loving them or fulfilling an intention toward them.

The morality of our time has far more to do with the question of active and passive than with any notions of doing one's duty or resisting temptation. To do our duty easily becomes almost a matter of course; to obey circumstances we have brought upon ourselves in one way or another is enormously satisfying because it makes for a good conscience, but it leaves part of our abilities unused. But to go to a brother or sister we are not particularly fond of and ask, like Parsifal, 'What ails you?'¹ is to *discover* another part of oneself. Even in the midst of dreadful circumstances and harassing storms, this is the still centre — it is our free and upright humanity; it is the silent, modest light from which springs any esoteric Christian striving.

BOTTON VILLAGE NEWS, 27 XI 1968

gold & wheat

I feel the Spirit-Child
Now disenchanted in the womb of soul
In clarity of heart
The holy word of worlds has now begotten
The heavenly fruit of Hope
Which grows rejoicing into farthest worlds
Out of my being's ground divine.

*Calendar of the Soul,*² verse 38 (Christmas)

It is only at Christmas that we can fully appreciate the reality of these words, and our deep need for the course of the seasons. Out of the being of everyone we meet, a divine child surrounded by a golden halo like the child in the arms of the Sistine Madonna looks out at us. It is only at Christmas that we become aware of the holiness of each person. Usually we rush past each other as if in a hurry, and because of this inner hurry our souls do not stop in front of each person and say: '*Ave!*' ('Greetings!') This spirit child is not in one place only, and it would be wrong to say it is more in one person than in another: it is in everyone, surrounded by the golden halo of Hope. The inner '*Ave*' and the child of Hope in the other person can meet, and the mood of Christmas — a mood of infinite, deathless comfort — arises.

Earlier, the gold of the Spirit-Child found expression in the crowns of kings and the jewels of palaces and churches. Physical splendour and costly ornaments denoted the grace and presence of divine worlds. Later, this physical splendour degenerated from being a reflection of grace into a sign of the possession of money. The gold of the Spirit-Child became the gold of money, the Gold Standard emerged and 'Whatever money can buy' became the only measure of physical pomp. That which had once been the privilege of priesthood and kingship — precious garments and buildings, the shining symbols of holiness — became the privilege of those with enough money to buy them.

All this turns into the unreality of a bad dream if we imagine that the counter value of money is not gold but wheat, as Rudolf Steiner once proposed. It is far beyond our thinking to imagine that money might lose its customary value simply because our notion of price and all it entails is based entirely on money having a lasting value. To us it is unimaginable that a price could be based on something that grows and decays, as Rudolf Steiner suggests in his lectures on *World Economy*.[3] But if it were, it could then be founded on the needs of human beings and not on something rare and precious. We would be able to express the heavenly world in appropriate substances independent of their 'cost', and only in this way could there be a Christian union of heaven and earth.

The humble stable, the place of the birth of Jesus, is poor because of the deep gulf between heaven and earth: the things of the earth were beginning to cost money. Human morality is dependent to a large extent on what people can afford. Christmas is the festival of the poor stable not because shabbiness and poverty are Christian virtues but because the things of the earth — food, garments, cars, ships, journeys, jewellery, etc. — have to be seen not in terms of money and how much they cost, but in terms of human need.

BOTTON VILLAGE NEWS, 23 XII 1966

the breathing of the year

Spiritual science can be no more than a guide for us, but Rudolf Steiner's *Calendar of the Soul*, with its fifty-two verses, one for each week of the year, is so impressive that we can easily forget the year itself and the rising and falling of its seasons. Yet it is up to us to observe, understand and interpret world phenomena with the help of spiritual science and the *Soul Calendar*. If understood in this way, its verses can be a key to the door of the rising and falling seasons.

Once our gaze has been directed to it, it is obvious that each year is a natural unit within which there is a self-contained sequence of seasons that transform themselves one into the next. As long as we merely stare at the words 'spring', 'summer', 'autumn', 'winter', the phenomenon revealing itself escapes us, but if we look closely at the variety of expression in nature around us, we can understand the unit of the year as a phenomenon of breathing, of inhaling and exhaling. When the northern hemisphere is breathing in, the southern hemisphere is breathing out. From winter through spring to early summer in each hemisphere life is breathing out — warmth and light through the growing arc of the sun, unfolding leaves and blossoms, birds and insects filling the widening space. From later summer through autumn and late autumn to winter, life is breathed in — trees become bare, meadows brown, the reducing arc of the sun leaves us surrounded by cold and dark, while underground the buried potatoes, carrots, etc. stay unspoiled in the winter earth despite being embedded in cold, wet mud. Rudolf Steiner often pointed to the summer nature of the etheric warmth underground, within which the earth wakes in winter.

These are the outer phenomena, and we have a tendency to regard the seasons merely as facts which present themselves in the course of the year. We have become used to looking for causes — it is the custom of our time — yet the seasons also have a Christian, prophetic and moral nature. They demand something of us, they call to us because they are complete only through our co-operation. We can only transcend impersonal causes if we begin to grasp that their 'original' meanings 'fell' into being expressed as cause and effect, for example, the sun's arc rising higher or sinking lower as being the cause of summer warmth and winter cold. The chains of cause and effect become the expression, the servants, of particular meanings.

The *Soul Calendar* points to the meaning of the year, to the co-operation between the experience of our souls and the objective tread of the seasons. That is why it is called *Calendar of the Soul* and its main countenance is what was described above as the breathing in and out of the respective hemispheres. The verse for the week around the middle of November is an enlightening example of this, though we could probably take any of the fifty-one others!

> So now I feel the world which,
> Abandoned by my soul,
> Would be but frozen empty life,
> Devoid of might.
> If that would reproduce itself
> It would within itself find nought but death.
>
> *Calendar of the Soul*, verse 33, (two weeks before Advent)

In this verse the twofoldness of the *Calendar of the Soul* is distinctly formulated. In following the earth's in-breathing we follow nature's decay and destruction. Where in spring and summer we looked at leaves and blossom, in autumn and winter there is only bareness. But another layer of existence, that of the soul, opens. The sense part of the year, during which the soul part was a mere echo of the growing strength and abundance of the world, is meant to become the soul content of human beings.

> There thrive within the sunlight of my soul
> The ripened fruits of thinking:
> Into the certainty of self-awareness
> All feeling now transforms itself
> Full of joy now I can sense
> The autumn's spirit wakening.
> Winter will summon up in me
> The summer of the soul.
>
> *Calendar of the Soul*, verse 30, (end October/beginning November)

This in-breathing part of the year in which outer nature becomes gradually more bare, poor and condensed, reaches from summer up to December 24th. From then until the middle of January, the period during and after the Holy Nights, there is, seasonally, a kind of standstill (the same is true for the period after June 24th). The sun reaches its highest point on June 21st, its lowest on December 21st. The outer sun becomes stronger in the out-breathing part of the year; the inner, soul's sun does so in the in-breathing part.

> Thus speaks the cosmic word
> Which I through senses' gates
> Could lead into the depths of soul.
>
> *Calendar of the Soul*, verse 17, (end July/beginning August)

Meanwhile, the Christmas verse says:

> I feel the Spirit child
> Set free in womb of soul
> The Holy World Word.
>
> *Calendar of the Soul*, verse 38, (Christmas)

We are meant to look at the year in such a way that in its first half we begin to see the unfolding of outer creation ['In the beginning was the Word,' John 1: 1], and flow out in our seeing to become one with that which is seen, to become part of nature, of divine Creation. In the second half of the year, the Word as such starts to come to itself in the soul space widening within us in contrast to waning, decaying nature. This widening comes to its climax at Christmas with the birth of the Spirit child in the womb of our soul. The real joy of Christmas (triumphing over all the commercial trappings of modern times) is the ability to feel that the Spirit child born in our soul is as widespread as the summer was in the outer physical world. We feel that the point-like 'I' is really as wide as the world. The physical unfolding of summer does not just become a memory in winter — the being of the Word rises in our own soul. In summer the soul was spellbound in Creation: at Christmas, that world's variety appears as the Eternal Child in our soul space.

But there is more to it than this. Time appears to flow in one direction, namely forward (Monday is followed by Tuesday; May is followed by June, spring is followed by summer, etc.). But there is another, a hidden, invisible stream that flows in reverse (Tuesday to Monday, June to May, summer to spring, etc.). How else could we explain the experience that over the course of eighty years, with eighty springs, summers, etc., the seasons are always new? We can be tired of life, but never tired of a season coming round. It is the illusion of the one-way street of life that makes us tired. When once we notice, if only dimly, that to time and its onward flow there is a reverse flow hidden in the background (from evening to morning, old age to childhood, winter through autumn to summer), life acquires new and fascinating dimensions in which we are not mere onlookers and victims, but also astonished participants. This becomes clear in any biography. The story of a life is not just a line which begins at birth and ends at death, with various events strung out one after the other along it. Rather, it is a single whole and can be likened more to the composition of a work of art than to a chain of cause and effect — the karmic powers are divine artists, not logical judges or scientists — and this whole is a 'time-space'. One half of the year (winter to summer) mirrors the other half (summer to winter). The first half displays itself before our senses, the second half within our soul. The soul is the mirror which is finally shattered at Christmas when the Spirit child, the World-creating Word, is born within it. The reality appears after it has gone through the two evolving images of the sense world and the soul world. (In the *Calendar of the Soul*, each pair of verses with the same letter identifying it represents this time-space year.)

Rudolf Steiner's huge wooden sculpture of the Representative of Man between Ahriman and Lucifer is also the god of the year. As July changes to August, the glory of summer just beginning to be invaded by the first decay of autumn can be experienced in the verses for this time. They speak of the growing world-width of the Word in human souls, the Word which is born at Christmas as Spirit World child. The year with its seasons is a continual education towards this image of the Representative, the Ideal of Humanity who has separated from and objectified Lucifer and Ahriman. The whole of the year contains Luciferic and Ahrimanic threats and dangers, the four cited verses (33, 30, 17 and 38) being the overt climax of these. The World-Word is interwoven throughout the whole year with its seasonal Ahrimanic and Luciferic tendencies.[4] There are fifty-two stations, as it were, at which the soul is educated to stand, each year a little more firmly, and experience the Word both inwardly and outwardly. It is vital that the year is absorbed not only as a sequence in time but, with the help of the experiences of the opposite season, is transformed into a 'time-space'. There we can know ourselves and the world as an ever-fluctuating interplay between Lucifer and Ahriman — more Lucifer-Ahriman in springtime; more Ahriman-Lucifer in autumn — with the Son of Man in the middle. The Son of Man has freed Himself, has become manifest and brought the Luciferic and Ahrimanic powers to a point of balance. It is He who will in future be identified with our ego.

There is yet another aspect. The two halves of the year arising from the in- and out-breathing of the Earth obviously divide the year into two. But there is also the division, at right angles to the first, created by the Easter-Michaelmas axis. The verses belonging to these halves are an exact mirror of one another, the verses A to Z of one half mirroring the verses A' to Z' of the other half. The verses are also numbered from one to fifty two so that as we progress through the 'year-time', each verse bears a letter and a number: A1 to Z26 being one half, A'27 to Z'52 the other half. The circle of the 'year-space' therefore has the cross inscribed in it arising from the two axes of Easter–Michaelmas and Christmas–St John's, which creates in turn four quarters, each quarter containing thirteen sectors or weeks. The four verses which always belong together unite the two halves or four quarters, one each of the four being positioned in a spring, summer, autumn or winter quarter. Thirteen four-sided, geometric figures can thus be formed — the first being the thin horizontal rectangle A1–Z'52–A'27–Z26 around the Easter-Michaelmas axis through G7–T'46–G'33–T20 which produces a square to the Christmas–St John's axis, again a thin but now vertical rectangle, M12–M'38–

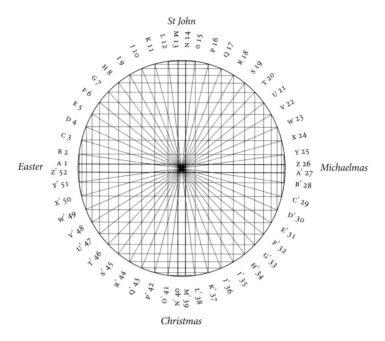

P'41–P15. The respective figures appear if one first finds the mirroring verses (A–Z', Z–A', B–Y', Y–B') and then join up these four sections or weeks to make thirteen figures within the 'year-space'.

We then find that the half from Easter through St John's to Michaelmas belongs to the time where our senses, and therefore our thinking, are increasingly fed but also fettered by the power of the sense-world, while the winter half of the year throws us back into our soul, our sense-free thinking, and therefore our freedom. Christmas, the time when we experience the greatest nearness of Christ to each one of us, is in this latter, invisible half. And why do the two halves mirror each other? The winter half, with Christmas at its centre, is the world of the great spiritual archetypes, of the etheric warmth, the invisible world of our thinking. The summer half, with St John's at its centre, is the world of the physically appearing archetypes, the world which tries to convince us of the various kinds of materialism. As anthroposophists it behoves us to relate these two halves to one another, as the *Soul Calendar* does in the thirteen squares. The visible half is lit up by the light of the sun, the invisible half by the light of our thinking.

The year-space halved by the axis Christmas–St John's is an event of creation, of 'great creating nature', of the arc of the sun and its relation to the earth. The halves resulting from the Easter-Michaelmas axis represent the basis of our freedom. The thirteen 'squares' gradually lead us not just to accept the course of the seasons (as spread around us in their apparent sequence) as a fact of nature, but to experience this course as needing our complementary activity. That is why the squares make a space out of this sequence, and why the fifty-two verses are called the *Calendar of the Soul*.

We have looked at the mystery of the two halves of the year, the rising and falling course of the sun with the falling half enclosing the waxing summer of the soul. As we saw, each of the fifty-two verses has its opposite divided along the axis from Easter to Michaelmas. Always two verses from the two rows 1–26 and 27–52 mirror each other (1–52, 2–51, 3–50… 24–29, 25–28, 26–27, etc). Alongside our lives' progression from verse 1 to verse 52 run the verses 52 to 1, the mirroring verses moving in the opposite time direction, for example the April-May-June weeks are mirrored in the March-February-January weeks.

In addition to this, the four quarters of the year express their quality in forward and backward directions too. January to April is about thinking — not the usual dead, 'head-thinking', but real thinking, embracing our whole body; indeed our whole existence — suffused with life. April to June is about the senses' flowering. July to September is the slow transformation of the senses' flowering into receiving the Word into our souls. From October till Christmas is the fruiting of the soul, and with it the endowment of the world with these fruits. And Christmas through into January crowns this part of the year with the birth of the Spirit Child, and the leading over once again into the birth of thinking.

All this means that in the course of the year we are concerned not only with the *complementary* verses, identified by the same letter (at opposite stations in the in- or out-breathing process), but also with the *mirroring* verses (A–Z, B–Y, C–X, etc.) Our existence in the world of nature, the seasons and the weather, shows us how bluntly and crudely we experience things. The mirroring of verses expresses what in the foregoing article was called archetype. We could think of the end of the second part of Goethe's *Faust*[5] where the 'Chorus Mysticus' begins:

> All earth comprises
> Is symbol alone;
> What there ne'er suffices
> As fact here is known;

All past the humanly
Wrought here in love;
The Eternal-Womanly
Draws us above.

Through the outwardly manifest, foreground ambience of the verse of the actual time we are in, and in which we immerse ourselves, the mirroring verse shines through, adding its soul-completion to our meditative understanding.

The split which began to separate human existence from the cosmos after the Fall is tentatively joined together again. The four verses, G7–G20–T46–G33, are the most poignant expression of this split between human being and world following the Fall. But what a blessing that split was! In the beginning there was the Garden of Paradise where nature, in a state of warmth, was completely at one with the human being. In the course of condensation through the airy and watery elements down to the earthly, the human being increasingly separated from the world of nature. Christ, the Word in the *Calendar of the Soul*, has given us moral, creative courage so that, having become united again at the end of time — although now with the transformed earth — we may be able to experience the New Jerusalem. When we take mirroring verses into our soul we are building the foundations of that heavenly city along whose golden streets the trees bear fruit twelve times a year. (Rev 22: 2)

CAMPHILL CORRESPONDENCE, MAY/JUNE & NOVEMBER/DECEMBER 1990

the soul's calendar — the wheel of the year

The verses of Rudolf Steiner's *Calendar of the Soul* can never be independent of the actual experience of the course of the year, nor become an object of study in themselves. They are meant as a clarification, expressing and making us aware of our own experiences of the seasons which escape us because we glide over them unconsciously. Anthroposophy as a whole, and the *Soul Calendar* in particular, is a call to activity. We must take hold of the world, and through the interpretation of anthroposophy we are more able to do so. Without our understanding of the world we would lose a great deal, and thereby block all roads to self-knowledge.

Around the middle of the months of August, November, February and May we discover something of a stationary grey in the mood of each respective season. Other times of the year seem to follow one another. By interpreting the words of the *Soul Calendar*, we find the verses not only follow each other sequentially, but also our relationship to the course of the year changes. Within these months, however, time seems to come to a standstill, as if there might never be anything else but summer heat, the bareness of late autumn, the promise of as yet invisible spring in the rising sun, or the advent of autumn in the first signs of decaying blossoms. In these four verses it is as though our soul condition touches the life of nature, the rotating wheels of sun and stars. The separation of 'I' (ego) and World is an existential experience which began in the 16th century, increased into our time, becoming more and more a concern of poets and philosophers, and was overcome (in principle) only in Rudolf Steiner's early book *The Philosophy of Freedom*.[6] The separation is an illusion for the sake of our freedom. But in these four weeks (G7–T'46–G'33–T20) the illusion seems to tear at our soul condition and the wheel of the year. The greyness of the soul and of nature become one for a short time.

These four weeks in the year are remarkable because the verses express our accustomed relationship to nature throughout the year. It seems as if nature holds her breath and halts her progress for our sake. On the other hand, feeling part of the movement of the seasons in these weeks, we can become aware that we are excluded from the life of nature and the universe, excluded for the sake of our freedom and self-consciousness. In May, August, November and February we stare into our souls as if excluded from nature and, through being excluded, we therefore 'come to ourselves'.

Towns were founded from the 10th century onwards (in pre-Christian times they were quite different), thus furthering this exclusion from nature so successfully that even when we live in the country we are actually town dwellers. Our consciousness is the same in winter as in summer, in spring as in autumn — it would displease us greatly if timetables became unreliable in spring — in short, it is the consciousness of our ordinary 'I'. The *Soul Calendar* is one of the pathways from the ordinary 'I' to our higher 'I'.

It is one of the ways. The year rolls on, wheel-like. The verses follow each other and in any calendar week the verse is a transition from the previous to the following one. Thus the past verse and the coming, future verse shine into the present one. It is our eye, our words and concepts that freeze what develops into still pictures and divides the year into fifty-two segments. We must swing our feeling and thinking on to the year-wheel, and get into the rush of thought-content of the three verses (past, present and future), not just the present one.

And the festivals? The wheel of the year has two layers — the inner, from Michaelmas via Christmas to Easter (which is called soul-summer in the *Soul Calendar*), and the outer, especially from Easter via St John's to Michaelmas, which is the glory of the sense-world. The layers of the *Soul Calendar* are led and ordered by what is expressed in the Michaelmas verse. The centre of the inner layer is the Christmas verse; the centre of the outer is the St John's verse. Easter is the end and the beginning of the layers of the wheel.

CAMPHILL CORRESPONDENCE, SEPTEMBER 1991

e u r y t h m y

> In the Beginning was the Word, and the Word was with God and the Word was God. The same was in the beginning with God. All things were made by Him; and without Him was not anything made that was made.
>
> John 1: 1–3

Something of an afterglow of this creating Word was present in the primal, archetypal language, the language everyone spoke before the time depicted in the story of the Tower of Babel (Gen 11: 1–9), when the break-up into different languages began. But we should not imagine that that ancient speech was anything like ours today. It was more like the moving gestures in eurythmy, a thinking-feeling garment of empathy. Before the Tower of Babel, Creation was word and sound forming itself into shapes — of mineral world; of plant world (dying and becoming); of the animal world (suffering and enjoying) and of human beings (able to pray). The human being was first poured out into this great diversity of enlivened and ensouled physical form, and then, in drawing back from being completely at one with the world-creating Word, he became gradually a coalescence of *all* forms. One might say that human beings started to speak within an increasingly silent world.

Eurythmy gives us this process in reverse. The fruits of human speech are thereby freed and offered back. The spoken word, more and more empowered by Christ, gains volume, as it were, in eurythmy. Written words in novels — but especially in verse, rhyme, rhythm and verse-plays — are all words which do not merely give information but express a soul or sense event. And it is not just a question of words, letters, or sounds as such (A or L or I*) on their own;

---

* In eurythmy, the German pronunciation of I (ee) is used,

it is their harmonious relationships one to another which lift the reading soul into a higher reality. This expressive quality raises what was dead, silent form into life again, and because in eurythmy the whole body gives voice to it we see the flesh becoming Word again, as once the Word became flesh. And here also it is the relationships between the pertinent eurythmy gestures which make the beholding soul aware of this.

The eurythmical movement rises, like sacrificial smoke, out of creation, and the relationships within the overall movement contain the meaning. There are three ever-widening yet inversely relating layers: the event itself which the words describe; the language expressing it and, finally, the eurythmy expressing the language — the 'eurythmic language' or 'sounding eurythmy' expressing the event. A part of the universal human being has gone into the event, and the death of the Word has created its silent form. The human word arises out of it in starry warmth, but it is a human word consisting of sound-relations and not of sounds in themselves.

The gospels are an archetypal image of this. Firstly, the earthly life of the Word is expressed in a fourfold way. It is not any single event that counts; rather it is the relation and sequence of the various events, their composition within a chapter and between the chapters, which counts. Christ is the Word. How the power of the Word appears in the gospels — not in any abstract or intellectual interpretation such as 'the Feeding of the Five Thousand means...' but in actual sentences and sentence-sequences — seems to be of great importance for the life of the human being and for eurythmy training. The human being is formed out of, and for, the Word.[7]

Examples of the principle of composition in the gospels, to which Rudolf Steiner repeatedly referred, are the so-called apocalyptic passages which we read during Advent (Luke 17 and 21, Matt. 24 and Mark 13). One has to connect, 'In the beginning was the Word...' with 'Heaven and earth will pass away, but my words will not pass away.' (Mark 13: 31, Luke 21: 33). And between these: 'They shall deliver you up to councils; and in the synagogues ye shall be beaten: and ye shall be brought before rulers and kings for my sake, for a testimony against them.' (Mark 13: 9) 'Take no thought beforehand as to what you shall say [because] it is not you that speaks, but the Holy Ghost.' (Mark 13: 9, 11).

The many catastrophes described in these apocalyptic passages, even the signs in sun, moon and stars, show a world that shakes and is splitting open. Just as the walls of Jericho once crumbled because of the power of the holy trumpets, so now it is the power of Christ entering human words which shakes the world, for the clouds in which He appears can only be in human hearts and souls. We must not imagine that these passages contain anything prophetic in a physical sense; it is events of the soul and spirit which are meant, some of which may also have a physical reflection. There will always be wars, but today war means something very different from what it did as recently as a hundred years ago.

Human language, if it is not merely informative, serving the needs of the day, but perhaps a poem, a lecture, or a deed of the selfless spiritual life, is a speaking before councils and kings. The power of the Prince of this World[8] is tremendous in our time (both in the East and in the West) threatening the purely human and reducing it to a mundane level.

In the time of the catacombs, the Sun of Christ melted the fear of death. In our time, it will again light up the essentially human in each one of us.

1 JANUARY 1971

～ *epiphany*

p e a c e

The mystery of Communion — the bread, wine and peace — is as wide as the known and unknown world. So also with Christmas and the Holy Nights. As the Transubstantiation is a continual Holy Week, from the entry into Jerusalem to the first Easter Sunday, so Communion is the continual presence of Christmas, from the annunciation to the shepherds (Luke 2: 8–15) to the dream of the kings 'to depart into their own country another way' (Matt. 2: 12).

In the Communion, the permeating of the temporal by divine Love is the same thing as the eternal Word entering into our earthly, temporal world. The light shines into the darkness, but our cold and hard darkness (although it can appear quite bright during the day), has grown very far away from the heavenly light. Love and warmth — the bread and wine — bear the glance of the eternal brother and friend of humanity.

However, this glance contains not only the grace of Christmas, but also the glory and fulfilment of Easter; not only the bliss of the glistening green Christmas tree, but also the dread of the harrowing of hell and the majesty of the Apocalypse. Christ, who during the Holy Nights is as near to us as the air we breathe, is the Son of Man, standing amid the seven golden candlesticks, the image from which the whole of the Apocalypse unfolds.

The peace following bread and wine in each Service is a peace in which the world-choir of the nine hierarchies resounds: 'I fell at His feet as dead. And He laid His right hand upon me, saying unto me, Fear not; I am the first and the last.' (Rev 1: 17)

Between Christmas and Three Kings' Day the light of the Holy Spirit shines into human souls during the night. This year particularly, the lectures each morning seemed to bear something of the night time's gold into the day: of human spirits in the apocalyptic light of the Holy Spirit. And something of this golden aura, too, was in the music framing each lecture.

DATE UNKNOWN.

st joan — torch-bearer of our time

Inscribed over the portal of the consciousness soul are the words: "Blessed are the pure in heart: For they shall see God." (Matt. 5: 8). 'Pure in heart' means to be less and less darkened by desires, illusions and drives, to be an increasingly faithful mirror to one's experience of events, and as a result to become an ever stronger source of light and warmth, because the two things go together. The 'purity of heart' provides the faithful mirror; the 'seeing of God' results from our being ever more a shining sun. All this was exemplified in Joan of Arc,* and the people around her felt it. Those who were against her — the English, Burgundians and dignitaries of the Church — were forced to ward off her divine grace.

Joan's whole life, but particularly her last year, was a parable of the process of knowledge and its fulfilment in the consciousness soul. Her courage, her faith, her fortitude and her bearing in battle are all pictures of the ideal of the modern human being. Had she stayed in Domrémy and looked after the farm, married and become a mother, she would have conformed to our modern-day science (prodigious in its own way, but developing in a one-sided manner). But in beholding the fairy-tree and hearing the voices, she *knew* there was more to life than Philistine custom allowed — she knew there is a spiritual world. The silent conviction with which she spoke to Baudricourt contains something of heavenly fortitude, an echo of Christ's words from the Cross, 'Father, forgive them for they know not what they do' (Luke 23: 34).

This conviction was also mingled with the faith that her mission was an earthly, historical, but divinely ordained event (as hens lay eggs, or cows give milk), and she would be heard. It is like a picture of someone today who sets out on the esoteric path because he wants to confirm his own spiritual origin, goal and mission (however humble). The changing of the wind to the west and the miracle of the occupation of Rheims are like the fulfilment of the Class meditations† as the Michaelic, esoteric path of our time; as the crowning in Rheims is like the seventh day of the chymical wedding of Christian Rosenkreutz.[9]

What was separate in her — the Maid and her mission, her grace, the voices — is united in us as bearers of the consciousness soul. As people of our

---

*Jeanne d'Arc, b 6.1.1412, Domrémy la Pucelle, d 30.5.1431, Rouen. This article was written in response to a play by Helmut von Kügelgen, translated and produced in Botton by Kate Roth.
† Meditations of the First Class of the School for Spiritual Science.

time we are all Joan of Arc. We all bear our temperaments and constitutions, our likes and dislikes, our individual destinies. But our observing, objective consciousness need not be cold or heartless (and thereby standardised), in order to work towards the incarnation of the spiritual on earth. Enthusiasm need not be only subjective: it can also be a part of an objective reality.

Joan is the patron saint of our time. What in her was the Word of God, grace given from above, which she had to carry like a precious, fragile vessel, also dwells in each one of us today if only we could become aware of it, wake up to it and take hold of it. If we experience that our individual reality is not meant to be something in and of itself but a beginning, a school in which we learn responsibility and selfless caring for the other person, and that our reality lies in the ideals which Joan served and was inspired by, then in a selfless and humble way we can say 'I' to these ideals if we choose them, and, like Joan, are inspired but not overwhelmed by them.

BOTTON VILLAGE NEWS, 14 II 1976

bio-dynamic farmers and the catacombs

It seems a remarkable fact of history that in the early days of Christianity there were the dark catacombs, while at the beginning of the new, anthroposophically-illumined Christianity there is the bio-dynamic farmer with a dim awareness of where he or she stands. It is dim because for the farmer the balance between consciousness and work is difficult to achieve. The work is heavy and therefore the body swings between activity and tiredness — with great contrast between the two — and the consciousness of the farmer is therefore easily crushed under the weight of self-righteousness.

Just as the catacombs were an effort to find Christ in His new garment, the earth, so the bio-dynamic farmer is meant to imbue himself with anthroposophical experience and insight which finally lead to Christianity. These will allow him to understand landscapes, forests and the upper layers of the earth-organism in order to make farms the ground for a new Christian culture. This connection between the activities of farming (for example, the spraying and making of preparations), and enlightened world-insight, can be achieved only after years of labour and experience, and the handing over from one generation to the next.

Herein lies the power of anthroposophical knowledge. Books and theory are only of interest if they are transformed into actual activity, by which they are brought to earth. (It is the same for the teacher or doctor.) But a question that is especially relevant to the farmers is: What is the relationship between Christianity and the limitless variations of the earth? Christianity must pass through human souls before knowledge of the relationship between Christ and the earth in our time will be achieved.

An agricultural training along these lines will no doubt be a powerful lever in this, especially here in Britain with its Celtic past. There seem to be two streams in the history of Britain. One lies with inventions, the Industrial Revolution, the factories, the towns and the Empire. The other lies deeper, where the *basso ostinato* seems to be, and is the Hibernian priests' non-physical experience of the birth and appearance of Christ, on which is built the mystical relationship of the British to the earth. This explains the British people's unending talk of the weather, with the garden as their field of activity for the weekend! A bio-dynamic training here in Botton, because of its religious basis, may further considerably the otherwise slow progress of anthroposophy.

DATE UNKNOWN

towards candlemas

Candlemas is a festival of the invisible, like Christmas, and follows it forty days later, on 2nd February. Outside all is bare, is nothingness, but around this time in temperate latitudes the crystal-forming powers in the interior of the earth are at their height. The plans of farmers and gardeners are inscribed upon the interior powers of the earth and become visible reality in spring and summer.

The person who is concerned with the earth in thought and deed is among those who bring about the transition from creature to creator. In our time, the farmer and gardener think, and a new creation arises, even though it is, to begin with, still in the garment of the old. (The corn — yes, but not only corn — the cornfield, too.) But in the words of the Soul Calendar for the second last week of January (verse 42), warmth of heart must be the element within which these plans are made — the farmer must love his plans. And in addition, today he must make them with others or the warmth will remain egoistic.

It is the task of the farmer to convey to his fellows not only the bare plans but also the warmth of heart out of which they are made.

In this dark winter's gloom,
The manifestation of its own strength
Strongly urges the soul
To turn towards the darkness
And dimly apprehending, already to feel
Through warmth of head — the sense-worlds revelation.

Calendar of the Soul,[10] verse 42 (third week after Epiphany)

BOTTON VILLAGE NEWS, 1 II 1981

clairvoyance

The concept of clairvoyance presupposes that there is not only a world around us that we recognise and know fairly well, but also an 'invisible' world which we know of only through seers like Rudolf Steiner who are able to perceive it. But in his epistle (1 Cor 13: 12), the apostle Paul maintained that the world becomes illusion because of our faulty understanding and knowledge. Rudolf Steiner's *Philosophy of Freedom*[11] is the reborn Pauline theory of knowledge, the Christian epistemology.

Nothing is more tempting (and natural) for us than to look at a tree and say: 'I see the tree, but I do not see its etheric body, or its elemental beings. But my esoteric exercises will make me clairvoyant one day, and then I will see its etheric body, and elemental beings.' However, esoteric exercises are concerned with clairvoyance only very indirectly and individually; rather, they lead to a gradual widening and waking up of our consciousness. In our inadequate understanding of the tree it is the torpor of our thinking, not our sense perceptions, that makes us wish to be clairvoyant. When we try to overcome the paralysis of staring, the torpor of our thinking and understanding freezes our sense perceptions, like insects fixed in amber. But if we follow the ideas of *metamorphosis* in our thinking, we become aware of the etheric body. Thinking that is able to understand and create metamorphosis is nothing else than our longed-for clairvoyance — but a different clairvoyance, a beholding of the 'physical' world.

Christ's words to the paralysed man waiting by the pool at Bethesda for someone to take him to the water when it was troubled by an angel: 'Rise, take up your bed and walk' (John 5: 2–14), is really the story of the world understanding of our time. Speaking metaphorically, we should not only sit on a green leaf with our 'flea-like' understanding, then hop to a coloured, scented petal and exclaim: 'This is something quite different'. We should understand that through colour and scent the leaf has *changed* into a petal. Or we could say that the plant kingdom has a peak pointing upwards, which is the flower, and the kingdom of the insects has a peak pointing downwards, which is the butterfly: or that the butterfly is the blossom torn loose from the plant; the flower is the butterfly fixed to the plant.[12] We could scan through the world and find many phenomena that we could point to in this way, although far more remain inexplicable to us for the time being. But to become aware of such a riddle is already a step towards this 'clairvoyance'. More important than anything else in Waldorf School education is that the children should learn to look at the world in this way and so acquire a store of metamorphic phenomena. Our 'flea-science' is not wrong — it can lead men to the moon — but it is only one element in understanding the world.

To understand more and more of the world is the only way to make life worthwhile. Marijuana, TV and such things give merely temporary satisfaction. Only a mobile understanding rejuvenates adult bodies, young or old. We should not imagine that in our time this 'mobile understanding' can be anything more than bright intervals. But Christ's words 'Rise and walk' are nevertheless the constant, exhorting comfort of our existence.

BOTTON VILLAGE NEWS, 22 VIII 1969

∼ toward lent

dimensions of human relationships

The meetings we have with other human beings and the relationships that may develop out of them seem (at least to start with), to depend on feelings alone; above all on the dominance of sympathy or antipathy. If we are alert to this, we soon discover how sympathy and antipathy are influenced by the physical impression which the other person gives, and by his general appearance. But although we easily notice the rôle that his ego, his self, plays in all this, and the way in which it centres and enlivens his physical composition, we can still fall prey very easily to the illusion that the physical body creates its own order.

At this point the unprejudiced observer must become aware that the ego is the composer of the body, and that we have a choice: either we can have a relationship to the ordered physical body alone, or we can extend it to encompass the organising ego as well. Relationships based on the flesh (physical/sexual), are a legacy of the Fall, and the split between body — the accomplished work of Creation; the ordered physical — and ego becomes increasingly marked as time goes on. Between these two extremes lie all possible shades of emphasis. However, it is really quite easy to distinguish between true ego-relationships and those which are chiefly focused on the body of the other person. While the second kind of relationship allows us to bathe in the soothingly warm waters of passivity, the first can (and usually does), require a high degree of inner activity.

If by means of self-observation we try to distinguish between the two, then the true ego opens majestically before us. We can begin to grasp something of the essential nature of the ego which, as Rudolf Steiner indicated, should become the chief actor or instigator in the karmic drama through repeated earth lives. As all this begins to widen out in front of us, albeit in a shadowy way, then the relation from ego to ego takes on the quality of love, because true ego-to-ego meetings always engender love. And the recognition dawns that although human beings may be at different stages, they are fundamentally (or potentially) equal in their soul-life.

Quite remarkably, the reality of the eternal ego is experienced by people, albeit in a rather vague way — for example, in the various books about life before and after this present earthly life, and in current discussions on abortion and euthanasia. The eternal ego will come into its own when we allow the whole sphere of social life to be lit up by it: when money ceases to be the thermometer of human worth (as when individual efficiency or ability are recognised by a rise in salary, or when status is judged by such symbols as cars, yachts and the like), and is replaced by the direct recognition and experience of one person by another.

BOTTON VILLAGE NEWS, 26 II 1993

m i t h r a s

One of the most remarkable signposts in the religious history of humanity is the Mithras cult.[13] In the first century after Christ, the Persian cult of the adoration of Mithras was celebrated between India and the Black Sea and swept into the then Roman world. It passed by the Hellenic countries (North Africa, Egypt, today's Israel, Libya, Turkey, Greece, etc.), but in a very short time became the religion of Roman soldiers. Many Mithras stelae and reliefs have since been found in Spain, France, Austria, Germany, England and the Balkans, and they always depict the human being inspired by Mithras, or perhaps Mithras himself, riding on a bull. The bull stumbles because the rider's dagger is thrust deep into its shoulder. The bull and its rider are surrounded by the signs of the zodiac, and a scorpion or a snake crawls under its belly.

The bull encircled by the zodiac is a picture of world cosmic life, the life which swells seeds and buds, makes the sap rise, initiates the lambing season and changes winter's brown into spring's green. This life bears within it the sting of the scorpion; of autumn, of death and decay. Within the round of the year it exhales into the shapes, forms, colours and scents of summer, and inhales into the vanishing and decomposing of winter. Human beings are meant to ride on this advancing and retreating life; to be superior to it and dominate it, which means that humanity is essentially higher and greater than the creating powers of the zodiac. The living form of the bull is the creation of all the stars, but in the human being something more than the stars has come together. In all Mithras stelae we notice that, although in relief, the zodiac signs and the bull are comparatively flat, while the riding man stands out clearly: he is almost a sculpture. But why does he have to kill the bull?

In the Parable of the Sower (Luke 8: 2–15), the seed occupies the same position as the bull; it swells and germinates, life streams into it from the world widths. This parable is preceded by the mention of women (Luke 8: 2–3), in particular Mary Magdalene from whom seven demons were cast out, and is followed by the story of the Gadarene swine (into which go the devils that had possessed the madman), that race down a slope and are drowned in the lake (Luke 8: 26–35). What stirs so powerfully *outside*, (although not yet visible in the second half of February and the first half of March), turns into all kinds of illusions, half-conscious dreams and wishes *within* the human soul into which, at least in olden times, demons may enter. In so far as the bull is a soul phenomenon, the rider has to kill him.

The sun moves consecutively through each of the zodiac signs during the four seasons. But it is the physical sun, whose arc is short and low in winter, long and high in summer, and passes through the equinox in spring and autumn. The Spirit of the Sun once lived as man on earth and now abides in human souls. Mithras riding on the zodiac-bull is not only Michael as the countenance of Christ; he is also Man as the king of the year, Man empowered by Mithras-Michael.

Today the chronometrical calendar has the different positions of the sun as its main cause and reference, but in olden times human beings had no calendar. However, the priests were able to experience intensely the constantly varying stream of the life of the year, either in the outer surrounding nature; in specially built sun-shadows (standing stones, stone circles, etc.), or within their own organs. This was a qualitative calendar in contrast to the quantitative one that we have hanging on our walls, or carried in our pockets. With its changing verses for each week of the year, Rudolf Steiner's *Calendar of the Soul* is a new beginning of this qualitative calendar, with the different positions of the sun fashioning the life stream of the year. We only have to imagine the sun as being within our soul, the outer physical sun being merely its reflection.

The image of Mithras riding on the bull, thrusting his dagger into its shoulder, the rider and the bull surrounded by the zodiac, the rider hovering above and over the remaining relief, as it were — all this becomes a picture not only of the past, but also of the present. Our observing soul is the fruit of the evolution of our time.

It is the task of our age to observe the life stream of the seasons, not as an outcome of a *quantitative* calendar, of geometric relationships, but as a qualitative embrace, a changing element within which we live. The geometric relations should be abstracted from the *Soul Calendar*, not the other way round, as we do at present.

BOTTON VILLAGE NEWS, 21 II 1969

the 'social soul' or 'honest politeness'

In a talk with Franz Löffler in 1924, Rudolf Steiner said, 'Because human beings lose their soul-substance, their soul-like qualities...'[14] He uses the word *Seelisches*, an adjectival noun to *Seele* (soul), which is very difficult to translate. It is difficult not only in itself — quite apart from the fact that the concept 'soul' changes its meaning, taste and flavour from people to people (German, French, English etc.) — but also because its value and importance in the whole human make-up evolves over time.

However, although the soul, or soul nature, does have various layers, it is always the well-lit stage of our consciousness on which our sense impressions, our thoughts and memories, our feelings and will, play out their parts between birth and death, and between waking up and falling asleep. Just as a stage has around it dressing rooms, lighting galleries, orchestra pit, etc., so also, in a manner of speaking, does the soul. Not being as well lit up, the 'dressing rooms' of the soul are not easy to discover, but they belong to the stage and enable it to be the earthly, named geographical location on which the 'play' — our personal biography — proceeds.

But Rudolf Steiner's expression '*das Seelische*' ('soul-likeness', let us say), refers to a specific aspect of the soul-life, namely, that place where one 'play' or biography is connected to another, talks to the other, or where one person looks at another: in short, where these plays are part of social life. Soul-likeness is more the social side of our souls than our strictly individual biographies. It is not the part of the soul which is emotionally, karmically, involved with the other person (whether through love or hatred of them), but that part which interacts with *all* human beings simply because they *are* human. This is very important for our social life, both in Camphill as well as in the world at large. It is the generally human in us that is open to what is enjoyable in life: a well cooked meal, a beautiful landscape, a complete work of art or a particular person simply because of who he or she is. It is open, therefore, to values, but also to grief and happiness; able to weep but also to laugh. While one part of the soul is like the still surface of a pond, able to reflect in purity, the other is a troubled surface whose waves cannot reflect because of inner storms. The still surface enables one to participate in the world, to be a brother to it. The rough surface throws us back into the loneliness of our individuality, without which, nevertheless, social life could not exist.

Past forms of politeness are hollow and have become empty. We need a new art of politeness that is nothing else than participation, but an honest participation. A good deal of the devil in our time comes from not listening properly, or listening but not properly understanding what the other person says or means. As a result, we are all continually wounded and withdrawing. We have achieved a certain amount of tolerance, especially the younger ones among us. Politeness born of honest participation is yet a promise of the Christianising of our time.

BOTTON VILLAGE NEWS, 29 II 1980

rudolf steiner

(b 25.2.1861, Kraljevec, Croatia, d 30.3.1925, Dornach, Switzerland)

Every year in the northern hemisphere, around the time of the anniversary of Rudolf Steiner's birth, we see waves of life beginning to rise out of the earth. The birds sing more distinctly, the light grows stronger, the air becomes gentler, the buds swell. But at the same time we feel that human words, feelings and thoughts do not do justice to this rising tide.

In the past, long poems, day-long dances, different kinds of music — perhaps also festivals with candlelight and incense, or religious and artistic performances of many kinds — would intermingle and unite. These were once appropriate at this time of year. Today, however, we have become more and more separated from the world, enclosed in our small souls, so that we can say 'I am' to ourselves and achieve self-consciousness. The majestic life and decaying of the world would never have permitted this in the past, in much the same way that a word spoken when an orchestra is playing cannot be heard, not even by ourselves. But this tender word-thought, 'I am', is the only place in the human being where he can approach the Christ.

Two historical events have done more than anything else to separate us from the unity of the world, to fetter and condition our soul, and thereby to bring about a kind of brainwashing. They are the invention of printing in the 15th century, and the discovery of electricity in the 18th.

The black art of printing has gradually resulted in knowledge becoming equal to what one reads in a printed book. People had knowledge before the appearance of books, of course, but it was more a knowledge acquired through living in different circumstances, like the travelling journeyman (consider the travels of Paracelsus, typical of many other, less well documented journeys), or the bard, singing and reciting at market places.

Today, many more people can partake of knowledge, but increasingly our universities and schools have become social phenomena and only ostensibly places of learning. The faculties required by these institutions are entirely based on our ability to read and write which we have learned from printed books, but knowledge based on or originating from the printed word is biased and one-sided. Apart from its social relevance, this kind of knowledge has a persuasive effect. Although it is obviously limited, it nevertheless seems to prove itself by its success (nuclear fission, rocket propulsion and other technical feats), and so by contrast it seems to make other kinds of knowledge appear pale and insignificant.

Electricity, which is the other pole, fetters and conditions us. As the printed letter is black, so lightning and electric arcs are blindingly white. Electricity forms the basis of nearly all invention and technical progress of the last hundred years, although to begin with technical progress occurred without it, as evidenced by the mechanical loom and steam engine which now seem quite old fashioned. Today, push-button automation makes the exertion of the individual will more and more superfluous in achieving the maximum effect with the minimum effort, as in the electric guitar or the electric typewriter. This will become increasingly desirable as time goes on. If these two powers — print and electricity — do not enter the service of a third power, we shall become ever more narrow-minded, stupid, inhuman, inefficient and clumsy. This third power is the experience of life itself.

Rudolf Steiner's lectures were never meant to be written down and printed. On the one hand, his insights were conceptual, but nobody should be under the illusion that they did not belong to, and were not carried by, the realm of life waves. At the same time we should not imagine that these insights were to be expressed only in religious and artistic forms — they are understandable and therefore they rescue human existence. But they cannot belong to the realm of the printed word. They are like a great procession of ships of many kinds: rowing-boats, sailing ships, air-ships, all gliding with unimaginable peace, floating majestically on the waves of life. Through the appearance of the vistas Rudolf Steiner opened, we can again love the earth. A knowledge reduced and confined to the printed page and earthly objects, or moved by electricity, excludes love but invites fascination. In contrast, Rudolf Steiner points toward a sphere of humanity where love and knowledge are reunited.

One of the consequences of the technical development of printing lies in the form of art reproductions. Thus we can decorate our rooms and stairwells with reproductions of great masterpieces, while our own individual creativity slumbers and snores.

Many social responsibilities of our time arise from the fact that art is imprisoned in the famous 'ivory tower', resulting in the gifted but anti-social bohemian artist — and it was thought that in order to be creative one had to be like them, perhaps even to the extent of drinking absinthe! But this is no longer true. Because we are human, everyone can create artistically. The reproductions on our walls are but signs of our shame. With a certain amount of guidance we can all decorate our own and each other's walls.

Günther Lehr will be good enough to cut chipboard in various shapes, and glue inviting white paper on to them (we will be able to buy these potential pictures very cheaply), and we will draw on them with coloured crayons. Those who wish to have crayons will also be supplied with them.

These pictures have the great advantage that because they are not great masterpieces they can, and should, be changed after a few weeks or months. Perhaps we may come slowly into a seasonal and festival change of pictures, so that our daily life, and not only our Sundays, have something of the course of the Act of Consecration of Man throughout the year.

Günther Lehr has agreed to start a group for those who would like to try this, and he will supply the above-mentioned guidance.

Insofar as these newly created pictures supplant printed reproductions, they are available free of charge. At the moment five hang in Hall South.

BOTTON VILLAGE NEWS, 26 II 1971

m a s k & m i r r o r

Mask and mirror have something in common, namely the fact that both have their primary meaning in what they do to the human *face*. A mirror can reflect anything, of course, a tie, a dress or whatever, but in such cases it merely serves a utilitarian end. A mask *hides* the face. But with regard to the human countenance, both mask and mirror present us with revealing and pertinent exaggerations. We must say human *countenance* here, because for animals neither mask nor mirror has any meaning. (Dogs bark at their image in the mirror, thinking it to be another dog, while for them a mask is merely an annoying encumbrance.) Why, then, are we human beings so drawn to looking in the mirror?

It is a complex phenomenon because we seek the assurance that 'I am I', the unique individual, unmistakable, unrepeatable, baptised and called by my own Christian name. But we also want to confirm that this unique face reflected in the mirror is in some way beautiful. And at that moment, as a result of our question 'Why do we love to look in the mirror?' a huge vista into the past suddenly opens before us, at the beginning of which is the Fall of Man. Lucifer appears in a blinding light, and vanity — of which our own is but a reflection in miniature — must be put on in front of a mirror.

Vanity is a short cut to self-assertion, self-recognition and self-conscious-ness. Self-consciousness is not meant to arise through fame, praise, gratitude, pride in one's beauty in the mirror, or applause from an enraptured audience — although all these may have their place for other reasons. It should come through the compassion of Christ for each one of us. It is by grace that we become aware of our Self. Through what we do, what we feel, what we think; through being interested in our near or distant surroundings, in people, in the earth, in the stars — in short, through becoming selfless in our interests — to that degree we lighten the veils of vanity and become aware of our Self.

Vanity is far more depressing, and selflessness is far more enlivening than we think. Our vanity is an expression in miniature of the world vanity that is connected with the Fall. Because it stems from Lucifer, this world vanity is magic. Hence the magic mirror in which Faust sees Helena, or the witches' mirror in which appears not the face of the person who looks in it but the countenance of some other, invoked from the past or future by a spell. The mirror reflects a supersensible world, a world conjured into our sense-world through magic spells. So when the wicked queen in the fairytale asks:

> Mirror, mirror, on the wall,
> Who is the fairest of us all?

and the mirror answers:

> O Queen, in all this land
> Thou art the fairest of them all.

then the unity of vanity and magic becomes not only a soul reality, but also a physical one.

Our self-consciousness depends upon our having two sides, left and right, and upon these two crossing or touching; it depends on this axis. But the mirror reflects its image without any such crossing: there is no axis; left is left and right is right. It is a sham self-consciousness that emerges because vanity only serves to bolster our picture of ourselves.

The mask, of whatever kind and whatever it depicts, (a totem mask, a carnival mask, or the masks worn by the ancient Greek actors), always exaggerates, turning the human face into something less human, less individual, although it can also make it appear more powerful or divine.

That which is human is unique and expresses itself in the individuality of the unique human countenance. It can only have as much power as the single human being possesses. Nevertheless, the human countenance is both memory and promise at the same time — memory of the time when the human being was created in the image of God, and promise of the time to come when Christ, because of the Fall, will restore and fulfil the divine image in each individual human being.

BOTTON VILLAGE NEWS, 1 IX 1967

the temptation to turn stones into bread

In Bible Evening and Service during the time of Lent we read the story of the temptation. As the divine Word, the being of Christ, begins to permeate Jesus of Nazareth — and fallen humanity — from the baptism in the Jordan onward,

He meets the Tempter: He confronts temptations which are the archetype and source of all the temptations and sins to which human beings have fallen victim since their expulsion from Paradise.

Because they are archetypes, on earth they appear in a thousand facets, but it is only the facets that appear. Just as the archetypal plant remains invisible, or light (being super-physical), reveals only colours in the earthly world, so also with the three temptations. The demands of the Tempter, and Christ's rejection of them, are essentially spiritual events. Hence these dialogues belong in the realm of archetypes and not to the events portrayed.

The first temptation (in the order they appear in St Matthew's Gospel, Chapter 4) belongs to the body, the second to the soul and the third to the spirit. We will consider here only the first command — that stones be turned into bread — since it is perhaps the most important for Lent.

One aspect of this first temptation is work. If stones could be turned to bread (lifeless substance into food), all work would become unnecessary. Essentially, work has two sides which, over the course of the ages, appear in ever differing forms. One is that we work in order to eat, to make life possible for our dependants and ourselves, and the other is that we work because someone else needs the products of our labour. Today, these two sides are very artfully fitted together and the seam has almost disappeared; through advertising, schooling and by manipulating public opinion. Only by enlightened self-observation and through spiritual science do we know that they are really two, or the devil would persuade us (one-sidedly), that our needs are more or less equal to what we earn. We are like the knight in König's *Michaelmas Play*,[15] thinking that the world between birth and death is the best, is 'heaven upon earth'. All the divine curses laid upon Adam and Eve at their expulsion from Paradise turn into karma, into that which, through Christ, educates the human being into becoming a selfless individual.

One side of the injunction 'In the sweat of thy face shalt thou eat bread' (Gen 3: 19) is that only through the effort of work do we earn our daily bread. The *need* felt by the other person belongs on this same side, but the moment you *work* for the needs of others, the second side, the purely Christian aspect of work, appears. The parable of the Good Samaritan (Luke 10: 30–37) also holds good for work. The wounds were inflicted by the Tempter in Paradise, but the Good Samaritan cares for the needs of the wounded traveller. Therefore he is imbued with the power of Christ.

The words of God in the *Oberufer Paradise Play*[16] are becoming truer today

than they were before:
"See how rich Adam has become,
Like unto a God is he."

BOTTON VILLAGE NEWS, 4 III 1963

the transfiguration & sense perceptions

Life in a spatial world presses in upon our eyes, ears and our other senses.
We cannot escape seeing, hearing, etc., and so are chained to our sense
impressions. These perceptions make the world seem solid and real to us, in
contrast to the contents of our mind or consciousness (thoughts, memories,
images), which appear thin, unreal and subjective.

In the onrush of spring our sense perceptions become richer and more
varied — especially so as we observe thickening stems, buds, and slowly
unfolding leaves; colours extending over the land; the prospect of scents and
blossoms and all the insects. In autumn, all this is doomed to wither and
perish until finally it disappears in the cold and empty darkness of oncoming
winter. But we would be quite unable to cast off the chains of these sense
perceptions if we could not *think*. For example, if we add one perception to
another — budding leaves to mature leaves to flower bud to flower; or egg to
caterpillar to cocoon to butterfly — seeing the many visible manifestations as
so many expressions of an invisible idea, we arrive at the concept of 'crocus'
or 'butterfly'.

Ideas and concepts can be thought, but *only* thought — we cannot see or
perceive them. But we are so bound to our perceptions that we confuse the
visible butterfly we see with the invisible concept of 'butterfly' in which egg,
caterpillar, cocoon, as well as the butterfly itself, are all encompassed. The
same holds good for the growing and decaying of plants; they appear in their
various stages, all of which manifest different aspects of their unchanging
idea. The idea begets these various waxing and waning sense-appearances in
space, but in conceiving the constant idea, we think in *time*. To behold and
understand the changing sense-images as expressing the multitude of created
ideas demands a kind of transfiguration. The spiritual light and power shines
within the earthly form; the ideas appear and enlighten objects in earthly flux.

We should not imagine that this appearance of ideas in earthly forms is
merely a thinking process as we know it, a product of our day-consciousness.
Mixed into this kind of thinking is something of the dreaming and darkness

of night. Goethe, the protagonist of the idea of the archetype, was in this respect the first 'hero' of the Transfiguration (Matt. 17: 1–13, Mark 9: 2–13). Because his waking life was permeated by dreaming, his thinking was actually able to behold the idea within sense objects. Today, the difference between our dreaming state (when asleep), and our perceiving state (when awake), is enormous. Through the power of Christ this difference will diminish until a single consciousness permeates both day and night — as was foreshadowed in the feeding of the five thousand. Our thoughts will become more filled out and alive; our sense perceptions purer.

In this connection, the Soul Calendar verse for the last week in February could perhaps be borne in mind.

> Out of the lap of worlds
> There will spring up sheer joy in growth
> Which will refresh the senses' sheen.
> May it seek out that strength of thought,
> All armoured with the gods' own strengths,
> Which lives strongly within my being.

Calendar of the Soul, verse 47 (week before Passion)

BOTTON VILLAGE NEWS, 29 III 1968

empathy

Empathy means experiencing the world — its people, events and oneself — in and through others. It is not just feeling or reacting to the outer world within oneself, nor a melting into the outer world away from oneself, but the widening of experience from a central point out to a periphery. In a way, compassion is the opposite of empathy. To have compassion one is still the central point; the person who has the experiences, feelings and insights. In empathy we move away from ourself and step into the shoes of the other.

The word empathy describes a relationship between human beings. One aspect of anthroposophy is an infinitely widened empathy, not only for human beings but also for the non-human world of stars, rocks, plants, earth, etc. This empathetic attitude has one immediate consequence — we do not ask the other 'How and what are you?' but rather 'How did you become as you are now?' We should cultivate an interest not only in the present standing of a thing, a person, a situation or constellation, but also in its history, its evolving.

In former times, what drove someone from within was the main incentive, whether they wanted to play the violin, paint or lay bricks. Today, the motive for our actions will increasingly have to be found elsewhere; in answering pleas for help, or undoing spells cast on parts of our marginal landscape — in the calls and needs from without. To be selfless will become the only thing that makes life worthwhile.

Each part of creation needs something of us: a flower, a star, a sunrise or mountain, the wind or soil. With the help of anthroposophy we have to unriddle this need. Empathy means experiencing not only the present situation of human beings, but also their becoming and their potential goals and glory; everyone we meet needs the sun-rays of our hope and recognition. This idealising, however, should be in accord with the other person's station in life and their present circumstances, whether they be co-workers, parents, council members, or whoever. In other words, we should be 'polite' to them, but politeness is a dying virtue — dying because the 'rules' of politeness seem now to have a veneer of hypocrisy — and so young people hate to practice it. Yet politeness must one day become the visible manifestation of this attitude of hope and recognition towards all human beings.

This transformation from centre to periphery probably has its roots in the sun's movement through the zodiac in the course of 25,920 years, the so-called Platonic year. From being in the sign of the Ram at the time of the Mystery of Golgotha, a couple of centuries later the sun entered the sign of the Fishes — anatomically, from the sign for the head to the sign for the feet and hands. The head makes our 'I am' consciousness possible, but in a point-like, concentrated form. The feet and hands, with their spread-out toes and fingers, gesture to the widths of the world. But because they are my fingers, my toes, they therefore seem to include the world in my 'I am' consciousness. Through the power of Christ the 'I am' has expanded from a point to being as wide as the world.

BOTTON VILLAGE NEWS, 10 IV 1976

faith as a power of the human soul

Among the many images of faith in the gospels is that of the disciples in a boat, fighting against wind and waves, while Christ sleeps. In their growing fear the disciples wake him and He chides them, saying, 'Oh ye of little faith' (Matt. 8: 26), and calms the wind and waves.

From this picture we take the message that we must uphold our faith like a flag in battle, above and beyond vicissitudes; that we should have faith in the will of God, and that to be a Christian means believing in good outcomes in what appear to be hopeless situations. In the teaching of the Christian denominations, faith became a moral virtue against which stood (and today increasingly stands), the findings of natural science and technology.

But faith is a power of the human soul, and if it is not consciously directed it sinks into the unconscious and plays into our life without being noticed. We already have tremendous faith — in natural and applied science; in the authority of experts such as doctors, politicians and university professors, without our noticing it. And this unconscious faith leads us to believe in their findings, both of facts as well as theories and hypotheses. But these theories and hypotheses construct a world that excludes faith because they reduce it to vague belief, a pre-stage of knowledge.

In a lecture on 2nd December 1911,[17] Rudolf Steiner remarked that there were people who did not say 'I believe what I do not know,' but rather, 'I believe what I know,' and 'through this belief I know it better.' Knowledge is the only basis of faith. The 'faithless' disciples in the boat are not a picture of moral cowardice; they are a picture of our faithless consciousness, our faithless knowledge, which the powers of the elements, of the outer world, threaten to overcome. Through the power of faith within His consciousness, Christ has control over, and calms, the outer world. From then on, Christ should ever more and more become the god within us. We ourselves will be at peace through knowledge which has become the basis for the power of faith. Thomas doubted the resurrection and was only convinced by touching the wounds. Christ said to him, 'Be not faithless, but believing.'

It is a deep but necessary prejudice of our time to equate knowledge with sense perceptions. For us, faith is mere belief. A person who 'knows' everything would have no need for belief. But this is a complete illusion. We 'believe' in the account of a traveller in New York or the Gobi desert even if we have never been to either. We 'believe' in the findings of experts despite never having looked through a microscope or telescope. Why, then, are we like the disciples amid the wind and waves, dependent on (and conscious of) only the sense impressions of the stormy waves and so, like Thomas, demand to lay our fingers in the wounds?

Sense experience confirms nothing: only *thinking* makes faith possible. Archetypes can be *thought* but not perceived. Rudolf Steiner often said that the findings of spiritual science can be followed and verified by ordinary thinking, but the findings themselves can only be achieved by a seer.

BOTTON VILLAGE NEWS, 14 II 1964

l i e s

The great challenge of our time — the time of the consciousness soul which began in the early Renaissance period, around 1413 AD, and will last into the fourth millennium — rests in our social life. The challenge is how to combine becoming a strong 'self' with the demands of many other 'selves' living together, quarrelling as well as enjoying one another, interlinked beyond sympathy and antipathy through the complex circumstances of life. And nothing obstructs social life more than lies! Why is this?

We live together in the world, are all part of humanity, and yet we are all very different from one another. Nobody argues about whether an ocean is an ocean, or a mountain is a mountain: a tree is obviously a tree; a lion is a lion, and a trumpet sound is not the song of a nightingale! But where we ourselves are concerned it is different. We agree whether someone is a man or woman, black or white, fully dressed or in bathing suit; in short, we agree on the externals. But our *freedom* — our opinions, emotions and inner life — is invisible and is unique to each of us. True, it is perceivable to an extent in his or her words, gestures, actions, facial expressions, etc., but even these must be interpreted in order to be understood.

In all the kingdoms of nature only the human being is able to lie, and he can lie only to another human being; not to an animal, to plant or a stone. There are many motivations for lying, of course, and anyone with a modicum of honest self-knowledge will recognise them: ambition, vanity, self-aggrandisement, lust for power, jealousy or defamation.

There are two kinds of lie: the self-confirming, self-righteous lie, and the lie that falsifies the facts. If the truth reveals us in a less favourable light than we might wish, as being less inefficient or cowardly, for example, then we lie; we *alter* the facts. We may say to a friend, 'I'm late because I was held up in a traffic jam,' when in fact there was no traffic jam: I simply started out too late. Many such lies are perpetrated in daily life. They may be small (the so-called 'white lie'), but have a very complex psychological background, or they may be large, often on the historical-political level.

Dictators lie in order to increase or impose their powers. For instance, it is asserted that armaments 'have' to be increased due to the threat of attack from other nations, when in truth armaments are increased partly as a means of employment. We can see very well how a dictatorship paralyses independent thinking. Our mass media must lie to an extent (or withhold information, which is really the same thing), because our democracy is not a *real* democracy.

But it seems to me that *every* lie, large or small, tears the web of reality which unites human beings. It undermines the ground on which we walk, and the web of geographical, historical, social and personal human conditions. And it has unforeseen consequences. The smallest lie reverberates into the widest reaches of the universe, as well as into the unknown beginnings of a future life within our souls, in both cases destroying the work of the gods. We have a definite feeling for this due to our conscience being tempered by spiritual science (although we choose often to ignore it).

We are all, in very different degrees, children of the earth. (The separation between earth and humanity — the races of mankind as distinct from the zones, continents and landscapes of the earth — was a fashionable concept in the 19th century. Before then, people were thought of as being conditioned by East or West, North or South, Asia or America, and were experienced as different 'tribes' living near by or far off in deserts, sea shores, alpine climates, the Mediterranean or Arctic, etc.) Although human beings have developed a certain independence from the earth, today they are still dominated nevertheless by their nations. As children of the earth, we play out our karma in very different conditions and circumstances, whether in desert, oceanic or African landscapes, as well as through being French, Italian, Bohemian, Chinese, etc. But *the earth and its variety is part of human karma* to such an extent that we can understand the significance of Christ writing the karma of the adulteress on the ground without judging her in a legal or religious sense. (John 8: 4–11).[18] Human beings have had to endure the dominion of the earth, the conditions in which the gods placed them. In future, humanity's power and karma will increasingly *transmute* the earth.

The web of reality that is our karma is laid out on the common ground of our earthly existence. Every lie tears a hole in the infinite variety of this common web, for only the good gods are allowed *wilfully* to change it. As soon as a human being alters it, even to a small extent, he interferes with the work of the gods, he disturbs the common ground and thus disturbs the individual karma which is interwoven, intermingled with the common ground. And the common ground is not just the physical world; not just the sunrise or the cycle of the seasons — it is also the reliability of what is seen and what is heard; it is the rules of common sense. All this is part of our wider karma and freedom.

In anthroposophical terms, our lying wounds the etheric sphere. Lying may seem to have more of an astral, emotional nature, but that is to look at it superficially. When we lie we interfere with the progress of the world, even though we have little idea of the consequences that the smallest, even the well-meant, lie has. In lying, we seem to make ourselves stronger than we really are, but at what a price! When we lie, we are not free; we have become servants of Ahriman.

BOTTON VILLAGE NEWS 22 XII 1989 / BOTTON MIRROR 23 XI 1990

toward doctor könig

(b 25.9.1902, Vienna, d 27. 3.1966, Überlingen)

Little more than a week has passed since Dr König's death, and it is quite impossible to place him with some degree of objectivity into the stream of the historical development of humanity regarding the fields in which he contributed — curative education, villages for the disabled, medicine and spiritual science. Perhaps it may never be possible. We are like Hermann Grimm who, when trying to write a life of Raphael,[19] could only manage to write an outer history of his fame. At this moment we can only try to describe a light which Dr König kindled in us and which fostered connections among those working in the Camphill centres. This is because his personality was by no means contained merely between birth and death.

He not only kindled a light regarding spiritual science; whoever met him felt the being of Anthroposophia and the striving towards her in his own most inward being. Through his love of Rudolf Steiner he founded a community of brothers and sisters who loved one another both as co-workers and friends. Rudolf Steiner is one of the great teachers of our time because he not only reveals the earth, the human being and the spiritual worlds in a new light, but his teachings also engender responsibility by rousing the conscience of humanity in a hitherto unknown way. In the literal sense of the word, 'religion' is the relation of one's self to the tangible and the intangible, both in interest and responsibility.

In Dr König this light of interest and responsibility shone with great intensity. It is a light which does not merely attract people as a moth is drawn to a candle; it arouses the latent flame of interest and responsibility in many who come into contact with it, and those in whom Dr König kindled that light owe a tremendous debt of gratitude to him because they have become aware of the need for interest and responsibility in the world. In this cool, self-centred age, the light which Dr König kindled in the souls of each one of us was so bright that his parting seemed merely to open a gate through which more light and more love could stream in. From him we received infinite strength and wisdom.

Dr König taught us our responsibility towards the child with special needs, towards our fellow workers, for our land, our houses and gardens; a responsibility which, without the warmth of interest, would remain lame. Those who helped him to build the spiritual network of Camphill, and those who have helped the helpers learn that unless the light and warmth of interest and responsibility shine forth in each person, the Camphill Movement dwindles into nothing.

Dr König was a physician, at first in Germany in a large home for children with special needs where he had many private patients. He then moved to Vienna, the town of his birth, and again built up a practice of several hundred patients. He gave numerous lectures and wrote many articles. He started a youth group which became the seedling of Camphill. When Hitler annexed Austria, the members of that youth group emigrated and most of them found one another again in Britain, in Scotland, where they began to live and work together with Dr König, which then led to the founding of Camphill in 1940. Since then not only has Camphill grown into the worldwide Camphill Movement, but Dr König himself has reached the ears and touched the hearts of thousands of people through his lectures, books and articles.

The work will continue — the realm of spiritual science will grow in the soil of mutual recognition. He was a knight of the cross entwined by the roses. Through his devotion, the community he founded, the community of those who love each other because they do their work out of enthusiasm, may help transfigure this valley of earthly existence.

BOTTON VILLAGE NEWS 6 IV 1966 / THE CRESSET, MICHAELMAS 1962

faith & the cursing of the fig tree

In the last days of Christ's life on earth following His entry into Jerusalem, we read the cursing of the fig tree, after which Christ utters the words: 'If you have faith… and say unto this mountain… be thou cast into the sea, it shall be done.' (Matt. 21: 18–21; Mark 11: 12–14, 20–23). In other passages, too, many references to faith, although comparatively short, can be found. But in connection with the cursing of the fig tree and the entry into Jerusalem, it is as if faith rises like an island out of the stream of the gospel narrative.

Rudolf Steiner referred to the fig tree as a symbol of the old initiation and enlightenment, recalling the picture of Buddha sitting under the Bodhi tree, for example.[20] Such ancient initiations lifted the spirit-soul out of the body of the neophyte with the help of the priests, but this initiation was the consequence of the old clairvoyance when, in pre-Christian times, the human being was still permeated by streams from the spiritual world. All humanity still drew varying degrees of spirit knowledge and nourishment from the heavenly order, as shown in the Egyptian temple drawings of Keb and Nut. By the time of Christ, however, these streams could no longer penetrate the hardening bodies of human beings, for the body had become tainted with the after-effects of the Fall. The innocent spirit entered bodies whose ensouled life had experienced the Fall. The spirit itself was not tainted, but the way that human beings approached the spirit was burdened with the guilt of humanity. When Adam and Eve clothed their nakedness with fig leaves, as described in the biblical story of the expulsion from Paradise, this expresses the condition of their spirit-consciousness following the experience of the Fall.

At the moment of Christ's entry into Jerusalem, the shouts of 'Hosanna' from the crowd (Matt. 21: 9, Mark 11: 9) was something like a rekindled flame of that ancient guilt and clairvoyance, fanned by the presence of Christ. Indeed, a few days later, on the morning of Good Friday, this same multitude would shout 'Crucify him!' (Mark 15: 13–14, Luke 23: 21, John 19: 15) Their dim awareness of the ancient spirit-presence in the flesh, fanned by the presence of Christ — the Word made flesh riding to His death — released the old clairvoyance from the shackles of guilt of the earthly body and made possible a new, innocent clairvoyance. The cursing and withering of the fig tree was one of the prophetic preparations for Christ's death, and only if the fig tree in the human being withers can any new spiritual awareness, free of ancient guilt, become possible through Christ's continued presence on earth. However, we should not take the cursing of the fig tree as the cause of its withering, otherwise the curse takes on the flavour of faith in a sentimental sense. Material cause and effect never appear in the gospels, although sometimes it may seem so — the cursing is the expression of the withering.

The old clairvoyance was a power, a real power in humanity, as varied in its expression as human beings are different from each other. Instead of the old clairvoyance, the new power arising in human beings is faith. Faith does not force human beings, though the old spirit-awareness had something instinctive and compelling about it, something moon-like; bound to the family, to the generations. Faith (the 'new faith' as it is called in the Act of Consecration of Man), is sun-like, depending only on the efforts of the individual in freedom, and is completely selfless. It will be a power based on the insights of the science of spirit.

Our body depends on the Fall, and through Lucifer's temptation our soul delights in the body, its senses and functions. Rudolf Steiner called our astral body the body of faith, indicating thereby that our soul will one day regain its innocence, using the body without being fettered to and tempted by it.

This new power depends upon new relationships between human beings; upon the new community as foreshadowed in the words of the Man with the Lamp in Goethe's *Fairy Tale of the Green Snake and the Beautiful Lily:*[21] 'A lone individual does not help, but rather he who unites himself with many at the proper hour.' The new community depends on the free will of people who have decided to live together and remain friends with one another. In contrast, the old clairvoyance depended on the blood tie of the generations, of family and tribe, that eventually deteriorated into something witch-like. Through faith, the human being will become a magician in a new way, together with others, for one cannot be a good Christian alone.

All this arises in connection with the cursing of the fig tree and the passages on faith in the twenty-first chapter of Matthew and the eleventh chapter of Mark. In Luke's Gospel the same thing is described, but from a different angle. (St John's Gospel is quite different from the other three in that it shows a very different aspect of the Christ Being, and so we will not consider it here.) In Luke 17: 5–6 Christ is reported to have said, 'If you had faith as a grain of mustard seed you might say to this sycamine tree:* be thou plucked up by the root and be thou planted in the sea.' After this, there follows one half of the description of the Second Coming of Christ, which is also reported during the days between the entry into Jerusalem and the Crucifixion, after the cursing of the fig tree. The Gospel of St Luke makes no mention of the fig tree in the events of Holy Week.

The old clairvoyance, of which the fig tree is a symbol, is connected as much with the entry into Jerusalem, and therefore with Christ's death, as faith is connected with the Resurrection and Easter Sunday, but both are linked with the earth.

In earlier times the earth was infinitely larger than the human being's consciousness of it. Human beings living in one part of the globe had no inkling of the existence of other human beings living elsewhere. As we see from the journeys of the Vikings, the relation between known and unknown was quite different from what it later became after the voyages of discovery began in the 15th century. Where geography is concerned, today we all know more or less the same. In the past, some people were aware that the northern part of the American continent was known to the Vikings, for example, but it was unknown to most of the peoples of western Europe.

And similarly with the old clairvoyance. It was local, confined to and coloured by the locality on earth where different peoples lived. The spiritual vision possible in Delphi differed from that in various parts of India, or in what today is southern Sweden, and so on. The earth and its inhabitants were still so connected with the heavens that different 'windows' opening into the spirit existed in the different regions — the heavens shone differently upon the different landscapes of the earth's surface.

Today our knowledge of the earth and the geography of its surface is the same for all of us. In olden times, maps and globes did not exist, but today no blank, unexplored areas are to be found on the maps of the world. This experience of the unity of the earth accompanied the gradual loss of the old clairvoyance as the different windows into the heavens slowly closed. From this modern consciousness of the oneness of the earth (which is

*Sycamine belongs to the family of the fig tree.

overwhelmingly confirmed by newspapers, radio and television), faith will arise and a new window will open, a window available to all human beings. Because Christ is connected to all human beings, the many localised windows need not exist: just one window, shared by all. The power of faith in every human being will endow us with a new power and energy for our lives. This power will be engendered through a renewed involvement with the earth, for the time will come when every human being will be engaged, in one way or another, with the earth, its soil and the production of food. The era of towns, to which we owe our civilisation and our picture of human life over the last thousand years, is drawing to a close. An era of faith is dawning.

THE CRESSET, CHRISTMAS 1971

spring thoughts

In Rudolf Steiner's *Calendar of the Soul*, the verses pertaining to the rising and falling seasons of the year point increasingly to the senses, to their weakness in winter when a deepening soul-space opens, and their subsequent rise following life's waxing glory in spring, and waning through summer and autumn.

It is an ever-renewed wonder and delight to see the slowly unfolding buds, the shining, innocent beauty of the opening flowers of crocuses, primroses and daffodils amid the surrounding bareness. At this time of year we increasingly experience the earth — with Rudolf Steiner's guidance — as a living being whose physiognomy is expressed in a mass of different features.

As human beings, we have only the human face and moving body with which to understand our physiognomy. Through our feelings we are able to interpret and understand the expressions, both fleeting and lasting, of another person, the inflections and sounds of their voice, and their movements. But the plants, bushes and trees do not speak or make noises as animals do, nor can they move. Their expression lies in their colours and forms, which everyone can understand if they develop in the right way. But boundless empathy is needed if we try to forget our selves and attempt to experience the being of a crocus or a primrose. We discover that we cannot; we discover that our soul abilities to experience other beings are hopelessly limited by normality, but we also discover that we are actually limited by fear and that we only feel secure within the bounds of our normality.

We must move 'into' the crocus, however. We will discover that we can do so without losing ourselves — something of the greatness of world-life touches us and we become part of it for a few moments. It is one of our illusions that we will lose ourselves in becoming part of our environment. In fact we only become wider; we go beyond the confines of our sympathies and antipathies, our likes and dislikes, our prejudices and egoism, our cowardice and our 'keeping up with the Joneses'. After a time, the wall preserving our deafness and blindness crumbles and we become part of a deathless world. We feel a slight shame in such moments because, for the sake of self-protection, we have excluded ourselves from the reality of the world. (The beauty of creation is, after all, only visible to us; of all creation we alone have selfless senses and can see and hear our surroundings objectively.)

To see, and then to experience, the plant world as a unique creation rather than just thinking: 'Aha, a primrose,' really means to experience it as divine art. By noting colour, texture, form and gesture in all growing things we are led to this experience of divine art. The great artists and poets of our time, such as Cézanne, Rilke, Eliot and Marc, demand the same empathy from their audience.

The great parable for this empathy is the Washing of the Feet (John 13: 5–16), the first step on the ladder of a Christian initiation.[22] From Christ's hands we feel the waters of life washing round our feet. We are meant to feel that for the sake of gaining our ordinary 'I' we have excluded world-life from ourselves, and ourselves from it. But we must become strong enough to carry our person into this selfless world-life. The more we can take spiritual science into ourselves, the stronger we become — not just by understanding as we normally do, but in the sense that we should love what we understand. We should take the composition of chapters, lectures, verses, etc., as works of art. Only then do we understand them as they should be understood; only then do we study them in a Rosicrucian sense.

BOTTON MIRROR, 6 IV 1990

the forty days

The story of the walk to Emmaus (Luke 24: 13–35) epitomises the forty days between Easter and Ascension as a parable-like background. On Easter Sunday afternoon, two of Christ's followers walk from Jerusalem to the little village of Emmaus and are joined by a stranger whom they invite to share their supper. 'Abide with us; for it is toward evening and the day is far spent.'

When the stranger breaks the bread they know it is Christ: and then He disappears.

When listening to the words of the Easter service and the appropriate gospels, and seeing the red of the altar and vestments, we can feel that all these accompany us in the surrounding world throughout the forty days. But it remains unrecognised, as was the case with the stranger who approached the disciples of Christ on their walk to Emmaus. And He disappeared at Ascension, as Christ does at Emmaus. It is as if the blood of Christ, shed on Golgotha, surrounds us invisibly like air and light, and that the pale green leaves of spring are a visible sign of this.

Throughout these forty days we live in a state of grace as if the sun, which once shone from within the earth in our paradisal past, had returned from distant skies as the blood of Christ. The outer spring with its budding green evoked by the external sun, and the inner spring with its enlivening, lighting and warming Spirit-sun of the blood of Christ, are one and the same. The Easter chasuble, red with a green rim, is an expression of this spring.

In the farewell discourses (John 15: 14), Christ said, 'You are my friends.' Human beings are the friends of God. The blood of Christ has flowed into the earth. Human beings shine again in the image of God, and therefore they are His friends.

BOTTON VILLAGE NEWS, 25 V 1962

equality

Equality was only given to human beings when on Golgotha the blood flowed from the wounds of Christ into the earth. His blood and our blood are permeated by the '*I am*'. The evolution and history of humanity are, in a sense, the paths towards equality.

It is clear that there was no real equality before Christ. The pre-Christian cultures, culminating with that of Greece, were made possible only because of slaves, and this was necessary and justified. After Christ, the way towards equality first showed itself clearly in the demands of Wycliffe and Hus in the religious life. All Protestantism — its strife in the Thirty Years War, the Calvinists, Covenanters and so on — had a common basis: the longing for a direct connection between the individual and god, with no mediating by the church. In our time, religion has stepped into the background and social and economic life have come to the fore.

The three ideals of the French Revolution, liberty, equality and fraternity, are the ideals of our time. 'The Rider on the White Horse' in the 19th chapter of the Apocalypse also embodies these ideals with the three names, the three garments, the crown, the vesture dipped in blood, the sharp sword coming out of his mouth. This is the threefold word of God, the threefold 'I am' — it is the human being who has at last become equal to his fellow brother, because both liberty and brotherhood are consequences of equality. The time when we will feel ourselves to be human only if our neighbour is our equal — no matter what he or she may do — is not as far off as we might think. Rudolf Steiner said that every meeting with another human being must become a sacrament.[23] In this, our sense of the equality of the other person will be immeasurably heightened, which is an *Easter* event.

The most difficult thing in earthly life is to experience the sphere of equality and make it real. It is not unlike the walk to Emmaus when the two disciples recognise Christ only after He has vanished. (Luke 24: 13–35) We recognise the different abilities of one another and reckon with them; we try to act in a brotherly manner towards each other; we continually experience and feel the equality of each other — but as though blindfolded. The taking of communion is somewhat like an ever-renewed Emmaus experience: the disciples recognised Christ through the breaking of bread, but at the moment of recognition He vanished. Although it is an element in which we live, the sacramental sphere of meeting another human being is far removed from our conscious grasp of the present. In all our relationships with others there is also attraction, repulsion, greed, possessiveness, blunted or warped cruelty. Christ's words, 'If any man come to me, and hate not his father, and mother, and wife, and children, and brethren, and sisters, yea, and his own life also, he cannot be my disciple' (Luke 14: 26) should be understood in the sense that 'hate' in the authorised translation of the Bible is best taken to mean 'leave', or the ability to free oneself — something entirely inward — when in unselfish freedom one aims at the sacramental sphere of equality.

But we are all equal before the altar. We feel this equality only dimly because in our consciousness lie our faults and failures, our gifts and our destiny. It is our selfishness which makes us blind. I can behold the first dawn when in taking communion I feel it is not I who take communion but the congregation through me. But my 'I' is the eye of the needle through which the event of communion passes.

Rudolf Steiner explained that the betrayal of Christ by the kiss of Judas

(Matt. 26: 49, Mark 14: 45, Luke 22: 47) was necessary because Christ could dwell within, and speak through, the apostles.[24] They could never be sure who was Christ. So also all members of a congregation are like the apostles whose limited ego-consciousness was extinguished through the ego-power of Christ. The Christ can dwell within each of us.

BOTTON VILLAGE NEWS, 26 IV 1963 & 10 V 1963

art in our time

When we see a council housing estate we could ask ourselves, Is art (in this case architecture) possible in our time? We may have leafed through an illustrated book on the history of art and seen pictures of statues, buildings, frescoes and paintings of various periods, and been impressed by the fact that they are all expressions of the spirit of their time. But when we look at the buildings, statues, etc., of *our* time we must ask the question, Does any art expressing our time exist at all? Perhaps not every age expresses itself through art. But should we not first ask, What is art *for*?

Before we consider this question further, we might look at three kinds of picture. First there is the icon — a Madonna and child, perhaps — created anonymously over centuries of culture, its object being to show in its faithful repetitions a heavenly-inspired pattern rather than the personal genius of the named artist. A second kind would be a fresco by one of the great Renaissance masters — Leonardo, Michelangelo or Raphael — as exemplified in the eternal grace and beauty of any of Raphael's Madonnas, or his apostles in the light of the Risen Christ at the Sea of Galilee. They are examples of painting which idealises the physical event, making it a parable for the heavenly glory. The relevance and reality of the prophets and sibyls by Michelangelo are highly personal and realistic. Rudolf Steiner said on a number of occasions that a being from Mars would be able to grasp the purpose of earth evolution when he saw the Old Sun stage of shine out of Leonardo's 'Last Supper'.[25]

In the icon, both physical reality and to a lesser extent colour, almost disappear in heavenly forms. Later, in the Renaissance, an inter-penetration of the heavenly with the physical took place. Where previously the icon had no weight, Renaissance painting portrays moments in which the lightness of heaven embraces and lifts up the darkness and gravity of earth.

Displaying pictures within a frame is seen only from the Renaissance on. Long before that time, the icons were pictures in this sense too, of course, but realism in painting (the use of perspective, a blue sky, etc.) really began with Giotto, and from then on an interest grew in displaying pictures in frames, first in the house and later in galleries. This realism culminated in Impressionism, but transcended it with a new beginning in Expressionism. In essence, Expressionism burst open the frame of the picture, and all these pictures would have been very different had they been drawn as frescoes; had they not been constrained within frames. We can see this in the frescoes in the first Goetheanum [since reproduced in the second Goetheanum].

Thirdly we note that in the 19th century people started painting what they saw; their pictures show a heightened realism. 'Realistic' pictures are really a contradiction in terms. From one point of view we could say that painting from Giotto to Renoir (apart from Raphael, Claude, etc.) had a single goal, namely the coloured photograph. Expressionist painting is apparent in the style of Cimabue and Duccio, as well as in icons, altar pictures, frescoes, and even stained-glass windows. The likeness of swimming water-nymphs to barmaids in the pictures of Böcklin show how the apprehension of the heavenly dissolved into a pale longing for it, and *Realism* — stark, expressionless, earthly objects, sometimes thinly clad in a vanishing aura of meaning and sentiment — called itself art. Materialism prevailed in all walks of life, led by the rapid development of science.

We became accustomed to pictures appearing somewhat Buddhist in nature despite their inherent materialism. They assumed a higher reality, a flight from our daily environment, although they had to have frames so as to protect them from being contaminated with the atmosphere of everyday reality. But paintings are meant to permeate, to transfigure our daily environment; they are meant to make us love our everyday surroundings, to suffuse the dark heaviness of our daily tasks with light.

Used as the characteristic expression of a certain historical period, the term 'art' is inadequate because different arts were prominent at different times — sculpture in ancient Greece; Romanesque and Gothic architecture during the Middle Ages; painting and literature from the Renaissance on, and music since the time of Bach.

Before we come to the question of the art of our own age, we should note the progression: icon to Renaissance painting (15th/16th centuries) to Realism in painting (19th century). Or we might say from heavenly forms to a marriage of the heavenly and earthly then to materialistic sense reality.

Now, what is the purpose of art? It is a step towards the spiritualisation of the earth. Our inner and outer surroundings are seen through the modes of different times and different artists. Therefore — especially in painting — it is also the manifestation of a higher life, a clear counter-argument against atheism. Every one of us is an artist (at least in our understanding), and all we need is enough confidence to allow our experiences to mirror the outer and the inner world. And not simply mirror it, but transfigure it!

What about art in our time? Today, we seem to have difficulty in going beyond art as decoration. In our so-called arts (music, painting, sculpture and poetry) it seems that an existential earnestness or necessity is lacking. But if art did not exist nothing much in life would be transformed, as is the case in architecture which today is reduced to mere utilitarianism. The arts have become simply adjuncts to what already exists, and although we ordinary mortals still go to concerts, exhibitions, theatres and museums, art as an *active* ingredient in our life is absent.

It seems to me that the seeds of an appropriate art lie dormant in the soil of our time. Our time is the beginning of the age of the consciousness soul, the time of social and anti-social drives. It is the time in which the anti-social tendency, the most selfish and self-centred egoism, will give birth to, and coexist with, both altruism and brotherhood — and our artistic efforts will have to do justice to both. Our concentrated endeavours, our gifts, will have to serve the others with whom we live, not in order to bask in their admiration, but so that their lives are made lighter. We will first have to cultivate what is called the 'social art', both within as well as beyond Camphill. Art will have to become a fruit of the warmth and moral intuition of our social life, of its fundamental creativity. Social art must precede all the other arts: gentleness will have to arise out of the deafness, the cruelty and the ambitions of our life so that the question 'Am I my brother's keeper?' (Gen 4: 9) may become the recognition: 'I am my brother's keeper!'

When a song is written to celebrate a festival it need not necessarily be a wonderful composition, but it should enhance our meeting in the mood of the festival. Anything we do as artists must have a social note. We do not create something because of our own greatness but because we bend our knee in humility and sacrifice our gifts to the other person. Thus we can shine in the light of the other's star. Our relationships are lifted up above sympathy and antipathy, above love and indifference: the arts can then become servants of Social Art.

The arts, especially in the Christian era, had a selfish note. The gifts of artists became bearers of a higher life. In our time the Christianising of art can only go through the renewal of the meeting between human beings. We have to divest our gifts of all pride and not work for fame. In the anonymity of the Middle Ages the artists were devoted to the divine. In the same way we have to be devoted to the other for that is where we see the divine today.

BOTTON VILLAGE NEWS 30 XI 1990 & ARTICLE OF UNKNOWN DATE

the new faith

The phrase 'the new faith' in the Act of Consecration of Man does not mean that there was ever an 'old faith'. There was 'provisional faith', and from our time onwards the new faith will become increasingly strong.

Faith is a Christian concept not only because in pre-Christian eras there was a direct experience of the higher worlds that gradually disappeared over the course of time, but mainly because it is a soul power which is especially related to Christ. It is a power, not a belief; not something pale and insipid compared to knowledge, but a power of soul which is meant to increase in the future. It is a quite mistaken idea that faith is a renewal based on the old scholastic duality of the world — direct *knowledge* of the sensory world, and indirect experience of other beings and of god which humanity can know nothing of except through divine *revelation*.[26]

Since the 15th and 16th centuries, knowledge has become very specific. But natural science and the science of spirit will continue to make real knowledge possible, and only then will faith assume its rightful place. We might otherwise think that with the coming of anthroposophy faith is now unnecessary.

As a power within the soul, faith is connected with the earth. At the very moment when the blood flowed from Christ's wounds on Golgotha the aura of the earth changed: it shone, star-like, into the World-All, and by receiving His blood, the earth became the body of Christ. Faith is connected with the blood which flowed into the earth, and so there is a magnetic bond between our power of faith and the blood of Christ through which the earth became His body. Therefore it is important that we should interest ourselves in the great multitude and variety of plants and animals of the earth; in its geology and fossils, and in the seasons, the climate and the weather. This interest not only makes us feel at home on earth in a far wider, less exclusive, less biased sense than if our interest is limited to our natural and national home, but it also kindles the broad flame and breath of faith. It is the power which longs for, which thirsts for, the earthly Christ; which wants to eat, to drink in and unite itself with the earth for the sake of Christ as a means of becoming ever more a bearer of Christ, a 'Christophorus'. It longs for the time when the earth is not only the human being's surroundings, but is like his own flesh and blood.

BOTTON VILLAGE NEWS, 12 II 1971

between easter & ascension

As human beings we tend to be imprisoned in a succession of static moments which are like film stills. Life around us, its growth and decay, its winter and summer, evolves comparatively slowly. As the sun's arc rises towards summer and the growth of plants and the ripening of fruit slowly proceed, we stare at the different *states* in which sun, plant and fruit appear at any given moment. We are caught in the 'stills', as it were, and cannot follow the evolving movement. But these 'stills' of nature are illusions caused only by our fixed staring, just as, conversely, the 'movement' in films is an illusion created by the quick succession of static frames.

It is one of the tortures of the consciousness soul to feel separated, alienated, an observer. The majestic powers of nature slowly emerge and disappear, engulfing us then retreating again, but we are always outside them. One aspect of our annual holiday scramble is the desperate attempt we make to be 'inside' them. But in truth the remedy for this despair is not only to observe and to stare, but also to *think*. Then the 'still' created by our staring melts and its own form and colour gives it a past and a future: it becomes the visible point of the invisible process to which it belongs. The invisible part is precisely what we add to a sense impression when we think. If we can see imaginatively that the green leaves of a plant near the ground are of rather simple form, while higher up they become more shaped and refined until suddenly growth stops, and coloured, almost transparent petals appear; and if we can supplant the one-after-the-other sequence with their unique at-the-same-time-ness, in that moment we are 'inside' the plant.

Once we feel the warm breath of thinking melting the shackles of sight, we will also feel something of the responsibility we bear towards the world. We live in the world and only we can be charged with this responsibility because we alone can unite sense impressions with thinking. (Animals, for instance, unite their sense impressions with movement.) We live in a world of illusion not because *it is so*, but because *we make it so*. We will achieve, increasingly, the most surprising results by uniting our sense impressions with our intellect. The past and the future, the origin and the goal of our natural surroundings, must be added by us to what we see, hear, feel, smell, taste, etc. Anthroposophia enables us to become responsible both within, and for, the world.

In learning to behold the natural world as a continuum of evolving movement, as an enormously varied multiplicity of time-organisms, we are led to the gradual Christianising of our powers. The more Christ can awaken in us and work upon us, the more will the variety of the world become a slow, majestic procession from the invisible thinking past to the visible present, and into the invisible thinking future.

BOTTON VILLAGE NEWS, 14 V 1971

faith & the gospels

Nothing has contributed more to the apparent decline of Christianity than the meaning assumed by the word 'faith'. When Christ says, 'If you have faith as a grain of mustard seed' (Matt. 17: 20, Luke 17: 6) you can remove mountains, we think that this pale word 'faith' (which has become synonymous with belief), is meant to shed its pallor and prove the might of Christianity. Too often today it induces a kind of powerless cramp in the soul.

Since the beginning of our modern age in the 15th century, as knowledge increased it gradually transformed faith into mere belief, meaning what is not known. Up to the present day, knowledge has won victory after victory, not simply as knowledge but as the practical, technical achievements resulting from it. Technical invention dominates our world while belief, or faith, has sunk to pale insignificance. Because of its technical prowess this kind of scientific knowledge seems to be the only knowledge possible. But what if faith were not merely belief? What if faith were a power, a power which unfolded its wings only when it was backed by the right knowledge? What if we could have faith today only when we *know*?

Knowledge as we understand it today, and as it has developed since the 15th century, does not need faith to be effective. Space rockets, for example, must rely on clear thinking and execution in order to do what they are designed to do. What, then, is the difference between a knowledge which can support and release faith, and knowledge that has no need of faith?

Among the many characteristics we might describe, two are especially helpful in relation to our theme of faith. The first is time. All our ordinary knowledge in the West regards time as a straight line where one point lies before, the next after. In the West we seem to live in a universe where time is an irreversible sequence from past to future: 8pm, 9pm, 10pm; 1970, 1971, 1972; March, April, May, and so on. There is, however, another time, consisting not of a series of befores and afters but a multitude of time spans. At what moment do we see the plant itself? Each stage of the cycle from old seed to newly formed seed (involving growth, flowering, fruiting and decay; from spring to autumn), is really only a visible part of the whole, invisible plant. This time-space, of course, differs in length for annuals and perennials, and differs again with trees.

Innumerable time-spaces exist on earth. The time-space of our consciousness is actually a mixture of roughly two-thirds waking and one-third sleeping — it extends from awaking to awaking and in that one time-space we wake and sleep. Our liver has a rhythm of gall- and glucose production. Perhaps the longest of all rhythms is the so-called Platonic year, the return of the vernal point of the Sun to the same place in the zodiac, a span of 25,920 years. Although all these processes unfold in rhythms, they all return to their initial state (seed to seed, awaking to awaking, etc.), and that which lies between the two initial states is the time-space. The science and technology of time-space, and therefore of rhythm, is almost entirely undiscovered as yet. (There is even an institute for rhythm research.) Many more time-spaces exist in the world than those mentioned above, and these the reader may discover for him- or herself.

Another characteristic of knowledge which enables faith to unfold in the human being follows on from the first, and has to do with thinking. The unit of time-space comprising a sequence of moments is invisible. For example, the complete plant is invisible; only single moments of its growing and decaying are visible, and consciousness itself, including our night-consciousness, is not really 'visible'; only our day-consciousness is. But we can *think* it.

In the world there is a phenomenon in which thinking is as constant and, although invisible, as real and ponderable as are objects in space, namely the human being himself. I walk, sit, take hold of things, smile and gesticulate, but I would never consider my 'I' to be merely my ponderable, shaped, moving being. My 'I' is the sum of my memories from early childhood on, my ideals and motivations, my feelings, the actual and potential content not only of my consciousness but also of what is vaguely called my identity. In every human being the visible and invisible are constantly before the mind. Although time-spaces are invisible, we can think them, so why should they not be real just because we only think them? The science of spirit describes the invisible worlds and beings of which the physical sense data are but signs and indicators. Knowledge that makes faith possible is the knowledge of the invisible that permeates our visible, heavy and measurable world.

After having ascended one height, however, another rises before our view, which is that if spiritual-scientific (anthroposophical) knowledge makes faith possible, why are all those whose thinking accepts anthroposophical knowledge unable to release the power of faith and move mountains?

There is a mysterious connection between our thinking and the gospels. The latter have become increasingly unreal owing to the knowledge that has led to technical achievements. They seemed to be accessible only to a paler and paler belief, as described above, and when thinking was followed to its logical conclusion they all but dissolved into loose strands of myths, words and beliefs — as the 'higher criticism' of modern biblical scholarship apparently reveals.

Meanwhile, Rudolf Steiner came and shed immeasurable light on the gospels, and in the light of his explanations meaning appears. But his light is not enough; the science of spirit, the knowledge of anthroposophy alone is not enough. In order that the otherwise dark country of the gospels resolves itself into familiar landscapes, we must walk through it in the light of these explanations, which means that our thinking must conquer its mountains, lakes and villages — its dimensions must come within the grasp of our thinking. We can only conquer it with our thinking, however, as we recognise the composition of the various chapters, discovering which event or saying follows another; against which background the same event or saying appears in another gospel; how their surroundings relate to each other, and so on. Through this we learn to avoid reading the gospels with the intellect alone and thereby dissolving them — no longer comprehending one event after another, one chapter after the other — because with this kind of reading we soon become tired and bored.

The gospels remain locked for us unless we unlock them with our activated thinking. To work with the gospels in the light of Rudolf Steiner's explanations has a twofold effect. Through the written words of the four gospels we begin to understand how the world-Word, which once created the world, rose and resurrected. On the other hand, in the effort of tracing their composition through activating our thinking in a creative way, we begin to discover that we and the gospels are really one. From walking in the realm of the gospels, to discovering their landscapes, we become conscious that the walking is possible only because of the landscapes, inner and outer, while the landscapes themselves only come into being because we walk in them. The gospels fulfil their meaning and are complete only if our thinking unlocks them.

Compared with the gospels other books are really monologues, lovely melodies sung and played to the world for the admiring reader or listener, but although we admire them we add nothing to them in the form of empathy. In contrast, the gospels sound and speak only when we touch them with our thinking. They are only half the dialogue; the other half is spoken by us when we try to read them with our activated thinking. They are dependent upon us.

In the past, people could simply read the gospels and their unthinking devotion and faith made them meaningful. In the future, other human efforts will be needed to complete the dialogue, but in the present it is our thinking. However, we should not imagine that this activated thinking is anything more than our effort to trace the composition. Until the end of the Earth-age the gospels will always need us and without us they are, and will remain, incomplete.

THE CRESSET, CHRISTMAS 1971

ascension & whitsun

the conservation year

In reading how much more seriously the pollution of rivers, lakes and the atmosphere is now regarded, along with the harmful consequences of radiation, artificial fertilisers, pesticides and so on, and of how governments are preparing appropriate legislation to deal with all this, one cannot help thinking that everything is taking a turn for the better. One feels that Nature in her ever-renewing strength has a chance to reassert her pristine glory: that she will be cleansed of mankind's attacks and become better able to imbue human beings with health.

However, in a quite different spirit of earnestness, one thinks again of Jean Jacques Rousseau, one of the forerunners of the French Revolution, with his glowing ideas of 'Back to Nature' and the 'Noble Savage' in his classic *Emile*.[27] The adoration of nature and the fight against pollution that springs from it is a step *backward* in the evolution of humanity! Of course pollution is bad, but less pollution — such as in the time before the discovery of atomic energy when there were fewer cars, factories and so on — will not make things better because pollution is not just a physical but also a moral question. The moral fabric of the world has become so weak that pollution has invaded physical life, with the result that through their unenlightened actions human beings are corrupting and despoiling Creation (for instance, by the thousands of satellites circling the earth, the moon shots, or the layer of algae in the American lakes as described recently in *The Observer*). As a result, quite new conditions will arise in the material world.

All such thinking considers the earth only as the creation of the Divine Father and the Powers (the Exousiai or Elohim). But the earth has since become the Body of Christ. It is not only the ground upon which human destiny evolves under the challenging conditions of natural forces, the climate and seasons, but what was once created by the Powers of the Father Ground is now also permeated by the presence of Christ, which means that matter is now imbued with morality. Chemistry and counter measures against pollution, healthier food, etc. are no longer sufficient: natural laws alone will no longer serve to tip the balance. Rousseau was a forerunner (more of the blood and terror aspect), of the French Revolution because his caring, his craving, for unspoiled nature was one-sided. It left out the human being, transformed and renewed by the Mystery of Golgotha.

> Near, but difficult to grasp, is God.
> But, precisely where there is danger,
> There also grows what can save us.[28]
>
> Friedrich Hölderlin

Christianity demands consciousness otherwise it can be of no help, and the human being, both in his nature and in his economic, political and cultural life, will be overcome by inhuman forces.

If we allow ourselves to be spellbound by the phenomena of pollution we are simply letting the polluting agents — in other words the various branches of human society — run wild and unobserved. If anthroposophical agriculture, medicine and science do not develop within a renewed social organism, they will remain ineffectual. If, on the other hand, these renewed social organisms remain self-righteous, self-satisfied and complacent, instead of looking at themselves as the basis upon which a truer agriculture, medicine and science can grow, we will forgo the means of catharsis and the consequences of pollution will overtake us.

It is questionable whether the dark and dubious appearance of a second Napoleon could rescue us in the way that Napoleon I was an inevitable outcome and saviour of the French Revolution. Indeed, Rudolf Steiner said that while in our time humanity will have the power to destroy the warmth sphere of the earth, in the final two periods of earth evolution it will be capable of destroying the air and water spheres as well.[29]

BOTTON VILLAGE NEWS, 13 III 1970

ascension as an abyss

It behoves humanity in our time to feel the abyss between Ascension and Whitsun. Historically, it was an abyss for the disciples too, because the Risen One who had lived, walked and spoken with them for forty days disappeared into the realm of the clouds. For ten days He vanished and then reappeared in a quite new way at Whitsun.

It is also an abyss for us today. In the unfolding nature around us the varied abundance of greens, of blossoms and scents, assumes more and more weight and our soul is happy to abandon itself to this ocean of light-filled beauty. We gorge ourselves on the sights, sounds and scents, and hardly notice that we are being poured out, drawn like water into a sponge. To feel this threat is like a first attempt to stand upright in spite of the abyss.

> My self now threatens to escape,
> Attracted powerfully by cosmic light,
> Presentiment do thou assume
> With forceful strength thy rights,
> And take the place of thinking's might
> Which tends to lose itself
> In all the senses' glory.

Calendar of the Soul, verse 7 (Ascensiontide)

Both socially and communally, the groups within a social organism today share this mood of the time between Ascension and Whitsun. Christ having disappeared, with the consequent danger of the rise of materialism because the presence of the Risen One is doubted — as the belief of our age loudly proclaims — is an abyss. But the reappearance of Christ in the etheric world (the World-Whitsun described by anthroposophy) and the advent of the Holy Spirit of Truth are like a shining rainbow spanning the abyss. Our groups (Stewards, Cultural Group, Land Group, etc.) lead towards the rainbow because in their discussions of various issues something else is happening in them. Listening to each other and feeling that the group belongs to the whole fabric of the social organism in which we live, endows us with strength and health.

The congregation, the heavenly Holy Spirit Mother, creates the organs of the body social — the *Botton Village News*, the Village Assembly, the groups and the new, as yet unborn, social forms. These are the mountain peaks reaching into the light of the rising sun while the valleys still lie wrapped in darkness. Like all social structures they are far larger than the individual and his thinking and can only be approached with devotion. It is devotion to the social organism and each of its essential organs which saves us from the threatening abyss.

BOTTON VILLAGE NEWS, 28 V 1965

what are we living for?

When the apostle Peter speaks to the multitudes in Jerusalem on the first Whit Sunday about the darkening of the sun, and the moon becoming blood (Acts 2: 19–20), he is actually referring to human loneliness, self-reliance and freedom — 'the Kingdom of Heaven is within you'. Celebrated on the fiftieth day after Easter, the Christian festival of Pentecost is the festival of the out-pouring of the Holy Spirit; the festival of human freedom and decision, of taking responsibility for one's own ideals and actions, which is entirely a matter of individual freedom.

Since then, individual human life has become much more earnest. The flame of the Holy Spirit, which two thousand years ago was seen *above* each disciple, now flames *upward* out of each single heart. As human beings we have been thrown back completely on our own resources. We have physical needs (we must eat and sleep) and there are ways in which we may be forced into situations (we may become refugees, or be imprisoned), but in neither case are we involved in the decision so they cannot be said to be our direct responsibility. But regarding morality there is no longer anything that can force us, and we do not like it. Being less bound to what is given, less driven to do this or that; being less and less inwardly restricted but increasingly prompted to act out of our own initiative, is uncomfortable. That people take more and more drugs is partly an 'anti-Whitsun' reaction: they long to be moved by something stronger than themselves.

But Whitsun also has a historic, social aspect. When we compare people in a western European and an eastern European town, we have two different impressions of social life. In the West, the area of individual moral freedom is becoming limited simply through a degree of economic satiety, and with it the human being is reduced to a kind of resignation — a small family, a small house, a small car. The western citizen has the inescapable tendency to become a mass item and freedom is reduced to keeping up with everyone else. In the East, the thoughts and feelings of individuals have no weight: the party and its goals are everything. Life seems worthwhile because it serves something greater. But in both East and West the question must arise: What are we living for?

In the West, the sheer momentum of life propels us on, but the more people falter the more they are driven to suicide. In the East, the Communist party can only become increasingly dictatorial. The threat of dictatorship is still linked to a sham idealism, while in the West it is a sham moral freedom.

We should recognise that both *East and West are in us*. The party system has lost its meaning because there is no 'they' in the world. The Vietnam war is my responsibility not because I can do anything about it but simply because its complex moral issues are *in me* at a soul level rather than on the level of physical events. The Christian answer to the question: 'What are we living for?' can only be an individual one. Moral responsibility can no longer be a corporate question. Only the individual can act, and only on his own decision. With Christ, the answer to the question: 'What are we living for?' can only be: 'To augment the kingdom of Christ on earth!' Whitsun is the festival of selflessness.

BOTTON VILLAGE NEWS, 7 VI 1968

kaspar hauser play

What a magnificent performance! Not only were the individual characters portrayed superbly (Kaspar, his Higher Being, his Mother, Daumer, Meyer, etc.), but they were wonderfully and harmoniously balanced. Through their unity all of them attained a higher, more powerful reality. The constellation of Feuerbach, Daumer, Meyer, Stanhope (and perhaps to a lesser extent the others around Kaspar), have an archetypal character, as the play shows. It is one of the archetypes woven by the gods into world history for the education of humanity. The superhuman quality of each character appeared most impressively, as did the nature and being of Kaspar Hauser — the inextinguishable light and apocalyptic aim of the image of the human being, steadfast within the changing waves of time.

Various questions arose. Because Carlo's play* is art it poses the questions: What is the destiny of art in our time? How should it be presented? How should audience and actors interact? More and more the word 'is' loses its immediacy. Today we hardly know what it means for something to simply be, or be present: we distance ourselves from experience. The actors must turn a script into a play; musicians must make a composition into something that attains reality, but not without the listening of the audience. The being of a play (or any work of art) must arise between actors and audience. A tuning-in of the audience to the play, and *vice versa,* is a necessity of which we know too

---

*And from the night… Kaspar. In: *Who was Kaspar Hauser?*[30] by Carlo Pietzner, published by Floris Books, Edinburgh 1983.

little and on which we expend too little effort. Another aspect linked with this, physically and concretely, is the preparation of the room which (speaking of our recent performance) had to seat 200 people for 2¾ hours.

The Light Age wants to sweep away all customs and institutions. Over the centuries the words 'play', 'actor' and 'audience' have assumed certain meanings which are entirely time-bound. In medieval times, plays were performed outside churches. In the first Goetheanum (destroyed by fire) the huge statue of the Representative of Man would have stood at the back of the stage during every performance. In ancient Greece the dramas were taken from mythology and the actors wore masks, but the audience filling the amphitheatre watched the performance as a festive religious rite. (And they did not have to pay for the tickets!)

BOTTON VILLAGE NEWS, 16 IV 1977

groups I
whitsun: archetype of the therapeutic community

The age of the gifted genius is past. Ours is the time of the therapeutic community in which people group themselves around various concerns in mutual recognition and acknowledgement, and in listening to one another can gain greater insight than each could achieve on his own. Objectivity, responsibility and reliability will increasingly be vested in groups. Ideas will spring from people being together in active inter-relationship with one another, and less and less from individuals working alone.

This group responsibility for ideas and their implementation is already well developed. Take, for example, the many groups we have in Camphill: the sectors and circles of the Inner Community; groups arranging cultural life and the festivals; groups considering practical goals (waiting lists, finances, Council, regional meetings, etc.) — all are composed of people sitting together, deliberating on various topics, each member playing a different rôle.

But a manifold variety of groups is not a blessing *per se*. If each member does not make a distinct effort the group will sooner or later find itself at an impasse — the impasse of wasting time, of failing to reach a decision regarding the matter in hand, or its members hurting one another. Then the group becomes merely the sum of the worst aspects of its members and each will feel more human when he is alone than when he is in the group. When that happens, people will feel with dread, 'Not another group!' How can the single individual prepare him- or herself so as to avoid this impasse?

As children of our time, we are endowed with the consciousness soul and have the innate ability to observe and to judge. These are intellectual qualities and therefore isolationist and antisocial, separating people from one another. It is in the very nature of observation and judgement to be unemotional and cool. Anxiety, love, faith, greed, etc. are simply not meant to enter the process for fear of soiling the purity of the observation and/or the judgement. It is this emotionless purity which separates us from one another, and ultimately sets our own loneliness against the other's so that wasted time, wounding and lack of clarity ensue.

But the purity reached through observation and judgement is only the first of the qualities to be attained on the path of the consciousness soul. There is a second quality which has to permeate the first, as into a cup-like vessel, and that is the quality of devotion. Only devotion will overcome all the wasting of time, the wounding and loss of direction, without at the same time losing its purity. Only devotion will transform purity from something that isolates people into something inter-personal and social.

But devotion must be more than simply a word. The matter or concern of a group should be approached not in a bull-headed way, but gently and with care. If in our attempts to observe and judge there could be idealism for the matter in hand (which may be quite mundane such as finding enough beds for people, production issues or money questions, or something a little more spiritual such as considering themes for Chapter or Community meetings), and if we could meet the other person's concerns, even if quite different from our own, with a little more positivity — and not a blind, passive positivity but one which actually invokes our observation and judgement — if we could do all this we would feel a quality enter the group which raises it above the sympathy and antipathy, greed and hate, which otherwise soil its purity. Devotion would then become something tangible, substantial, and not just a mere word. It could become something that lifts the members of the group out of the confines of their own person. The group would then become *more* than the mere sum of its members, just as the group of disciples at the first Whitsun became a vessel for the Holy Spirit, capable of being understood by people of many tongues.

Whitsun is the archetype of the therapeutic community. Today the Holy Spirit is the *Healing* Spirit, which makes people not just healthy but *whole*.

BOTTON VILLAGE NEWS, 24 V 1974

groups II
turning the other cheek

The modern human being finds himself in a dilemma: his capacity for purity of observation leads him into loneliness and isolation. Groups of whatever kind — administrative, neighbourhood groups with the task of caring for one another, or community groups — are the carriers of new endeavours which raise us to a better existence than we could manage on our own, and they depend for their success on devotion to the matter in hand.

This is easier said than done. We all benefit today from a wave of new awareness of the other person; contemporary efforts at community living are based on a new feeling of brotherhood among human beings. In my youth between the wars, people were more entrenched in convention, family or nationality, more bound to sympathies and antipathies, and because of it they were more dependent on *reactions*. We were interwoven with a world which we knew and accepted, and which knew and accepted us. We were less able to judge or simply to observe (which always involves stepping back and *not* reacting). Documents from other times can be misleading: writing things down always involves a certain measure of objectivity that was not necessarily present in the moment itself.

There are many things which prompt our reactions when we meet other people: the way they dress, what we experience as their mannerisms; their way of speaking or moving and, particularly in groups, their opinions. There is not only the *anti*-reaction but also the *pro*-reaction: somebody I love can do, wear or say what he or she likes and I will find it delightful! Thus many of our reactions are prompted by sympathy or antipathy and not by pure observation. Yet, if we were only observing beings we could never fall in love or choose a tie. Taste is, quite rightly, very subjective. Different people want different things and therefore an economic system based on choice still seems justified. Reaction, sympathy and antipathy have their place. But with a little self-observation we can distinguish whether our interplay with other human beings is in the nature of 'an eye for an eye, a tooth for a tooth' or whether we are trying to put forward an opinion based purely on observation and judgement, and not swayed by sympathy or antipathy.

It is in such moments of self-observation that we can experience a transition: the transition from subjective reaction to *freedom*, and not only our own freedom but also the other's. As long as we simply react, subjectively, we are bound and imprisoned by our feelings; we give way to them, and our surroundings are coloured and shaped by them so that in the end it is not reality that surrounds us but so many mirrors which reflect back to us our own intentions, suspicions, loves and fears. The other person who lives in these surroundings is chained to the fetters of our reactions. When we feel outraged ('How dare he say such a thing?'), we wound him so that he feels only the pain of our selfish antipathy and is imprisoned by his wound. As long as we merely react there can be no question of freedom. Our freedom —and we can observe this exactly — begins only when we reach the pure plateau of selfless judging. In that way we shatter the mirrors; we escape the prison of our own self-centredness and lift the other person to the plateau of his own capacity to judge, not swayed by emotion but free. When the gospel says, 'Whosoever smites thee on thy right cheek, turn to him the other also' (Luke 6: 29), it means precisely this. The other's aggression slaps me on the cheek; I feel attacked and my antipathy is roused, but if I turn the other cheek I overcome myself and set the other person free. If we simply retaliate, we are Old Testament Jews.

The more we cultivate an attitude of devotion the less we will react blindly. Moreover, our lonely freedom will become a fount of love for the other because we will discover that the other's opinion is worth hearing.

BOTTON VILLAGE NEWS, 5 VI 1974

groups III
schools of love

Everything described in the first and second articles — devotion to the theme, turning the other cheek — can be summarised by saying that we are trying to climb the path towards a plateau where our higher, our truer egos, the *Person* in our all too human *persons*, meet. This pilgrimage is protected, accompanied and sometimes hindered by the Guardian of the Threshold.

The Guardian of the Threshold in our time is not merely concerned with the individual but is pre-eminently a *social* phenomenon. It resembles the transformation of the ancient Egyptian epoch into our own. For example, in the Temple at Karnak which is outwardly vast and visible, everything leads through the dark entrance to the inner chamber, the realm of the dead, the place of initiation. Today, when I look into the pupil of your eye,[31] into its black nothingness, and you look into mine, I meet you and you meet me. It is a meeting where your soul and my soul, your body and my body, your world, and my world all fall away. There remains only the nothingness of our pupils, our age-old, eternally young truth. In this black nothingness the Persons within the persons gaze into the world and into each other. Everything that is not black is unreal — the world, the soul and the body, which in one sense are only mask and mummery, and in another sense, karma and biography. In fact, everything is unreal that has to be borne and overcome.

In a group we can concentrate on the non-black, but *truth* can only be found in the black, in the gaze itself, and not in the 'gazed *at*'. We, the Persons within our persons, are chained in various ways to the non-black, the 'gazed at'. But groups and inter-personal relationships exist in order that we may help one another to dissolve some of these fetters. The other person can see our limitations better than we can see our own. In ordinary society, to courageously seek out the true self of the other person is not considered fashionable. We keep our awareness of other people's fetters to ourselves; or, alternatively, talk about them behind their backs, which makes all such awareness useless. 'Village gossip' is merely cowardice. But the inner courage to discover the true self of the other person dissolves his chains. To become aware of the reality of the other means to love him. Only our fetters, i.e. our limitations, prevent us from loving one another.

Groups are schools of truth, and therefore of love. They belong to the humanity of the Light Age; they are esoteric phenomena and yet manifest. Accepting the presence of the Guardian and his relation to our development, recognising the eternal truth of the other person, and achieving love are the tasks of modern humanity, as well as grasping these by means of our ordinary, earthly understanding. Since the Fall, 'our eyes have been opened,' meaning our gaze becomes fettered to outer glamour, to the outer appearance of Karnak, without realising that the higher reality lies within the dark chamber. We relate to the glamour, which becomes our karma. By hindering us, the Guardian forces us to turn to each other, allowing us to find the truth of the other person; the innocence of the consciousness soul in the black pupil.

In paradise we were dependent children. Since then we have grown up, and now our individual existential innocence isolates us. Christ lived on earth in order to enable us to combine innocence with adulthood. Rudolf Steiner is our guide in this and, as such, shows us the way towards a renewed Christianity.

BOTTON VILLAGE NEWS, 19 VI 1974

a visit to egypt

Anke Weihs, Gisela Schlegel, Ann Harris, Kate and I went to Egypt together. We spent the first few days in Cairo, a squalid, sprawling city of six million inhabitants which has grown so large that it almost engulfs the Pyramids and the Sphinx at Giza. The usual skyscrapers, Victorian houses which have not been redecorated since they were built, and a shanty town of Heath Robinson-like* contraptions, are all enlivened by a completely disorganised flood of traffic.

We then flew down to Aswan, over two hours away, near the Sudanese border. At the first cataract are two dams, the first one British-built in 1902 and the other, a little higher up, built with Russian help sixty years later. The newer dam creates Lake Nasser, a huge reservoir, the largest in the world, along with a greatly increased electricity output, and millions more fertile acres. Although the yearly deposit of mud along the Nile no longer occurs, there are all kinds of soil problems, and overcast skies, especially in Cairo. We stayed for almost a week, then took a half-hour flight to the north to Luxor-Karnak, the old Thebes, the centre of ancient Egypt.

In Karnak there is the magnificent temple complex dating from roughly 1500–1000 BC and a large temple in Luxor (now a biggish city) dating from about 1200 BC on the east bank of the majestically-flowing Nile. On the west bank of the river, amid desert and rocky escarpments, is the Valley of the Kings, where queens and nobility are also buried. These tombs are cut into the rock and there are steep staircases and passages leading into chambers, now mostly empty, yet with wonderfully painted reliefs on the walls. These have hardly faded in thousands of years and, along with the cascading veils of hieroglyphs, depict the journey of the soul after death and its meetings with the gods, finally encountering Osiris.

Our holiday ended with a further two days in Cairo where we visited the outstanding Egyptian Archaeological Museum.

* * *

After viewing the ruins and antiquities of Egypt we were left with the overwhelming impression of being engulfed by the ancient past. Egyptian culture has its roots in prehistory before the onset of the Dark Age (3102 BC to 1899 AD), or Kali Yuga as it is known in Hindu esotericism and in

---

*W. Heath Robinson (1872–1944), a cartoonist who drew bizarre contraptions for everyday tasks.

anthroposophy.[32] Up to that time life was still lived to a large extent in the companionship and embrace of the gods. The difference between waking and sleeping was not pronounced and the boundaries of birth and death were transformations rather than closed frontiers. The human being still lived in a relatively transparent body and was less weighed down than later when history as we know it began with the development of art and a relatively independent earthly existence for human beings.

The yearly flooding of the Nile began in July. That event ensured Egyptian supremacy for over two thousand years (roughly 3000–700 BC) and it coincided with the rising of Sirius, the star of Isis. There is no doubt that the Egyptians felt the covering of the Nile valley with fertile mud and the rising of Sirius to be a single cosmic event; their life was one with the life of the whole universe, macrocosm and microcosm were still not quite separated. But within this unity in which the Nile was mysteriously representative of the greater universe, the reality of death caused the achievements of earthly life, an earthly consciousness and the light of day, to be pushed increasingly into the foreground. The tombs, the mummies and the dwellings of the dead on the west bank of the Nile in the end became more weighty, and the contents of the tombs, the nature of the objects which accompanied the dead on their journey after death, became more and more physical in character, more earthly, with more everyday meanings. Meanwhile, the gods (Thoth, Hathor, Anubis, Isis, Osiris) dwindled to little more than images of an unknown world.

Yet the power of these forms and the configuration of material objects, both indicative of the increasingly urgent process of incarnation into earthly matter, were so strong that, although later on Greece flourished and Egypt was eventually reduced to a mere province of Rome, the forms, hieroglyphs and gods were imitated far into the future — indeed well into Christian times.

BOTTON MIRROR, 7 III 1984

stars & old egypt

Human life at the beginning of the age of the consciousness soul is a day-life created by our senses which only functions while we are awake. Illumined by electricity, our sense life reaches above the unlit, undifferentiated earthly darkness into the majesty of the night sky which we know but rarely see.

The stars in the night sky always have something of an alien and unearthly beauty. Our experiences are accustomed to earthly illuminated phenomena;

the stars have something incomparable about them. In the beginning of old Egypt (2907 BC), they were still known to be the seats of the gods, quite near, while the day was not as light nor the night as dark as they are today. Heaven was not yet the sky: heaven and earth, night and day were not divided. But as time went on the seats of the gods retreated into far distances and became small shining stars. This transformation took place during the waning of ancient Egypt. In the beginning of the Graeco-Roman epoch (747 BC), the gaze of human beings was directed earthward. The stars then became stars in our modern sense, withdrawing into a mysterious distance. But with the retreating stars the divine perfume that once permeated all earthly existence and kept the gates of birth and death unlocked also withdrew. These gates became firmly shut, but through this separation from the godhead, human beings gained not only the greatest goal of earth-existence — the ego (which they had possessed since Lemurian times) — but ego-*consciousness* and, as a consequence, *responsibility*. Slowly, freedom, and therefore responsibility, developed. Today we are at the point that is described in the gospel, 'and then he came to himself', for we all are prodigal sons. We all are free to return to the Father because we have been empowered by the Son. (Luke 15: 11–32)

But the 'return to the Father' contains within it increasing responsibility for the course and tread of history (in the sense of the 'historic conscience') — responsibility not only towards the outer world but also toward our own souls. Jealousy, greed, ambition, selfishness, laziness, all manner of critical attitudes, wasted emotions and thoughts of a petty, all-too-human gossipy kind have developed in us because the stars left us alone.

In the year 869 AD a synod took place in Constantinople[33] in which it was dogmatically stated that man did not consist of body, soul and spirit, but only body and soul, the soul having some spiritual qualities. This was the final step of the withdrawal of the gods. The shining stars remained behind as mere signs in mysterious distances.

Rudolf Steiner explained tirelessly that the visible stars are only the luminous points of the star being which is as wide as its course. Venus and all the other planets are not somewhere in the sky far away, but embrace and permeate the earth, the colour and the forms in the plant world (yellow to the sun, blue to Saturn, and so on), and human beings.

Our consciousness will be at home once again in the cosmos if we not only know about the expression of the stars in their configurations, but if we also experience them.

The stars spake once to Man.
It is World-destiny
That they are silent now.
To be aware of the silence
Can become pain for earthly Man.

But in the deepening silence
There grows and ripens
What Man speaks to the Stars.
To be aware of the speaking
Can become strength for Spirit-Man.[34]

This experience will certainly lead to the stars widening to the realities of the gods, but it will also lead us to a widening and awakening of our knowing heart. The untrue dogma of the 869 Council of Constantinople will prove to be an illusion. The stars and what they signify will again become part of us. The horoscope will no longer be some dark guidance in our lives, but part of our widened and awakened consciousness. We will have travelled from the end of Egyptian times — the divine heavens reduced to stars in the night-sky — towards the start of their manifestation when in our speaking and singing the stars reveal themselves again. The stars in the night-sky become signs for our own person and spirituality.

BOTTON VILLAGE NEWS, 27 IX 1991

Botton Village News
St. John's

~ *st john's*

social organisms of ancient egypt & today

In the past, one of the most detrimental factors to learning was the way we were taught history as a series of kings and battles, or cultural and artistic styles, which became hazy and incoherent in our minds. The only thing that can make history relevant is the importance which the past holds for the present and future. We ourselves all have the past in us and transform it since we are important links in the historical process. The spiritual-scientific insight of repeated earth lives — the revelation that in the past we were ancient Egyptians, or perhaps Greeks, or American Indians — shows this existential importance.

There are special links between ancient Egypt and our time, particularly the being of the pharaoh and what corresponds to him today. We can hardly imagine the divine majesty, power and glory issuing from and surrounding the pharaoh, who could be likened to the sun illumining all the works of man, his private as well as his external life. He was surrounded by court officials, scribes, generals, priests, keepers of various domains of Egyptian life and its land. Egypt was a well-ordered, extremely conservative country whose glory remained almost undiminished from about 3000 to 800 BC.

The power of the pharaoh was an objective fact. He was a priest-king initiated into the divine worlds, the sign of which was the Uraeus snake on the crown of his forehead. No one would have dreamt of rebelling, just as no one would rebel against the sun. His glory was a fact as the sun is a fact.

The relationship of Egypt to our time is that today we are all on the way to becoming priest-kings, pharaohs. Although we are greyer, smaller and do not have the symbol of the Uraeus snake on our heads, each one of us is his own master, having his own thoughts, forming his own opinions and taking his own decisions. As Westerners, it is inappropriate for us to enlarge our existence in obedience to the warmth and light of a guru or leader. We have to rely on our own courage, our own guidance, and following a guru would feel like we were betraying the achievements of the West. We would become caricatures, like Hitler's puppet government. (Hence it is quite wrong to look upon Rudolf Steiner as a guru.)

With the discovery in the 15th/16th century AD that the earth is a globe, we all stepped down onto the ground. Whether tall or small, genius or fool, we are now all on the same level. Since then, the equality of men and women in any social organism has become the greatest problem in life on earth, and it is made greater still through the problem of work. An apparently limitless reservoir of raw materials was opened up in those voyages of discovery, and a further reservoir of infinite technical possibilities dawned with the invention of machinery in the 18th/19th century. This is known as the Industrial Revolution, the outcome of which we (as also the French and the French Revolution), have not yet resolved.

In Egyptian times the earth was thought to be flat and its interior no deeper than the tombs. The individualisation of human beings was so little developed that the living and working together of people was not a problem. Everything was held together and enlivened through the will of the pharaoh and his court, as the cells of our body are held together and enlivened by the blood.

In contrast to the uniqueness of the pharaoh, in our time the equality and uniqueness of *all* human beings underlies many of our contemporary problems, both social, psychological and work-related. The pharaoh was a priest-king. We are on the way towards a kingship that we can read about in the Epistle to the Hebrews (Heb 2: 6–8) in the New Testament. We are aware of our uniqueness. We say 'I see, I walk, I feel' because all our abilities are centred in our uniqueness. But we are also aware, whether dimly or clearly, that this uniqueness is still full of undeveloped potential; its greyness is but the outer shell of an inner content that is golden.

One consequence of the singular uniqueness of the pharaoh as distinct from the general uniqueness of people today is the possibility to arrange social life into three spheres — a threefold order as opposed to the unity of Egyptian theocracy. This threefoldness is the cultural-spiritual-religious realm, the sphere of social rights, and the field of economic life. The first should be permeated by freedom, the second by equality, the third by brotherliness. This offers the possibility for the right relationship of work to the three spheres to arise. These three spheres do exist today, but in a wholly distorted way due partly to their inter-dependence. The distortion is due to our warped view of the human being because the notion of a threefold social organism stems from the threefoldness of the human being.

In ancient Egyptian times the human being was not yet a threefold, independent, circumscribed unit as he is today; he was but a tiny part, a cell of the spiritual realm of the pharaoh. This theocracy — a social pyramid of which the apex was the pharaoh — did not allow for the appearance of three independent spheres, nor had humanity developed, historically, a soul into which the three spheres might have shone.

Although Egyptian art and culture were extremely conservative, it was also a culture preoccupied with death. By far the greatest number of preserved objects are from graves, the contents of which were to accompany the soul in its journey through the heavenly underworld. The main point of this preoccupation was the preserving, mummifying, of the physical body.

The identification of the self with the physical body is very much a characteristic of our time. We have to bear this identification because we have to imprint the stamp of our 'I-am' on all our experiences. The increasingly common practice of cremating the body is like saying good-bye as quickly as possible to the fetters of the physical body. The opposite tendency in America — or in Russia, as shown by Lenin's glass-coffin in Moscow — are materialistic efforts to prolong the earthly life, at least as a picture. But mummification in Egypt was a world-historic means to create and intensify the feeling of the earthly self. After death, the one who had died was forced to look at his mummified body which he had used too little while on earth. It filled him with the urge to be more bound to the physical body in a next life in order to develop the 'I am'.

The lack of earthly 'I am' feelings and the gold on the sarcophagi, hide the black mummy in Egyptian times, while in our time the multitude of grey 'I-ams' hide the pharaohic gold in each of us. A fuller understanding of the conscious development of this relationship between the Egyptian epoch and our time, and of our relationship to the work we do, would cure many of our social difficulties.

CAMPHILL VILLAGE TRUST NEWS, AUTUMN 1981

the innocence of the consciousness soul

The understanding of our own souls is a complex problem. We not only have an individual biography and soul-constitution, but we are also participants in the general soul-state of the 20th century, the so-called consciousness soul. This has been developing over the last four hundred years, and its development will continue throughout the next two millennia. We are so deeply entrenched in the soul life that we cannot but identify ourselves with it. It permeates all our thoughts, feelings and actions as well as our self-consciousness.

Our past soul-frames, ordained for us by the gods, conditioned the way in which we experienced the world. We had to endure it. In the course of evolution through repeated earth lives we were educated to bear continually changing outer and inner conditions. But the consciousness soul is quite different. The gods have given us the ability to *observe* and, because of this difference, human beings can *grow up*. The consequence of this has been the development of natural science, and the founding of the Royal Society its first great manifestation.

But *sense* observation is only one part of the consciousness soul. The other part is certainly not a gift of the gods! It can only develop through our own individual will. *Supersensible* experience is only possible if our will shoots into our consciousness, will that can only come from ourselves, never from an outside source. Will from outside would make us like children again, or perhaps marionettes. All facets of life, where observation is not sufficient — religion, art, the social organism, politics — have become paler and lacking in guidance over the last centuries because the will now lies entirely within personal freedom.

This personal freedom, which has been available to us since around the 16th century, is something holy; it comes from the gods, and because it is holy it is innocent. It shines in the divine heights and is beyond earthly darkness, weight and guilt. While sense observation alone is a continuation of the Fall: 'And the eyes of them both were opened' (Gen 3: 7), sense observation when lifted up into the realm of freedom and contained within it becomes divine: 'Ye are gods.' (John 10: 34)

More than any other time of the year, St John's places the human being at a crossroads. We recognise John the Baptist in the white innocence of the vestments, which are white at Christmas also. In our northern regions of the earth it is summer, the time of the greatest abundance of our outer sense experiences. The warmth, the light, the scents, the bird song, the whole ripening glory around us — all this threatens to drown our self-consciousness in sense experience. If our self-consciousness does not derive its strength from morality and will we become materialists, drawing in sense impressions as if all the glory around us were only matter. Sometimes in summer we long for the bareness and colourless chill of winter so as to have fewer sense impressions and, instead, to feel the glow of our soul and spirit. The whole of natural science is like having a surfeit of one-sided St John's experiences.

Permeated as it is by the consciousness soul, our soul life is a mixture of guilt and innocence. If we remain as we were born, namely as observers, we remain cold, old and guilty. If we put our will into this consciousness soul, as we do when we allow the gaze of the service to fall upon us, or when we undertake any of the exercises given by Rudolf Steiner, our consciousness becomes warmed with spiritual beings. Then it can be as innocent as the white vestments at St John's and Christmas, and it can be rejuvenated by the steps of deathless rebirth.

BOTTON VILLAGE NEWS, 3 VII 1964

st john's & the act of consecration of man

Summer bears the imprint of St John the Baptist and of his birth and beheading. 'The voice of one crying in the wilderness' (Matt. 3: 3, Mark 1: 3, Luke 3: 4, John 1: 23) reverberates through the beauty and fullness of creation. It announces the advent of the Word to a creation which had been created by It but which had become guilty through the Fall.

In the Gospel of St Mark, the story of the beheading of John is preceded by the forming of the disciples into a brotherhood of twelve and their 'going out', and is followed by the Feeding of the Five Thousand (Matt. 14: 15–21, Mark 6: 37–44, Luke 9: 13–17, John 6: 5–14). The light and majesty of this 'twelvehood' shines in its fullness, feeding the multitude of our age, the thousands of the fifth post-Atlantean cultural epoch. John was beheaded, meaning he sacrificed his head, the seat of his consciousness, his thinking, beholding and speaking, in order that it might become food for the many with the blessing of Christ.

In the Act of Consecration of Man, there are two kinds of so-called seasonal prayers, prayers which change according to the festivals or their preparation times. One precedes the whole Act of Consecration like a gate through which one enters the temple. The colour of the gate and the words on it change (the vestments and altar are black for Lent, red for Easter and so on), while the temple itself, with the exception of the Gospel Reading, remains. But there is another gate, further into the service which also changes with the festivals and which leads into the holy mystery of the temple.

The words on this gate are usually spoken before the Offering begins, before the priest lifts the paten with the bread from off the cup, before the uncovering of the cup: *only* at Christmas and St John's tide are these inner words spoken after the Offering and before the very Holy of Holies itself, the Transubstantiation. When the priest speaks these words, one feels that when the cup is filled with wine and water and the incense is put on to the glowing charcoal, the sacrificial life of John flows into the offering. When the seasonal prayer precedes the Transubstantiation during St John's Tide the consequences of his beheading flow into the transformation of bread and wine.

Throughout the year, the beheading of John takes place on the brink of the valley separating the second and third parts of the Act of Consecration, between the Offering and the Transubstantiation. There is something like an allusion to the beheading of the archetypal human being in the so-called silent censing. After the book is carried from the right to the left of the cup, the priest censes the altar: the clouds of incense rise from the four sides of the holy table top. Incense is the purifier, carrying the prayers of human beings *up* to God, while in its scent, its life, grace *descends*. The coming about of our closed head-nature (in the baby the closing of the fontanelle), intrinsically separated us on earth from the spiritual world.

Something of that grace, of that warning of the summer heights, and therefore something of the scent of incense, is in one of the summer verses from Rudolf Steiner's *Calendar of the Soul*.[35]

> And when I live in senses' heights,
> There flames up deep within my soul
> Out of the spirit's fiery worlds
> The gods' own word of truth:
> In spirit sources seek expectantly
> To find your spirit kinship.

Calendar of the Soul, verse 13 (week after St John's)

BOTTON VILLAGE NEWS, 15 VII 1966

astronautics

One of the most world-shattering events of recent times was the pictures taken from Gemini iv, in which we could see the astronaut dangling on a line outside his spacecraft, with the globe of the earth behind him. It was world-shattering because the earth, looking as if it were made of cardboard, glass or plastic, was exactly as it is depicted in all the atlases, and as we have learned to think of it since our early school days. It looked like the proof of popular science, of Copernican theory, and of a material universe, the universe looking exactly as we have come to think of it. The picture of the astronaut, the globe of the earth and 'space' behind it, like those taken on another occasion (from Ranger ii on the surface of the moon), looked as if it were a photograph of earthly objects, within earthly space. For earthly eyes or for an earthly camera, it looks as we see it. For cosmic, World-All eyes or for a cosmic camera it may look completely different. It is quite wrong (and futile), to ask 'What does it really look like?' Earthly laws, not only those of gravity but also those of logic and proof, have validity only on earth. They, too, decrease with the square of the distance from the earth, just as the law of gravity does. We have no reason to believe that these earthly laws are valid for the entire universe. Only pride in our logical and mathematical thinking makes us believe this to be so.

One of the reasons why pictures from outer space create such terrible illusions is our concept of time. We measure time by means of the different positions of heavenly bodies in space, in particular the sun. In the West, we think of time as a tunnel, a road, or a rope — as something linear with the past behind, the future in front, and the present (and us) in between. But time is not just a category like space, within which events take place; it is a power which can be observed in the process of ageing, in physical changes such as white hair, wrinkles, etc. These effects can be likened to erosion caused by the power of time. Living through a day from morning to evening is not simply a succession of moments but a conglomeration of various modes and states of existence. The souls of the elderly are filled with memories of childhood, and their reactions make it apparent that time is a *circular* power. The journey from birth to death does not follow a straight line, for the gate of birth and the gate of death are one and the same. We make our life journey in smaller or larger circles, always returning to the starting point. Time becomes space. People who were near drowning and then rescued have described this panorama-like, circular time-world. Their memories appeared to be all round them; they were no 'further away' from their childhood memories than from their memories of yesterday. Their time-tunnel expanded into a time-world, completely squeezing out and obliterating space, spatial sensation and spatial experience.

The familiar movement of the heavens, the rising and setting of stars with their arcs across the sky, have remained unchanged throughout millennia, steeper towards the equator and flatter towards the North pole. In the zodiac, tilted over against these arcs, the moon, the sun and the planets trace their paths, with orbits lasting a month, a year or several years. In the sun's course and appearance varying throughout the year, this majestic, rotating universe is like an image of golden arcs against a dark blue background, where 'time becomes space'. These arcs are like an architecture of time, like time frozen into spatial forms.

Photographs of the earth's globe, of the moon's surface or of other heavenly phenomena, do not take account of the fact that earthly objects appear to us as they do because they seem to be strung on a rope of time, like snapshots of a plant in which we see the seed, then the leaves, then the blossom, each separately.

Baptism by John caused the consciousness of those baptised to be immersed in this time-world, the time-world into which shone the fire of the approaching Christ.

BOTTON VILLAGE NEWS, 25 VI 1965

visit to nürnberg

We had our Christian Community Synod in June in Nürnberg, one of the oldest German towns. Nürnberg is not only one of the oldest, it is also one of the most Germanic. We should recall that Germany emerged in 1871 at the end of the Franco-Prussian war, when a conglomeration of kingdoms and dukedoms was united into a German nation under the leadership of the Prussian King and his chancellor, Bismarck. Nürnberg and the landscape of Franken, North Bavaria and Thuringia are situated at the very centre of what we imagine as Germany. It was the home of Albrecht Durer, of Cranach, Behaim, the Fuggers, the Meistersingers and Hans Sachs. If you visit the German Museum there, you find the most wonderful pictures, illuminated manuscripts, sculptures and craft work — a rare blend of mystical spirituality and realism. But Nürnberg was heavily bombed during the war. Most buildings were damaged, and many were obliterated. It is a strange sight to walk through the newly-built streets and houses in which the architects have tried as far as possible to tastefully incorporate the old facades and reliefs.

In politically pre-German times there was also a German folk-spirit which was at first close to, and then farther from, the German landscapes and their inhabitants, breathing in, incarnating, and then breathing out, excarnating.[36] Nürnberg must have been a pivotal point in this process, which is perhaps why Hitler loved it so much. Between the 15th and 16th centuries, between Renaissance and Baroque times, there must have been a period of physical intensification of this ultra-German mood. But the task of Germany was never to be herself to such a high degree; rather, it was meant to unfold cosmopolitanism by delving into foreign nations, their culture and modes of existence, though in a completely non-political way. Bismarck was therefore a traitor to this task because he forged Germany into a nation and hence it became a political unit, a physical rather than a human reality.

This physical densification of the German spirit in Nürnberg at the end of the Middle Ages (symbolised today by the huge stone steps just outside Nürnberg which Hitler erected for his march pasts), has a remarkable similarity in its mood to the atmosphere of the concentration camps.

If the spirit of the German people does not remain human, with all the spiritual heights that the selfless human being can attain to; if it sinks down into the physical or threatens to become a political power (as it did under Hitler and as it threatens to become again), then something like the holocaust of the Second World War will become a possible outcome again. Humanity as a whole, the variety of all its nations, depends on Germany not being a political nation. That the Allies managed to physically destroy Germany had as its ultimate aim the emergence of the human reality which Hitler had betrayed. The present German and Austrian refugees living and working all over the world fulfils, perhaps, this cosmopolitan task far more than the millions of Germans living in Germany.

The Camphill community which Ursel Herberg has established in Nürnberg — a day school for 30 (soon to be 50) children with special needs, full of gentle, though energetic humanity — was a very moving sight. It is truly a place of German refugees within Germany. It reminds us of Kaspar Hauser who appeared in Nürnberg on Whit Monday, 26th May 1828, a refugee not just from a country which was occupied by a dark, hostile power, but from earthly life which had become increasingly ruled by dark powers. However, he persisted in this earthly realm, full of courage and light, full of confidence and trust in the final victory of the good on earth.

BOTTON VILLAGE NEWS, 30 VII 1977

uriel: the window of history & the window of summer

Summer, St John's Tide, is the time of Uriel, the Archangel of summer, the lord of the earth's sleep. Uriel is also the lord of historic conscience.[37] Nature and morality at this time flow together in a kind of higher alchemy, and human sins and mistakes arising from humanity's endowment of freedom intermingle with nature's regularity and perfection.

Rudolf Steiner described how humanity is not yet able to experience history in a fully waking state.[38] One can well recognise this in one's own inability to grasp history. In spite of the guiding insights of spiritual science concerning the periods of humanity's evolution, we can only imagine in a half-dream the consciousness of people in bygone ages. And it is remarkable how for us the history of the past fifty to a hundred years separates out into single events, into individual clumps, but does not gel into real history. It is also surprising how similar this inefficient grasp of history is to our summer consciousness, such as when contemplating a summer landscape, a rose, the light spreading from morning towards noon, or a thunderstorm. We do not notice the similarity because our summer perceiving is so mixed with bodily conditions (delight in warmth, light and scent, or the horror of wetness), and emotional states (being swayed by beauty or overcome by fear).

Through imbuing oneself with the words, verses and composition of Rudolf Steiner's *Soul Calendar*, we become aware not only of the structure of the year's course, but also of the different values of the social organism and the social relevance of our connections to others.

It is difficult to discern the similarity of our dreaming history to our dreaming summer nature because both are overlaid by different veneers of normality. History is drummed into us in school in an unimaginative way; our summer nature is characterised by tourists and holidaymakers, leaving only a few bare patches of loneliness, earnestness and majesty.

We are surrounded, one could say, by stained-glass windows which are engraved from outside, but engraved not only by the physical surroundings. We sit gazing at these coloured windows with varying degrees of conscious understanding: we look at the two windows of summer and history with a dreamlike consciousness; at others with different states of consciousness.

Both windows have in common the idea that something only intended or promised is coming to its peak, to its outer, visible fulfilment, like the change in season from spring to summer, the change from archaic to classical Greece, or from early to high Renaissance. In history there are, of course, many peaks or waves, lesser and greater, some like the ripening of fruit in late summer and autumn, others like the change from Minoan culture to archaic Greece, or from Baroque to the Rococo.

Through the many windows which surround us, different realities ray in upon us. Through the window of history, reincarnation and karma may shine. We ourselves may emerge in our past lives from the stream of history in Egypt, in Crete, on the shores of the Black Sea, in Scandinavia or in Iceland. Because our existential consciousness was once in those places, so different from now, we might have a taste of reality through the figures, documents and events of history.

And the window through which summer shines in earnestness and majesty is that through which we look at a dark red rose with its long stem, or at a mountain mirrored in a still lake on a clear, warm morning, or at a rounded, perfectly green, strong tree. We may then feel that we not only look at them, but that out of their uncreated perfection they also look at us with our incompleteness and longings. From the blending of these two perspectives or angles of view there may come the alchemy of which I spoke at the beginning, the blending of the perfect with the imperfect.

'In the beginning was the Word, and the Word was with God, and the Word was God… And the Word was made flesh, and dwelt among us…' (John 1: 1, 14) If the Word had not entered the imperfections of our flesh, this alchemy would never have occurred. Human striving and failure would never have been able to enter and thereby renew the perfection of creation. Uriel's earnest gaze would have broken in sorrow. Now world hope can permeate this earnestness.

BOTTON VILLAGE NEWS, 31 VII 1982

~ toward michaelmas

fritjof capra

Fritjof Capra's book *The Tao of Physics*[39] was a world-wide success because it seemed to answer the question which human evolution is increasingly posing: How can we rediscover the spirituality which has become lost in the course of evolution? Contained in this question is a step which our conscience must address, and which will be described in this article. The answer, as dealt with in great detail in Capra's book, is that in mathematical concepts, modern physics is that which Eastern mythology and wisdom expresses in poetic and imaginative ways — the hidden essence of matter.

Equating these two different approaches has became possible because Newtonian physics is increasingly replaced by modern physics, which shows that matter is not simply made up of ever smaller solid building-blocks, but that these building-blocks reveal themselves to be processes. The theories of atomic and sub-atomic physics have shown the existence of elementary particles to be very unlikely. These theories have revealed a basic inter-connectedness of matter which shows that energy of motion can be transformed into mass, suggesting that particles are processes rather than objects.[40] Hindu mythology, the psychology of Zen Buddhism and the ethos of the various Chinese holy writings, speak about these processes, and the processes arising out of their relationships. But the essential unanimity of occidental physics and oriental spirituality shows itself in the concept of *maya*, namely that outer sense-realities are projections of the mind — illusions, basically — arising from a particular state of consciousness.

When the oneness of all things is not recognised, then not only is there ignorance but there is also particularisation.[41] The variations, the variety of the outer world, play the same rôle in both Western and Eastern approaches. According to quantum-field theory, all interactions between the constituents of matter take place through the emission and absorption of vital particles. More than that, the dance of creation and destruction is the basis of the very existence of matter. Every sub-atomic particle is an energy dance, a process of creation and destruction. For the modern physicist, Shiva's dance is the dance of sub-atomic matter. The dancing Shiva is the dancing universe, the ceaseless flow of energy forming an infinite variety of patterns that dissolve into one another.[42]

The reason why the equating of Western thought with Eastern imagination only *seems* to be an answer to the question of our lost spirituality lies precisely in the phenomenon of the variety of the sense-world, its multifarious forms and colours. Present-day science explains the chemical content of red or green, the physical properties of the many existing forms, but it never explains *why* the geranium blossom is red, or why oak and oleander leaves are different greens, and so on. St Paul's words in connection with the glory of the Resurrection come to mind:

> 'All flesh is not the same flesh: but there is one kind of flesh of men, another flesh of beasts, another of fishes and another of birds. There are also celestial bodies, and terrestrial bodies: but the glory of the celestial is one thing, and the glory of the terrestrial is another. There is one glory of the sun, and another glory of the moon, and another glory of the stars: for one star differeth from another star in glory.'
>
> (Corinthians I, 15: 39–41)

The consciousness appropriate for perceiving this variety in the sense-world is simply ignored if the sense-world is declared to be only *maya* (illusion) by the East — for fear that we will become entangled in it — and by the West because it sees it simply as a non-material, cosmic dance.

In its infinite variety our sense-world has two poles which threaten to attract us. One fills us with fear (a prowling lion, a chasm, an earthquake, etc.), and the other with greed (a food shop window, a picture in a travel brochure, etc.) The observer's mind hovers between fear and greed. There are various ways of stating this basic polarity. Another would be the evolutionary approach: 'How did this tree, this animal, this stone become what I see now?' or alternatively the aesthetic approach: 'Is this phenomenon beautiful or ugly or sentimental?' But it is the cultivation of a third attitude, however, which offers an advance over the spiritual possibilities of the East. To declare the sense-world to be *maya* is only the first rung on the ladder which a human being can climb. To approach this third attitude the following deliberations are necessary. There is no doubt that a direct relation exists between one's consciousness and the object it perceives. *Maya* therefore relates to a consciousness which in its nature perceives the variety of the world — the acceptance of the illusory nature of the solid outer world is only due to our ignorance of the potentials of this consciousness.

But what if the variety of the world were in fact a challenge to our consciousness, asking us to do justice to it? Children perceive the world very much on their own terms. Only gradually does a consciousness emerge in which the variety of the world can be observed and mirrored with objective neutrality. Fear and greed are soul moods stimulated by what comes to us from outside — fear is caused by aggression or by something stronger than ourselves, while greed stirs up our soul from within. The third attitude, that of the *observer*, is one of stillness. We must cultivate stillness in ourselves, and in observing it we discover that within stillness lie hidden sources of activity which everyday life does not tap or challenge. The scientist's observation of phenomena out of his soul-stillness is only one side of the scientific activity of observing by which he proves himself in the technological achievements of the real world.

Another activity is connected with art. Painting and sculpture are not just imitations of Nature. (This becomes immediately obvious when we think of music or architecture.) Nor are these arts random or anarchic fantasies, but rather they are activities which make manifest the hidden nature of whatever is depicted. The variety of the world and of Creation is overwhelming, and yet for those of us who experience it so often, spring in European countries is overlaid with the grey veil of the 'accustomed', the 'normal', the 'named'. Even when faced with all the variety of a Greek spring, its differences in leaf colour and form — not to mention the glorious colours of geranium, bougainvillae, convolvulus, hibiscus and oleander blossoms — even when faced with this, we are capable of reducing everything (whether leaf, petal or fir needle), to processes similar to the investigations of modern physics. The variations of the world are quite beyond this kind of investigation.

The colourless sub-atomic world of pathways, patterns and relationships, of different electrical charges, is a world which has led to great achievements in medicine, armaments and technology. The variety of creation, however, has remained entirely unobserved and unused by technology. If art is neither an imitation nor a reproduction of nature; if it is not a subjective, random or anarchic fantasy, then what is it? In the past, this question was answered by describing art, especially painting and sculpture, as representing the idea in physical form. Rudolf Steiner described art as fulfilling nature — taking nature as incomplete, art is meant to complete it. How is this completion to come about?

> 'For the creature was made subject to vanity, not willingly, but by reason of him who hath subjected the same in hope. Because the creature itself also shall be delivered from the bondage of corruption into the glorious liberty of the children of God. For we know that the whole creation groaneth and travaileth in pain together until now.'
>
> (Romans, 8: 20–22)

So the answer is by letting nature take part in that which is the privilege of the human being alone: morality.

The history of painting in the last hundred and fifty years is simply this — an attempt to imbue nature and one's own reactions to her phenomena with love, hate, tragedy and drama; solutions that let the world of nature and the world of the human soul interweave and interact. The human being speaks: nature is silent. The soul is invisible, apparently colourless; words, gestures and appearances are her means of expression. Plants express themselves in form and colour; animals, additionally, in movement and sound. The word of the human being is in its early beginnings. When humanity learns to let nature take part in the word, plants and animals will also take part, out of their innate goodness and empathy. This will require not only an acquiring of knowledge but one's will, one's activity, will also have to enter this process. Art is the first step. The red of the hibiscus, the leaf-form of camomile, the needles of a fir tree — all of these were once a part of the human being in order that his '*Gestalt*' could become a fitting vessel for his spiritual efforts. Nature seems to glow and appear to us from the outside. But we can, once again, widen our soul so that that which has become externalised may be internalised and become part of our soul-world.

> 'Earth! Invisible!
> What is your urgent command, if not transformation?'
>
> (Rainer Maria Rilke, *Ninth Duino Elegy*)

Surrealist art is the first sign of this. Rudolf Steiner described how in the future we will hear human speech in colours,[43] because empathy and goodness will entail listening to the forms and colours in which sounds and words are hidden.

In Indian mythology and Eastern spirituality, the human being was still an integral part of the world. Only the will of human beings retained the ability to lift itself back to its origin, to the creative worlds of the gods. Now, human will is strong enough to become apocalyptic, and gradually to permeate nature and the earth. As knowledge becomes part of human intercourse, part of social life, so knowledge and art will not only become interlinked, they will also become tools for each other — the creative will of the human being will have to enter knowledge. Paul's words quoted above point to this. The more our being is lit up by Christ, the more it will be able to permeate the earth with His Life.

CAMPHILL CORRESPONDENCE, VI 1989

'judge not, that ye be not judged'

This passage from the gospel (Matt. 7: 1) is akin to the exhortation of the fifth auxiliary exercise:[44] 'Look at your surroundings, including people you know well, every day afresh, unbiased by your feelings and judgements of yesterday.'

How can this be done? First of all, judgements imply something almost fixed, unchangeable. Once we have judged, it is not easy to change our mind, be it about a person or how to hammer in a nail. This fact concerns our time, a time that strives towards the 'I am', towards self-righteousness, towards the security of my opinion. But only those who have achieved a certain level of 'I am' can feel free and able to climb the ladder towards the 'Self' — a selfless self, a choir in which the 'We' arises, not out of the security gained from the opinions of many 'I ams', but in listening to and praising the other one. Our judgements are usually wrong because they are too narrow. The context in which somebody acts in a certain way has to be discovered. It usually reaches back and around, covering unexpected areas. In making this discovery our judgement is thereby transformed into understanding.

But there is another major reason why it is so difficult to transform our opinions to make groups work successfully. Faced with the Mont Blanc of our ego, the other reasons are mere molehills in comparison. I exist because of my 'I am'; I have my own opinions because I achieve my 'I am', and if I lose them, I lose my existence. But it *is* necessary to lose the ground under our feet. In the second scene of the *The Portal of Initiation*,[45] Johannes, one of the main figures, says, in ascending one of the first steps of his inner development:

> I was in each; [in each one who spoke]

But for myself, I died.
(From springs and rocks there sounds:
O Man! Know thou thyself)

We are all like Johannes. Living here in Botton, we are all undecided whether to stay for a day or for thirty years, but we also have a desperate fear of losing ourselves, of letting the other person be heard too loudly within ourselves. However, we will rise again out of the others, from the periphery, from the 'springs and rocks', as a different 'I' from the one we were before. But we are afraid of becoming different. We are deeply in love with ourselves as we are and as we were.

All social rifts are simply fear. On one bank a small group huddles together, leans against each other to gain a sham safety. This is because our fear is an esoteric fear — fear of the threshold that divides our ordinary existence from our supersensible existence.

This transition from 'I' to 'Self' is an individual process lasting not just a day but usually decades (although it could also be just a moment). If we took seriously the admonition to 'judge not', either in the context of the gospels or in the context of the auxiliary exercises, we would feel an unspeakable relief. The ability to judge is one of the thorns of the consciousness soul, one of the main burdens of our time. We will only learn to use it without wounding the other person, and thereby ourselves, if we transform its aim and participate in world citizenship of our time.

BOTTON VILLAGE NEWS, 31 VIII 1990

the moon landing and the atomic bomb

The world in which we live reveals itself to us in a threefold way:

1 There are the material, measurable objects in space.
2 There is the whole realm of our feelings, of sympathies and antipathies, of aesthetic values, of colours, sounds and speech.
3 There is the sphere of morality and of goodness, the realm of deeds.

What was so frightening about the astronauts' landing on the moon (21st July 1969) was that all of a sudden the moon was reduced from a threefold world to a purely material totality. This material totality is different from our earthly one, but the spacecraft overcomes earthly conditions such as gravity and atmosphere by reckoning only with matter (*see 1 above*). Karl Marx 'invented' dialectical materialism — for him everything that is ideological rises like smoke from the only reality there is, namely the economic field. Photographs of the moon are like Marx's conception of the economic life. And one day feeling and moral evaluation (*see 2 and 3 above*) may rise like smoke from the ashes of a purely material consideration of the moon. The spacecraft and the moon landing seem to prove that there *is* nothing but matter (*3*); colours and sounds are reduced to their wavelengths etc., and everything works according to the calculations of physics. Unfortunately, we have only material science, not an aesthetic or moral one. 'Proving' is therefore the only 'scientific' touchstone we have.

Another event took place in a different set of circumstances, although it was also based on physical scientific and mathematical calculations. Perhaps the two occurrences will illuminate each other. Dropped by the Americans, the first atomic bomb fell on the morning of the 6th August 1945. On that occasion, and without any warning, hundreds of thousands of people were maimed, burnt or killed in the course of a few short minutes. And then, induced by the tornado-like suction of the air, an inferno of indescribable fire storms raged for hours afterwards. The yellow-orange light of the exploding bomb was infinitely larger, more intense, more blinding than anything human eyes had ever seen.

There was a time when the world was reasonably secure and human life was comparatively easy because a stable relation existed between all three realms (*see 1, 2 and 3*). These two events — the moon landing and the dropping of the atomic bomb — are both beyond the frontiers of earthly material events. Who knows what aesthetic values or moral judgements (*2 and 3*) may arise to equal their oversized nature? The moon landing revealed an apparent lack of feeling and morality (*2 and 3*). The atomic bomb, on the other hand, left an enormous amount of pain and destruction in its wake, although Japan's surrender followed four days later.

But what if quite different feelings and morality (*2 and 3*) were added to these two materialistically considered events (*1*); events which, like metal tempered in fire, would have to prove Christianity in a quite different way from the way in which the early martyrs proved it in the Roman arena? We might imagine that, just as the atomic bomb was dropped on Japan by the Americans, so will Japanese zest, industrial efficiency and a certain un-European exuberance explode into America. But it will explode in an inhuman, gigantic way that is as yet unimaginable. We can only hope this will be accompanied by what should belong to our understanding of the moon landing. In the future, to be Christian will mean remaining faithful to the totality of what is human, and to that alone.

BOTTON VILLAGE NEWS, 21 XI 1969

space

The mastering of space is one of the most impressive aspects of mankind's evolution. Only the human being has the unique experience of space as a composite of the senses of sight, movement, balance and the varying stages of self-consciousness. In space there are animals too, but they experience themselves in a network of sights, smells, surfaces and time. Movement seems to presuppose space, but only human movement — animal movements are complete because they are space-less. A human being's movements, whether free or restricted, are as incomplete as the individual who moves; they are dependent on the individual. But one fox moves like any other.

Only the human being builds. Animal buildings are nests (whether simple or complex), but architecture — buildings in space — exists only in the world of the human being. In Hindu culture, 'to have space' not only meant belonging to the ruling class, it also signified belonging to the Brahmin caste, to those who were endowed with heavenly wisdom. The palaces of kings or the nobility were built not only with a lavish use of space but, both in their forms and in the gardens surrounding them, they retained an after-glow of priestliness in their pomp. They can be contrasted with the hovels in which the majority lived; those who did not belong to the ruling class.

From the French Revolution on into our time this has gradually changed. The skyscraper is the exact opposite of a palace because its form derives from the premise of 'no space'. There was no space on the island of Manhattan so they had to build upwards. In the hovels of the past there was no space either. It is one of the most unfortunate errors of the 19th century Liberal and Labour Movements to think that overcrowded housing was essentially to do with lack of money — it had to do with a lack of spiritual qualities and knowledge as well as of money.

Rudolf Steiner said that our spatial knowledge (astronomical, terrestrial and chemical) is of the greatest importance for the gods.[46] Only we human beings can have spatial knowledge; knowledge determined and fashioned by space. In bearing it up, in spiritualising it (for instance in objective thought), we fructify the spiritual worlds. But we do not spiritualise our spatial knowledge by building skyscrapers. The 'upward' is a materialistic imitation and has a certain similarity to the Tower of Babel. It is significant, even ominous, that the United Nations Organisation is housed in a huge skyscraper.

We spiritualise spatial knowledge if we live in space with compassion. Only by so doing can the eternal problem (at least here in Botton) of wanting to put too much into the timetabled evening activities, or how many we can squeeze into a house, be understood. We must live, but without self-sacrifice we will simply exist, and we will never have space. Only in having no space do we re-conquer the social organism for the heavenly wisdom; we penetrate our 'pariah-ness' with 'Brahmin-hood'.

To arrange space is an extremely Christian, and therefore difficult, virtue. If we want to have space, we are victims of an Ahrimanic illusion, and some future guillotine (although perhaps not a steel one), will kill us.

BOTTON VILLAGE NEWS, 26 VI 1964

august nature: the shadow of death

It is a stirring sight in an August landscape to see the contrast between the darkening greens of the deciduous trees and the ripening yellow of the corn, both of which started as the light green of spring in April. In the August light those darkening trees give a particular roundness to the landscape against the brightness of the cornfields; they give it a sculpted look which it did not have during the preceding quarter of the year and which seems to be endorsed by the rising arc of the moon's course in the heavens — which will be as high at Christmas as the sun's arc was at St John's time — and the lowering, autumn-heralding arc of the sun. In autumn, the corn will be harvested and the leaves, after their short flaming-up in orange, yellows and reds, will turn brown, wither and fall, leaving the branches bare.

For the observing heart this August picture contains the first fading of summer and expresses the path of nature from St John's to Michaelmas: to the radiant, heat-ripened corn that we will later eat. The August picture celebrates the entry of high summer into the fruits of the earth, its fire-hot light creating new form in the landscape before the leaves drop and sink towards darkness. Our souls are suffocated by the growing, darkening weight of matter and we long for the autumn winds to blow away all that is decaying, and leave us only the concentration of matter in corn and fruit.

The interaction between nature and humanity is very much more complicated than theories about pollution would have us believe. The human being is not merely a higher animal. Science in the future will discover how the digestion and metabolic processes work quite differently in animals and human beings. Animals are principally at one with their food, as much a part of nature as their food is. We, on the other hand, stand apart, opposite to our food. For us eating is not merely the interiorisation of something external, as the grass is for the cow or the hazelnut for the squirrel. It is an event, shared if possible with others, a moment where the 'I' meets the 'not I'. Our breathing is also different. There is a special relationship between human beings and the plant world in that we breathe in that which the leaves breathe out.

The aim of evolution is the development of consciousness; not just of an intellectual kind, but as a progressive heightening of actual experience. From that level of consciousness there could arise the morphological understanding of plants as pioneered by such luminaries as Goethe, Portmann and Rudolf Steiner[47] and which gives rise to the *creative* consciousness out of which new knowledge, art and social deeds evolve. Plants — with which, in the far past, we enjoyed a close kinship — are an image of what we will become in the future and we are already allowed at least to breathe them in.

The August picture of nature, focused in the ripening yellow and the darkening green, seems to be issuing a call to the human being — summer's unfolding is completed and her embrace is loosening.

As Christ goes into Jerusalem for the Passover, He speaks to His disciples about His death and resurrection, but the disciples understand nothing of what He says. Outside Jericho, Christ heals a blind man; the blind man is the blindness of the disciples.

The growing, thickening heaviness around us during August envelops us in a dark curtain. More and more, we are fettered to a prison of matter, and are thus forced to become blind to Christianity.

In the *Soul Calendar* verse for the third week of August (although it spreads its mood over the whole time between summer and autumn), the August mood is taken for granted and then goes a step further:

> Thus do I feel my own existence
> That it would, far from the world,
> Become extinguished
> And if it would build only on its own foundation
> Would kill itself.

Calendar of the Soul, verse 20, (late August)

If the surfeit of matter succeeded and throttled the soul, the soul would die; it would kill itself.

What the Book of Revelation calls 'the second death', the soul's death, could then take place. We die many deaths and are born again many times. Because we have many lives we can fulfil and redeem our destiny, and our soul can stay alive. Christ died once and rose, and the image of the human being was rescued once and for all. We can preserve and rescue Christ's deed for us only through many deaths and births. The second death, the soul death, can only happen once. Nature in August, and our condition in it, is a picture of that.

Arise! Fill yourself with courage in the gathering darkness of autumn to remain faithful to *your* light and warmth. If that summons is answered, nature will have a friend in the human being, a friend who does not wish to become one with her, to return to her enveloping summer, but a friend who through his understanding returns nourishment to her in his breathing and in his eating.

By reading the gospel passage and the *Soul Calendar* we fashion a coat of armour which will enable us to walk upright towards Michaelmas.

BOTTON VILLAGE NEWS, 25 VIII 1967 & BOTTON MIRROR, 22 VIII 1981

thoughts from vienna

Summer is much more 'summer' here in Vienna than in England. From my window in a house in the suburbs I gaze at orchards, trees and hills. The apples glisten red in the dark green foliage; a warm summer wind wafts through the trees and summer clouds throne the purple sky. The veiled tenderness of English summer days, as though the light and colours were gently wrapped in a cocoon, is completely absent. Here, the awesome beauty of nature gazes at you, yet it does so without attacking you. In Italy, or elsewhere on the Mediterranean coast, one can sometimes feel one is succumbing to the strength of the light, of the sun — the colours of the plants, the earth and the houses can be overpowering beyond endurance. Here in Vienna, the beauty, although awesome, never overwhelms.

One of the remarkable features of Vienna is its parks. They reach their glory in Schönbrunn, a large area of trimmed and tamed nature which takes about half an hour to traverse. Its wide avenues leading star-wise from roundels with ponds are lined with huge old trees, all cut back so that both sides of the avenues look like high walls. The other Viennese parks are smaller and seem like shining dew-drops fallen from the cascade of Schönbrunn — some more French in character, some more English, but always with the trimmed and clipped French style predominating. Despite their artificial forms these parks retain something of Nature in a special way that is connected with the famous Vienna Woods which surround Vienna in the northwest and west, a curved belt of wooded hills, vineyards and fields — a landscape of remarkable, eternal beauty. Its spirits must have inspired Vienna's special brand of culture, particularly its music, but also its theatre, its art, and architecture (not to mention the Viennese way of life), from the middle of the 17th century until the Second World War.

Within Nature, the human soul does not feel self-contained moods. The rushing of wind through the trees; light through the branches of a forest; a darkening of the sky by clouds; the drama of thunder and lightning — these are all events, but the human soul takes only an insignificant part in them. In a park there is also Nature, but blunted and unreal, as if it were holding its breath, and so the moods of the soul gain all the more reality. The colours, the forms, the air and the scents from the branches, the reflection of the ponds, the curve of the avenues, the flower beds and lawns demand not so much observation as moods; a tuning of the soul. They are *in themselves* not so much events as causes and conditions for soul-moods. Surrounding the park are its walls outside which is the town with all its noise and bustle, while inside the walls there is an area of stillness into which the soul can expand. And into these areas of stillness come the chords of music from the Vienna Woods, giving the soul-moods a background of reality.

What Rudolf Steiner meant by 'Middle Europe' is becoming a little more understandable. Nature, not static like a photographic still but changing through the course of the seasons is, in our time, one of the main portals leading towards Christ. The more the self, the ego, finds itself within this changing nature, the more the self becomes Christian. The more the self can behold the metamorphosis in the dance of the seasons, the more it grows and evolves.

'Middle Europe' is the ground, the lap of the evolving ego. Britain — not as a nation but as the constitution of its people — is the land of the consciousness soul. The British character is that of an observer. The veiled light, the shrouded vagueness of the English seasons with its mild weather, these do not involve the ego to the same extent as in central Europe and so the observer tends to come to the fore. Through the strength of Nature in central

Europe the ego evolves more strongly, but without the consciousness soul it tends to become violent and nationalistic, just as the consciousness soul without the involved ego tends to become self-righteous.

Britain and Middle Europe belong together.

BOTTON VILLAGE NEWS, 6 & 13 IX 1963

central europe and the east

Over the course of the past 250 years the area that is now Germany, although comparatively small, has been very active and important. First there were the many small 'states' (Saxony, Prussia, the Palatinate, etc.), each headed by a king or duke. Then, at the end of the Franco-Prussian War, in 1871 Bismarck brought about unification, and Germany was born with the King of Prussia at its head. Before, it had been an idea; now it was a nation, a legal, political reality. And eventually came the First World War.[48]

For central Europe, one of the worst outcomes of this was the birth of nationalism. Its evil flavour did not taint England, France, Greece, etc., nor had it anything to do with the many states which were formerly embraced by the idea of Germany. It arose out of the history of the empire created by Bismarck and led, first of all, to the rise of National Socialism and the re-founding of states which had once belonged to the Austro-Hungarian Empire. Among many consequences of the Second World War were the loss of the British Empire and the division of Germany again, this time into East and West, as well as a still further intensification of nationalism. And now a third stage, at the beginning of the Light Age, is our present situation. Increasingly the world is becoming westernised, and the fruits of nationalism are being spread. The so-called European Community is looming before us, as well as the threat of chaos in the East, now much intensified by events in Russia.

The mass emigration from Germany and Austria in the years between 1933 and 1939 seems to me an important event. People threatened by the concentration camps of the Nazis, the dissidents, a good many of them Jews, emigrated from central Europe to other parts of the world for artistic, human and political reasons. These people, though naturally integrating to various degrees into their new surroundings, created cultural islands wherever they went. They all felt themselves to be not only 'refugees from Nazi oppression' (as it was then called) but also bearers, missionaries of the ethos, the culture and humanity of central Europe, who could fructify their host countries (the Americas, England, France, etc.) with this spirit. Among them were anthroposophists and, especially, those who moved into the many Camphill communities. These felt themselves consciously to be offering their work, life and destiny in a Christian way to Anthroposophia.

Rudolf Steiner described how the 'German' folk-spirit incarnates and excarnates, how it breathed *in* during the 13th century and again at the turn of the 18th/19th centuries, and breathed *out* in the intervening periods.[49] It is conceivable that this folk-spirit incarnates for a third time into these small groups of German people all over the globe, instead of into the actual geographical entity of Germany in central Europe. The 'chaos from the East' only shows outwardly what is true inwardly for the United States, and also England and France. The longing for sovereignty of Croatia, Azerbaijan, the Kurds, the Palestinians, etc., is something very different from the longing to be an independent state. The spirit of our time moves towards federation and assimilation, not the creation of artificial states and boundaries. It moves towards income sharing and not individual possessions; towards a world economy rather than national economies. Could it not be that these little groups of refugees could become the vessel for the German folk-spirit, especially as the humanity of this spirit contains the mirroring of the nature of the other nations? While integrating into their host nations, those central European emigrants nevertheless maintained something of Middle European culture and humanity, including the ones who came to Camphill. Anthroposophical centres will begin to arise in the East as those countries come to themselves, including East Germany. Perhaps this 'East' will one day become part of the European Community?

With the emigration and then the partition of Germany, the geographical middle was gone. But more and more the heart will become a global one with any slight traces of nationalism that adhere to it disappearing. Rudolf Steiner mentions a lecture which the Austrian poet, Fercher von Steinwand, delivered to the King of Saxony in which he prophesied that the Germans would suffer the same fate as the gypsies and be scattered all over the world.[50] And a few years later, Rudolf Steiner also wrote a verse containing the line: "The German spirit has not reached completion or fulfilment."[51]

In the dawn of the Light Age, the destinies of the folk-spirits also change. Regarding the 'chaos from the East', the further east one goes (although not in the case of Germany itself), the more the *soul* comes to the fore while the unensouled western intellect recedes. When the concrete lid of (western inspired) communism is finally lifted, the previously suppressed soul will predominate in this chaotic element. This chaotic soul abundance is very much more human than the intellectualism of our westernised society, but another element is necessary — the idealistic thinking which, in the decades around 1800 in Germany, reached such an astonishing peak of glory in philosophers and poets like Goethe, Schiller, Novalis, Lessing, the Brothers Grimm, Herder, Hegel, Schelling and Fichte. It was as if a great flame from above set a whole sleeping forest alight. Idealistic thinking appeared not only in their philosophical works but also in their feelings. Generally, it permeated them with particular strength, clarity and purity.

The East has nothing of this. It does have strength and humanity of feeling, but it does not have the purifying element of the power of thinking. It was only that power of thought which dawned in Germany at the turn of the 18th/19th centuries that gave sufficient strength to these feelings from the East so that they were able to withstand the full brutality of the democratic intellectuality of the West. This Ahrimanic brutality tries to annihilate the ego, and rule the ego-less masses with 'statistical' goodness, while the East tries to swamp human beings with individual yet ego-less goodness. Only the power of idealistic thinking will hold the ego-balance of human beings between East and West, between intellectual democracy and sentimental goodness. We don't need a geographical 'between', but a middle must arise within each human being.

There are various obstacles to the permeation of the East by the Middle, and later on the East-in-the-Human by the Middle, the Lion in the Human. The main obstacle is that old shadow of nationalism, the geographical middle. Germany looks on Goethe, Herder, Fichte, Schelling, Hegel, etc., as part of an old-fashioned past, compared with the Neo-Marxists, Adorno, Habermas, etc., of present German culture. But these latter are not part of idealistic thinking because such thinking is a *quality*. It not only signifies a certain category of thinking which makes that thinking appear in strength, as a shining life, but it transcends the narrow confines of a certain period in the history of Germany. What is called German idealism is really something generally human.

Anthroposophy is without doubt the genuinely human idealism of our time, with Camphill as its social facet. Rudolf Steiner not only gave the name Goetheanum to the anthroposophists' central building but also described how those 'German idealists' would assume their real importance only in the future. When Camphill began, Dr König imbued us with a kind of thirst for these idealists, as the abundance of their books in each Camphill centre bears witness. If each anthroposophical island in the East could house such a library, something of that spirit of the 'thinking idealists' would develop which was all but crushed by an inhuman nationalism and the Ahrimanic world-economy — by the materialism of the later 19th century. Its blessing would be bestowed on that part of humanity which is 'of goodwill', and the Christianity of the sixth epoch might have a chance to permeate.

CAMPHILL CORRESPONDENCE, VIII 1991

the human being & the world

Describing the relationship between human being and world in the middle weeks of August, the Soul Calendar (verse 20) says that if the human being leaves the world and dwells only in him- or herself, then he slowly destroys himself. This means that anthroposophy can prevent the 'suicide' of our time. Such self-destruction is prevented not by Green parties, CND protests or whatever, but by anthroposophy — not merely by intellectual encyclopaedic knowledge of the human being and the world, but by being spiritually alive and dependent on one another.

The enormously successful endeavour of recent centuries was to separate the human being from the world. Through his one-sided knowledge the human being has increasingly come to dominate the world (surgery, artificial fertilisers, technology, etc.) and he now destroys it (pollution, atomic power). Sublimated and rarefied, this knowledge was expressed 'theoretically' by the philosophers of those centuries — by Locke and Hume, but mainly by Kant and Husserl — who all asked how the human being can approach and know the world.

Then at the end of the 19th century, against this prevailing view, Rudolf Steiner demonstrated in his *Philosophy of Freedom*[52] that the human being's thinking is part of the world, not in a subjective way but such that the world thinks in the human being. The idea of the world thinking in the human being became the foundation for anthroposophy — anthroposophy is the world transmuted into thoughts. The human being is encouraged to transmute these thoughts back into the reality of their origin, while being enriched and Christianised by his own karma and achievements. The Rosicrucian books from the first centuries of the consciousness soul (collected by Paul Allen,[53] mainly in English), show from different sides how the human being is a microcosm into which the macrocosm has transformed itself. Through his world-historic concept of metamorphosis, Goethe took this relationship a step further, and it was as if human thinking only then came into its own. The philosophers had taught human beings to be passive, unaware that their central ability was to think creatively with the forms of Creation, and thereby transform their passivity.

The human being is the microcosmic key to the macrocosm. Anthroposophy is the unfolding of the human being and the world. But the great danger is that we stare passively at what anthroposophy shows us and forget to think, to relate the various statements of anthroposophy to one another: forget to transform the human being from microcosm into macrocosm. The right kind of thinking enshrines freedom. Therefore Rudolf Steiner put the various building stones into our hands, but he left the actual building to our own activity.

The metamorphic relationship between human being and world is made more complicated by Nature, and also by the fact that our head is the metamorphosis of the body in our previous incarnation.[54] It is interesting that our speech originates between body and head, in the larynx. The World-Word, the creator of everything, is contained within the constellations of the zodiac and the planets. We know, as a kind of external appendage, that Jupiter corresponds to 'O', Aquarius to 'M'.[55] When we speak, the origin of the world is manifest in our words, but our language has been reduced to mere communication and has lost its creative power. This is a blessing because if the words we speak were not powerless, our social life (which is really founded on strict equality), would never be possible. When the managing director speaks to the messenger boy it is not his words which carry the power but the fact that he is the director. There will come a time when words, too, will have power. Even now the infinite number of people who speak express themselves in the tones of their language, and the spoken words themselves — not the content — convey tenderness, enlightenment, enthusiasm, sadness or goodness. It will become obvious that the divine in each person speaks, and as a result that the Divinity has as many shades as there are human beings on earth. The World-Word speaks as human word through each person. Their words will become an individualised starry firmament.

This can and will happen, but only when metamorphosis enters human experience; when we see (and do not simply stare at) how the various objects of our perception are not mere separate entities but that they transform one into another — branch into leaf, stem into blossom, will into consciousness, and many other still undiscovered transformations. The whole subject of metamorphosis is unexplored today. Art will play an important part in its discovery.

The metamorphic skeleton — the bones of the body becoming bones of the head (leg and toes, for instance, forming the lower jaw and teeth), with the invisible larynx and speech as the sign and symbol of the present — is an earnest image of the ongoing evolution of humanity and the world.

BOTTON VILLAGE NEWS, 31 VIII 1985

listening to music in vienna after dr könig's death

Music in Vienna sounds different from anywhere else. Whether it is chamber music in a small hall, the four holy players in their starched white shirts sitting on a podium, their instruments strangely at one with their movements, or an orchestra in a grand hall — a host held together by the flame of the conductor — the musicians are intent upon and devoted to the worlds which the music builds up and transfigures. Dressed in Sunday clothes and completely removed from daily life, the audience listens, and the listening (together with the devotion of players and conductor) has such a power that ordinary life becomes distant. Joys and sorrows, fears and expectations, all lose their weight and coarseness. It is like a play on a stage. Then, through the sun-like thunder of the music, the listening souls are as though clad in white garments, standing round the Throne of the Lamb.

The music may be Mozart or Beethoven, Schubert or Bruckner, but through this union of playing and listening within the unique setting of Vienna, these different sounds of music seem like variously carved doors leading into the same space, a space with a huge golden ceiling where the Spirit is present on earth, and the souls of those who have died are as truly present as those still living.

The central temple of this overwhelming and timeless mystery is the 'Musikvereinsgebäude'. Forty years ago it was exactly the same as it is today (but with a different audience, of course). On the ceiling of its main hall Apollo is painted with the nine Muses* because it was built in the middle of the last century in the mediocre, costly and ornate style of that time, a

---

*Urania (Astronomy), Clio (History), Thalia (Comedy), Melpomene (Tragedy), Terpsichore (Dance), Euterpe (Music), Erato (Love Poetry), Polyhymnia (Hymns), Calliope (Epic Poetry).

Baroque-Renaissance. The Renaissance meant the rebirth of learning, and Apollo seems to be the one who opens this mystery temple. Apollo slew the dragon Python in whose vapours the Pythia prophesied in Delphi. The dragon would have made the rise of the human soul impossible but because Apollo slew Python, a harmony of thinking, feeling and will in human soul life could emerge. Apollo as the god of music, Orpheus; Apollo as the god of medicine, Asclepios; and Apollo uttering the Greek mystery words 'O Man, Know Thyself' are but different facets of the power of killing the dragon. And it was Apollo who was later born as the Nathan Jesus described in the Gospel of St Luke.[56]

The immortal 'I' is meant to shine more and more in the human soul, and with the killing of the dragon a soul space was won into which the light of the 'I' could radiate. Music was (and still is) like the windows that carry this light into the soul, and musical instruments are like the weapons with which the dragon is fought. Mars is the god of war and of sound, and there is something of war and weapons in the shape of the bows of violin and cello, in the sound of trumpet and drum. And it is the iron of Mars that makes our blood red.

We have our soul life on earth. Through the killing of the dragon a soul space developed in which thinking, feeling and will were able to balance each other and incarnate. But this killing was at the same time a taming, a taming through music. The longing for the angel who carries our immortal 'I' wafts through us more or less unconsciously, for within our soul space we are like prisoners in darkness. Music — but especially music in Vienna — carries us into the golden, innocent space of our existence. The primeval power of the Golden Fleece seems to be not only Apollo's garment but also our own soul's angelic fount. Eternal youth breaks in on us borne on the streams of music.

BOTTON VILLAGE NEWS 13 V 1966

compassion

The sun, moon and stars accompany the earth's out-breathing wherever it happens to be spring or summer. In winter our home is the house, in summer our home widens out into the widths of the world and we find ourselves sheltered in the air, warmth and light, enclosed by mountains, under the vault of the stars. In autumn all this changes, the dark and cold increases, the leaves on trees and plants wither and decay but the fruits ripen, harden and sweeten. And that which is fruit in nature is equal to compassion in our souls.

The whole world is interconnected and interwoven. Each created form and each substance is the outcome, the crossing point or point of densification of world powers streaming downwards, upwards or horizontally. For a human being to have compassion, empathy, there must be objects and events outside him which give rise to inner feeling. But the inside cannot be soul alone — otherwise animals would also feel compassion — it must be soul permeated by will and the being of a self, a human ego. Growth always has something selfish and self-willed about it; the powers and forces which make plants and us grow allow us to become visible.

Fruits are selfless, they ripen in the midst of growth that has decayed, they feed us and they contain the seed for the next generation. It is the same with compassion; human thinking and feeling are resurrected within the inner soul space of the surrounding creation. The reverence of a Buddhist or the declaration of an Albert Schweitzer are but single stones in the vast edifice of compassion. We can have compassion not only for the world of life, but also for the inorganic world; for dirt or disorder in a room or passage, for roads, rivers or quarries. We can feel compassion for animals and human beings but we should not pour sentimentality over things and beings, we should see things objectively. We can have compassion for everything in the world (even, for instance, tram rails, a sentimental view of which might be 'O dear, they always have to bear the weight of the tramcars!'). Or we can have compassion for the embarrassment, tiredness or frailties of human beings. Then something happens; our soul, although we cannot see the change, starts to become weighty and real.

Our time imbues us with a continual autumn mood. Our soul is always half slipping into the withering decay of autumn and is in danger of being engulfed by the sadness and growing darkness of the end of the year. It is in danger of being swallowed by or fettered to the physical world, which is bound by the law of becoming and dying.

If we do not strengthen our souls through compassion, we will never learn about an existence beyond death, or even about freedom. The teacher of this freedom is autumn when the physical world decays and threatens to engulf our soul. And the guardian of this freedom is Michael whose gaze evokes the dignity of humanity. This dignity can unfold only in the freedom found through compassion. The human soul then shines as a sun. The verse of the *Calendar of the Soul* preceding the Michaelmas verse calls upon this reality of the soul in the light of Michael:

I may now to myself belong
And radiantly spread inward light
Into the darkness of all space and time.
To sleep inclines all natural Being.
The depth of soul shall waken
And waking carry sun-filled glow
Into cold winter-floods.

Calendar of the Soul, verse 25

BOTTON VILLAGE NEWS 30 IX 1966

~ michaelmas

the seasons as macrocosm of the microcosm

From Rudolf Steiner's teaching we learn that we human beings cannot just be regarded as separate from the world around us. Our soul, our consciousness, is not simply life *inside* our skin, but extends beyond it into our surroundings. It is very moving to ponder the seasons in this respect.

Human will and metabolism correspond to heat and summer, while human thinking, nerves and brain correspond to autumn and winter. That which is *outside* is simultaneously within our soul and body space, breath/air and pulse/blood connecting the two poles. Through our senses of sight, smell and hearing we can experience an autumn or winter landscape, a symbol of thinking, while the growth of leaves, flowers and fruits of spring and summer are symbols of our metabolism and will. Our waking, head-nerve organisation looks like an autumn or winter landscape; our sleeping metabolism like a summer one.

Here something is revealed stretched out in time which, within ourselves, takes place only under exceptional conditions, namely, the separation of thinking, feeling and willing.* Within our soul-space, thinking, feeling and will are intermingled, as depicted by the Mixed King in Goethe's *Fairy Tale of The Green Snake and the Beautiful Lily*.[57] Thinking always contains an element of will — we *want* to imagine something. And likewise, our will is always guided by a thought, an idea. Both thinking and will are therefore always tinged by an element of sympathy or antipathy, interest, love or disgust. In the course of the year, however, the pole of consciousness (thinking) is not just autumn and winter magnified enormously, majestically, but is also completely separated from the pole of will, which, similarly magnified, is spring and the height of summer.

The course of the year reflects our whole soul. That which is compressed in

---

*Unrestrained will can lead to violence or terrorism; untempered feeling to religious fanaticism, drug dependency etc., and abstract thinking can lead to cold indifference. Ed.

a continual 'now' in the continuous moment of soul space expands into a time sequence in the unit of one year.

BOTTON VILLAGE NEWS 24 XI 1967

magic & faith

When Moses threw down his rod before the Pharaoh and it turned into a snake (Exodus 4: 3–17), we have the exact transition from magic to faith. To turn a staff into a serpent is a magical act. But in the Biblical description of Exodus, a 'sign' presupposes something like faith — an inner concentration, not simply an outer sequence of actions or words. The historical exodus, the rising of the Hebrew people to their essential destiny, had its fountainhead in the burning bush out of which the words 'I am the *I am*' came to Moses. The plagues preceding the exodus were, superficially, like a struggle between Moses and the Egyptian magicians, or, to put it another way, between the Jewish god and the Egyptian gods. But it was chiefly a struggle between faith and magic. Therefore, Pharaoh's heart was often hardened. Faith is something invisible and again and again Pharaoh doubted its reality. But it was not only Pharaoh who doubted; the Israelites worshipped the Golden Calf when Moses was called to Mount Sinai. Jewish history preceding the Epiphany of Christ is a history of the battle between faith and doubt, from the judges, Saul, David and Solomon up to the Roman occupation.

There is a great difference between the faith required of the Jews in the laws of Moses and the faith of which Christ spoke. The Christian faith is connected with the *transformed* serpent — the serpent which tempted Adam and Eve; the serpent which had been the staff of Moses; the brazen serpent which Moses lifted up on a pole whose sight healed the Israelites from the tortures of the fiery snakes, as well as the 'sons of the serpent' (wrongly translated as 'generation of vipers') with which words John the Baptist addressed the multitude. Goethe's *Fairy Tale of the Green Snake and the Beautiful Lily* is one of the great creations of the age of the consciousness soul. In an archetypal, precise yet pictorial way it contains the main purpose of our time.

The life and death of John the Baptist was the end of the age of magic. The following words in Goethe's *Fairy Tale* herald the beginning of the age of faith:

Old Man: 'Whether I can help, I know not; an individual helps not, but he who combines with many at the proper hour.'

Old Man: 'Let each perform his task, let each do his duty; and a universal happiness will swallow up our individual sorrows, as a universal grief consumes individual joys.'[58]

The snake symbols are facets of the individual self. We had to be cast out of Paradise for the sake of the development of the self, which lives in the warmth of our blood, which suffers and creates our karma. But until Christ came to earth humanity had developed increasingly towards egoism. Magic is something essentially egotistical — the power of the snake is needed to overcome the laws of nature, to transcend human consciousness. Even in 19th century spiritualism, in stories about Mme. Blavatsky, we can recognise this in a vague, misty way.

Faith also presupposes our ego but as something essentially social, 'who unites with others'. It was the mistake of Protestantism to think that faith takes place only between the lonely individual soul and God, thereby trying (in vain) to make faith into something selfish. Faith recognises, and at the same time believes in, the other person. Brotherliness, in the sense of becoming aware of and beholding the 'You', is the basis of faith.

The ideals of the French Revolution — freedom, equality and brotherhood — although an outcome of the same spiritual time period as Goethe's *Fairy Tale*, were the same as St Paul's faith, hope and love. They are the three sides of the incarnated human ego.

The snake played its part in order that faith, hope and love could develop but its rôle has come to an end. Faith is the basis for love and hope, as brotherliness is the basis for equality and freedom. The sacrifice of the snake forms the pillars of the bridge of love between the earthly and the heavenly land on which the children of hope, no longer sons of the serpent, can walk.

BOTTON VILLAGE NEWS 7 IX 1962

the french revolution & the idea of metamorphosis

Rudolf Steiner said in the lecture cycle *Karma of Vocation*[59] that the same impulse, the same 'world-historic soul blood', flowed in Goethe, Schiller, Herder and Lessing as in Mirabeau, Danton and Robespierre. He then showed how through their different constitutions the same impulse resulted in numerous works of art in Goethe, while in Danton etc., it had strong effects in the physical world. But what impulse was it? It was the impulse to become aware of and understand, celebrate and praise, *incarnation*.

For about thirty years before and after 1800, a wave of artists swept over

Europe. A great many men and women were stirred to dramatic, literary and philosophic creativity — Keats, Shelley, Blake, Kraszynski and Mickiewicz, Manzoni, Lavater, Troxler and Carus, Goethe and Schiller, Novalis, Fichte and Schelling. From this list of names we can see that nationality was relatively unimportant. It is a European brotherhood united by a single bond; that of love for the human being 'created in the image of God'. This does not refer to being in a theological sense but in an idealistic sense; not a denominational phrase but one heralding a new scientific religion or religious science. Goethe was undoubtedly the peak of the wave for not only are all his writings illumined by the invisible light of the human being, but at the heart of his output is the idea of metamorphosis:[60] metamorphosis is the apex of the wave. Because the idea of metamorphosis was forgotten, the materialistic world view began to dominate and became the chief way of explaining the world, and the headlong advance of technology (nuclear energy, space travel, etc.) seems to confirm this materialistic conception of the world.

In a hidden way thinking became paralysed. Matter with its attendant chemistry, its atoms, molecules and their apparent structures, caught and fixed the human gaze. But the *form* of matter, the shapes of creations, the universe as a vast physiognomy, matter as a vessel for the spirit — all these ideas became shrouded and hidden. For science today, the idealistic humanity of the artists around 1800 is unfounded and meaningless. And yet the idea of metamorphosis, the idea of the invisible all-embracing archetype appearing in physical space in various and successive forms, will cause the idea of incarnation to alter present day illusions through its very truth.

In France this idealistic wave took quite a different form. There were no artists to speak of, but there was the French Revolution that began in 1789. Here, too, the dawn of the divine human being inspired the souls preparing the revolution. It was the same invisible archetype but it appeared in social forms rather than in natural ones, although it is difficult to discern in the turmoil of those events amid the abolition of kingship, aristocracy and hierarchy. But what was root, leaf and flower, or light, colour and darkness[61] for Goethe, was liberty, equality and fraternity for the revolutionaries. What for Goethe was the oncoming flood of materialism, was for the French Revolution the goddess of Reason — but the unity of liberty, equality and fraternity led in the end not to a new social order but to a blood bath, and the rise of Napoleon.

Incarnation — only through spiritual science can we understand that the archetype appears in many successive metamorphoses. It is only today that the way to an active understanding of it can be found in the social order as well as in nature. The fountainhead is the golden, the silver and the bronze kings of Goethe's *Fairy Tale* embraced and constituted by the human soul.

BOTTON VILLAGE NEWS 29 III 1968

on the consciousness soul

'I let the objects quietly impress me, then observe their effect, and then try to reproduce them faithfully, unfalsified.'[62] (Goethe)

This seems to me to be the perfect description of the consciousness soul, the soul activity, quality or ability of our time, which will develop, expand and metamorphose for hundreds of years to come. It began seed-like in the 15th century Renaissance. This ability of the consciousness soul to *observe* both itself as well as the world around it has two consequences. With one gaze it can look inwards, but to begin with it is unable to distinguish between reaction and observation, while with the other gaze it learns to say 'I' (I think, I walk, etc.), by distancing itself from the world, from the observed. Before the 15th century the world and soul were too closely interwoven to enable people to say 'I'.

For the hygiene of our soul as well as for our social life, it is vital to distinguish between reaction to, and observation of, an object. In social life it is only by distancing ourselves that we are able to observe, but we cannot love, we can only *judge* the other one. By reacting we gain our opinions but we are biased. Science reduces its findings to what can be measured, weighed and counted. It is obsessed with observation through apparatuses, but has no theories for many of its findings. This is because of its great fear or prejudice that the human being can never really observe, he can only react. As the quotation above shows, Goethe was the first to try to base science on observation, and because anthroposophy does this too, the Goetheanum was named after him.

To tear observing and reacting apart is an effort of will. If we succeed in doing so it becomes possible, through a thinking observation of society, to understand the reality of a Threefold Social Order, the three kinds of money[63] (gift, loan and purchase), and the Fundamental Social Law. But we are surrounded by remnants of the fourth post-Atlantean epoch, by the old modes of thought, feeling and will that gave rise to universities, hospitals, banks and other arrangements and which force us to experience the world of nature and of society through the distorting 'spectacles' of past customs and habits. With active, understanding observation both fresh and immediate — with childlike, 'unbespectacled', unbiased curiosity — we could then get to grips with the world.

We now take learning and working as *one* human activity. In the past they were separate and hence castes and classes were necessary. They have become one because in our time the human being, man or woman, *harbours* in his soul the ability both to work and to learn. It seems sensible that industry (or in Camphill, our workshops) feeds on money as well as engaging with the spiritual, the learning activities of life, because these belong together, as they do in the human being, with thinking and will.

The illusion that money is something solid, something which can be shifted from place to place, also belongs to the aforementioned remnants of the past. Marx was quite right in denouncing the selling of labour. The spiritual life seemed to him to be the ideal because the economic life was so full of injustice. In using the phrase 'dictatorship of the proletariat' he showed that he believed the spiritual life to be no more than ideology. He saw the cultural life of the non-proletarian classes as ideology and he could not distinguish ideas from ideology.

Anthroposophy is the guide to unbiased but active observing which is the outlook on life that is appropriate to the consciousness soul. Without this guide we would be unable to rid ourselves of our prejudices. To say that salary differentials in our time are inhuman is merely to react, but reacting always has something self-righteous about it, spawning short-sighted thoughts and opinions. Rudolf Steiner's guidance in active observing is seen in his insight that the distribution of earnings among those who work in a social organism should be according to their needs (whether manual or white collar worker), and the surplus donated to a cultural organisation. The human being must not only work but also learn; he has limbs and a head, and his Spirit and ego-bearing blood flow through both, making them the bearers of consciousness or will; making them light or heavy. If we love to work manually and earn our livelihood thereby, our cultural longings and abilities may remain untapped, but with non-manual, professional work it would be the other way round (i.e. not doing justice to our 'manual' side). What could be more reasonable than that the surplus of our earnings goes to the cultural life? Those who work do so for the cultural-learning side of the life in which they also live.

Observing seems to us to be something passive — active, unbiased observing means the rescuing of present-day humanity.

BOTTON VILLAGE NEWS 28 II 1992

goethe the poet — goethe the scientist

The question of why and how Goethe's art and science originated from the same source, and why and how this common source was the historic and spiritual precursor of anthroposophy and of the Goetheanum, is indeed an interesting one. The following is one possible approach to an answer.

If we try to imagine conditions on Atlantis, guided not only by descriptions but also by the thoughts and insights of Rudolf Steiner's spiritual science[64] concerning evolution, we notice first and foremost that compared with our time everything was less formed. Earth and stones were not separate as they are today. Swamps abounded, mists clouded the air, and the light of sun, moon and stars never penetrated the water-laden atmosphere. There were hardly any flowering plants and only during the course of Atlantis did the animals develop into mammals. Atlantean times were dominated by water and by life forces. There was no dry land as yet, and it was not until after the submerging of the last remnants of Atlantis that the separation of water and earth was completed.

On Atlantis, the ground resembled strange, mossy pillows of hard and soft textures. The life forces gave a kind of living quality to these mossy pillows. Nothing was inorganic or dead; even bark, nails and cartilaginous materials were permeated with life forces. Leaves, plants and tree-like forms were enormous. Amongst all this the human being was a tender, flexible, transparent being. Only in the course of Atlantean development did he acquire a more stable, more material, and at the same time a more human form. Before that, his physical aspect (though not his immortal soul) was either in the image of a lion, a bull or an eagle. However, he was an upright being whose motion was a swimming-cum-walking one.

Around the middle of Atlantean development all this gained a certain stability. From then onwards, consciousness started to override and suppress the abundant life forces. The human being's sense of his own inner being, which had hitherto been experienced primarily through memory reaching back through many generations, became transformed into the ability to think. The living world expressed itself through sound. The human being made sounds too, and he related to all that was around him, communing with it. But this world was somehow dim and colourless, even though it was alive in its multitude of sounds.

Only when Atlantis submerged, when the fog and clouds dispersed and sun, moon and starlight could shine down and illuminate the earth — only then were the tremendous life forces tamed and transformed, becoming the landscapes and seas that we know more or less as they are now. Through the taming of these nature forces, humanity lost the ability to commune with nature, and all became silent. If we are to understand Atlantis we should also know that there was no beauty there. Beauty is an essentially human concept and experience, of course, and since there was no beauty there was also no art which is so closely connected with it. It was necessary to describe this background in order to make the phenomenon of Goethe as poet and scientist understandable.

Newton, who was both a scientist and a theologian, had interests that ran parallel to Goethe's, but the latter's poetry and science were two branches arising from the same root. This is only possible if the artist feels his own creativity and the creativity of nature to be one. 'Beauty is the manifestation of the hidden laws of nature,' Goethe said.[65] If we try to imagine the development of nature in the time of Atlantis, from a state in which everything was transparent and diffuse to one of condensation and form; from the simple, vague, child-like and seed-like into differentiated, manifold, mature forms, we can imagine that humanity was, to begin with, simply part of evolution. Then, as Atlantis submerged and creation dried out, dry, barren land emerged among the waters and the multitude of plants and trees. The human being, however, developed consciousness, and by virtue of his consciousness he is no longer part of nature but an observer of it. At the same time he felt himself to be a messenger of the divine.

Humanity carried a multitude of formative forces in its consciousness which were destined to become paralysed in order that this consciousness could reach ever greater clarity and so achieve the individualised 'I am'. The height of this clarity is the intellectual, individualised thinking which is able to comprehend spiritual-scientific insights.

In the succeeding post-Atlantean epochs, art has been a kind of forerunner of advancing knowledge. In the future, knowledge will again be transformed into art, and art into a new nature. But in the first three post-Atlantean epochs, art was the creative power within our consciousness, the power which did not express itself in created nature but was used to express the divine.

The Egyptian epoch is the first post-Atlantean period from which a multitude of art objects has been preserved, representing the divine in a variety of forms — in the form of animals (mainly heads) such as lions, monkeys, birds; in the human form (sitting, standing or walking) and in plant forms, mainly the lotus flower. These nature forms, reverberating in human consciousness, were used to express the divine whose emissary the human being felt himself to be. But he was not simply an emissary because there was something divine in him also. With the development of knowledge, and especially of Greek philosophy in the fourth post-Atlantean epoch, art distanced itself from the divine, becoming an end in itself.

Goethe was the first who was convinced that art needs to become Christianised. Nature was created by the gods (stones, plants, animals, stars and the human being), but in artistic endeavour Goethe experienced a higher realm than that of Nature. Artistic creativity was for him an enhanced creativity of Nature. This kind of artistic endeavour is close to the pursuit of knowledge and the search for truth. In the course of millennia, not only has art become an activity in itself, but knowledge has also become a separate field, totally unrelated to art and just as distant from the divine as art has become.

Both art and knowledge are expressions of human destiny and purpose, but they have become separate, and because of this separation a third branch has sprung from the same root — religion. In the mysteries of antiquity the three were one, but these separated views of the world were necessary in order that each could develop its own distinct identity. Thus the human being was able to develop his predilection for one or the other without tearing himself apart. It is one of the miracles of our time that Anglican bishops can talk about the Gulf crisis* from a completely different standpoint than the politicians.

No doubt one of the tasks of our time is gradually to reunite these three separate strands, and it is understandable that Goethe was one of the first to try. His way of looking at nature, and his discovery of the archetypes, was the beginning of the divine art of Nature once again receiving recognition. Compared to divine Nature an artist is a dwarf, but it is only human activity that can create works of art. Hence Schiller's little verse is amply justified:

---

*Refererence to the impending Gulf war to liberate Kuwait from its Iraqi invaders.

In diligence the bee can be your guide,
A worm can teach you efficiency,
In knowledge higher spirits instruct you,
Art alone belongs to you, O Man.[66]

It is only in art that the human being creates. Only in creating works of art does he exist in the realm of freedom. And, as a human being, he has had to endure his long evolution through history in order to learn to be free, and out of this freedom to do the Good.

CAMPHILL CORRESPONDENCE, I/II 1991

proof

Seen from one point of view, there is no doubt that science plays a dominant yet sinister rôle in our time. Its way of thinking — strictly causal and logical — cannot encompass those aspects of life where causality makes no sense: in a work of art, for example, because here it is composition, not cause and effect or logic, that is essential both in producing it and enjoying it. Neither can causality apply in questions of morality in the widest sense, such as in the guidance of one's life. It cannot apply to human relationships, nor to inner or outer social and ecological standards, nor to what Rudolf Steiner calls 'moral intuition'; nor, even, to religion itself.

Someone may ask you whether you can prove something. If you are talking about reincarnation, or the greatness of Raphael, you become aware that proof is not applicable to moral or aesthetic questions, nor in the sphere of truth (except for scientific truth) in the same sense that a medicament can be proven 'scientifically' to be efficacious. But what does this mean? It means that regarding our relationship to the world, a large part of life seems to be a matter of taste, while a comparatively small part obeys what can be proven. A side-effect of this coercive power of proof is a laming of our individual thinking, of our common sense. Vast areas of our lives seem to be 'proven', although only some authority, without any proof, has declared it so. The enormous influence of Hitler can only be explained by the lameness of our common sense. Common sense is always something individual, while by its very nature proof compels each individual, obliterating the power of their differences of opinion.

There is, however, another mode of thinking. Thinking need not proceed from one detail to the next. It may take in the phenomena of the inner and outer world by grasping their forms and meaning, leading to an archetype, so that our experiences are at the same time creative, invisible, divine, and not, as it were, literally isolated from each other. Plato and Goethe[67] thought like this. Goethe's 'discovery' of the archetypal plant[68] in the botanical gardens in Palermo in 1787 is an example of an endless hierarchy of archetypes. With his understanding, naked eye he perceived how the leaves of palms, firs and deciduous trees, roses and columbines — *all* plants — are variations on the same theme, as also is the relation of leaf to stem or the bursting of the blossom. Each is another step towards understanding and being able to explain the plant organism. For this mode of thinking the metamorphosis of *forms*, of *Gestalt*, is as much a 'proof' as the physiognomic expression of smiling is for the one who smiles, whereas 'natural' science only researches the detailed muscle state of the 'smiling' event.

These ways of thinking have their dark and beleaguered shadows in today's reductionist and holistic thinking. Holistic thinking did not achieve much. Only anthroposophical thinking, combining both the intuitive and the modern scientific approaches, will bring about a renewed excellence of thinking, a thinking in which the archetypes will become *thoughts* because *concepts* are but the pale, lame images of the archetypes. In a saying which Rudolf Steiner often quoted, 'A wolf that is fed only on the flesh of lambs never becomes a lamb; it remains a wolf', we see that concepts (e.g. wolf) have a regulating, even a creative power. The moment we draw or paint a wolf we feel, and do not only think, its concept. By lifting it into the realm of the artistic we feel something of the creative power which conceived the wolf. But at the same time we feel something else: that the concept is not static. The wolf developed from being a baby wolf which was once an embryo, and it will also become old and die. The different concepts will then hold sway as time enters, which leads to an understanding of the truth.

One mode of thinking leads to the concept, another to the invisible archetype. In the second mode (that of the wolf remaining wolf in spite of eating lamb, and the various plant forms leading to the archetypal plant), art helps to guide our thinking. In the first mode, counting, weighing and measuring are the causal axioms which create the concept.

We can imagine our gaze beholding the radiance of the stars while our ability to think is reduced to concepts and thus the star map presents itself to our ordinary upward gaze. But the stars can also be seen as signs for the shining thrones of higher beings, not as they present themselves to our fantasy but as the result of metamorphosis, as in the archetypal plant.

These relationships also have a socio-political aspect. Governments, parliaments and newspapers would not dare to speak or think in the language of metamorphosis, of archetypes or the holistic mode of thinking. But many ordinary people in the electorate of the various countries feel and direct themselves not to the stars, but to the ones who sit on the thrones. The question of our time is not 'Should we vote Labour or Conservative' but rather, 'Are governments, parties and political powers appropriate to democracy, to the will, the insight and the understanding of *all* people?'

BOTTON MIRROR 22 XI 1991

the red window in the west

The red window of the Goetheanum lies in the west of the building. Light flooding in from outside makes it visible and, although there is the wall of the auditorium in between, the window looks towards the east of the building where the statue of the Representative of Man should have stood, carved in wood — wood which is the result of death in streaming life; death into which came the power of the incarnated Christ.

The red window depicts a face with a nobly earnest countenance and an overwhelming innocence. Surrounded by the hair, the beasts, the lotus flowers, the face seems to enfold paradisal life, and above it is the quietude of the planet Saturn.

All those leaving the Goetheanum have to pass this gaze. Stepping out into ordinary life, into our profession or to meet our earthly circumstances, we always go to the West, so to speak. America is the land in the West whose light shines through the Red Window. The Red Indians are the Saturn race which had colonised that huge continent,[69] but as a result of their physical disappearance an enormous space has developed which longs for the Light of the Holy Spirit but which appears to be filled only with roads, cars and skyscrapers.

However, the West is also the direction from which the Fifth Gospel[70] comes, with its centrepiece the Reversed Lord's Prayer. On 20th September 1913, the foundation stone was laid for the first Goetheanum. The words that Rudolf Steiner spoke on that occasion culminated in the Reversed (or Macrocosmic) Lord's Prayer, which is really the original Lord's Prayer. The version with which we are familiar was turned round by Christ, line by line, so that the meaning is changed from looking down into the abyss to looking upwards. The original prayer begins with 'The Evils hold sway' and ends with

'And forget your Names, Ye Fathers in the Heavens' while our present day prayer begins with 'Our Father who art in Heaven, hallowed be Thy Name' and ends with 'and deliver us from the evil.' The original prayer stresses the fallen nature of humanity and the split in the cosmos caused by the Fall, but nevertheless we can call it the prayer of hope, as we can call our Lord's Prayer the prayer of love.

The central part of both prayers contain the question of the 'daily bread'. Our life on earth is about nothing else. The great human, Christian question is: How does each human being, in justice to both his eternal and his earthly being, receive his daily bread? Enlightenment can only provide a gradual answer. The Prayer of Hope and the Prayer of Love are words of freedom, and Michael is the guardian of freedom.

Anthroposophia was meant to have a home in the original Goetheanum but it was burnt down and something like a renewed seed of it was given in the Christmas Foundation Stone Meditation, in the centre of which are the lines, devoted to the Christ:

> Let enkindle from the East
> What is formed through the West.

On earth, physical form is always due to the powers of death. In the soul-house of the Goetheanum, death becomes the fount for a new form. The innocence of the gazing countenance shapes and moulds forms. Innocence is restored to earthly life as it is lit up through spiritual permeation. The Goetheanum is the physical expression of this spiritual light.

In an impressive way the American region of Camphill lights up the Red Window with great brilliance in the Goetheanum which Camphill tries to build. Anthroposophy has a home there because the gaze of the Red Window looks out upon everyone today who goes out from the Goetheanum to his earthly place and task.

BOTTON VILLAGE NEWS, 26 IX 1969 & 16 X 1970

hans heinrich engel

(b 29.7.1921, Greifswald, Germany, d 30.10.1973, Bern, Switzerland)

To think, feel and write about somebody who has died is difficult because one's feelings about the person change so much, as the one who has died rises and passes through many spheres.

Before and during the first part of the funeral, as he lay in the coffin with hands folded over his chest, his countenance was like that of a knight — an infinitely tender knight whose sword was bent moon-like (as described in the old Polish legend of Michael), into the frame of a lyre. He was a knight of music. And when the candles were lit for the first part of the funeral, and the host of lyres began to play, it was majestically moving to remember Hans Heinrich's compositions and all his efforts with music therapy. Music therapy is a virgin soil for curative education, and for the whole of music today, a soil which he began to plough and sow heroically.

Part of this majestic earnestness was to see, the night before (on the 1st November), the waxing moon and Mars, the planet of 'creative sound' (*des Mars erschaffendes Klingen*), shining in solitude and with great brilliance in the heavens.

As time went on, our meeting in St Prex in the first days of October, and Hans Heinrich's contribution to it (although it was far greater than this), came increasingly to the foreground in my memory. The autumnal setting of that meeting, the yellow-orange-green leaves against the blue sky, the thunder, the rain and storms, enhanced our endeavours in the light of Michael. And when we talked about the windows of the old Goetheanum, Hans Heinrich spoke in a new way about their progression; the two pink windows leading into the darkness of a threshold that opens into the space of the small cupola in which the Representative of Man stands in the centre.

He is now within the World-Word; he whose human voice came forth from the pulpit at the threshold leading into the darkness of the small cupola. Now he will be able to stand before the Son of Man whose image is the statue; the Son of Man whose earnestness is so full of comfort and relief, who places the karmic burdens that each of us carries into the setting of the whole of our being, before whom the load and guilt of earthly life melts into the boundless — the one who overcomes Lucifer and Ahriman.

BOTTON VILLAGE NEWS 16 XI 1973

the duality of evil

A new Christianity which tries to do justice to the Second Coming of Christ can arise only out of a new understanding of the human being, an understanding that appears in Rudolf Steiner's statue of the Representative of Man. This great carving was intended to stand at the back of the stage in the first Goetheanum, but because Steiner had not completely finished it, it was still in the studio and thus escaped the fire of midnight 1922–23.

In this statue the figure of Christ is seen between the two figures of Lucifer and Ahriman[71] both of which are depicted twice, each in their microcosmic and macrocosmic forms, the five together representing the full human being. We are shown that the main pillar which builds a new understanding of the human being must be a knowledge of the duality of evil. Knowledge of this duality is now dawning in the souls of human beings. Our hearts and minds mirror the reality of the world and humanity more truly than we like to believe. But the common contemporary world conception — a hazy composite of our education, popular opinion, newspapers and popularised natural science — comes between the world and our individual experience. As with rows and rows of identical houses, 'popular opinion' covers up all individual differences, and thereby blurs the experience of Luciferic and of Ahrimanic evil.

It is instructive to find, for instance in novels, that these two evils are described but not *met* by adequate comprehension. It seems to be part of the history of the Second Advent of Christ that the duality of evil was described more often in the period between the two world wars, and not so much before the first or after the second. In the great novels of the 19th century (by Dickens, Proust, Tolstoy, etc.), the two evils are intertwined in the dense emotional and physical realities described, but after the Second World War the duality is again hidden from human experience. In the books of Iris Murdoch, J.D. Salinger or Günter Grass, life separates into incoherent lumps which make the purpose of earthly existence appear wholly doubtful. In *The Outsider*[72] by Albert Camus and *Look Back in Anger*[73] by John Osborne, the last evening light of the sun of morality seems to be setting. It sets because knowledge of the two evils, which could have made a *new* morality possible, did not arise between the two wars.

Books convey the element of human experience and its metamorphosis over the course of time. But before describing two books which serve to illustrate my meaning, reference must be made to an aspect of Lucifer and Ahriman spoken of by Rudolf Steiner in his lectures *The Mission of Michael*.[74] He points out that one of the things which prevents the rise of Christianity in our time is the setting up of *one* evil — the Devil — against the Good. In this way the Good is not encountered but rather its Luciferic counterpart is. 'Thus,' he says, 'we must emphasise the fact that if a person wishes to conceive the structure of the world in a factual manner, he must acknowledge the triad, the two opposing elements of the Luciferic and Ahrimanic, and the Divine which holds the balance between the two. This must be contrasted with the illusion that has arisen in mankind's spiritual evolution through the erroneous concept of the dyad of God and the Devil, of the divine spiritual forces above and the diabolical forces below. This illusion forces the human being out of his position at the fulcrum by concealing from him the fact that a sound comprehension of the world can only arise from a proper conception of the triad. It is as though he is made to believe that the world structure is in some way determined by the dyad. Yet the highest human endeavours have fallen prey to this error.' Rudolf Steiner then cites John Milton's *Paradise Lost*[75] and Friedrich Klopstock's *Messiah*[76] as examples of works in which this dual principle is assumed. 'What does this really signify?' he asks. 'Nothing less than the removal of the Divine from consciousness and the usurping of the divine name by the Luciferic principle...'[77]

One modern book which seems to be an example of this is George Orwell's *Nineteen Eighty-Four*.[78] Though it was written soon after the Second World War, it belongs very much to the time before and during that war. Evil has shrunk to the Ahrimanic image of Big Brother and his state system, while Good has been transformed into the sentimental, Luciferic love story. This love story, which is meant to be the divine and human contrasted with the diabolic, is in reality merely the Luciferic against the Ahrimanic.

Another book showing that a real understanding of our time is not possible without the concept of the two evils is *The Innocent Ones*[79] by Hermann Broch. Though partly written in 1949 it ends with a description of Hitler assuming power. It describes the diabolic regime as the outcome of many individual jealousies, cruelties, envies, pleasure-seeking and ambitions of the years before. But the Ahrimanic can never be the outcome of the Luciferic; individual guilt can never become mass terror. The sum of individual guilt can hollow out the substance of the soul so that there is room for the other devil, but there can never be transition from one to another. One can never be the root and the other a flower of the same evil plant. Many other books could be described in this way, one of the greatest and most famous being *The Magic Mountain*[80] by Thomas Mann in which the world of Claudia Chaudrat and Mynheer Peeperkorn come up against the sanatorium organisation, modern medicine and the First World War.

Today's world view excludes the two evils, and because they are excluded the mystery of the two Jesus children remains hidden. There cannot be a new Christianity without knowledge of the two Jesus children. This knowledge belongs to our time because it belongs to the Fifth Gospel. Ahriman chains thinking and sense perception to a material universe, a closed dungeon in which incarnation and excarnation do not exist. Lucifer stirs up illusory and egoistic passions, the highest of which is the lust towards self-perfection.

The meaning of the two genealogies of Jesus — the one in the Gospel of St Matthew, the other in the Gospel of St Luke — was described by Rudolf Steiner in his lectures on *The Gospel of St Luke*[81] and also in *The Spiritual Guidance of Mankind*.[82] There were two Jesus children, not one. One child came through the Solomon line of the house of David, the other from the Nathan line of the same house. The significance of the two children and the nature of their subsequent union in preparation for the incarnation of Christ can be found in detail in Rudolf Steiner's course of lectures on *The Gospel of St Matthew*.[83]

In the lectures on *The Occult Significance of the Bhagavad-Gita*[84] it is made clear that the impulse of the Nathanic Jesus alone would have driven the human being into the arms of Lucifer. He would have gone back into the light and wisdom of Paradise but carrying with him the power of egoism which the ego has gradually developed since his expulsion from Paradise. Only through the power of Christ Himself can the separate ego become an integrated part of humanity and fraternity experienced, and thereby the taint of egoism be removed from us. Our aim is no longer self-perfection but the common perfection of humanity in brotherhood, which is the New Jerusalem. The Solomonic Jesus represents the reincarnating human soul. He is at the side of the human being who has been expelled from Paradise and who is learning to gain his ego by walking through the dark valleys of repeated earth lives, through the guilt of humanity; the human being whose guilt and karma has been woven into the karma of mankind.

ANTHROPOSOPHICAL QUARTERLY, AUTUMN 1967

h u m o u r

On the huge wooden statue which was intended to stand at centre back stage in the first Goetheanum, depicting Christ between the two devils of Lucifer and Ahriman, carved in the upper left hand corner appears a being whom Rudolf Steiner called the Being of World Humour.

The way in which the face of the Spirit of Humour was carved is remarkable for its rôle in the future of humanity. Looking at the half finished sculpture, Rudolf Steiner felt that in the left upper corner something was missing and he carved the Spirit of Humour there. This feeling that something was missing was not just an aesthetic feeling (which could have been answered in several ways), and could be resolved only by the emerging face of the Spirit of Humour. We can think clever thoughts about him such as the connection between Christianity and humour, but he came about as a work of art through the observing creativity of the artist.

This Being looks down on the majestic group. Christ between Lucifer crashing downward and Ahriman fettered, between Lucifer and Ahriman locked together, is a picture of human life on earth. Gustav Vigelandt's sculpture 'Pillar of Life'; Munch's many attempts; Rodin's 'Gates of Hell' and Gaugin's 'Whence come we?' all try to depict the tremendous upsurge of life stamped by the ages of humanity. But human life is always stamped, not only by the ages, but also by destiny. The moral life of humanity always veers either to the Ahrimanic or to the Luciferic side, it never reaches the pivot of perfect freedom. But this deviation is always destiny, karma, and karma is nothing other than the many balances made necessary by our deviations. In the statue, Ahriman and Lucifer are the source of karma. The whole statue shows Christ as the Lord of Karma, making the counterbalance not only possible but also beneficial to others.

The tragedy of human existence cannot be overcome in our time, but it can be borne through humour. The ability to have humour is one of the rising abilities of mankind. It behoves the human being to rise above himself and his condition, and it is one aspect of Christ, empowering and humanising him more and more. It is also, incidentally, a very English characteristic, a part of the instinctive consciousness soul.

The Spirit of Humour (and he is as much 'I myself' as the rest of the statue), gazes down upon the sufferings and achievements, the joys and sorrows of earthly life, and in looking at them is not completely involved in the movement of the scales. Our involvement in our own destiny is always something felt, something passionate, surrounded by clouds of emotion. Humour blows these clouds away and the mountain ranges of our destiny appear in shining clarity. Because humour is so connected with our freedom, with the innate Christianity of the human being, we suffer under the wrong kinds of humour — from cynical jokes or jokes which make us forget or ignore the clouds instead of blowing them away — thereby making us aware of our condition. For we are aware of our condition only when we behold the mountain ranges, and not the clouds.

Humour is an earthly accomplishment of the Christian, for without Christianity there can be no humour in the real sense, only heavy jokes. Humour does not balance our tragedies. It is not a fulfilment of responsibilities but the tragedies are necessary and are borne by countless beings in order that we may become useful bearers of responsibility in the World-All. We bear the clarity which we have won through humour into our pathways and landscapes after death.

BOTTON VILLAGE NEWS 15 I 1971 & 5 IV 1975

s o u t h

It is one of the archetypal human experiences to go through the Gotthard tunnel and experience north and south as qualities, not simply as abstract spatial directions. From knowing the northern side of the tunnel, with its grey clouds, cold winds, rain and mist, you go through the Alps in darkness for twenty minutes and emerge into the light, warm softness of the South. You see the romantic shapes of the mountains around Lake Lugano, the colours of the little Italian houses and churches, the sloping vineyards, the mulberry and olive groves, and you smell the indescribable and quite overwhelming abundance of the light-filled blossoms. It is a special bliss to traverse the dividing line between the wet, cold, dark North and the dry, light, warm South in twenty minutes.

One thinks of English and German poets, both famous and obscure, as well as painters who, at the turn of the 18th and 19th centuries and later during that century, crossed the Alps from the north and found in Italy a new home, a heightened form of earthly existence.

One of these was Goethe.[85] It is interesting to learn what influence his sojourn in Italy had on his thoughts and feelings, his artistic and scientific production and ideas. Like an image of the impact of the South, the whole Mediterranean splendour and culture on Goethe's central European soul, is the figure of Helena in *Faust*.[86] Faust sees her for the first time in the magic mirror in the witches' kitchen in *Faust: Part One*. In *Part Two* this is enlarged to the apparent union of Faust and Helena. It is surrounded by a host of mythological beings and events — they even have a semi-human son,

Euphorion — but Helena and her world remains a picture of a mythologically rich past conjured up by Mephistopheles. But what is real is the present; is what takes place in the last scene after Faust's death. The bliss which breathes into us from the South is past, as Helena herself is past. And being in the past, it gradually changes into a mere image.

Faust, who is the representative of our time, is shown at the back of the small cupola of the first Goetheanum with the word *Ich* (I), and flying towards him is a child. The mystery of the ego is the mystery of our time, and the South, the Mediterranean culture represented by Helena, is what the ego (Faust) should love, but it can only fill him with unfulfilled desire. Within the ego, however, lies the power of rebirth, of rejuvenation — the powers shown as the child flying towards him. These childlike powers do not tempt the ego with unfulfilled desire, but enable it to say, 'Not I, but Christ in me.'

BOTTON VILLAGE NEWS 11 II 1966

america: soul rejuvenation — michael splendour

On this my third visit to America, even though I was there in Beaver Run and Copake for only one month, my impressions were very distinct. I was particularly impressed by its vastness; its hills, its roads, even its cars, compared with which everything in Europe seems tiny. On our return journey we flew over France in the early morning, looked down and saw the tiny fields and villages, tidy and ordered. In America — at least in that small part of the east coast which I know — things seem not only vast but also heroically untidy, as if the tidiness we are used to in Europe gets lost, or is inappropriate, in the elemental power and space of the United States.

Those elemental powers! I had the impression that whatever corresponds to them humanly is not yet born. In American culture and art, in history and religion, there is a great indebtedness to Europe, but this imitation does not really fit, it only appears to. I became aware how much European landscapes and forms correspond to a human inwardness which responds to its environment with poems, music, houses, work and emotional behaviour. This presupposes a certain thoughtfulness, a contemplativeness which is not present in America, where human strength lies in the will and manifests as yet only in technology. In America the elemental powers ask for a quite different human response from that of Europe, no doubt on the basis of spiritual insight and the new Christianity.

America is the land of the West, of the sunset and of autumn. Nowhere do the autumn leaves glow more brightly, especially in September, when the first yellows, oranges and reds appear in the midst of the green. In Rudolf Steiner's *Soul Calendar* we read of how the human soul revives when outer nature starts to wane. Perhaps this second birth, this soul-rejuvenation, this Michael-splendour, is meant to develop in America, unfolding the soul, while in Europe it is rather the spring which lifts the wings of the soul, endowing it with the life of nature, but thereby chaining it to itself. The opportunity for spiritual insight is much greater for this autumnal American soul than it is for spring-bound European inwardness.

BOTTON VILLAGE NEWS 1 XI 1974

～ *advent*

advent — ending & beginning

Looking out on our first Advent Sunday over a bare, snowless landscape was a remarkable experience. Seen through the silhouettes of the leafless branches under an overcast sky, the slopes of the Yorkshire moors were brown, misty and withdrawn — an image of final, deathly tiredness. There was no comfort to be had from the memory of summer with its brilliant light when the moors exploded in vivid colour. Yet the blue altar and the vestments in the Christian Community service, the seasonal prayer which speaks of the chariot of the sun and the rainbow, the prophetic words echoing in the inner places of the soul — the experience of these rises above the outer nothingness to give an enormous strength filled with hope and the promise of eternal youth: the victory of inwardness.

The younger generations today reap the fruits of 'natural' science. It is a science which by its very nature has to extinguish all feelings of awe, love, fear and conscience. It is a science that owes its greatness and achievements to *observing* and, in its battle cry for 'objectivity', marks the first stage in the development of the consciousness soul. Knowledge has become reduced to the results of this science, and only that which has been tested and proven by it attains a degree of reality that counts. Everything else is dismissed as subjective and blurred, or regarded as being somehow unreal, such as, for instance, the values of other human beings. Yet it is a science which uses only a small part of the human being. Its objectivity is nothing more than a November consciousness with death as its star.

Three powers should stream from the human being: wonder, compassion and conscience. These powers should clothe the youth described in the Gospel of St Mark who fled naked from the soldiers in Gethsemane during the night of the Last Supper (Mark 14: 51–52). That youth is the Christ impulse[87] whom we human beings should clothe with soul qualities, life forces and physical form. From the concentration of awe, compassion and conscience within the human being will be fashioned the soul, life and physical body of Christ.

The earth with its seasons is the body of Christ. Nature is full of marvels if only we would develop our sense of *wonder*. Human beings suffer, but we would also experience *compassion* and empathy if only we felt that compassion has relevance in the world. And moral intuition, *conscience*, must be rekindled in human beings once more.

In its darkening mood of finality, Advent can be seen as the promise of a new year with its spring, summer and autumn, or it can be seen as a challenge and admonition to build up a soul nature, a soul year; to combine science with awe and wonder. Our consciousness soul must not remain at the stage where it is a breeding ground for demons. It is meant to become a bridge to the awareness of our spiritual background.

BOTTON VILLAGE NEWS 4 XII 1970

stations on the path of sacrifice

All sacrifice has the same exalted aim: that a higher power can reveal itself through the one making the sacrifice. We have only to think of the great sacrifice of the Thrones offering their Will to the Cherubim, a sacrifice that became the substance of all ensuing creation.[88] Or that of Abraham who, obedient to the command to sacrifice his son Isaac (Genesis 22: 2), brought about the revelation of the biography (as well as the identity), of the Hebrew people which can be recognised in the being of the Archangel Michael.

Of all creation, it is we human beings who are the ego-bearers and so have the potential to be like the candle which sacrifices its own wax, its own substance, in order to shine. No doubt many of us would be prepared to sacrifice ourselves if we had any idea of how to begin. Our time is very different from all other times in that it is given to us to *know*, while in the past we were only able to *believe*. The further back we go, the greater the strength of that belief, as witness the ancient certainty of divine kinship. Today, we need to know, we need to find the certainty within ourselves, because we no longer have that belief. We have grown up; only adults can know. But with knowledge comes responsibility for what we know, namely to uphold that knowledge in our *deeds*.

We see sacrifice all around us. The plant must sacrifice its growth or the scented flower could not emerge, and fruit can only ripen when the blossom is burnt away. The speed of the stag, the cruelty of the tiger, the ingenuity of the beaver are all part of nature because those creatures have relieved us of the overbalancing extremes of our own cruelty, speed and ingenuity.

In the *Calendar of the Soul* verse for the second week of Advent the last line is spoken by the World Word, the Christ:

> To offer up yourself through Me

It is necessary for evolution that we achieve this present stage in which individual beings are free to become an 'I'. Now we can say: I think, I feel, I will, in all its forms — I walk, I grasp, I hate, I imagine blue, I remember my grandmother, etc. Without this evolutionary stage and the development of the 'I', all these thoughts, feelings and will impulses would have no home in human souls. In this, however, there is the sting of the Fall, in other words, of selfishness. It is only when our wishes are warmed by Christ, when our 'I' becomes an organ of Christ, that we are able to lose our selfishness. If this doesn't happen the soul forces assembled around the individual ego accumulate a strength of their own and appear as our greed and prejudices, operating in many ways and on many levels. They must be sacrificed, but how? The *Soul Calendar* verse for the first week in Advent says:

> I feel that strength is lent to me
> To member my Self in modesty
> Within the World Self.

In the second week we find:

> Imbue the aims of your work
> With my bright Spirit light
> To offer up your Self through Me.

And in the third verse it says:

> To carry spirit light
> Into World's winter night
> Is, full of bliss,
> My heart's desire.

So I am 'to feel my Self as member'. But then we read, 'to offer up your self through Me', and finally that I am 'to carry Spirit light into World's winter night'. In this we can find the strength which will permeate the New Year, along with the strength of the Christmas verse in which warmth, light, and life are united.

Later in the third verse it says:

and Divine Word...

transfiguring all Life resounds.

The Christmas light which we may then experience through the sacrifice of the security of the sense-lit world, begins to shine. Through this sacrifice, all existence begins to echo with the divine Word and is meant to go on echoing throughout the year. Through the Advent verses we become aware that our individuality is only a preparation for saying 'I', not as separate from the world, but as being one with it, and that we are approaching a time when we will be able to say 'I' in this selfless sense.

Within this tremendous widening lies the offering-up, the sacrifice, of the second verse. It contains the promise to feel and understand spring and summer, no longer as outer facts, but rather as parables, as *images* for the spring and summer within us, of a humanised and ensouled Advent and Christmas. It is not within our small 'I' but rather within our world-sized 'I' that the world and the seasons can arise and be renewed. The Advent and Christmas verses lead us, via the threshold of sacrifice, to this world-sized 'I'. On that threshold stands modesty, not the small modesty which is personal to me, but World Modesty.

CAMPHILL CORRESPONDENCE, XI/XII 1992

jakob wassermann

(b 10.3.1873, Fürth, Bavaria, d midnight 31.12.1933/1.1.1934, Altaussee, Austria)

Many of us in Camphill, and others too, have read his only book translated into English, *Caspar Hauser: The Enigma of a Century*.[89] It was one of his first books, written when he was a little over 30 years of age at the beginning of our century. In the course of time it became a bestseller. In those first thirty years he was extremely poor and lonely, outwardly and inwardly, and living on the edge of despair.

After *Caspar Hauser* he wrote several other books and became famous. In my youth he was one of the three or four most reputable European novelists, the others being Thomas Mann, Hermann Hesse and Franz Werfel. Wassermann's later books written in the last ten to fifteen years of his life are ponderous and have a certain similarity to Dostoevsky. His characters present an enormous panorama of humanity, fascinating in their variety and the complexity of their relationships. He wanted to write a *comedie humaine,* and just before his death he produced detailed sketches for it: a multitude of sharply delineated, concrete situations in a dramatic procession of events and characters, including the wandering Jew, Ahasver.

We must bear in mind that he was a Jew. In central Europe this fact played an ever increasing part in the years from 1900 to 1945, not only in his inner biography but also socially and historically. It later reached its climax in the rise of Nazi Germany and Austria, the Second World War and the holocaust. But Wassermann died during the night of New Year's Eve 1933/34, the year after Hitler became Chancellor.

In many lives one can distinguish three stories that can be represented by the threefold Rosicrucian motto:[90]

> *Ex Deo Nascimur*
> *In Christo Morimur*
> *Per Spiritum Sanctum Reviviscimus.**

'From God we are born' describes the genealogy, his Jewish origins and ancestry, his darkness and poverty, the landscape and traditions of the 19th century. 'In Christ we die' represents the conditions, activities and experiences of the actual biography, which in Wassermann's case encompassed the end of the Kali Yuga and the beginning of the Light Age. 'Through the Holy Spirit we are resurrected' represents the heavenly biography promising a future waiting to be transformed into a new present.

Every biography orders itself in these three 'layers', but each has its own individual colouring, of course. The first layer is always linked to the roots, to his German-Jewish background, the chaotic, poor, dark proletarian conditions of his first 25 years.

The second layer depicts the famous novelist writing a large number of increasingly expansive books, each a stage or crowded marketplace of humanity with the greatest abundance, fantasy and varied tensions. It is the tension which makes you read these 500- or 600-page books as a thirsty person drinks fizzy lemonade on a hot July day. The tension is as fresh today as it was 60 years ago, its strings as taut as if the books were written yesterday. But the background against which they were written is permeated by a stern composition — the light of a new spiritual-social future. It was permeated by an ethos which really belongs to the third layer, an ethos of ideal innocence,

---

*The Latin endings of the verbs 'nascimur', 'morimur' and 'reviviscimus' imply an unfinished event, and therefore mean 'in the process of' being born, of dying and of coming to life again. There is no completely satisfactory English translation.

humanity and purity.

This light had been reached to an astonishing degree in *Caspar Hauser*, but it was laboured for in a great variety of ways in his other books because this background with its stern themes became ever more grandiose, and the light increasingly difficult to reach. A question that presents itself here is whether the potential of Anthroposophia, and also the rôle of youth which played such an important part in Wassermann's age, is hidden in there somewhere, for in spite of his money and fame, Jakob Wassermann was noted for his *modesty*. This seems to point to the innocence of the Kaspar Hauser figure, its spirituality never reached — a spirituality akin to the real nature of the German Spirit, the Buddha-angel permeated by the Nathanic essence,[91] serving the other nations of the earth while trying not to dominate them (cf. the aim of the Nazis).

His earthly life is a mystery because in trying to reach the light these copious books contain, though in a hidden and somewhat barren way, aspects of conscience and of the Guardian of the Threshold. In his adolescence he wrote in a short novel, *My Path as a German and a Jew*[92] how he felt torn between darkness, loneliness and poverty and the continual Sunday of a higher life and divine guidance, whose pictures shone with a kind of wildness but surety into the darkness of the weeks. To the end of his life he could not reconcile the darkness with the light. He seemed to live in a perpetual Advent without ever reaching Christmas.

CAMPHILL CORRESPONDENCE, XII 1991

the meaning of the seasons

Modern man is never more strongly confronted with the reality of the seasons than through the seasonal prayers and the accompanying colours of the Act of Consecration of Man. It will take some time, of course, before more people understand the colours and know that the words of the seasonal prayers are spoken by the gods of our time whose powers are increasing — indeed, are beginning to reveal themselves. Yet gradually, greater numbers will become aware of these words and the background colours, in the same way as the trumpets sound in the Book of Revelation. The words express the Christian festivals within the setting of the seasons, and the seasons become the Father Ground on which the festivals of the Son can grow. These contain the germ of a rebirth, a renewal of the seasons in our time, because the Earth has become the body of Christ. The seasons, with their growth, flowering, fruiting and decay, are as much a part of the earth as childhood and adulthood are parts of humanity.

Today it is possible to see photographs of the earth as it appears to an astronaut far out in space. The oceans and continents, partly covered by cloud, appear on the globe as on a map. But these pictures are 'stills' and do not show what else belongs to the condition of the earth, namely the circling course of the seasons. In a 'cosmic' film we would see the oblique earth axis which, during May, June and July, causes the arc of the sun to be high and long in the northern hemisphere and low and short in the southern hemisphere and, in November, December and January, the other way round. To make such a film would require a complete year.

It would be illogical to suppose that these mechanical, astronomical conditions *create* the seasons. That would be about as sensible as saying that the lengthening and turning up of the sides of the mouth creates a smile. The mechanical, astronomical conditions make it possible for the seasons to *appear*. Very obviously the seasons also have a moral value beyond their mechanical aspects — the uplifting mood of spring, the earnest mood and indeed the courage of autumn, or the conscience-searching, evaluating nature of summer's perfection. Were it not so, they would not have inspired so many poems. The seasons reveal Michael, Gabriel, Raphael and Uriel as the countenances of the seasons, just as our face is our countenance and reveals us.

Because the deeper being of the seasons is personal and therefore moral, our freedom is connected with it, for morality cannot exist without freedom. In our connection to another person, both freedom and morality enter in. We should learn to feel that the seasons *need* our freedom for their existence — not for their mechanical rhythm, but for their moral, personal being. This new relation to the seasons would constitute a first step towards the actual realisation of the Earth as the body of Christ. The centre of the seasons is, therefore, in the human heart.

BOTTON VILLAGE NEWS 15 XII 1967

third year

~ christmas & the holy nights

the three stages of christianity

The triple celebration of the Act of Consecration of Man at Christmas — at midnight, dawn and Christmas morning — can lead to an understanding of the three steps which Christianity took, and continually takes, to arrive on Earth.

Christianity originates in the night, with the Son of God. In the course of human evolution, the spirituality of our earth existence had to withdraw into the unconsciousness of our sleep, of the night. If our day consciousness had found access to our night consciousness, it would have started to eat away the Tree of Life. The Fall of Man is the gradual development of consciousness within human beings, but at the same time the godhead had to remove the Tree of Life. (Gen 3: 22) Every night when we become unconscious, we enter paradise. Every morning we are expelled from it because we wake up and eat of the Tree of Knowledge. We must pass the Lesser Guardian, the sum total of our past weaknesses, failures, imperfections and inhumanities, because we have not yet learned to combine our waking consciousness with our freedom. We were expelled from the embrace of the godhead so that we could gain our individual freedom which we would not have gained had we stayed in God's embrace. But Christ has endured the Mystery of Golgotha; He has come from the night — the Son of God has entered our day, yet without touching our freedom for He does not force us to accept Him. He has combined in Himself the Tree of Life and the Tree of Knowledge. Now our day-consciousness can enter our night-consciousness, our sleep existence, without destroying it — as long as the power of Christ is with us.

If the first stage of Christianity is the descent of the Son of God from the night, the third is His standing on the Earth and permeating earthly existence, thereby fulfilling the Trinity in whose image the human being is made. The reality of the Trinity — the three aspects of the godhead as Father God, Son God and Spirit God — had to be darkened for a time for the sake of our freedom. Particularly from the 17th century on, the term 'Holy Trinity' was no longer fully understood. Since the coming of the Light Age, the dawn of the Second Coming and the emergence of spiritual science, the human being shines divinely once again, even in his day-consciousness. Spiritual science explains divine intentions in terms of our day-consciousness. The special Christmas prayer inserted into the Act of Consecration of Man before the Transubstantiation, from the third Christmas service onwards, expresses the restoring of a divine origin to the human being. The Divine song sounds forth, and in spite of our imperfections, we, too, sing *with* the heavenly choir. The evolution from creature to creator has happened. With youthful modesty, we enliven our aged glory.

And what of the second stage of Christianity? The skills which develop in a child's first three years, namely walking, speaking and thinking, are manifestations of the Trinity. Speaking, the manifestation of the Son God, has a special place in this development, because as adults we use speech only as communication — of thoughts, feelings, intentions or concerning outer events. But nevertheless our speech contains within it the promise of the Creating Word which it possessed in the beginning. Wherever speech is used not just for communication but as a power (in speech therapy, drama, recitation or speech formation) the palest glimmer, the first promise is seen of what is to come in future through the Word. The second stage, the Act of Consecration of Man celebrated at dawn, is the stage of the Word.

These three stages of Christianity are confirmed and expressed in the three-part celebration of the Act of Consecration of Man at Christmas. The white and gold of the altar vestments manifest the Word entering our earthly existence, emerging from the Son God as Son of Man.

BOTTON MIRROR, 8 I 1983

an incentive for living

As time goes on it will become ever more difficult for human beings to exist, to find the incentive and will to live. Fifty years ago, quite mundane things — the longing for a car, enough money for a holiday, the search for humane political ideals or the simple enjoyments of life — all seemed a sufficient incentive for living. Today we can hardly call the longing for a car or a holiday an incentive for living: we can only call it a wish. Reading the advertisements or looking in shop windows enormously increases the number of such wishes but they do not add up to incentives.

However, there is another landscape in which we can live, although for the most part it is invisible with only the faintest allusions here and there to proclaim its presence. This landscape is the gospels, and for it to reveal itself two conditions are necessary — the enlightening words of Rudolf Steiner (although we should not accept them blindly, as a guide they are helpful), and our own efforts. Regarding the latter, everything depends upon trying to discover the composition of the gospels, whether of a single chapter or a number of chapters placed side by side. If we imagine one event or scene and see how it fits artistically with the one that follows or precedes it, we will be amazed at how the composition supports the words of Rudolf Steiner — indeed, as long as the gospels do not shed light on themselves in this way and make their landscapes appear, his words remain like straw. But we must also learn to endure unanswered questions.

This is a complicated process, but insofar as our own activity is involved, the landscape of the gospels is filled with the power of life. It is a landscape which brings us near to Christ and then we learn that it is only our awareness of Him that gives us the incentive for living. A moment of realisation arrives and the words of Rudolf Steiner spring into life because we have discovered something of the composition. His words then aid further discovery. They are like 'the lightning that lighteneth out of the one part under heaven, shineth unto the other part under heaven', to quote the phrase in St Luke's Gospel (Luke 17: 24) used to describe the Second Coming.

In the context of all this, let us look at the second chapter of St Luke's Gospel. At Christmas we read the first part of that chapter and, during the Holy Nights, the second part which is about Simeon, and there is a clear link between them in the composition of the chapter. Verses 1–7 correspond to verses 41–52, and verses 8–20 correspond to verses 25–40. This correspondence is not a simple mirroring, but it opens our understanding. Verses 8–20 tell of the shepherds sleeping in the open fields, their sleep enlightened by the angel and the singing of the heavenly host. In verses 25–40 there is Simeon, not out in the open fields but inside the Temple, yet more than awake through the light of the Holy Spirit. In both cases the light, the power of the Spirit, breaks into the sphere of Earth existence — the first time in the night, out in the open fields; the second time within the confines of the human mind. Both the shepherds and Simeon worship the Holy Child — Simeon, old and perhaps learned, from the town of Jerusalem, and the shepherds, younger, living in simple country conditions on the fringes of civilisation. In Bethlehem the child lies in the crib, with Mary and Joseph as archetypal figures behind it. In the Temple, Mary takes the place of the crib and holds the Holy Child, while Simeon, and later, Anna, are in the place of the shepherds. We know from Rudolf Steiner that the being of the Buddha is interwoven with these two events — with the revelation to the shepherds and to Simeon — and with the being of this particular Jesus child. Verses 1–7 correspond to verses 41–42, and in a similar way the first chapter of the gospel corresponds to the third, in which the Christ becomes manifest through the Baptism in the Jordan. (All this can be found in Rudolf Steiner's lectures published in *The Gospel of St Luke*.[1])

This is a weak attempt to open this subject, yet it is an attempt to lift the stone of passivity, paralysis and resignation impeding the fountain of activity and rejuvenation.

BOTTON VILLAGE NEWS, 3 I 1969

the beginning & end of st john's gospel

One of the missions of our age is to understand the gospels in the light of their composition. This means not only understanding them as a sequence in time, the 'after' following the 'before' and perhaps being caused by it, but rather being able to see their unfolding in space, viewing the whole more and more as a landscape with peaks and valleys, lakes, rivers and pastures. As we begin to let the various parts stand side by side — having them all present at the same time — we will become aware of consonance. One such consonance is between the opening and closing chapters (chapters 1 and 21) of the Gospel of St John. The following is a very tentative beginning in this direction.

The twenty-first chapter begins with seven of the disciples fishing in the Sea of Tiberias. At dawn, John recognises Christ standing on the shore beside a coal fire. They share a meal with Him which is then followed by a conversation between Christ and Peter. The chapter ends with John's words about the world not being large enough to contain all the books that would be needed to record Jesus' doings.

The first chapter begins with the Word. Then comes the scene with John the Baptist speaking, baptising and pointing out the Lamb who takes the sins of the world upon Himself. Then follows the calling of the first six disciples.

The two chapters are like a reflection of each other — the end of the twenty-first corresponds to the beginning of the first. The Word, which created the world, mirrors the world which cannot contain all the books filled with the words and deeds of Christ. Likewise, the beginning of the twenty-first chapter with the seven disciples corresponds to the end of the first chapter with the calling of the first six apostles.

The baptism by John takes place in the flowing waters of the river Jordan while the setting of the twenty-first chapter is at the broad stretch of the Sea of Tiberias. The twenty-first chapter is, obviously, steeped in the presence of the Risen Christ, while the first chapter dwells on the beginning of the cosmos, the annunciative voice and figure of John the Baptist and the very beginning of Christ's earthly appearance. In fact, Christ is present in both — in the twenty-first chapter He is standing on the shore, then He shares the meal and talks as Himself, while in the first chapter He is present at first as the world-creating Word, then He is with John and finally, passing by John, he talks up until his prophetic words to Nathaniel at the end.

In the first chapter we find John the Baptist's words 'I baptise with water', (verse 26) and '... He baptiseth with the Holy Ghost', (verse 33) — or as given in other gospels; 'with fire' or 'fiery tongues'. In the last chapter this fire has become the glowing coals that cook the common meal. In the first chapter John the Baptist says 'Behold the Lamb of God which taketh away the sins of the world.' Then in the twenty-first chapter, inspired by the twelvehood of the disciples, Peter says 'Lord, thou knowest that I love thee', to which Christ replies 'Feed my lambs.'

I am sure there are many further treasures to be discovered in these two chapters, but I would like to point out one more. It might be that something of the mystery of John the Baptist and John the Evangelist is contained here. According to Rudolf Steiner, and further elucidated by Emil Bock,[2] the being of John the Evangelist is the mysterious union of Lazarus and John the Baptist, and so from the middle of St John's Gospel onwards he is called 'the disciple whom Jesus loved'. In chapter 1, the sixth verse says 'There was a *man sent from God*, whose name was John', while in chapter 21 the seventh verse reads '... that *disciple whom Jesus loved* said to Peter It is the Lord.' Later, Christ foretells Peter's martyrdom at some length and shortly afterwards He says, referring to John, 'If I will that he tarry till I come, what is that to thee?' (John 21: 23) John recognises Christ in a deathless and eternal way.

There will come a time when the hidden, underground stream of esoteric Christianity — the stream of John the Evangelist — will unite with exoteric

Christianity. Like Peter, church Christianity will have to die, but a quite different side of Peter will live on. Peter was renamed Cephas, meaning a rock or stone, as was the servant Hagar in the Old Testament.[3] Peter became the rock or foundation of the Christian churches, as Hagar, the second wife of Abraham, became the mother of Ishmael who would later be the father of the Arabs, while Isaac was born to Abraham and Sarah to carry on the Judaic line. Nevertheless, something of Ishmael's 'Hagar-stone' descendants entered Jewish orthodoxy.

John the Baptist is the representative of the old creation of humanity, John the Evangelist the beginning of the rebirth, the renewal of humanity.

BOTTON VILLAGE NEWS, 23 X 1970

midnight thoughts between 1966 & 1967

Antoine de Saint-Exupéry, pilot and author of *The Little Prince*, was killed in the last war. In a letter written in 1943 he said: 'One supplies humanity with a standard, a paper-flower culture, as one supplies cattle with hay. This is how the human being of today looks. The meaning of humankind is at stake, but no answer is offered.'[4] From the standpoint of the insights given by spiritual science, and also from an observation of the past decades, we would have to add that answers *are* offered, but that human beings seem unwilling or unable to accept them.

The world as perceived by popular science sees nothing but material space throughout the universe. It regards the human being as existing only between birth and death, with nothing before or after; with neither a pre-earthly past nor a post-earthly future. Because of this outlook a lameness, even paralysis, has descended into human will.

But even if our consciousness did reveal wider vistas of humanity and the universe to us, they would be forced to relinquish their power to compel us. Although it is the sun that draws us upward, human ideals should be created by us alone. We must create our own ideals — and woe betide if they are mere subjective opinions or viewpoints! Lacking any compulsion from outside, kindled only by individual conscience and self-propelled as it were by its own insight, the will of the human being would be able to spread its wings and fly, obeying solely its own command. Human will would then grow enormously, and that power of faith which moves mountains would become a fact.

The powers of will slumbering in the human being are gigantic but they are like glaciers, they can melt and flow again only if the human being marks out his own ideals. Any example, precedent or external law is but an anachronism from the past and is powerless. That is why dictatorships can only compel human beings through fear. The kingdom of Heaven is within you. The Three Kings in the Gospel of St Matthew give away their gold, frankincense and myrrh; the content of their wisdom, their conscious knowing. They receive the fire that enlightens their will because the will can only be kindled by a new knowledge. Spiritual science must become a flame of inner impulse in the individual.

What is the difference between old and new knowledge; between outer and inner; between knowledge and mere opinion? The difference is linked to the fact that the Mystery of Golgotha, the death and resurrection of Christ, takes place in spring. Knowledge (including spiritual knowledge), remains external and ineffectual as long as the seasons remain no more than changing physical conditions — wet, dry, hot or cold — which make us comfortable or uncomfortable, or at most alter our mood a little. But the moment each season receives its countenance (as described by Rudolf Steiner in *The Four Seasons and the Archangels*[5]), a spiritual being looks at us — Gabriel in winter, Raphael in spring, Uriel in summer, Michael in autumn — and the season loses its physical coarseness because the gaze of the archangel shines above its mere physical attributes. Then the outer, physical aspects lose their compulsion and soul events become real. Belonging entirely to the world of the soul, human will wields a magical influence, while nature wanes.

The winter-spring quarter of the year from Christmas to Easter seems to be the time of Christ's earthly incarnation. Death and resurrection certainly belong in that quarter because each year there is the same sequence of the despair and painful contraction of winter, followed by the hope and blissful expansion of spring. But it only seems so, for Christ's incarnation comprised *all* seasons. And 'spring' also comprises 'winter'. In that inner, free spring lies Christ's resurrection, and His coming to dwell in the body of Jesus makes of winter a parable of incarnation.

The moment that the seasons cease to be mere outer conditions and start to become parables and images of spiritual events, their physical 'weight' diminishes. The physical world loses something of its denseness, and the fetters which numbed and bound our will begin to loosen. *Inner* light and *inner* warmth overcome outer light and darkness. Our will gains the strength to strive and to achieve. We should not treat ourselves as prisoners. The future depends on our will.

BOTTON VILLAGE NEWS, 6 I 1967

conscience

Conscience is the Cinderella of psychology, mainly because it seems to be present only at important, decision-making moments, but in reality it accompanies us in a hidden way from morning to night, every day of our lives. We are not aware of it because it does not judge us; it does not speak but rather it is like the tolling of a bell or the gaze of an eye. The language of conscience is of a different order from our ordinary language. Were it not so we would not be free. With unbiased observation we can feel that conscience is mightier than we ourselves are (it was just a matter of convenience when Freud reduced it to a kind of Moses-like father figure), yet if it were to exert its power it would lower itself to the level of our consciousness.

Rudolf Steiner explained that our present concept and experience of conscience only emerged around 500 BC.[6] Before that it was experienced as an external power, the Erinyes (or Furies) described in Greek mythology as goddesses of fury and revenge, for example Orestes being pursued by the Furies. After 500 BC that which had been outer was transformed into the inner experience we have today. Rudolf Steiner also tells us how, starting in our own time, what was inner will slowly become outer again. The new conscience will consist in pictures and visions arising in our soul, prophesying the future consequences of our present deeds, their karmic consequences in a later life.[7] This new conscience, this new prophetic vision, will be an enhancement of our power to think. At present, both thinking and conscience are blind, but they contain the potential for vision. They are like the bare, black branches of a tree in winter which the light and warmth of the Second Coming of Christ will awaken into bud, leaf and colour.

The time of the Holy Nights from Christmas to Epiphany is a well from which the new conscience can draw water. These nights were always holy because during them the soul had a direct connection to the spiritual worlds. In our time it is Christ who, full of grace, connects the human soul with the heavenly worlds, and in the course of the year Christ is never closer to us than during these Holy Nights. Therefore, the days belonging to them have a golden halo about them; the night shines into the day. The Christian

Community vestments are white, as is the altar, while the letters above and on the altar are gold. This innocent white and gold of the days during the twelve Holy Nights is meant to permeate the content of our lives. It is the new conscience; the revelation of the tolling bell, the gazing eye, in our newly-found and enlarged sensitivity towards our wanderings, and their consequences, in the landscape of destiny.

That is why it is so important to celebrate the twelve Holy Nights in some way. *What* we do doesn't matter so much, but what is important is that *we* do it. If we do, we can hope that the well of the new conscience will not just overflow and run down the mountain slope of the year but will be contained and preserved.

BOTTON VILLAGE NEWS, 24 XII 1964

Olaf Åsteson

Picture based on a tapestry by Torvald Moseid "The Dream Poem"

∼ *epiphany*

the three kings & the image of humanity

In the Epiphany celebration each year, the Three Kings remove the symbols from our Christmas tree along with the apples, roses and candles and, finally, take away the tree itself. At that moment *we* are as poor as *they* were when they had knelt in adoration of the Child and left their gifts with Him. Before the birth of the Child the Three Kings embodied the peak of wisdom, shining in pure splendour; after it they merged into the fulfilled, divine Image of Humanity. When the three gifts lay beside the cradle — where, in fact, the Mystery of Golgotha began — the Image of Humanity rose again.

When the Mystery of Golgotha was completed, the Three Kings became the patrons of the threefold social organism which is based on the equality of all human beings; not, however, the equality of their destinies, but the equality of their creation in the image of God. In pre-Christian times, the social order required hierarchy; at its peak a shining, superhuman wisdom, and on its slopes (according to the culture), castes, gentry or slaves, etc. The totality of the social organism of the particular tribe or nation was humanity. Now, after the Mystery of Golgotha, each individual human being bears the power of the Three Kings within himself. Human threefoldness is fulfilled and so the social organism can become threefold in the human likeness.

Each one of our [Botton] neighbourhoods bears within it the light of the Three Kings, warmed by the brotherly powers of the Shepherds. But our neighbourhoods are as yet little more than ideals, stars of hope rather than facts. We can see a powerful counterpart to the royal gifts of the Kings. In their time it was the return to their own lands, the flight into Egypt and the slaughter of the innocents; in ours it is the disappearance of the Christmas Tree and the end of the Holy Nights. We are no longer graced with the heavenly shelter which the Holy Nights gave us, but are thrust out into the dangers and uncertainties of the New Year, into the raw winds of daily life. Yet *the responsibility for one another within a neighbourhood* can become a tremendous comfort and an unending source of strength. This responsibility for the other person is the soil out of which the more objective tasks of a neighbourhood will grow in the course of time. Responsibility for one another quells self-righteousness and pride. It means nothing less than to face up to Cain's question regarding Abel: 'Am I my brother's keeper?' (Gen 4: 9) The gifts of the Kings shine within the human soul against a background of guilt.

The *Soul Calendar* verse for the week after the ending of the Holy Nights seems to point to the responsibility which human beings will increasingly have for one another:

> When I live in the spirit's depths
> There streams within my soul's foundations —
> Out of the heart's worlds of love
> And filling the empty delusion of myself —
> The fiery power of the Cosmic Word.

> *Calendar of the Soul*, verse 40, (first week after Epiphany)

the threefold social organism

The following sequence of thoughts is, of course, based on Camphill and its way of life. I believe that ideas and insights on the threefold social organism have arisen in Camphill not by being forced theoretically or abstractly onto life, but out of its spiritual, economic and human striving. One can therefore say that what appears outwardly as threefold ordering of the social organisms in the various Camphill places is inwardly motivated and created by the power of the Community.

I

What does a 'free spiritual life' mean? Obviously it contrasts with an unfree life lived under an authority. It is easy to recognise authority when it is backed by physical power — under the Nazis, Communists and other dictatorships, only certain concepts are allowed to be publicly stated or taught, and the fear of imprisonment or death ensures that the limit of what is permitted is never overstepped, except secretly. It is more difficult to recognise lack of freedom in spiritual life if the authority is not physically seen. What we learn in school, college and university has authority because both public opinion and its apparent success seem to prove it to be true. And there is also a third authority which excludes freedom in the spiritual life, namely the authority of a beloved person who is assumed always to speak the truth. His seeming possession of all spiritual (or mental) truths paralyses the spiritual abilities in others. He becomes a kind of opinion-dictator who, despite the best will in the world, turns the thoughts of others into taboos. Because there is a streak of this tendency in all of us, we should emphasise it as an enemy of any form of human community. It may be a relic of oriental forms of guru-leadership, in which we owed absolute obedience to the guru.

One of the peculiarities of the threefold social organism is that, as in all organisms, we can understand one sphere only if we understand all spheres. Therefore we will now speak of the economic realm, then of the social, and finally of the spiritual realm.

II

Freedom in spiritual life would be pointless, of course, if it had no practical outcome. Schools, hospitals, universities, farms, manufactories and so on, would have to flow out of the respective theories of education, medicine, science, agriculture, technology, etc. The two arch-enemies of this multitude of physical undertakings born from a free spiritual life are well known: the Welfare State, and advertising. Both are caricatures of producer-consumer associations. The quality that should be developed in these associations is brotherhood, but brotherhood is a very personal and hence a spiritual virtue. The caricature arises if the association becomes only physical. But if the need for shoes, say, corresponds to the output of shoe factories, the balance between need and production is an infinitely varying one according to locality, productivity and current needs. In such an association we can imagine an escalation of meetings which have their basis in person-to-person relationships. But unless production is determined by need (rather than amassing wealth through advertising), the personal factor disappears and money is then the only link between producer and consumer.

The same relationship exists between teachers and parents regarding their children. Parents need education for their children; teachers are enthused by the idea of a school, and the need of the parents is answered if the teachers can fire the parents with the same enthusiasm. It is a similar situation with patients and doctors in the case of illness, and with students and universities in the case of higher education. But where does the money come from for shoes, schools, hospitals and universities?

III

As time goes on, money will become separated from work and we enter the social sphere, the realm of justice and equality, which is also the sphere of compassion, of caring for each other. It is the sphere of *real* democracy and therefore in this realm we can never vote. The reason why profit exists in the world, and human beings continually chase after it, is because of the gulf between individual needs and earnings. The fact that earnings of any kind are meant to cover needs becomes, in this case, less and less important.

Economically, every undertaking must cover the needs of its participants: the shoe factory its workers, from the board of directors to the cleaning staff; the school its teachers, the hospital its staff, etc. This can only be done if the participants of any undertaking meet together at regular intervals, say once a month, and share out the available money according to the ascertained needs. Among these needs are the schooling of children, the care of ageing relatives or the need for books. Empathy, compassion, care for the other person will eradicate what we might consider are needs but which in reality are born of the old idea of profit — the 'need' for a Jaguar limousine, for instance!

It is a mistake to think that a secret dossier which the government may hold on every citizen is the only serious weapon against freedom and an intrusion into private lives. Much more serious is the threat that 'the state knows best', and the consequent levelling down to one standard in medicine, education, food, etc. Certainly the Welfare State has brought enormous benefits, but if it lays down anything other than purely physical standards it becomes a kind of dictator and paralyses individual common sense. The 'nationalisation' and inspection of schools at a physical level (upholding cleanliness, prohibiting caning, etc.) is wonderful, although over-rigid regulation of air space and fire escapes is perhaps a bit unnecessary. But if it encroaches on the moral level of teaching methods and curriculum it is inhuman because in doing so it presupposes that 'government knows best'.

IV

All this is, of course, initially only applicable to small numbers and small units, not to millions. But it is probable that threefold social organisms will be built up from small units; street neighbourhoods, village communities, etc. Rudolf Steiner said that the propagation of the idea of a threefold social organism was a test of the ability of human beings to kindle their devotion to Michael, but the test failed.[8]

Nevertheless, our time harbours a longing for community, particularly among young people, and no doubt what is now dawning as supra-national, tolerant relationships is connected with the approach of the etheric Christ.

But these communities have a tendency to dissolve, mainly, I think, because their economic basis is not durable enough. An economic basis demands brotherhood, but the full reality of brotherhood appears only when true economic conditions prevail — the separation of work and wages, producer-consumer associations, and so on — otherwise it is mere sentimentality.

In former times, communities like this did not form because they had to have one ideal, one world-conception. Now, the purely human connection from man to man is the dominant and immensely Christian motive. Because of the great tolerance of the younger generation this does justice to the free spiritual life, but it does not do justice to the economic sphere. The economic sphere is looked upon as part of the 'establishment' and as such is therefore hopelessly irrelevant, hence the basis for real brotherhood is removed and only equality and freedom remain. But mutual recognition, acknowledgement of the fullness of each human being, entails recognition of the other as free, equal, and as *a brother* — but brothers are just *not* equal.

It is this recognition of each human being in their full reality which necessitates the effort towards a threefold social organism, and it was the failure of this recognition which led to the collapse of the first attempts at social threefoldness.

In its endeavours as a community, as a social organism, Camphill strives towards this recognition, not towards common ideals since these must lead to sectarianism and fanaticism because ideals can ripen only in freedom. To combine freedom with brotherhood will result in real equality, an equality which is not state-dominated.

BOTTON VILLAGE NEWS, 27 I 1973

the two jesus children

The decline of Christianity is due to the fact that for hundreds of years people have imagined a straight line leading from the child in the manger, from Mary and Joseph with ox and ass; from the announcing star and singing angels, to the cross and to resurrection. The image of the human vessel which was to bear the Divine Word only from the baptism in the Jordan onwards became completely blurred. It is idle to speculate whether the mystery of the two Jesus children was known in the past. In our time we must not merely know it but also understand it, and that means we must insert it as a building stone into our world conception and comprehend it more and more as reality.

The two Jesus children were by no means simply 'special' children. They were infinitely more. One, the so-called Solomonic child, was the reborn Zarathustra,[9] the most highly developed individuality of all mankind. We may perhaps have a faint idea of what this means if we realise that not only the Persian but also the Egyptian and the Hebraic civilisations sprang from him and were nourished by him.

The other, the Nathanic child, had never before incarnated. The closest he came to incarnating was an 'overshadowing' of Krishna in old India.[10] As this child was that part of Adam which had not gone through the Fall, he was infinitely alive, infinitely innocent and compassionate, but not highly developed intellectually. We might imagine him (which is hardly possible) as the radiating power of the human 'I' — not in an intellectual sense or a self-centred way, but softly, dependent on his compassion. This was the world majesty of the 'I'; it was not feelings, nor was it sentimentality, but the infinitely enhanced power of the 'I' to transform itself through what it loves. In Jesus' twelfth year,[11] at Easter, this impersonal power merged with the other Jesus child (Luke 2: 41–52). The Zarathustra child died: his soul permeated the Nathanic child. When Jesus sat among the learned doctors in the temple, he was already Jesus of Nazareth who in his thirtieth year would be baptised by John the Baptist and thereby become the bearer of the Christ.

The Solomonic child, the one described by St Matthew to whom the three wise men come from the East offering gold, frankincense and myrrh, is something like the human soul as it had evolved through the ages, the human soul enduring and becoming one with its repeated earth-lives. It is the ballast of the karma-laden 'I', the growing personality — the human powers of thinking (gold), feeling (incense), willing (myrrh), that previously were distributed among types of human beings. The Nathanic child, the one described by St Luke (2: 1–20) to whom the shepherds came, is also soul, but without a destiny and therefore without death — soul which is one with the power of the original, primeval egohood of man. In the twelfth year, the Nathanic Jesus becomes something like the charioteer soul driving and steering the three horses of thinking, feeling and willing. Since the baptism in the Jordan, when the Ego of Humanity entered Jesus of Nazareth, every one of us is a human being only if he becomes part of this Ego of Humanity — not I, but Christ.

Our time is the re-birth of the Egyptian era. The decline of Christianity occurs rapidly because event and consciousness must become one. Events take place only when our consciousness accompanies them in an appropriate way. Hardly anything happens by itself. The nice, safe borderline between knowing and happening is becoming fluid. The deity of consciousness has solidified into plaster in Catholic churches — the devotion to a plaster effigy of Mary has developed a consciousness which dreams of a materialistic universe. But it should be remembered that in old Egyptian times Mary was Isis, the divine Sophia.[12] Through an understanding of the two Jesus children[13] a new Sophia, a new Isis, will deify our consciousness.

BOTTON VILLAGE NEWS, 4 II 1966

christ & the sun

Rudolf Steiner described the sun as a huge mirror which transforms all the streams of the cosmos into light and warmth. It has this transforming quality because it is negative space; it forms a suction. The light and warmth in which we exist on earth are not the result of explosions of some kind or other, but rather of this macrocosmic in-sucking activity of the sun.[14]

We should always try to imagine that Christ descended to mankind from the sun (although this knowledge was suppressed in the 4th century AD and the idea of 'church' — increasingly the Roman Church — substituted as the vessel of all Christianity). Therefore we should imagine the deeds of Christ after the first Easter as sun activity on earth which, since then, has been enacted through human beings. The sun's activity known to modern astronomy is but the physical epitaph of an unimaginable moral action in worlds and times beyond our experience. What for us is an astronomical mechanism measurable in degrees, is the remnant (or perhaps the outcome) of the moral deeds of beings. Our earth is now the setting for forging the world-mirror, but out of the hearts of those who try to approach Christ within through an understanding of spiritual science, because in its apocalyptic development the earth depends entirely upon human beings. The shining sun is the image of the world as sacrifice. In the stage of old Saturn, before our planetary evolution began, the Thrones sacrificed their being and warmth in what became the beginning of the world.[15] Sacrifice is now demanded of us human beings, not once but on many levels and through many lives.

It is the tragedy of Christianity over the last two thousand years that the relationship between Christ and the sun was forgotten. Morality became something that belonged to the sphere of belief and Christianity therefore became the religion of belief. But understanding and knowledge are beyond morality. Spiritual science explains morality (and therefore Christianity) for the understanding and cognition of humanity, and only thereby can human hearts begin to shine into the cosmos.

In the second part of the Act of Consecration of Man, in the Offering, the elevation, the lifting up of the cup with wine allows fragrance to ascend in a mood of devotion to the Creed. This is followed by the rising smoke of the incense in which Christ begins to unite Himself with the offering human hearts. This elevation corresponds to the elevation of the paten with the bread and the cup, after the Transubstantiation — the permeation of bread and wine with the being of Christ in the third part of the Act of Consecration of Man. The Sun being of Christ rises at the altar as the outer sun rises every morning over the horizon: every altar becomes east, wherever it faces. Human beings can offer sacrifice only if Christ permeates the Offering, and Christ can only permeate it if man increasingly takes Transubstantiation into his thinking. The archangel Michael is the guardian of the Act of Consecration of Man because he is the guardian of human thoughts. These world thoughts fell into human minds for the sake of our independence and freedom. It is up to us to recognise them as being held in Michael's guardianship and to use them, with Rudolf Steiner's help, for Christ's illumination.

The Gospel Reading in the Act of Consecration of Man has two sides. One is the Evangelion, the message of the deeds and words of Christ; the other is the beginning of a process which ends in the Communion. Christ, the Word, becomes bread and wine in the Transubstantiation, which is then taken by the communicants. Thus we have it that the Sun quality of the Word becomes Christ's body and blood. The words of the gospel spoken at the altar by the priest are a beginning of the new creation. (Another beginning is the silent words of a meditation.) So long as human words remain, as now, predominantly 'information' (telling the other person one's thoughts, feelings, actions, etc.), an impotence is cast over language — although ever since the Tower of Babel this has really allowed human freedom to develop. If words had retained their magical power, the simple information-use of language would have been impossible because the power over others, whether or not the speaker intended it, would have continued to work.

As the sun transforms all streams of the cosmos into light and warmth through its negative space, so our listening will change the words spoken by others. A school for such listening is the two moments in the Act of

Consecration of Man when first the cup as the draught of health is raised and offered; secondly when paten and cup, the bread and wine as body and blood, are elevated and offered after the Transubstantiation. Into this descends the Sun sphere of Christ, not 'positive' as is outer light and warmth, but negative, a resonant human space created through our listening. In the first elevation we reach into the Sun sphere which has come to us through Christ; in the second we ray out into the cosmos because Christ has empowered us.

DATE UNKNOWN

the threefold social organism & the son of man

In the course of observation and experience guided by Rudolf Steiner's insight, it becomes clear that every social organism, be it a school, bank, hospital, university or whatever, is threefold. *Any* concern in which human beings have an aim in common — but not necessarily in an idealistic sense — is threefold. Whether two people or several thousand are connected in this way, the social threefoldness described by Rudolf Steiner should appear. It is neither dogma nor abstraction because it stems from, and is related to, the threefoldness of the human being himself.

In our time, however, social threefoldness cannot avoid being warped owing to a variety of other factors whose inhumanity becomes apparent if we measure them against pure, genuine threefoldness. It is distorted by nationalism, by nations and nation-states, and by all that follows from a centralised government. It is warped through the ethos of trades unions, political parties, courts, etc., and finally it is warped by the rôle that money plays in our society, objectively in the economy as well as psychologically in the individual.

Any social organism is inherently threefold. First there are the *ideas* which guide it. In a bank these are the current ideas about money in the economy — its deposition in client accounts, its lending with interest, the buying and selling of shares, etc. In a hospital it would be prevailing ideas about illnesses, their diagnosis and therapy, while in a tobacconist's shop it would be current ideas in the tobacco trade and how to manage the shop in relation to them. Secondly, there are *human rights*, *duties* and *relationships*. These are familiar to us today in complex hierarchical structures and differentiated salaries, from managing director down to messenger boy, for example, or the inter-relationship of superintendents, consultants and other doctors and nurses of various grades in hospitals. Structures govern the administrative, cleaning and cooking staff in institutions; bureaucrats and their staff in offices, and last but not least, the rôle of ordinary citizens — patients, clients, students, pupils, customers — for the sake of whom the respective social edifices exist. Thirdly, there is *economics*. This is expressed in the balancing of income and expenditure, the work timetables of various salaried staff, geographical trade routes of goods, producer-consumer relationships, and so on. In addition, everything that takes place in the first and second areas of a social organism has its repercussions in the third.

Threefolding did not exist in this way in former times, and in our day it is obscured by the three hindrances enumerated above — the centralising nation-state, obstructions to real meeting between human beings and the rôle of money. It stands to reason that the more each particular area can move freely, unimpeded by these three hindrances, the more its inherent gifts, riches and particular qualities can unfold. In a hospital, for example, this would mean that the money doctors and nurses need for their livelihood would be paid by present and future patients. The salaries and pensions of teachers or university professors would no longer be paid by the state, a situation that forces the government to make judgements about education which are out of place here, belonging as they do to the first realm. And ideas, thoughts and responsibilities for what is done or taught rests with the individual doctor or teacher, and should not be constrained by those to whom they owe their livelihood and their ability to survive after retirement.

As indicated above, this threefolding is also to be found in us as well as in our biography. We could become helpers to one another if we would only interest ourselves enough in the threefoldness of the other person. What we call a person's destiny is really the weaving together of these three strands into one thread which forms the biography of the human being in his earthly life according to his or her karma. Each person has his own ideals, thoughts and ways of looking at the world through his experiences with art and religion; he has a wide variety of human relationships (family, friends, loves, colleagues, subordinates, superiors, etc.), and he must brave and negotiate the economic ocean-currents of his time.

This threefoldness permeating the human being during his earthly existence is not merely something to be borne in a passive sort of way: the human being has to say 'I' to it. And while I can say 'I' merely within the small house of my opinions, feelings, likes and dislikes — within my own skin, as it were — I can also extend this and experience a tremendous widening of my 'I', and with it a widening of my responsibilities. If I am *responsible* for my opinions, feelings, etc., the whole world becomes my home rather than what is merely within my own skin. In this home my *activity* is called for, not just my suffering. And in being 'widened' I discover that in their interplay human beings can be greater than each is when alone in his singleness, with his particular worth or lack of it. In essence, a social organism is something greater than the sum total of the human beings comprising it. The politics of democracy, of voting and of parties, arose from the misconception that the numerical sum of a multitude of us, each in our smallness, constitutes the social organism. The widened 'I' encompasses the social organism and with it the natural, created world of our nearer and wider locality.

However, the pure threefold social organism into which we are meant to widen our person has a singular peculiarity: *it does not exist* — not even as an ideal or as a theory — unless human beings, imperfect human beings, *will* it into being. It must be willed by many so that individual imperfections can balance each another out. In prehistoric times there was no social organism, although in his cosmic sinless being Adam Kadmon encompassed the whole of nature. On the other hand, there was no singleness either, no uniqueness, no 'I' (in an earthly sense) and therefore no human 'we'. Something of this angelic, paradisal condition can be seen in animals and small children. Their 'I' is in the spiritual worlds and their togetherness is very different from adult social togetherness. Our intellect — which is based on our singleness, on our 'fallen uniqueness', we could say — can point towards a social organism but cannot actually bring into being what is in reality part of a restored, Christianised humanity that lies beyond the threshold. Rudolf Steiner often insisted that the social organism can only be grasped by knowledge from beyond the threshold. This is because the intellect can only state what is, but the will (when it flows into the intellect) can 'think' the Archetypal Unseen and bring about the full flowering of the consciousness soul. This is Goetheanism.

Goetheanism enables us to understand what is beyond the threshold. Initially, the consciousness soul can grasp the world only on the basis of our 'fallen' intellect, but true Goetheanism is a further step — a step towards a new 'we', beyond singleness, that uses our consciousness soul in a social way. Geniuses will arise in social life just as in the past there were artistic geniuses. But the genius in social life need have no grand social ideas since he understands the other person in his potential. That is what Rudolf Steiner meant by 'social art'.

The Christianising of the human being is possible only if the inner life and the social life can be brought together.

CAMPHILL CORRESPONDENCE, I 1981

∿ *toward lent*

to be social as therapy

This is not just a term.[16] Social therapy means healing by means of the social organism surrounding the person who is sick. We are all 'sick'. The intention of social therapy can only be to create a social structure that works on the members of that structure, otherwise it would not be a social organism but a kind of hospital — a hospital for 'cases', for exceptional situations. But a village settlement (even if situated in a town) for drug addicts, ex-convicts, or for the mentally ill, is there not only *for* these people, but *with* them. This means that it is not the variety of what take place there, whether work, cultural or religious events, art therapy, etc., but the social organism with its manifold structures and areas of responsibility that is decisive and healing.

This social organism encompasses not only the 'patients', those who need care, but also the 'normal' co-workers who made the decision to share their humanity with the patients and their handicaps, in order to elevate this way of living together. To a certain extent it means to give up one's own selfishness.

The concept of 'normal' is relative to any given period in history. We, the co-workers, are people of our time in the widest sense, thanks to the norm of today's intellect which makes possible our present ego-consciousness. The unfolding of human history has brought about mankind's development of ego-consciousness. Because of this development, so called 'normal' people today are barbarians compared to human beings in the past who had more highly developed spiritual-heart forces and physical forces (although they had only poorly developed ego-consciousness). Socially, however, our intellect is a useless soul faculty. It was on this provisional ego-intellect that Rudolf Steiner had to build, yet his lectures and books carry the garment of this intellect in the most exemplary fashion without deviating into the abstract and unreal. The intellect is the most 'human' property in relation to the spiritual.

Our greatest responsibilities lie in our social interactions with others. This holds good not only for this sphere but for every social organism, be it a state, a business or communal life. A patronizing attitude is no longer acceptable today, yet the mentally handicapped person needs guidance and consequently the social aspect is partly destroyed. In curative institutions for children and young adults we are often stuck with established forms. This applies not only to the co-workers — the difficulty of entering into a relationship of mutual dependence and equality also exists for the handicapped adult, insofar as he or she wants to remain childlike and is reluctant to grow up. But why?

To be grown-up means to be able and willing to carry responsibility. It is not whether one can do a task well or not, like cooking potatoes or sanding a piece of wood, but whether one can be responsible for the task as a whole — putting together an order of finished dolls for delivery; organising the household laundry or the entire mid-day meal. In other words, to be able to complete a task in its entirety. The moans that accompany the burden of responsibility — and often the tiredness of the co-workers, too — show that responsibility is not enviable. Our time offers a certain ease: the more responsibility, the bigger the wage. In this way responsibility becomes material, something to be striven for, and in addition, a halo is offered to the one who carries the most responsibility.

In future, the reality of responsibility will play a paramount rôle in social therapy. Hierarchy and financial gain will be replaced by responsibility. This statement can be confirmed by observation. When one of the co-workers cooks a meal, he or she is aware of what needs to be replenished in the larder. A villager can learn to cook, of course, but the social responsibility for the totality of the cooking, the keeping of stores and the ordering of them, is usually the task of the co-worker because not only can the virtues of reliability and responsibility be acquired intellectually, they also require a great deal of selflessness. We, the co-workers, have a need to carry responsibility for the sake of our self-respect and cannot easily let go of this deep-seated urge. But all too often society does not accept that a handicapped person *can* carry responsibility. On the other hand, the handicapped person often has the notion that to take responsibility is a step towards growing up; a further letting go of childhood, of taking his or her own destiny more seriously. Jealousy, ambition, envy and so on are caricatures of being grown up, as is dependence on praise and appreciation.

Important attributes and capabilities are called forth if we succeed in engendering elements of responsibility in the handicapped person. In this way, the demarcating line between handicapped person and co-worker will gradually be eliminated.

Although springing from the same root, anthroposophical curative education for children and young people is fundamentally different. The social circumstances surrounding the handicapped child is important, but the perception of his handicap is even more important. The child is still changeable and flexible, whereas the body of an adult is not. To create a healing social environment is only one of the therapeutic ways available to anthroposophical curative education. Medicines, pedagogy founded on the modified curriculum of the Waldorf school, curative eurythmy — all these are also available.

Difficulties in social therapy often arise because a co-worker has been active previously in curative education. The curative educator strives to diagnose constitutional deviations and typical pictures of illness (for example small-headedness or epilepsy). For the social therapist this can be a hindrance to accepting the handicapped person as a fellow human being. Today, the social element among adults plays an undefined rôle, but this does not mean that we should forego what has been gained from anthroposophical knowledge of the human being, which is the aim of curative education.

In his book *Who Was Ita Wegman?*,[17] J.E. Zeylmans van Emmichoven describes at length how medical knowledge of the human being is one of the pillars of a future ordering of social life. Naturally, people do not have to become diagnostic specialists, but individual human beings cannot really be perceived and understood, not even one's own wife and child, without an understanding of features such as pallor, obesity, breathlessness, etc. Without this more general medical knowledge of the human being, in which the activity of the heart is as strongly engaged as in any human relationship, medicine only corrects symptoms.

There are many social organisms. Humanity is the most comprehensive: single nations are multifaceted and diverse. Nationalities are connected to this, although they are politically defined. There are also the many human interest groups in the widest sense, from the family to world-wide organisations like Amnesty International, for instance.

In the field of anthroposophical social therapy, the social organism of a village community is novel in that it is not constituted by the individual 'type' as in curative education, but through work in agriculture, work gained and executed in workshops and life in the households with its all-embracing human quality. Moreover, it is a village *with* people with special needs, not *for* them. To learn to become part of a normal social organism is truly therapeutic for the adult person, whether in activities such as farming, cooking, housekeeping, dressmaking, carpentry, etc. Individual weaknesses, handicaps and clumsiness are actually remnants of childhood and should not stand in the foreground. The difference between 'villager' and 'co-worker' is gradually erased. The villagers learn to be less identified by their handicaps and the co-workers learn not to take their preferences too seriously, thus both can serve the being of work — in agriculture, workshop or household. An understanding compassion takes the place of sentimentality and lack of feeling. As we know only too well, every social organism has to deal with these two enemies.

Anthroposophical curative education is a fact but anthroposophical social therapy is not yet a fact in the same sense. Curative education can look back on decades of experience in the field of knowledge gained, as well as the activity flowing out of it. It is already an organism of achievement, whereas social therapy is very much at the developing stage. Village social life is dependent on the greater and ever-changing social life within the stream of time, and what has been said here so far is still to come. In the social therapeutic institution of Botton Village, for example, we can only say that in the light of the moral intuitions of its people, this or that has evolved over the past forty years. Different insights are being gained in other institutions, and out of these specific intentions a future social therapy will develop.

Two remarks should be added at the end of this general introduction. Firstly, König's lectures (published as *In Need of Special Understanding*[18]) are significant seeds out of which the many and varied ways of this village have grown, and further forms will also grow. The second remark concerns the fundamental question of training. Anyone who wants to work in the field of social therapy must acquaint himself with the anthroposophical world view and cognition of the human being. To live one's life in service to others cannot be taught: it must be acquired through love. Among other things, dramatised exercises can be helpful here. In a social therapy seminar, for instance, we may have to slip into another persona and then act as that different person.

Now, following these more concrete observations, social threefoldness provides an archetypal way of ordering the association of adults:

Work — Economic Life
Human — Social Life
Spiritual — Cultural Life

The Meaning of Work

Work was the centre around which the social-therapeutic organism of Botton began to grow when it was founded in 1955. The daily chores in the house, on the farm and in the workshops outweighed everything else. But we are talking here of work without remuneration. Essentially, the work is done for the sake of others – – cooking because others are hungry; land work for the sake of the earth, the animals, the harvest; work in the craft shops to fulfil the orders — in short, work because it affirms in the worker his selfless human worth. Living together in community is our remuneration. Furthermore, the sphere of work, around which to a certain extent the course of the day is ordered, also has a social aspect — camaraderie begins to grow among those who do the work, which in turn builds community.

Work in the craft shops has a central meaning: *it is done for others* (who may sometimes be in other countries), thus becoming the medium by which the worker becomes associated to all mankind. Work done for the earth lets the earth become the homeland for mankind.

Work, the spiritual life and the variety of human relationships are the three great social co-ordinates which have to be developed in every social organism. The communal, the inter-human element of work, leads to the human-social sphere.

The Social Sphere

As already mentioned, a social form that is built on mutual dependence and equality has not yet been achieved in curative education. In curative education, learning and healing are to the fore. However, in the shared life of adults (with or without disabilities) the social element is the deciding factor. Because the villagers are not only adults but also need to be educated, a social-therapeutic organism is not easily achieved. At the table we have to insist on absolute equality since meals are not only to quell hunger but also to help establish a social organism. Since meals are social events of the first order, this self-same equality holds good in relation to hygiene, where possible. Equality instead of hierarchy is in order when it comes to punctuality for meals or work, and also in the handling of money. This can only be achieved by mutual love between co-workers and villagers, and this kind of love can only grow gradually through enthusiasm for a spiritualised human understanding. In daily encounters it is less relevant *what* is said than *how* it is said. One must conduct oneself, inwardly and outwardly, in awareness of the other adult or older person. This is valid for co-workers as well as for villagers.

By now the reader may have noticed that something of a future-bearing social organism is growing up around and with the handicapped person. This must also develop in relation to money. Should the individual be remunerated for both good and inferior work? Should co-workers be treated differently from villagers? And what about a group of workers? Of course, a major share will be needed to pay for food, lodging, administration and other expenses, leaving very little for pocket money. Therefore, the system adopted in all the Camphill centres is better because everyone receives what he needs. In this respect also, the principle of equality among adults is acknowledged — one needs more, the other needs less; one smokes, the other buys books. To receive just enough for one's needs is no problem for villagers (although I dare say it may be for co-workers). In receiving a salary the advantage seems to be that one does not have to account to anyone how the money is used. But a religious or philosophically-minded person will perhaps concur that, ultimately, we may owe an account to the divine-spiritual world. This sphere of the divine is the Christian sphere which also manifests in human relationships, for in social interactions between people the Christian element can be at work. 'Behold the kingdom of God is within you.' (Luke 17: 21) Therefore, regarding spending needs in a social therapy context, each consults with the others as to how much money he needs for himself. Above all, the precept here must be: the eternally divine is in every human being.

'Discipline' only rightfully exists in schools, the army and in prisons, not in a living community directed to the future. Order in these communities is something other than discipline. Order should also be established in the family. It should become an aesthetic, living concept, even a moral one — disorder is ugly, like a discarded snakeskin. Order among adults can only be achieved by insight and responsibility, consciously carried together and not through coercion.

With regard to work in the home, on the land or in the craft shop, the concept of hierarchy makes little sense. The person who understands most about a work process is the workmaster who teaches and trains; and there could be two or even three workmasters. With regard to the various realms of the community such as production, agriculture, finance, households, etc., groups of responsibility should be formed, and could include villagers where appropriate. These relevant groups do not act as 'inspectors' but rather as sounding-boards for the respective work areas in which they operate. The individual circles of responsibility balance each other out. Astonishingly perhaps, a Board or Council placed above the whole is superfluous because a certain measure of heavenly reason incarnates in the groups of a particular community. Naturally, these groups have a certain 'power', but the 'word of power' of a group or an individual must gradually give way, or transform itself, in recognition of selflessness and the capacity to be receptive. Power is an old form of clairvoyance that has turned egotistical.

Money and hierarchy have obscured the real being of responsibility. This being is what enables the social organism to function, and makes hierarchy superfluous. This being is the angel of brotherhood and has the wellbeing of all in mind. Whoever catches even the smallest part of its rays will be recognised in his being, and will rightly become more transparent and more intelligible to others. So responsibility is the angel of brotherly recognition, and therefore a part of eternally true curative education. The element of this sphere appears — firstly in Goethe's *Fairy Tale of the Green Snake and the Beautiful Lily*,[19] as the Silver King, then in Schiller's *Aesthetic Letters*[20] — as playfulness and as art. The child shows clearly that playing carries no responsibility. Every other activity that could be called 'work', that benefits another, is the result of old karma, and thereby a wellspring of new karma is woven into the social fabric of humanity. But play is totally free; the one who plays is free of pressure or duty and does not follow desire. It is up to us as Christians to elevate work which arose as a consequence of the Fall and the expulsion from Paradise, ('in the sweat of thy face'). (Gen 3: 19) Co-workers, together with the disabled, move into the sphere of innocence. Here we can also think of Christ's words, 'Except ye be converted, and become as little children, ye shall not enter into the kingdom of heaven.' (Matt. 18: 3)

The Spiritual (Cultural) Sphere

Now we turn to the third realm of any social organism, the spiritual life. How does it metamorphose into a social form, including in the villages? It is the sphere of individual creativity, the sphere in which the true, selfless ego comes directly to expression — in the capacity to receive as well as in activity; in the communal upward gaze to the divine (in a concert, for instance); during group work in adult education or in a religious service. We co-workers only appear normal because we can grasp the world intellectually, and we have this faculty because we have an ordinary ego-consciousness. The villagers often lack this ability and cannot, for the most part, take hold of their ego in our world. But as a result their ego is much more selfless than ours; it is closer to the angel, although it may not seem like that. Their experience is far stronger than ours since it does not need to go through the intellect. So an adult education based on experience, on images and imagination and less bound to the concept of causality, is therefore stimulating and beneficial for co-workers and villagers alike.

As yet we do not understand how to awaken the productive and active element in the villagers. If we succeed in this they will become our teachers on the way to the spirit. The concept of our higher ego is limited; it is inorganic, so to speak, and ego-related. 'We' are separated from 'it' by our ordinary ego, having developed the latter through our intellect. The villagers are unfree, yet directly exposed to the vitality of the higher, and therefore the social, self.

In relation to the spiritual-cultural life we are completely dependent on our individual intuition. The Bible Evening, inaugurated by Karl König, is an institution in which the social element is lifted above the merely practical, into the sphere of the religious-spiritual.

Adult education groups for villagers as well as co-workers, and experienced by them together, enable the important balance between work and learning to be maintained. This balance is of the greatest importance, very much like the work activity in the craft shops, on the land and in the households. Through identification with human culture, creation in nature and the phenomenon of the earth in its manifoldness (as represented in adult education), the eagerly receptive souls are effectively helped in the development of consciousness and their 'becoming'. In this way the villagers become like co-workers, in a real sense, members of humanity.

The diversity of these concrete social therapeutic endeavours are connected by their development. As every human being is in the developmental stage, so also is the social organism. Whatever is in the evolving stage is incomplete and diverse, but in it the divine can be creatively active.

LEBENSFORMEN IN DER SOZIALTHERAPEUTISCHEN ARBEIT, 1995

camphill in the light of the fundamental social law

It seems to me that through the many years of the development of Camphill, the separation of work from money (i.e. a salary or wages) has been one of the main factors that has made (and still makes) everything else within Camphill possible. The determination to gain more earthly space for the incarnation of Anthroposophia lay at the foundation of what later became Camphill. It was then, and still remains, its ever-renewing fountain. For this the separation of work from money became the main instrument. Indeed, I wonder whether without that instrument, the flow would not have been seriously hampered. When we began we were mainly a place for handicapped children, but there was always the urge that within this place there should be a realisation of anthroposophy.

A veil of obscurity is laid over any kind of work if the notion of 'earning one's living' is in any way connected with it. People would love to work if the aim of their work (that its fruits should benefit others), could remain unclouded by monetary considerations. Originally, the lack of money in Camphill obliged each one of us to use only as much as we absolutely needed. We kept to this arrangement of receiving only such money as we needed when, later on, our undertakings earned enough income to pay us ordinary salaries. We did this because in our work — and therefore in our morality and conscience — we wanted to stay free of the shackles of a salary scale. Such money as was earned by everyone was available to everyone, and slowly something else in our non-salaried life was added to the freedom of our work: the need to care for each other.

In those early days everything took place within the confines of a place for handicapped children. We were all teachers, dormitory parents, gardeners, farmers or cooks. In time, some of us took on the work of conducting the Children's Service, and all of us felt that the work we were doing — digging, teaching, washing-up or dressing the children, etc. — was inspired by the service and enlightened and warmed by Anthroposophia. In doing our work we felt we were doing something that was needed by the world. We saw ourselves as servants of the world, and in serving and working for the new Christianity we would have felt it to be inappropriate to receive 'payment' for the work we were doing.

Later on, as money became more available, we felt it was justifiable that more ordinary needs such as holidays, clothing, books, etc., should be met. Other needs too (the cost of caring for parents in old people's homes, the education of children, etc.), had to be met out of the 'common pot'. Since our work was completely free of any purse strings, the assessment of our needs depended only on our conscience, and this again became enlarged and enlightened by the growing knowledge of Anthroposophia. But our own conscience depended also on the conscience of our fellow workers, not only in regard to the children and the estates we were caring for, but also regarding him or herself. The Old Testament words: 'Am I my brother's keeper?' (Gen 4: 9), assumed a very natural reality in our caring for each other. Because our conscience was continually stimulated by the presence of our neighbour, he or she became unconsciously the co-creator of our own conscience — through him it was, and is, nourished. No wonder that we felt, and must feel, impelled to care for him or her. Our conscience was aroused by him because through anthroposophy we had learnt to regard him as a unique and eternal being who, passing through deaths and births, has been sent to earth to fulfil a divine task. In understanding his or her divine purpose, our own Michaelic determination was strengthened.

*   *   *

In a lecture in Stuttgart on 21st February 1912,[21] Rudolf Steiner remarked that a civilisation which equates money with work — in which one 'earns' one's livelihood through work — has little possibility of understanding anything about karma and reincarnation. We were very happy to discover these remarks for the first time some ten or fifteen years after Camphill had come into existence, when our own lives had already been arranged in the way I have described, not out of theory but from our own moral experience of life. We did, indeed, experience that the situations in which we found ourselves, and how we tried to bear them unhindered by their monetary value, were our karma. We have to 'pay back' or put right what we have done in the past, whether helpful or harmful, but in the present we are also free to add helpful or harmful intuitions and duties. Our responsibility extends both from the past and into the future.

This experience of responsibility has nothing to do with clairvoyance but everything to do with conscience. Anthroposophy can be seen as an enormous augmentation of human conscience. As an anthroposophist, I become aware of how and for what I can be responsible (for the earth, for education, for others), and in this a salary — 'earning' through work — can be a great hindrance. We can only care for each other in a non-sentimental way if we see each other as developing beings who are educated through the different cultural epochs according to their karma. Therefore in Camphill we have tried to take in as much of our time as possible, culturally, artistically, socially and scientifically. Separating work from money also brings a certain equanimity in our attitude towards the work. At the outset we chose our work not according to our individual gifts or inclinations, but solely according to the kind of work that needed to be done. Our will was more something that responded to the needs of the world than a means of self-assertion. Later on, however, it came to be seen as rather wasteful that a book-keeper should be doing the gardening and a gardener doing the accounts, but we found that the selfishness sometimes expressed in the assertion: 'I am a gardener' or 'I am a book-keeper' and so on, was completely overcome by the fundamental attitude towards work in Camphill.

*   *   *

In the life of Camphill these three things:
- work as the tool of the gods for the balancing of karma,
- work for the sake of work,
- caring for each other,

perhaps best express the way in which we have tried to realise what Rudolf Steiner spoke of as the Fundamental Social Law: [22]

> 'The well-being of a community of people working together will be the greater the more the individual makes over to his fellow-workers the proceeds of his labour, and allows his own requirements to be met from the proceeds of the work done by others.'

There is, however, something else in which these three things are included. In its many centres in different parts of the world, Camphill tries to establish (for all who work there and all who are in care there), a day of twenty-four hours — a way of life which tries to be a whole. It tries to do away with the divided existence which so many people in our time have to endure: one part (mainly for men) devoted to earning money, another to 'culture', and another (mainly for women) to that other side of life which is called 'home'. Many efforts are being made to achieve something different, the Women's Liberation Movement being an example. But most of these efforts prove barren because they seek only to readjust the existing system, which is man-made. Without the recognition of that fundamental social law mentioned above, it is difficult to imagine how our society can develop towards something less divided.

One more thing should be said about Camphill and the threefold social organism. With the passage of time since Camphill began its work, the individual centres have increasingly evolved their own lifestyle, and have increasingly taken a direction away from central government towards a form of decentralisation in which the groups responsible for the different spheres of life and activity in the centre try to work out a balance between each other.

These groups distribute themselves within the three spheres of the social organism, and each has its own very different procedures according to the nature of its sphere of work. In spite of grave shortcomings, the balancing of these groups has been, and still is, fundamentally successful. It has convinced us that decentralisation is the only way towards achieving a threefold social organism, and with it justice for the human being — a being who bears his karma on the path from creature to creator.

ANTHROPOSOPHICAL REVIEW, SUMMER 1979

work, the fundamental social law & tiredness

Nowadays, work forms a major part of our lives, at least time-wise. This does not mean it was so in bygone days. Ambition, the desire to climb from one social level to another, is largely a consequence of our democratic tendencies which are apparently intended to eradicate social strata. In a way that is not quite comprehensible to us today, the slaves, labourers and craftsmen of earlier times were content with their position in society. Why? Because in the past work was more integral to one's existence than it is today. Imagine a glass of water to which a spoonful of salt is added. If the water is cold the salt will not dissolve easily but sinks to the bottom as a precipitate, dropping with its own heaviness. This precipitated salt could be compared to work today, especially bodily or manual work — perhaps to all duty — whereas in former times work was more comparable to the dissolved salt. It is only in our time (and the beginning of the 'social problem'), that work has become a *separate* part of our life, a part for which a wage is due to us.

When Camphill began fifty years ago it was considered very unusual to work without receiving wages. In the current climate of unemployment benefits, the younger generation particularly does not care much about money as long as there is enough to satisfy the basic needs of life, so it in no way colours their decision to join Camphill. Relatively late in Camphill's development we came to realise that not paying wages is only one part of the so-called Fundamental Social Law, as formulated by Rudolf Steiner in his essay, *Anthroposophy and the Social Question.*[23] The other aspect of that law is that it can only concern a social organism in which a common idealism is held, even if only slightly. In the past, idealism didn't require any specifically individual activity since it was inspired from outside the human being by mythology, the king and fatherland, or by the church. Then, with the advent of Protestantism and its denominations, nationalism arose, democracy evolved and groups and parties formed. But in our time it is individual activity, meaning the *individual human being* in the activity, that supersedes the groupings of democracy, politics and Christianity, and outer forms will have to do justice to this fact. It will increasingly be individual human activity which will carry morality in the future.

Work done by human beings will gradually be understood to be more than a purely physical fact. The *result* is physical, but the *process* leading to it is not — rather it is a spiritual exertion. Little by little this idealism must come to replace money as the incentive, because work is not something that can be bought like a pound of apples! As long as Camphill consisted of relatively few co-workers this idealism — an actively devoted idealism — was natural to their existence. Now, with thousands of co-workers, the salt has begun to precipitate in the glass of water, and the tiredness of which so many complain seems to be the result. The idealism is no longer strong enough to dissolve the salt in the water of our Camphill life and prevent it obeying gravity and sinking. As a result, the *process* of work becomes sheer physical effort.

An answer to this tiredness would be to fire our idealism in an individual way — to make Anthroposophia one's own personal, immortal love. With that fire under it the water will become warmer and the salt will dissolve. Anthroposophia must become our real, personal child, as in the beginning of Camphill it was our only child. Tiredness does not enter into a mother's care for her child, or the work which that care entails. Neither can the work we have to do for the sake of this 'world-child' called Camphill make us tired because we are all, individually, its mothers. If there is tiredness, it may lie rather in the absence of care, in our lack of punctuality, our unreliability, our lack of respect for the other person or in our feelings of inferiority, and as a result of all this, the subsequent blurring of profile in the child itself (i.e. in Anthroposophia).

It depends upon us whether the child shines and is worth caring for. To long for those bygone times (as we too easily do), when there never seemed to be enough money yet life seemed so much more simple, is pointless! While an individual salary for work can only be the expression of that materialistic egoism which we all possess as children of our time — and Rudolf Steiner pointed out that a culture which pays for work cannot understand anything about reincarnation and karma — any economic arrangements which try to separate work from remuneration can only succeed if human spirituality assumes a certain strength and acts as an incentive. We need to long for a time when our idealism will be strong again.

CAMPHILL CORRESPONDENCE, XI 1971

reincarnation & wages

Why did Rudolf Steiner mention in February 1912,[24] apparently in passing, that an age which remunerates work with the wage packet cannot understand anything about reincarnation? In thinking about it within the context of Camphill, where working without wages has been the practise for decades (and 'working without wages' often seemed to become a mere phrase), one arrives at this: the nature of work that is paid for becomes clouded because its essence is to be needed by others. But if work is coloured by the attitude: 'I won't do it if you won't pay for it,' something of its essence is lost. Any work contains a dialogue. The consumer should express (in whatever way) how the work he needs is meant to be done — whether lecturer or teacher, shoemaker or joiner — and via educating one another this social dialogue leads to brotherliness. But if money is built into the process in the form of the worker's wage or salary which makes his livelihood possible, the essential *social* tie of work is severed. The moment work is connected with money which the worker needs, the above-mentioned cloud obscures the phenomenon of work. It seems to me, therefore, that work can only shine if it is entirely disconnected from money. Our needs, on the other hand, must be reconnected with money. Today there are many efforts to separate work from money, but as yet none — apart from Rudolf Steiner's initiatives — to reconnect needs with the amount of money required to meet them.

Work and needs have to do with the kind of person we are — work perhaps more with our future; needs more with our past. In our work we *create*, and we will have to live with its fruits in this or future lives. Our needs are more an outcome of our past; our heritage, past conditions, even past conditions as human beings. Needs are more an outcome of our karma; work is linked more with our freedom. Money compresses our existence into a being between birth and death. Money seems increasingly to become the incentive for our life, but karma and reincarnation are meant to replace it gradually in this respect.

No doubt the knowledge of reincarnation and karma has yet to travel many paths. One of them is through the understanding of our own needs on the one hand, and of our work on the other. Once the cloud of money is removed, the phenomenon of *work* can shine. In almost nothing else do we experience so directly our own 'selfless, eternal world-self' than when working flat out — whether as doctor, farmer, or woodworker. It is more difficult with our *needs*. Over the last few centuries these have become overwhelmingly determined by the amount of money I have at my disposal. Are the things I can buy with my money really needs or are they perhaps a mixture of advertisements, fashion and wishful thinking? Some of them I require as a human being, of course, such as food and clothing. So it is therefore necessary that my needs should enter the social process of dialogue — with a single person or with a group, the members of which can also explain *their* needs.

Where is the transition between need and wish? As long as I receive a salary or fixed amount of money, it is *my* affair how I spend it, but it is *fixed*. One condition towards creating a new *flexibility* is that I have to *confess* my needs — the money which becomes mine has first to be drawn through a social bath, as it were. How the social bath happens depends on the social fantasy of those engaged in the dialogue within a social unit, whether it be a post office, factory department or social-therapeutic institute. What is important is the empathy and tact of other people.

It is clear that much depends on the insertion of such a fact into a social organism. The fixed amount is intended to avoid human beings having to come closer to one another, with the shame and fear such a 'defrocking' always entails. It makes clear that the only reason why we are not yet all clairvoyant is our fear of the spiritual world, but the kingdom of heaven is in each one of us — and therefore so is the working of karma and reincarnation.

CAMPHILL CORRESPONDENCE, II 1991

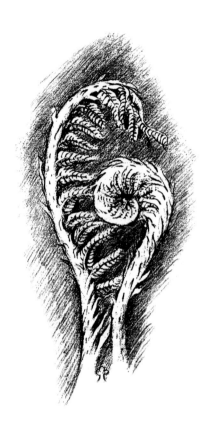

∼ *lent & passiontide*

the social side of lent

During Lent in bygone days we deprived our physical life of something we especially liked, sugar or tobacco, for example. Today this would be an old-fashioned, somewhat wasted effort. This exercise is the deprivation of an ascetic; it has a selfish nature, just as losing weight makes us feel better.

In our time an effort in courage, such as overcoming both sympathy and antipathy in our relationships to other human beings, is much more important. On the one hand, this is a positive activity because in overcoming we are looking away from ourself towards the other person, and on the other hand we are surrounding them with a reality which they themselves are not quite able to recognise. Courage in overcoming sympathy and antipathy must be based on one's goodwill towards the other, of course, but we will observe that their individuality becomes much more distinct through this effort. We will also notice how much cowardice permeates our own soul and how much we actually like to wallow in sympathy and antipathy.

We think that if we criticise someone directly we hurt them, although we do not want to. We are afraid both of our own aggressiveness and of theirs. Between these feelings lurks a great deal of cowardice. It can prevent us telling older people that they should not always have the last word, or it hinders us from offending or educating our neighbour. There are many occasions when we sin not by lying but by not saying something that might hurt but which, if it *had* been said, could have helped them. Because in some matters we do know best, this cowardice can only be overcome by separating the person from their words or deeds — through recognising their person.

Our social life would change tremendously if we could recognise each other as persons. When we do so, something like reverence for the other one overtakes our heart and soul. The idea of reincarnation, of the eternal essence of the other, becomes part of the experience of 'person'. It grows from being a theoretical idea to becoming a part of life, and the question of proving it recedes and pales — we would no more need to prove it than we need to prove the transparency of glass. The recognition of the other one as a person makes his heredity, his dependence on status, his being fettered to emotional patterns, all insignificant.

The threefold social organism, in all its manifold aspects, starts to make sense as appropriate for human beings only if the human beings who make up the social organism are recognised as persons, and thus as body, soul and spirit in their eternal essence. The complex involvement and interactions of human beings with one another can be understood. Arguing proves only the inorganic — for further realms of existence (like the threefold social organism) it is but a bridge, although a necessary bridge, to experience.

If we experience the other as a person, his peculiarities fall away. We are able to sense his karmically-laden but eternal and free spirit; his soul in combination with his everyday constitution and its eternal, holy flame, and his body as no more than a bearer or vessel. The expression of all this becomes a fact for us. The threefold social organism orders the three realms, spiritual, soul and physical — they must all be permeated by brotherhood.

We have been wrongly educated regarding thinking about the social life. We think about the ideas and theories of politics, but the threefold social order is not one of these. We have not been aware that the substance and basis of our social life is our own human individual existence and the human relations that we form. It is out of them that the threefold social order arises in the same way that a plant grows out of the earth and not out of sand. The relationships we form are like many and varied flowers, as tender as are the substance, colours and patterns of butterfly wings. But these flowers are, as in Novalis' fairy tale,[25] bred in the fire and glow of our determination and faithfulness.

BOTTON VILLAGE NEWS 27 IV 1985

transfiguration

The passage in the gospels called the Transfiguration depicts Christ on the mountain raised up and clothed in heavenly light between Moses and Elias, (Matt. 17: 1–13, Mark 9: 2–13) with the lunatic son and his father plus the nine helpless disciples in the earthly darkness below, (Matt. 17: 14–18) 'where there shall be weeping and gnashing of teeth'. (Matt. 8: 12, 22: 13, 24: 51, 25: 30, Luke 13: 28) In the gospels the two stories are told consecutively but we should imagine them in space, happening simultaneously, as in the picture painted by Raphael. What is depicted there is the earthly human self. Our eternal and inmost self is a manifold being but in our time only a very small and blurred image of it is visible to our waking consciousness. In reality this manifoldness extends into the heavenly light and into the arms of Christ. We ourselves are the nine helpless disciples as well as the father who begs of Christ: 'Help Thou my unbelief.' (Mark 9: 24)

What heals the son and overcomes the unbelief of the father and the disciples is the light shining into darkness, is Christ coming down from the mount of the Transfiguration. But on the way down there is a conversation between Christ and the three disciples who had been with Him but had fallen asleep, about John the Baptist and the return of Elias. (Matt. 17: 10–13 and Mark 9: 11–13) John the Baptist was beheaded not simply as a result of the evil power of Herodias but also as a sign and sacrifice for mankind. The 'voice crying in the wilderness' (John 1: 23) prepared the coming of Christ through this final sacrifice. From that moment on his voice merged into the Word of God, and so the Feeding of the Five Thousand could take place. The beheaded John stands on the path from the light of the mountain to the darkness of unbelief. The head is the source of unbelief but also of the first blurred image of the ego. The physical head encloses us in the boundaries of birth and death and robs us of the reality of reincarnation.

Three stages in the evolution of humanity can be discerned here. Firstly, the forming of the head which severs humanity from the heavens and plunges it into darkness but which nevertheless gives it the potential for ego-consciousness and with it the longing for Christ. The second stage is the whole picture described above — the Transfiguration, the conversation between Christ and the three disciples about Elias and John the Baptist, and the healing of the lunatic boy. The third stage begins with Raphael's picture; Raphael who is himself the returned Elias and John the Baptist.[26] Colours appear where light and darkness merge and Raphael's picture positively glows, its colours shining with the brilliance of the Transfiguration itself, light pouring into the darkness of sickness and unbelief. Every human being who tries to bring his life into relation to Christ takes part in the sacrifice of John.

In our time the third stage is developing further through all that has been initiated by Rudolf Steiner. Because of him, our age is the age of the Transfiguration.

BOTTON VILLAGE NEWS, 1 III 1963

the third world

By the term 'Third World' we refer to that part of the globe which, compared with North America, Europe and Russia, is under-fed, under-industrialised and, to a greater or lesser extent, developmentally dependent on the Western powers. The Third World consists mainly of parts of South America, Africa and Asia.

Nothing would be easier than to think that if those in the Third World were not starving, if the enormous differences in food intake between the countries of the world were more equal, then all would be well. This is true, but not completely true.

The impulse which sent out missionaries — first from Europe to Britain in ancient times; later from Britain to India, China and Africa — had at least two sides. One was to convert people to the Catholic or Protestant faiths. The other was to humanise them, to make them members of wider mankind rather than leave them localised as heathens.

There was (and still is) a tendency, especially in the Catholic Church, to cut religion off from the rest of life and make it into a shining, sinless world of its own belonging only to the Church. Against this, Protestants had the tendency to turn religion into something all-too-human, devoid of grace from above. In the Middle Ages, learning was fostered only by monks in the monasteries, as if learning was possible only for men who led an ascetic, devout, ordered life serving the spirit twenty-four hours a day, cut off from family, business and politics. Today, knowledge has detached itself completely from religion and has become an entirely secular (although largely technological) affair. The age of Irish-Celtic Christianity is long past when learning and knowledge was a Christian affair in which man's humanity was vested in a piety enlightened by learning. Learning causes responsibility to permeate the person's individuality and dignity, and it affects his neighbours.

To think we can rescue the Third World merely by feeding it is just as wrong as thinking (as the old missionaries did), that salvation could be assured simply by converting people to 'Christianity'. The inherent fault of Marxism was its materialism because matter alone (food, money or the means of production) can never do justice to the full human being. The educational impulse is as Christian as the economic one.

But education and money alone do not make life worthwhile. In the end what makes life worthwhile is the company of other human beings. It is the relationship to others which allows both learning and economy to shine in their inherent truth — only that which we do together with others lets the whole of life shine in its real warmth. Our ideal should be to found social units all over the world in which the social organism is lit up by mutual recognition and friendships — places which are neither communist nor capitalist, nor alternative-idealistic, but simply human. This could change the Third World. Such communities would be the yeast in the dough.

BOTTON MIRROR, 14 III 1986

understanding the act of consecration of man

For those of us who go to the Act of Consecration of Man, it is necessary to understand something about it — although not in an intellectual sense but rather as one understands a gesture, or the expression of a face. It is pointless to 'know' that left and right sides at the altar signify active and passive. It means far more if one feelingly understands that the priest moves by the same left or right World-power as when one uses right or left hand or foot for actions appropriate to left or right.

The veneration naturally felt in the presence of the altar — the altar itself, the picture, the candles and their lighting, the priest, the servers, the words — is not simply veneration of something supersensible appearing in the sensible realm; it is veneration for one's higher self because in the course of the service the priest's words 'Christ in you' are fulfilled, finally, in the communion. During the Act of Consecration of Man we ourselves become hallowed as Christ Himself descends from the space of the altar into those present as the service progresses. But this means that they look towards the altar as the source of Christ, the Spirit Who makes the human being whole, because in the course of its spiritual past humanity has lost the spirit. It lost the spirit slowly in the course of its historic evolution and is hardly aware of the loss.

In the past, this relationship between higher 'I' and lower 'I' was different. Human beings were just beginning to develop their ego consciousness, although they still had a strong connection to the spirit (the higher ego). Later, this incipient 'I am' consciousness evolved into the clear 'I am' consciousness we possess today. Increasingly, humanity lost its dream-like consciousness of the spiritual worlds, its god-willed past earth lives, its dreaming humility, devotion and piety towards a higher existence, and instead developed an earthly 'I am'; a consciousness of its own name. With this step came pride, ambition and illusion. Through this rising 'I am', a certain Cain-like nature came to the fore as opposed to his former Abel qualities. Earthly activity became increasingly more important.

As people of our time, we feel a certain wholeness in our selves. We call this wholeness by our own name and experience it as 'I' — the name and 'I' are one. No wonder we have lost the feeling for our repeated earth-lives. Our named 'I' in this life is only one facet of a majestic 'I' that comprises many earthly lives and many names, and the times between deaths and new births. It is this higher, comprehensive 'I' that lights up in the souls of those attending the service as Christ draws nearer.

The words of the Lent prayer 'Thou has lost the spirit', become a convincing experience. The words 'Christ in you' returns what is lost. At the same time the seeming wholeness filled by the spurious 'I am' (which is only a fragment of the many lives embracing the 'I'), crumbles. Outside the service (and also but in a different way, outside meditation), we feel we are not complete; we are a ruin but it is the best we can do. In the service we receive that which makes us whole again but in a new way, quite different from days of old.

This gradual loss of the spirit and the emergence of the 'I am' has taken place over the 2,000 years of Christianity and is one of the final steps in the evolution of humanity from Paradise to Materialism; from a belief in divine beings to our faith in 'cells'. The emergence of the 'I am' and the loss of spirit means that mankind must regain the spirit in a new way.

With our emerging 'I am' consciousness, the brilliance of the spiritual worlds has dimmed and slowly disappeared, and with the rising 'I am' has come what we now call psychology. Psychology presupposes a gradual differentiation in the powers of the soul: sense experience, thinking, feeling, willing and memory.

When we turn our thinking, feeling and will to the godhead in the Offertory, the second part of the Act of Consecration of Man, we do so in order that the splendour of the spiritual world may reappear because the strength of our psychology (our thinking, feeling, and will), will decrease. But through the help of Christ it is not the 'I' that is recreated but a new 'we'. 'We all lift up...' is the beginning of the second part of the Offertory.

It would be a mistake to think that we can follow the transition from 'I' to 'we' in the Offertory with our ordinary 'head' understanding. We also have to awaken our 'heart' understanding to comprehend the Act of Consecration of Man as a whole. Only by following the service with our hearts do we discover that it takes place outside time and that we are allowed to enter a new dimension of existence. When the candles are extinguished we realise that an hour of earthly time has elapsed and we have discovered a new dimension in which space seems to disappear and time is not progressive, earthly time. If we do not follow it with our hearts we are always tempted to look at our watch and measure its length in earthly time.

The second part of the Offertory is when 'we' — no longer 'I' — turn to Christ. From this moment on we are exhorted to follow the upward stream of the Offertory with the rising smoke and scent of the incense, in a praying mood. In the first half, we tried, individually, to divest ourselves of our usual biased thinking, feeling and will — to set aside our ordinary soul life to which we are so accustomed — in order to pray without our garment of normality because we are allowed to turn to Christ. And because our words of prayer rise upwards on the clouds of incense, Christ can descend in the Transubstantiation, the third part of the Act of Consecration of Man. The heavenly fire of love burns within our earthly existence.

At the end of the service we take communion by taking into ourselves the body and blood of Christ, the Being of Christ. The words 'Christ in you' are fulfilled. At the beginning of the fourth part of the Act of Consecration of Man, called the Communion, Christ speaks of the peace by which He is related to the world. The peace of Christ is obviously not the psychological feeling of peace we normally have. It is of existential majesty, and so also is the peace we receive after the bread and wine. In a miraculous way, as Christ's body and blood, the bread and wine are the earth. Through the Mystery of Golgotha, the earth has become Christ's body: Christ — and the earth as His dwelling place — are one.

At the beginning of the Communion, in connection with peace, comes the phrase 'world's evolving'. In the Transubstantiation, the third part of the Act of Consecration of Man, we recognised that the earth is also permeated by the power and being of Christ, and that therefore, at the end, the bread and wine contain not only the majesty, grandeur and promise of the earth, but also the 'world's evolving'.

Through the grace of Christ, three times in the course of its evolution the earth became increasingly adapted for human habitation, until the fourth occasion, the Mystery of Golgotha, when it became Christ's home. These four stages were steps of separation between earth and humanity, and thus increasingly a suitable environment for the human being's selfhood.[27]

The senses were not yet able to observe, but were variations of what our senses are today. They fettered man to the endless variety of the earth in his pleasure and pain, his greed and disgust, with a strength that made freedom impossible. Through Christ, humanity could become upright; the senses could disentangle themselves from the fetters of the earth.

To begin with, human beings were silent, but in the second and third steps speech entered the world and man began to use it. At first the sounds could only express his various inner conditions, not of his soul but of his life — his wellbeing, his bodily pains and discomforts, his hunger and thirst. Later, in the third step, by overcoming his subjective limitations the world and his experiences could become words, sentences and grammar.

The fourth step was the Mystery of Golgotha. Humanity's understanding, and the earth became one. Christ died into this unified whole. He permeated the earth as well as our understanding — he overcame death. His blood, His resurrection, shone into the cosmos.

In the beginning the earth contained humanity. The first separation between human being and earth took place in the Fall. Then, in the three steps leading to the Mystery of Golgotha, human beings became more and more independent, albeit forced to breathe the earth's air, to eat its fruit and to build shelters for themselves. But in freedom and through his connection to Christ, the human being will find his connection to the earth anew.

This and much more is contained in the bread and wine of Communion.

DATE UNKNOWN

reincarnation & responsibility

Towards the end of his life Rudolf Steiner said repeatedly that in our time the innermost task of spiritual science is the elucidation of reincarnation and karma. It was only towards the end of his life that he was able to devote himself to it unhindered.

We, his more or less fervent pupils, experience the majesty of this thought only occasionally, and when we do it is *our* one biography, *our* one life from birth to death that is dominant. But that we have many lives behind us and ahead of us remains a shadowy thought compared to the dense reality of our present life. This must be so because reincarnation has yet to become a *factor* in the Christian evolution of humanity, not merely a *thought* among others but a factor that alters many things in our present existence. These former lives are not memories in the ordinary sense, for if we could remember them they would not let us be free. Rather they colour the events of our present life with a certain moral sheen and are responsible for them.

It was not some blind power which determined *these* parents for me, *this* nation, *these* human encounters, *these* illnesses, journeys, life-conditions, etc. It is not random chance that I am faced with daily or lifetime decisions; it is my responsibility which colours them all — although the 'I' which is responsible for them is different from my everyday 'I'. After a while one senses that its nature is eternal and hence my freedom and my necessities, my birth and my death, belong to its star existence. In order that the person walking the earth becomes a *person*, his self (his eternal I) is hidden from him. At the moment of his birth, the stars (his horoscope) no doubt press him into certain forms. These forms are *his* responsibility in the widest sense and they are in accordance with his past lives. This responsibility is certainly very different from the ones we take on when starting a family or changing a profession, which derive from the freedom that earthly life offers the individual. The responsibility for our lives through the eternal self is wider than that of our earthly life.

In that we have a head and a body, we all bear visible signs of our past incarnation as part of ourselves. Our present head is the transformed body from our previous life, so therefore we have very individual heads and countenances but not so individual bodies. The head is the basis of our observing faculties and sense impressions, whereas the body enables us to *act*, and contains our metabolism, pulse and circulation, and our breathing. The head is of the past; the body is of the future. Our neck, our larynx, our voice and language is an image of what took place in the spiritual world, the land of transformation between our last death and the birth into our present life. Therefore Christ is the Word because He is the spirit shining into earthly matter. He unites head and body because His life on earth was lived only *once* — it was a karma-less life and therefore the repeated metamorphoses of body into head was unnecessary. It is karma, our responsibility towards humanity and the world, which extends our existence over many lives throughout the evolution of mankind and world.

To these responsibilities also belong our reactions, our mode of existence in the different evolutionary stages, both historical and natural, in which we are and have been placed, and in which we develop. We are part of mankind and must participate in its evolution because were we not part of it, what importance could it have for us? We are meant to become more and more the friends of Christ. He is the Alpha and Omega, and through Him the Word and all evolution unfolded. Through being virtually and ever-increasingly His true friends, have we not played — and do we not still play — a decisive rôle in evolution?

In the younger generation there is a general conviction that they are nothing, mediocre, or unimportant for evolution, and so they can flee the awesome task of becoming His friend. The burden of this task means to take earnestly not only one's freedom, but also the cross which we have accumulated through our many lives.

BOTTON VILLAGE NEWS, 3 V 1991

memory & kamaloca

Kamaloca is part of our life after death, lasting about one third of earthly life. We live through the actual events of our days and years in reverse order. It takes place neither within space nor in time. We move in a time-space, a panorama of our past life, seeing ourselves in the way that we might look at a number of pictures on the wall of an exhibition. The first pictures we see are of what took place nearest to our death, the next are ever further away in time, back through middle age to our youth, our school days and our infancy. But not only do we see ourselves in the different ages from the time of our death until roughly the third year of our life, rather we experience how those people around us in the course of our lifetime have seen, heard, loved and suffered us. If we once gave someone a box on the ear, we do not experience the situation in the same way in kamaloca as we did when the event occurred in life. In kamaloca we ourselves feel the blow on the ear that we gave the other person when on earth. We are required to become the recipients of what we did during life — we have to experience the consequences of our deeds.

The ramifications of kamaloca are manifold. What takes place in kamaloca forms the seed for our destiny in the coming life. With counter-words, counter-deeds, counter-sufferings and counter-joys we have to balance what we did, said, suffered and enjoyed in our past life. In this way our life is lived through in a very selfless fashion, since we are always part of a whole web of relationships.

Christ can interlock the balancing of our needs with the needs of others — our need fits the need of someone else because it is the opposite. In our effort to become Christian it is the awareness of this kamaloca time that we have to raise into everyday consciousness as we live our lives on earth. Our unconscious harbours all the suppressed thoughts and experiences we went through in kamaloca in the time between our past life and this present one, and our present life is partly the outcome of what we experienced then.

It is necessary to look upon one's life in this light, not only concerning the boxes on the ear and other such obvious things, but also in regard to memory. Our memory not only serves us regarding the past situations and stations of our life, thereby giving it cohesion and making it possible for me to experience it as my life. It is also through memory that we are inserted into the social order. To keep a promise, to remember appointments or stick to decisions, makes us into reliable human beings. The disappointments we cause through forgetfulness are incalculable, the more so since these disappointments go through a varying scale from unconscious to full consciousness. The result of not coming to a meeting with someone is seen plainly enough, but not sticking to a decision may affect many who do not notice it because it was only one's own responsibility to hold to the decision. Because they are part of a situation, all these lapses of memory will confront us in kamaloca whether we noticed them in life or not. We will be amazed to find how much social life depends on our memory. The emotional cruelty of not caring enough for each other is a consequence of our forgetfulness far more than we think. How often do we want to give each other a word of explanation but forget to say it, thus leaving the wound of the other person untended. Or we order something, then circumstances change and what was ordered becomes unnecessary but we forget to inform the person we ordered it from, and hours of human strength are wasted and stick out of the web of life like a sore thumb.

Human memory is becoming worse as the generations pass. The moral activity of our goodness will depend more and more on our ability to remember. The minutes of a group meeting are more valuable today than a poem or a picture.

BOTTON VILLAGE NEWS, 27 II 1970

MARCH 1996
BOTTON VILLAGE NEWS

∼ holy week & easter

the threefold social order in the light of easter

Hidden within the womb of the Lent and Passion space clothed in black, the red of Easter grows and shines, until at Easter it bursts forth and melts the black away. Because it is a world event, an event of the divine world reaching into the earthly world, it moves not only through the spirit-souls of individual human beings, but also through the social order, through our earthly living together.

The prophet Zechariah says, 'Tell ye the daughter of Sion, Behold, thy King cometh unto thee, meek, and sitting upon an ass, and a colt the foal of an ass'. (Matt. 21: 5) Christ riding into Jerusalem on Palm Sunday, into the approaching and thickening shadow of the Cross, is an image of a social order which came to an end on Good Friday.

That social order was determined through a king, a pharaoh, an emperor, but from the Mystery of Golgotha onward every individual is a king. At the entry into Jerusalem, the shouting multitude wanted 'thy King' in the sense of physical power, but the true meaning is individual kingship — the indwelling king — not a king that rules over his subjects. Therefore the cry of 'Hosanna' turns to 'Crucify' on the morning of Good Friday.

The social history of the last 2,000 years is the struggle between dying kingship and rising democracy. The form of democracy we have now is but a rung on the ladder towards a social order in which individual kingship is possible. The parliaments of modern times, in as far as their members are elected and that a government results from a general election, are still very much the beginnings of democracy —for what about those who voted for the losing side, which may be 49%?

The 'inner light' dwelling in each human being (the founding and guiding experience of the Quakers), is the only real basis for democracy. The social reformers of the 19th century in Britain (as well as others in many other countries), were directly or indirectly stirred by that inner light: Wilberforce,

Shaftesbury, Owen, Dr Barnardo, Elizabeth Fry, Florence Nightingale.

Rudolf Steiner's idea concerning the threefold social organism is to form social organisms, both small and large, in which this individual light is allowed to shine. It will take a long time before a fully appropriate organisation for the three spheres is found, but Rudolf Steiner said that only when the social organism is threefold will the true social problems appear. For that, the fully appropriate organisation is not yet necessary, but something else is necessary. The working together of the three spheres is no longer achieved through anything resembling a government. We must find out how members of *groups* can support one another. Rudolf Steiner often said, 'Truth needs proof as little as the stars need sticks to hold them in their position; they hold each other.' So also members of groups carry one another, on condition that one human being values the other, experiences the other far more intensely than usual.

In our time, the experience of the other human being is obscured. Rudolf Steiner therefore described as the inner core of the social question the words of Christ from the Gospel of St Matthew (25: 40), transmuted into our time: 'In whatever the least of your brethren thinks, you must recognise that I am thinking in him.'

Reality, not chaos, is found through unprejudiced listening. The inner light shines not through introspection, but because others acknowledge it. The warmth and light of the Easter red arises through groups striving for the organisation of the three spheres of the social organism, and carrying each other because in each one of the members the flame of Easter is listened to.

BOTTON VILLAGE NEWS, 27 III 1963

the temple legend

In an old legend[28] it is said that Seth, the son of Adam, was allowed to return for a moment to Paradise. There he saw that after Adam and Eve's expulsion, the Tree of Life and the Tree of Knowledge had intertwined so that one could no longer distinguish which branches belonged to which tree. Seth took three seeds from this tree, put them in Adam's mouth, and from them grew a bush with a threefold trunk.[29]

The wood of this trunk had a long subsequent history. It was the flaming bush from which the words 'I am the I am' came to Moses. It became his staff which turned into a serpent at Pharaoh's court and with which Moses struck water from the rock. The wood was found to be unsuitable as a portal or a pillar in the Temple that Solomon built with Hiram in Jerusalem. It became the bridge over which Balkis, the Queen of Sheba, walked when she visited Solomon. It was then submerged in water and brought healing properties to the pool of Siloah. Finally, it became the cross which Christ carried and upon which He was crucified and died.

This wood points to spiritual part of the human being — to Spirit Self, Life Spirit and Spirit Man — which he lost when he was expelled from Paradise, and which he regains the more he partakes in Christ's death.

King Solomon built the Temple in Jerusalem ten centuries before Christ. Although small, it was one of the miracles of antiquity because to some extent it reflected its builder, king Solomon, who was himself a human miracle, a man of surpassing wisdom as well as outstanding beauty. He was like a beautiful mask or shell, looking as if he had been carved from ivory, ebony and gold. He had seven names (of which Solomon was only one) because in him the seven constituents of the human being were radiantly clear.[30]

The Temple was the image of the human body, yet Solomon himself could not build it; he needed Hiram, a Phoenician priest-initiate and architect, to build it with him. According to the legend, Hiram was a descendent of Cain, while Solomon was a descendent of Abel. The descendents of Cain were skilled in the arts, in craft and building work, so Hiram was therefore able to build the Temple as an appropriate expression and dwelling place of the divine, and the descendents of Abel could thus be filled with the divine. This meeting between Hiram and Solomon, and the building of the Temple which resulted from it, was a turning point in the history of mankind.

Balkis, the Queen of Sheba, had discovered that Solomon was only a man — albeit a wonderful one — but that the promise of the future lay with Hiram. Hiram had three apprentices whose frustrated ambitions to become masters led them to subvert the building of that part of the Temple forecourt known as the Brazen Sea. Fueled by jealousy, Solomon instigated the death of Hiram indirectly through the apprentices, and thus the old guilt of Cain was atoned, but only by incurring new guilt. The Mystery of Golgotha alone could supersede and reconcile what had been split asunder in the Fall. The blood of the Redeemer had to flow into the earth on account of the blood of Abel and Cain.

There was, however, a counter-picture of the holy blood which had not yet flowed — the dark third part of the Temple, the Holy of Holies, into which

only the High Priest entered once a year. (For example, when the birth of
John the Baptist was prophesied to Zacharias he withdrew to that part of the
temple.) It was the curtain of this third, dark sanctum that was rent in twain
when Christ died on the cross. The Temple, with its dark third, is connected
with Solomon and the names of the human being as they have yet to unfold in
the future.

The Sermon on the Mount (Matt. 5: 3–12) opens with the Beatitudes. At
its centre is the sevenfold Lord's Prayer[31] (Matt. 6: 9–13) which represents the
seven constituents of the human being. One of the signs on our Christmas
trees is this figure (*see below*). The three points of the triangle stand for Spirit
Self, Life Spirit, and Spirit Man; the four points of the earthly square signify
Ego, Astral, Etheric and Physical bodies. The seven constituents of the human
being to which the names pointed were a plan, a design which would gain
life through the Son of Man. In the warmth and fire of His baptism these
seven constituents would melt from their rigid slumber and thereby gain
their divine independence. Only then could Man appear, created in the image
of God. That which had been only a silent, sevenfold picture in Solomon,
became reality through the baptism by fire, as foretold by the prophetic voice
speaking from the burning bush.

BOTTON VILLAGE NEWS, 17 I 1969

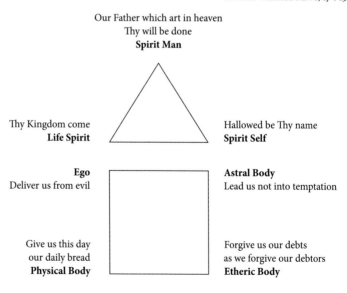

Our Father which art in heaven
Thy will be done
Spirit Man

Thy Kingdom come
Life Spirit

Hallowed be Thy name
Spirit Self

Ego
Deliver us from evil

Astral Body
Lead us not into temptation

Give us this day
our daily bread
Physical Body

Forgive us our debts
as we forgive our debtors
Etheric Body

the youth in the gospel of st mark

One day the gospels will be the strongest symbols of Christianity. Despite the many books on Christianity, it cannot be fully assimilated by the intellect, and the attempt to make the gospels 'understandable' is one of the most dreadful obstacles in our time. The substance and flavour of the gospels is so strong that for many centuries they have borne something of the impact of Christianity for millions of people, which historical criticism and misuse by the established churches have been unable to subvert. Rudolf Steiner's interpretations have helped our intellectual understanding a little, just as a beam of light makes part of some great structure visible in the darkness. But the Word-nature of the gospels does not reveal itself in a logically understandable, narrative sequence. Rather, they are a composite structure and to the extent that one can follow the composition (with the help of Rudolf Steiner), understanding dawns.

One part of the composition in the Gospel of St Mark is the enigmatic figure of the youth who appears on the Mount of Olives in the night of Maundy Thursday after the disciples have fled. The men who came to take Christ try to seize the youth but he leaves a linen garment in their hands and slips away naked. (Mark 14: 51–52) He reappears clothed in a long white garment sitting at the right side of the empty grave, speaking to the three women on Easter Sunday morning. (Mark 16: 5–7) When the beam of interpreting light is shed on him, he is revealed as the *Christ impulse*.[32]

We must imagine that from the Baptism in the Jordan onwards, the Christ impulse was united with Jesus of Nazareth — with His words, His deeds, His wanderings — and that it left him on the night of Maundy Thursday to reappear on Easter Sunday. The words spoken from the Cross: 'My God, my God, why hast thou forsaken me?' (Matt. 27: 46, Mark 15: 34) indicates this, but it remains beyond human comprehension. Yet it may be that the events from the imprisonment onward — the talk with Pilate, the scourging, the crucifixion and the darkness of the sun eclipse — are also expressions of this same fact. It was all borne by a human being, albeit a guiltless one, but one devoid of any divine power and presence. We are all guilty in the chain of repeated earth lives, but He is not. Although he was human, there was no karma, no destiny, which had to be balanced. Our head is the consequence of our body in our former life, but His head and body were *one*. The form of the Risen Christ is the transfiguration of our sins, the apocalyptic restoration of our divine likeness. For a day and a night He was merely Man in order to make us into future gods.

BOTTON VILLAGE NEWS, 17 V 1968

chlorophyll & blood

Again this year after Easter we see with wonderful clarity how a green veil starts to clothe the black skeletons of the trees, and the bare fields form a bridge between the warm, light, white air and the bare, black earth. The tender green seems a peach blossom red when the light shines through it.

The green of the leaves and the red of our blood have almost identical chemical compositions, the only difference being that the green (chlorophyll) contains magnesium, the red contains iron. The surface of the leaf 'breathes' — with the help of light the plant breathes in carbon dioxide and breathes out oxygen. Green chlorophyll is one of the results of this process. We inhale the air into our lungs and its oxygen makes the blood red and sustains our life. But air also contains much more besides oxygen, and too much oxygen would make us faint through a surfeit of life.

Our lungs are like folded leaves breathing in darkness; they inhale the air (mainly oxygen), and exhale carbon dioxide. The power of Christ was (and at present still is) a soul power, but it will become a physiological power, and from the Mars-like red of war our blood will change into the selfless, scented red of roses and we will no longer exhale poisonous carbon dioxide. The plants sacrifice themselves for us by exhaling enough oxygen for us to live. We can live out our karma only because the plants remain innocent, karma-less and faithful to the gods, balancing our sins and the equilibrium of the world with our errors and longings.

For the natural human mind, these things would be quite understandable had we not been trained since childhood into the black and white concept of cause and effect. We have been brought up to equate understanding with discovering the causal nexus. But by reducing phenomena to a mere cause-effect relationship — for example, 'because I put the seed in the ground the plant grows' — we think about the world far too narrowly, superficially and dryly. The world is a huge inter-related organism. The green plants and our red blood can also be related to each other artistically, like the colours and patterns in a picture or carpet, the artist being not human but divine.

This carpet includes the stars. A part of its pattern and colour determines the date of Easter — the first Sunday after the first full moon following the spring equinox — but if this were a causal relationship we would make sun and moon into something like heavenly bombs whose impact has the power to make the green appear, like an aeroplane that sprays insecticide. As soon as we get away from the cause-effect straitjacket and see a world picture on whose periphery circle sun, moon and earth, and in whose centre the spring part of the earth is clad in green, then we can behold the world in this divinely artistic way.

Easter, the Mystery of Golgotha, is inserted into this world situation out of Christ's being and freedom. The wonder of Christianity — although it is the very opposite of a nature religion — is that it inserts itself into the course of nature and the course of the stars.

BOTTON VILLAGE NEWS, 31 III/7 IV 1967

austria

It is moving but also important to ponder the destiny of Austria in the stream of time. Even in my childhood, Austria (or mainly Vienna) with the blue Danube, the lilac and the waltzes of the Wienerwald, was an alluring inducement for tourists to spend their money. Austria was, and still is, part of central Europe, which is a soul-and-spirit reality that has never yet found its physical expression in the social and political constellation of Europe, except in many, many individuals. This is the central Europe about which Rudolf Steiner so often spoke as the origin and source of what in a modern sense is 'human'; this central Europe which reaches from Burgundy to Bohemia, from Silesia to Northern Italy and Alsace, and also from the lower Rhine to Corinthia.

If this central Europe could have found its political-physical incarnation then its inhabitants would have felt themselves superior to the rest of mankind and would thereby have destroyed this fount of being. One could 'become' a central European, not simply be born one, as it is not a nationality but an individual task.

Historically, nothing was worse for Europe and for mankind than the unification of Germany after the ending of the Franco-Prussian war in 1871. Before that there was no Germany, only independent dukedoms and principalities, of which the largest and most powerful was Prussia. In the unification of Germany, the frontier between Germany and the Austro-

Hungarian Empire became one of the starkest lies of history. Austria was looked upon as 'only soul', soft and untidy (meaning female and sentimental), while Germany (or Prussia, really), appeared strong, masculine, efficient, idealistic (although it was merely intellectual) and militaristic. The army officer became the image of Germany, while *'das susse Wiener Madl'* ('the sweet Viennese lady') became the image of Austria. But both types are mere caricatures of the human image. The stupidity and inhumanity of the Habsburgs, who held the huge Austro-Hungarian Empire together, played a certain part in all this, of course. In the division of Germany and Austria, the image of the human being and the being of central Europe was blotted out, both for Europe and the inhabitants of the other parts of the earth.

The seeds for this anti-Christian division go back to the Thirty Years War. That war was really a conflict staged by the counter Reformation — in fact by the Jesuits.[33] If the Roman Catholics could not suppress Protestantism, then at least they would try to change the map of Europe so that the fruits of Protestantism would be intellectualism and not an enhanced humanity. From 1618 to 1648 central Europe became the battlefield between Catholics (mainly Austria, but aided by France), and Protestants (mainly the 'German' dukes, but supported by Sweden). With the preponderance of Prussia, the division between Germany and Austria grew. This battlefield destroyed wide parts of central Europe for decades by famine, fire, epidemics, etc., in an unspeakable way. The many Rosicrucian[34] efforts which began to appear publicly in the first decade of the 17th century were drowned in the waves of the beginning war. When it was over the Prussian king Frederick the Great, a genius of order and cruelty, made one of the first moves towards a social life arising out of the chaos.

What moves one when breathing Austrian air is her rôle in central Europe; the strength of her humanity; the theme or melody hidden in her history which Austria is meant to play openly one day in humanity's orchestra of the future. In the sense of a one-sided way of life, Austria is not a 'nation' at all. The Austrian earth, its landscape, is full of unused strength — as is ever more true everywhere in this last century, in the town, the capital, or any concentrated 'culture'. The human and spiritual potential which could not stream into the intellectual flowering of the town-culture, remained dormant, latent in the Austrian earth.

Two things seem to me a symbol of Austria's future. The first is that the memorandum which Rudolf Steiner wrote concerning the threefold

commonwealth[35] and its application to the empire, was appended to his
memoirs of the years 1916–18 by Count Polzer-Hoditz, private secretary to
the last Austrian emperor Charles, when he presented them to him. The
second is that in the first battle establishing Austria's nucleus and the rule of
the Babenbergs, Austria's flag became a white band across a red field because
blood had so drenched it. In the same way, the red stole and girdle is laid
across the white alb of the priest at Easter. At this festival, the priest expresses
Austria as well as Easter, humanly and spiritually.

BOTTON VILLAGE NEWS, 28 IV 1967

our neighbourhoods

In a lecture given in Dornach on 7th August 1920,[36] Rudolf Steiner spoke
about political parties and the threefold organisation of social life. He said
that what dominated eastern Europe as Bolshevism was really only the
end product of Western materialism, and what would later dawn as the
future reality has nothing to do with Bolshevism but is to be found in the
Russian village communities.[37] An understanding of these is necessary to any
understanding of the future that waits to be born. The village community is
the only reality in the East: everything else belongs to the institutional life that
will eventually perish. In the West we will have to learn to organise the three
spheres of the social organism out of the substance of life that is already given
expression in these village communities. They are beacons of an East-West
synthesis flaming in the night of present day social illusions.

Here it is our neighbourhoods that can encourage the brotherly element of
the Russian villages to take root and grow — the flavour of this brotherliness
is familiar to us from Tolstoy's stories — for the essence of our village lies in
the neighbourhoods. The groups (production group, stewards group, school
group, cultural activities group, etc.) exist merely to help in organising and
integrating our activities. The groups take up village issues generated in the
neighbourhoods and channel them into the three spheres of the social life
— cultural, economic, and the life of rights and justice — and so make social
life fruitful without the agency of a dominating, central government.

Because they are made up of all the individuals in the village, the
neighbourhoods are indeed the very stuff of the village. In the highest sense
they are its metabolism. It is into a neighbourhood that the individual spirit,
laden with its destiny, incarnates on earth, but it is the groups (working as

they do out of the threefold structure of the social life), which make the individual incarnation fruitful. In their working together, the neighbourhoods (presently three* but the future may suggest more), provide a brotherliness that is organised by the groups in an increasingly threefold way. In their totality, the neighbourhoods provide the harmonies, the keys and chords, on which the groups can play their melodies, themes and movements. Or to use another image, the neighbourhoods receive the pristine, heavenly glory, like the pure white snow. They are the fount from which all the remaining social intercourse and organisation flows. Therefore they are the only effective counterweight against centralised government.

It will take years of social insight and enthusiasm for the neighbourhoods to learn how and when to use the groups, and for the groups to see themselves as merely auxiliary experts.

BOTTON VILLAGE NEWS, 8 IX 1967

impressions from russia

These impressions are somewhat meagre. Ann Harris, Barbara Lipsker, Anke and Thomas Weihs, Kate and I went on a package tour — one day in Kiev, two in Leningrad and two in Moscow. As we could not speak a word of Russian we could not talk with anyone, although we would have had ample opportunity.

The distances between airports and towns is great. We drove through large stretches of country, through a wonderful, light-filled spring which substantiated Rudolf Steiner's description of the relation of the Russian soil to light in a miraculous way.[38] It also showed that the relationship of these people to nature, to the soil, can and will develop only in the sixth post-Atlantean cultural epoch (3573–5733 AD). Our ego lives partly in light, a light that is external to 'us' and our inwardness. How different, then, will human existence be when we become aware of it! No doubt this will also be the time when eastern Europe's kind of humanity will become valid again and play its part in the full symphony of humanity. Today the world lives in an enormous wave of westernisation. Western technology determines economy and life, but it also engenders the western reserve of the 'stiff upper lip'. It is as if eastern humanity engulfs you with a certain warmth, while western humanity leaves you alone.

---

* now five.

Russia is overlaid with a thick, cement blanket of western thought-forms of tyranny — because Communism is just that — which are a direct continuation from the past, from Peter the Great and the Romanovs. The West allied itself with Russian barbarism and invaded, enslaved and stupefied it from the 17th century onwards. Whether the enslaving tyranny came from the tzarist secret police or from the Communist regime seems to make little difference to the ordinary citizen. He sleeps and dreams (as is so tellingly described in Maxim Gorki's autobiography[39]), and will wake up only in the future. Rudolf Steiner said that the young man in Goethe's Fairy Tale is a Russian.[40] His time has not yet come, but 'the time is at hand'!

We visited two churches, one in Kiev, one in the Kremlin, painted inside throughout — the walls, the pillars, the ceiling with its huge iconostasis and wonderful golden decorations. All the spaces were filled with that especially deep, timeless Russian Orthodox piety stemming from a past with which we are only vaguely connected. But it is also an unsentimental piety containing a future which, although seed-like and sleeping, is enormous, majestic and full of world strength against which our present spirituality is small and weak. On entering one of the churches, a woman pointed to the beret on my head and said "Off in this place." The church, like all 'official' churches, was a museum, but she said it quite naturally, with a very ordinary humanity, as a matter of course. (One can imagine the effort it would cost an official not to say it.) To this timeless quality of Russian piety also belongs the attitude to look upon the earthly 'here and now' as a place of darkness, pain and lament, as opposed to the heavenly light after death. This perhaps explains why *western* communism has its emphasis on factory work, on industry and technology through which our earthly 'here and now' is meant to be transformed, since in its western materialism the communist system is convinced that after death we cease to exist. Connected with the timeless quality of this piety is the fact that Russian architecture and painting remained oblivious to developments in the West which progressed from the Romanesque via the Gothic to the Renaissance. Perhaps it is a consequence of the rape of what is essentially Russian through the force of the West from the 17th century onwards. Only in architecture (accompanied by icons) do we have a typically 'Russian' style up to the 17th and 18th centuries, after which it changes into a kind of westernised Baroque. There is nothing in Russian culture that parallels the enormous changes in the West brought about in our soul and consciousness by the Renaissance — printing, Protestantism, geographical and astronomical discoveries, and so on.

The Russian soul did not change with the 1917 Revolution. Contemporary literature is still as Russian and political as it was then — patient, enduring, suffering, somewhat sleepy and dreaming of a future in which its potentials will become manifest. We seem to think that the main soul-content of the Russians is what we read in our newspapers — atomic warheads, détente, lack of 'freedom', and so on. In fact it can be found more in the eternal queues that form not just because there are so few commodities, but because there are too few shop assistants, probably in order to save wages! The sight of queues and the special attitudes that queuing engenders — the faintly self-righteous seller gazing into some imaginary distance; the humble, bent attitude of the buyers patiently waiting their turn — contributes to the greyness which seems to overlay everything that has to do with people and towns. It is the cement blanket. People and towns seem to suck up the communist system, but nature, landscapes, weather — everything that is not man-made — shake it off like water from a duck's back, while everything man-made seems to be dyed grey and becomes lifelessness. The obedient queue is the epitome of it all.

In a completely different setting, the women of Greenham Common are like a homeopathic drop of the true Russia. Communist materialism makes us realise how much we live (and have lived) in a masculine society. All our civilised institutions are masculine throughout — police, army, law courts and prisons, government, parliament, ministries, even politics itself. The message of Greenham Common is peace, not as a set of circumstances or a part of politics, but peace as social order, as relationship to others — a relationship in which nationalities and passports dwindle to transparent insignificance; a relationship in which the gap between government and civil service on the one hand, and ordinary life on the other, ceases to exist. This was well-defined by C.P. Snow in *The Corridors of Power*.[41] Because it includes politics in the widest sense, this 'peace' has a female character — the *women* of Greenham Common.

Greenham Common is the most articulate expression of the movement for peace now springing up in many countries. When the Russian communist government (in its pamphlet *How would disarmament affect us?*) says that it wants peace and disarmament contrary to the wicked West, it really means something else. No government can want peace, because peace in the sense of the peace movements is something feminine, and governments are born of masculine thinking.

Just as when in Russia the thought of a feminine world order moves us, it is not through overestimating the feminine. Rather, it is a longing for the balance between masculine and feminine. The Russian gaze directed towards the Holy Sophia is a longing for the union of both, for what is purely human. This feminine element dormant within the Russian sleep has a sibyl-like quality. The saint of the consciousness soul, Joan of Arc, is the Christian sibyl. A humanity uninspired by this element, cut off from the spiritual world, must become a prisoner of the intellect. In the peace movements (as in Greenham Common) there is the sound of a future world order that is purely human. This world order will cause the Communist government to magically vanish, and at the same time awaken the dreaming Russian peoples. In them a humanity is longing to arise that would carry a Christian spirituality in its awakening, a future Christianity which has to be achieved by central Europe — although not as a geographical region.

BOTTON VILLAGE NEWS, 1 VII 1983

aggression

Aggression has many layers. Firstly, and most obviously, the physical one — seeing two people boxing on TV, or watching violence in the cinema or at a football match, etc. How we enjoy the aggression we see when watching weekend sporting events with thousands of spectators travelling from all over Britain! Less obviously, it is also evinced in conversations and dialogue in our not being able or willing to listen. Here aggression is always linked to being deaf to the feelings of the other person, not simply for the wounds we afflict on him physically, but also for the soul-wounds we inflict by being uninterested in him, concerned only with our own experiences or opinions. This is just as cruel as if, physically, we gave him a slap on the face.

Before turning to a third layer of aggression I should mention an ability in human souls which is of a rather recent date and certainly did not exist in my youth. It is called empathy — an impulse that seems to make people soul-brothers to each other, less enclosed in themselves and also more internationally-minded. In my youth it was not easy to speak to someone of a different nationality. The stream of empathy makes it easier for one to feel the human being in the other person. Although often still darkened and warped, this beam of empathy helps make one of Rudolf Steiner's mysterious descriptions a little more understandable. He described how Christian

Rosenkreutz sent Buddha to Mars in 1604[42] so that human souls on their passage between death and a new birth should experience the Mars-sphere in which an abundance of aggression is opposed and transformed by the power of Buddha, the bearer of compassion and love. It seems that in the balance and structure of the world, this occult event is slowly becoming apparent in the light of day as empathy. The Green parties, CND and the flickering hope for unilateral disarmament, to name a few, seem to point in this direction.

The third layer of aggression is what is called public opinion (fostered by mass media, education, tradition, etc.) blanking out individual thinking. In connection with Buddha's task on Mars, Rudolf Steiner also mentioned the combating of public opinion. Somehow the lord of compassion and love will have to overcome the aggression that lies hidden in public opinion. But how?

Many generations have been brought up on the popular natural scientific world picture, the essence of which is that in order to understand the living we must dissect the dead, thereby discovering cells, molecules and atoms; the laws of heredity; entropy, and the conservation of matter. Anthroposophy has made only a relatively small dent in this world outlook. In reality, this world view underlies everything contained in the mass media. The violence that erupts physically in Chernobyl (26th April 1986), or the war in the Falklands (2nd April—14th June 1982), is comparatively small, but the violence invisibly behind and causing these eruptions is enormous. Many armaments factories buy the produce of atomic power plants; millions of workers all over the world are employed in such factories and many workers, mainly in Europe, tried clumsily to repair the damage of the 'cloud' of Chernobyl! But consider the Falklands. Military schools have been educating soldiers for many years, it seems, to make it possible for a small part of the army, navy and air force to fight in the Falklands! Yet how much time do the governments of the world spend talking about or reckoning with the goodness of human beings! And how much time and effort goes into producing military deterrents, armaments which play on people's fear and cowardice?

It is indeed one of the amazing phenomena of our social endeavours in the West that on the one hand there is a great deal of social conscience, state welfare programmes, etc. but on the other hand the human being is thought of as having an evil nature to a large degree. It is as if only his evil nature is reliable, while his good side appears only at times, and in small glimpses. This evil side needs our aggression in order to 'let them have a go'. The good side needs our activity, our idealism, in order to redeem the evildoer, and to strengthen his experience of the goodness of the world. Future times will look upon the evil deeds of others as our fault — we omitted to elicit the good in the other one.

But back to public opinion. Based on our materialistic world view, the mass media have one thing in common — they paralyse the listeners', the readers', the viewers' powers of thinking, and thereby their power to act. In our time we can grasp our activity directly only with our thinking. The detrimental aspect of watching TV, listening to the radio or reading the newspaper is their power to paralyse. Our ego can find itself only in activity because in its activity the ego can only be good — its evil possibilities appear when it is submerged in the astral body and 'rests'.

From all this we can derive the picture of a vast field on which lie many sleeping bodies, while from a loudspeaker above them trumpet the words: 'The world is evil.'

Indeed, it is not so! The world and the human beings in it are full of goodness. But we expect evil and so we throw a mantle of evil, such as military armaments, locks on our doors and cars, over the orb of goodness.

BOTTON VILLAGE NEWS, 31 I 1987

BOTTON VILLAGE NEWS
31st MAY 1996

∼ *a s c e n s i o n & w h i t s u n*

a s c e n s i o n : t h e g o l d & t h e r e d

Inside its skin, the human body appears to be suffused with blood and if we injure ourselves, blood leaks or pours out. The organs are like islands — solidified mirages or clouds floating in the rivers, lakes and seas of blood and the various tissues — like solidified blood itself, or banks in a landscape drenched and inundated in blood. In our blood lies the strength and goodness of selfhood, as well as its guilt. Both larger and smaller elements of our destiny, of our former earth lives, are contained in the blood.

The counter-picture of this inner, red landscape of the body is the outer, green landscape of the earth. In spring, when the outer landscape is slowly beginning to turn green, the leaves of bushes and trees seem to emerge out of a misty, reddish haze. When still young and 'transparent' (before it settles into the solid green of summer), this green has a brownish, pinkish, or reddish tinge, looking as if green and red were intermixed in varying amounts.

This interplay of green and red appears in the Easter chasuble which is red with a green design and rim. The chasuble for Ascension and the ten days leading to Whitsun is also red but with a golden design and rim. This true golden colour is not found outside in nature, except in metal. At Ascension, Christ disappears from the sight of the disciples yet invisibly He permeates all being. The disciples' pain at this disappearance and loss cannot be compared with any other pain we may experience on earth, but it is this pain which is golden — the golden background in old pictures and the haloes of saints.

Our time can be likened to the period between Ascension and Whitsun. Although our gaze and experience are fettered to matter, to physics, to the anatomy of corpses, there is a golden background to our time, too. We may be persuaded to see only the grime of factories, the illusions of film producers or of astronauts, but as disciples of Christ we have to believe and allow ourselves to experience the gold out of the strength of faith of the red.

BOTTON VILLAGE NEWS, 1 VI 1962

scandinavia — a philosophy of the north

At the beginning of Rudolf Steiner's lecture cycle *Man's Being, His Destiny and World Evolution*,[43] which he gave in Oslo in May 1923, he said 'Norway… lies at a remarkable point in the evolution of European civilisation and it is precisely on Norway that much in the future of Europe will depend.' These words were then followed, as in many other places that year, by words about the burning of the Goetheanum.

In May 1974, Piet Blok and I made a tremendous journey to Norway and Sweden lasting two and a half weeks. We flew to Stavanger, took a hydrofoil to Hogganvik and then by car and ferry to Bergen, via Voss to the Sognefjord and on to the jewel of the Borgund Stave Church, and finally to Vidaråsen. Next we went to Stockholm and thence to Delsbo six hours to the north. After two days there it was back via Stockholm to Vidaråsen where we stayed for four days before returning to England, again via Stavanger. What a feast of brilliant landscapes and waterscapes it was, and manifold life conditions!

Under the influence of an ongoing spring, the enormous variety of the Scandinavian landscape unfolded — the vast coniferous forests of northern Sweden, in a permanent bluish darkness, with earnest hills, wild rivers and thousands of lakes; the awesome loneliness of the Sognefjord where you can take a morning's trip on the ferry and see only three houses; the towering rocks, glaciers and mountain peaks on the serpentine bends from Voss down to the fjord; the loveliness of islands and waterways leading to Hardanger Fjord. In Delsbo there was still snow in the ditches flanked by bare birches, while in Stockholm and at the Oslo Fjord the deepening green and the abundance of blossom in western Norway, all spoke of the power of spring and the majesty of the high, radiant course of the sun.

Although the landscape of Sweden is like a bridal prologue to the sombre earnestness of Norway, the two are really a differentiated whole. In the renewing spring — perhaps at the behest of the thousandfold meetings of land and water — the elemental world seemed more alive than anywhere else I had ever been. In the 'Foundation Stone Meditation'[44] for the resurrection of the original Goetheanum, each of the first three sections concludes with the invocation:

> The elemental spirits hear it
> In East and West and North and South:
> May human beings hear it!

In Norway and, although differently, again in Sweden, one feels that the landscape is permeated by elemental powers and beings in a quite different way than in the rest of Europe or Britain. This can perhaps be described in the following way. Our experience of landscape and the moods of the weather is usually either a purely aesthetic one — beautiful landscapes attract tourists; a remarkable sunset fills us with delight, etc. — or as a combination of the aesthetic and practical, with scientific insight — the farmer or geologist, for instance. In Norway and Sweden, however, the landscape is exciting rather than aesthetically admirable. One cannot but be stirred by the rivers, the forest lakes, the dark, grey rocks rising out of every meadow or the towering cliffs and crags where spraying cascades plunge into fjords, the ever-present sound of water confronting land and wind in the fir trees.

In Europe (in the Bernese Oberland, for example, or Westphalia around the Externstones), it seems that nature either does not care for human beings or is simply superhuman. But confronted by the natural wonders of the vast area that is Scandinavia — softer and more feminine in Sweden; more aggressive and masculine in Norway — it seems as if nature inclines towards the relatively smaller number of people who live there (only eight million in Sweden and a mere four million in the whole of Norway). Certainly, the Norwegians and Swedes succumb to a form of nature-madness from June to August, going out in droves — boating, sailing, climbing — and trying to unite with the powers of nature with which they appear to live in a certain harmony. That is why they are so successful at building roads, blasting rocks, etc., for nowhere is the human being alien. In Norwegian pictures (Theodor Kittelsen, for instance) trolls and other nature beings appear as a kind of condensation or imagination of these natural powers, and one feels that they look to human beings with a certain expectancy:

> The elemental spirits hear it
> In East and West and North and South:
> May human beings hear it!

Because people in Scandinavia are embedded in nature as nowhere else on earth, the spiritual-moral understanding of the world, together with the sacraments and the social coherence of this tiny scattering of human beings, is important in a special way. This interweaving of nature and humanity is more like it was in ancient, pre-Christian times, and some of the old clairvoyance still persists — not necessarily an actual seeing, but the peculiar strength arising from it. Yet this interweaving nevertheless has a Christian sheen.

Rudolf Steiner's 'Folk Soul' lectures of 1910,[45] also given in Oslo, speak of the dark powers of the Fenris Wolf being overcome by the new light of Vidar. But this interweaving has to be grasped and taken up with new faculties. Perhaps that is why another of Rudolf Steiner's tremendous lecture cycles, those on the '*Fifth Gospel*',[46] were first held there as well! Travelling through that dramatic spring one could feel the dawn of a new Christianity in which the old life of Baldur is not forced to go through the zero point of the intellect before Christ can appear in the etheric world. We may imagine that in the course of time a new relationship between humanity and nature will arise in Scandinavia — a new symbiosis between Christian spirituality and nature — founded on those powerful elemental forces. The human being in Scandinavia seems to be very different, not so much in his day-consciousness but during the night when he enters this elemental world. The promise of a more human, a more Christian humanity is very radiant there. The sixth rhythm of the Foundation Stone Mediation comes to mind.

> Light Divine
> Christ-Sun
> The spirits of the elements hear it
> In East, West, North, South:
> May human beings hear it!

Rudolf Steiner spoke of it on New Year's Eve 1923 during the festive week of the founding of the General Anthroposophical Society. That day was the actual anniversary of the burning of the Goetheanum which, ceasing to exist on earth, impressed its being into the invisible worlds. This sixth rhythm comes to mind because it speaks about the Christ light that shines fourfold through the power of the elemental beings in East, West, North and South, and it implies that that Christ light is carried from a physical centre to the elemental-etheric periphery from where it shines back towards the centre. This means that in the light of the Etheric Christ, the elemental beings rise and populate our world once again. In this context, fairy tales, myths and legends assume a new life. We human beings who had to become isolated loners for the sake of freedom, independence and strength, are slowly being surrounded by long-lost friends. The expectations of humanity held by the powers and beings of nature can be discerned more clearly in Scandinavia than anywhere else. This means that Scandinavia may become a teacher to us, leading the way towards a new Christianity.

BOTTON VILLAGE NEWS, 7 VI 1974 & CAMPHILL CORRESPONDENCE, OCTOBER 1980 pentecost & the colour circle

Of all the blooms that burst forth every year around Whitsun, the apple tree is the queen and essence. This is due to the mysterious relation between the green of its leaves and the colour of its petals. The green is of the earth but the colour of the petals hints at something more — it is like a promise that points towards the realm of the supersensible.

The half-circle of the seven colours of the rainbow from red to violet can be extended by two additional shades of mauve beyond the violet and by two additional reddish shades beyond the red, the mauve and red ends meeting in a pink or peach-blossom, thus completing the circle.[47] These extra five shades are not visible to us in the same way that the other seven colours are. Or rather, we cannot distinguish the difference between them in the way that we can between green and blue, red and orange, etc. Although in every plant there is a quite precise relation between the green of the leaf and the colour of the blossom, in the apple tree the green leaves and pinkish blossoms lie exactly opposite each other on the colour circle. There is something both satisfying and moving about this, as well as the unique scent.

The abundance of colour and scented blossoms on the bushes and trees at Whitsun brings the green expansion of spring with its unfurling leaves to a kind of apotheosis. A new chapter is about to open in the book of the year. Rudolf Steiner said that a plant blossoms when it is touched or kissed by the astrality of the world, by the soul-powers of the world. We need only imagine this astral ocean surging above, its waves ebbing and flowing through the swathe of blossoms, expressive of the descending astrality at Whitsun. No wonder the petals seem to point 'beyond' — they are washed by waves of colour, transformed and metamorphosed into transparent patterns.

These waves are only indirectly visible. But even so there is something infinitely blissful about them. The heralds of heaven make the human heart sing paeans for they fill the soul with bliss. But if the shades of green did not accompany all this coloured blossom there would be no music, no chord. The blossom alone would be a kind of unison that would be boring, even intolerable. The relation of green leaf to coloured blossom of the apple tree — the 'chord' arising from the opposite poles of green and pink in the colour circle — forms something of a mysterious middle, the fulcrum on a pair of scales, in contrast to other leaf-blossom relationships which are one-sided in some way or other. The rhododendron, for example, emphasises darkness and heaviness; the cherry emphasises lightness, etc.

The Latin name for apple is *malum*. The word also means evil — Eve gave Adam an apple to eat. But every spring the blossoming apple tree points us to Christ Who brought the 'beyond' into the earthly.

BOTTON VILLAGE NEWS, 4 VI 1971

groups: droplets of the holy spirit

Democracy is *the* social mission of our time but it has not yet been achieved by any means merely by having established parliaments and voting in many countries. Voting reduces a group of people to numbers. Their opinions can only be expressed in the larger number, the majority, against the smaller, the minority. Yet democracy is the Christian longing of our time in that people are equal, not because they can be numbered like so many carrots or apples, but because they have a human countenance. This means each of us has an individual destiny; each bears the star of a singular purpose and needs Christ through whom each can fulfil him- or herself as an individual human being. Every action, even the smallest, is coloured by this fact.

In Botton we have groups concerned with the various areas of our life — a group dealing with human questions; the stewards ordering our available money, the cultural group caring for our cultural activities, and so on. But in reality everyone belongs to every group and is affected by them. Although everyone understands (or can at least learn to understand) something about others, or about money, etc., meetings in which everyone takes part obviously do not work. Small groups of people come to a unanimous decision more easily than large groups. So what about those who do not belong to the various groups? They either feel left out or they think 'Well, others are doing it anyway, so we need not bother.' In both cases something that Rudolf Steiner described as significant for the future of a social organism fails to happen, namely that its members should feel towards work the way an artist feels towards his work of art. We could recall Steiner's 'motto of the Social Ethic':[48]

> The healthy social life is found when in the mirror of each human soul the whole community finds its reflection, and when in the community the virtue of each one is living.

Christ said 'When two or three are gathered together in My name I am in the midst of them.' (Matt. 18: 20) And also, 'He, the Spirit of Truth, the Comforter, whom the Father will send in my name, will guide you.' (a composite of John 14: 16–17, 14: 26, 15: 26 and 16: 13) Being open to the difference between the working of Christ and the Holy Spirit could play a great part in building up the social organism. The purpose of groups is that the various members can contain and balance one another in their opinions and the exercise of their common sense. In this way, a few people together may arrive at the truth of a question, especially once they have learnt to listen to and talk with one another.

Groups have the potential to realise something of the truth! These are small Whitsun events, little steps towards the destruction of the Tower of Babel. The organisation of social life therefore has something of the divine about it. This is why any conception of a social order formed by shadowy intellectual thinking such as we usually have on earth will always be useless. When they are together, members of a group have to feel that something holy wants to incarnate in their group. The more individual effort and courage they put into their deliberations, the more their souls can contain Mary who, at the first Whitsun, sat amidst the apostles. (Acts 1: 13–14)

But the light of the spirit shining into earthly matters signifies the approach of the Guardian of the Threshold. This is the threshold, the abyss between the physical and spiritual worlds, that works against individuals on earth who are trying to build a social order — the social question is an esoteric, an occult one. Words spoken in the group echo into the unseen cosmos. Out there they can be one of two things; either what the psalmist calls gossip, (Psalms 34: 13) or used by Michael for the building of worlds.

If groups are possible bearers of even just a tiny droplet of the Holy Spirit, the problem of non-members has still another slant. This is where the *Village News* comes in. (Newspapers have been part of the social organism for as long as democracy has existed.) Reports of what has happened in the groups will have to be not only informative but must *evoke inner, participating activity* in each reader who should feel that he can invite himself at any time to one of the groups in order to add his own viewpoint or initiative to it.

One can begin to see the task of the single individual and of the group in building the social organism. Eventually, everyone will come to look upon the social organism as his or her work of art. This entails a high output of unaccustomed energy, of course, but it is essential if groups are not to become little 'governments'.

In St John's Gospel, the Resurrection and the gift of the Holy Spirit take place on Easter Sunday, and then at the end of the gospel a story is told about a common meal, particularly featuring Peter and John. (John 21: 12) (The other three gospels end with the Ascension.) This is followed by the account of Whitsun given only in the Acts of the Apostles. By trying to combine the power of the single individual and that of the groups in our social organism, it may be that the villages will one day be able to partake in the grail-like conclusion of the St John Gospel.

BOTTON VILLAGE NEWS, 5 III 1965

science as social phenomenon: a whitsun consideration

Scientists are a caste in themselves, and with the growing prominence of natural science over the last hundred years the features of this caste have assumed ever greater clarity. Over that time there have of course been tremendous developments in all areas of research, in physics, chemistry and in medicine.

In the past, the conviction was that scientific research should be 'free', but today it has increasingly become subservient to the politics of the different countries (for example, the atom bomb), and yet the image of the scientist has remained largely unchanged. Every professional grouping past or present — artists, civil servants, guilds or trades unions — expresses to some extent the society within which it occurs. The social organism must need the group in some fashion otherwise it would not allow it to exist. This is easy to see in the case of plumbers or civil servants (and many others, too), but in another society they might not exist or, if they did, they would be linked and integrated in quite different ways. In the case of scientists the situation is different because we are led to believe that the purpose of their work is the furtherance of objective truth, and we are confirmed in this conviction by the practical successes of their research in technology, surgery, space exploration, etc. But what if the content of their work was not the gradual unearthing of objective truth but was dependent on the social organisation? Rudolf Steiner often described the origin of 'maya' in the East and 'ideology' in the West,[49] and how 'historic materialism' was not an 'objective' truth but a just description of a certain aspect of social evolution in the past 150 years.

What counts in science today — and until now there has been nothing but natural, physical science — is matter, but whether or not it was mineral, plant, animal or human was (and still is) irrelevant. The enormous success of medical and technological research seems to 'prove' material science.

If we want a society in which decisions are reached without voting (as in Camphill, for instance), we must have a science not only of physical matter, but also of life, soul and spirit. Everywhere, anthroposophical science is being strangled more and more. A new science can only be born and evolve out of a new social organism. Life in Camphill will have to *want* scientific enhancements. It will be useless to carry the attempts of a new social order into present-day science: it would be like putting new wine into old bottles.

BOTTON VILLAGE NEWS, 30 V 1969

substance: a whitsun consideration

Truth is not only what can be proven. Truth is also revelation since all manner of different facts and events balance each other, as the stars balance each other in the sky. More than anything else, the great variety of substances on earth show the truth of spiritual science: that there is a multitude of spiritual beings who, with their different powers, shape and fashion what appears in earthly matter. In nature, each genus exhibits tremendous variety and this presents an illuminating challenge; it stimulates an observing, a beholding power of judgement (Goethe) if we consider the many substances in the different kingdoms of nature: mineral, organic and animal. It becomes clear to our ordinary senses in a moving and awe-inspiring way that in their various substances, earthly bodies express different powers of existence.

When we imagine a stone, a leaf, a petal, the tissue of an animal or human flesh, we should consider it not just as varied matter but as an expression of different modes of existence. We can imagine the many forms of leaves — tender green in spring, dark green in August — growing on a plant on its way towards blossom and later to seed. The many-coloured, scented petals can seem more like a velvety butterfly's wing than a leaf. We can imagine the internal density of a stone, or the animals whose insides contain organs and which move about and utter sounds, and have a skin for sensing. Finally, we can imagine the human being who can be guided by conscience and who is always, potentially, a moral being.

There will come a time when we shall see that everything visible is only pointing, like a script, to its real meaning. Our 'natural' science examines only the composition of the printer's ink, so to speak, of the various letters of the script. The invisible spiritual powers and beings are only visible because space, within which we have our existence between birth and death, makes them appear. But we can 'think' these powers and beings — thinking is the angelic rung on the ladder of clairvoyance.

BOTTON VILLAGE NEWS, 6 VI 1969

trinity 1
consciousness and freedom

Our consciousness contains thoughts, ideas, memories and the thought-pictures of aims and feelings. Each of them belongs to a different process, but the main feature of each process is that it finds its result, its summit, in the light of consciousness. It is this light of consciousness which shines from our waking up until our going to sleep. Our named identity, our freedom, our conviction of being one human being among other human beings, rests on our day consciousness, and because we rely on it and owe so much to it (not always knowingly), it seems to us the very pillar of our existence.

We also owe our freedom to this day consciousness. With it we can choose, we can ponder, we can decide, which is something we cannot do when we are sleeping or dreaming. Our 'I am' — our being as a person with a name — reaches its reality out of unknown, unconscious depths. Our day consciousness is like the plateau of a mountain rising into the sun out of the swirling mists of its slopes and valleys. The peak of this mountain plateau is the 'I am'. The decisive thing about our freedom is not how far it is hemmed in — by constitution, natural laws, world conceptions or education, etc. — but that we know of the various possibilities within which we can move. Then we realise that our day consciousness, freedom and knowledge, are interrelated phenomena.

Whitsun is the festival of the Holy Spirit, the festival of the Comforter 'whom the Father will send in my Name, he shall teach you all things' (John 15: 26). It is the festival in which the disciples awoke as though from a dream-filled sleep. Like Peter, they could then speak about the life, death and resurrection of Christ, and for the first time felt the Being of Christ within; for them His presence was no longer external and they were therefore free.

Anthroposophia is a Whitsun event. Our knowing has been increased immeasurably so that freedom could be given to mankind, freedom which since the Fall had been given only in a limited way.

Whitsun is a festival of flowers, but the flower has an inherent tendency to become fruit and seed. Our present knowing is flat, a shadowy colour and powerless: it is completely barren. The effort of the concentration exercises in *Knowledge of the Higher Worlds*,[50] the effort needed for meditation, or the effort required to sit and take in the words, colours and events of The Act of Consecration of Man, all demand our will and not our intellectual understanding. Will enables our knowing, our thought, to bear fruit.

But Whitsun is also the festival of peace. 'Receive ye the Holy Ghost', (John 20: 22) 'Peace be with you' (1 Peter 5: 14) and 'These things have I spoken unto you, that in me ye might have peace. In the world ye shall have tribulation: but be of good cheer, I have overcome the world.' (John 16: 33) The shadowy unreality of our knowing, and thus of our consciousness, is only the outer expression of a host of murdering demons who follow 'The prince of this world'. (John 16: 11) The peace, the fruit-bearing will of Whitsun, is the armour against these demonic hosts.

BOTTON VILLAGE NEWS, 15 VI 1973

trinity 11
the catacombs and the council of constantinople

A famous church council took place in Constantinople in 869 AD in which the view that the human being consists of body, soul and spirit (in modern parlance) was condemned as heretical, and that the human being has only a body and a soul with some spiritual qualities became orthodox dogma.[51] As a consequence, Whitsun became a festival that was unattainable for the individual and celebrated only within the body of the church for believers. The Holy Spirit could be contained in the church but not in the individual.

The concept 'church' as we now know and use it emerged in the 4th century (325 AD) when Christianity became the state religion of Rome under the Emperor Constantine. Previously, when the Christians were still being persecuted and forced to meet in the catacombs, spiritual life was completely separated from ordinary life. They met in the darkness and stillness of a subterranean labyrinth, far from the noise and light of everyday life. Their altars were the graves of their dead. Christ, whom they encountered in the catacombs, embraced both the living and the dead. Therefore, when they went about their daily business, they were empowered to heal, to baptise (to admit people into the community of Christians) and to preach. They were endowed with the power of the Holy Spirit which they passed on to those whom they baptised. But this power was a day-conscious power. Although gained in the darkness of the catacombs, this power filled the one who was baptised with light. The Holy Spirit, prepared in the darkness of the catacombs, became the presence, the majesty and the power of Christ within the day-consciousness of human beings. When Christianity became a church, this power waned.

The consequence of the Council of Constantinople was twofold. The living reality and power of the Holy Spirit was reduced to a set of dogmas. Belief developed instead of a conscious awareness of the presence and majesty of the spirit. The minds of human beings became increasingly filled, not with the awareness of experiences, but with thoughts which soon deteriorated into intellectual opinions, or thoughts which, just because they were thoughts and flat, colourless and powerless, enabled the human being gradually to say 'I' to himself. Human intelligence was reduced to day-consciousness. That which is only the beginning of the consciousness soul, namely the intellect, is mistaken for the human 'I', his person, because it enables him to say 'I' to himself.

Because they have no reality of their own, these flat, powerless, mummified thoughts that enable us to become convinced of our identity, are holes in the web of worlds — they attract and draw into themselves the demonic hordes of the prince of this world. From this fanatical dogmatism the pyres of the Inquisition, the rigidity of Calvinism, etc., were made possible at the time of the emerging consciousness soul. The death of thousands of heretics was the tragic, hellish reality imposed by a lack of consciousness in those who judged them, and a lack of understanding of the threefold human being.

Consciousness, selfless day-consciousness, is the most precious human possession. What was sown in the catacombs might bear fruit in our time as a renewed Christianity. In its light, the dignity of the human being wants to rise out of the darkness.

BOTTON VILLAGE NEWS, 13 VII 1973

the trinity in europe and north america

Every instance of threefolding appearing in mythology, nature or the human being is a manifestation of the Trinity. But before Christ's life on earth these manifestations had a prophetic quality, pointing to a future reality. This became actual only after Christ had lived on earth, because only then could the way to the Father be found. The Father could send the Holy Spirit only in the name of the ever-present Christ. The Sundays of Trinity begin after Whitsun which is the last manifestation of Christ's incarnation on earth.

The prophetic nature of the Trinity becomes clear when we think of the Old Testament. Jacob had a dream of the heavenly ladder while on his way to Laban, his future father-in-law. Sleeping on a stone, he saw angels ascending and descending out of the opened heavens. (Gen 28: 10–12) No doubt this is a revelation of the Holy Spirit. It depicts the enlightenment of thinking: the head lying on a stone; the head enclosing our thinking powers and thereby becoming the portal into heaven — human consciousness enabled by the head to embrace the light of the spiritual world. But the heavenly ladder is a night picture, a sleep-image. Only in the night and into the sleeping mind can the heavens reveal themselves. The Holy of Holies, the third part of the Temple of Solomon, was always kept dark. Only during the Crucifixion was the veil protecting it rent in twain. The moment the blood of the Redeemer fell to earth, the Trinity turned from promise to fulfilment.

Since that time, waking consciousness is able to grasp the spiritual world. Jehovah was a god of night, a Moon god, whereas Christ encompasses both night and day and, as the Word, is the Sun god. The historic developments of the last two thousand years are nothing but the effort to reach out to the Mystery of Golgotha, but human consciousness must grow worthy of it.

It is rewarding to compare nature in Europe and North America because of the different manifestations of threefoldness. In Europe (both on the continent and in Britain), the forms and growth of nature seems tidy, and although 'tidy' is a rather uncomplimentary description, it is appropriate. In Europe, the trees are trees, mountains are mountains, meadows are meadows — what is sometimes called 'humanly penetrated nature' — a nature which in its threefoldness expresses the presence of the Trinity. In North America, however, it seems as if the Great Spirit of the Native Americans, who knows no Trinity, still permeates all nature, Therefore the growth of woods is often weed-like and rapid; mountains seem to adopt animal forms, and water has a primeval power. (In Europe, water only has such power during catastrophes like floods.) The vast American rivers — the Susquehanna or the Hudson — have an overpowering majesty. A primal, world grandeur is but a few yards from the turnpikes.

In Europe, stone, plant and animal each have their living space and so do the three elements of earth, water and air, and they are equally permeated by warmth. In North America, the borderlines between nature and the three elements are vague, and warmth by no means permeates the other three elements in equal measure — angry waves of excessive heat are followed by death-like cold.

In regard to the Trinity, North American nature is the very opposite of Jacob's dream. In the picture of Jacob sleeping on a stone, the third member of the Holy Trinity is kept back at night — it was only in sleep that the spiritual world could enter because during the day thinking consciousness resembled a stone. In North America there is no question of the obvious connection of human, stone and consciousness: it is nature which in its power has something of the undifferentiated Great Spirit of the Native Americans, something therefore of a primeval world power.

Europe is differentiated and formed; every realm has its breathing space. Humanity and nature correspond to one another. In Europe the Trinity has its natural home, therefore in Europe Christianity must always return to awareness of the Trinity.

BOTTON VILLAGE NEWS, 11 VI 1964

BOTTON VILLAGE NEWS
ST. JOHN'S 1996

~ st john's

baptism by water & baptism by the holy spirit & fire

In a narrow sense, the story of the earthly life of Jesus Christ lasts from the first Christmas until the first Ascension, but in a wider sense it lasts from the baptism by John in the Jordan until the first Whitsun.

John the Baptist said, 'I baptise you with water.' (John 1: 26) Asked by the multitude at Whitsun 'What shall we do?' (Acts 2: 37) Peter answers — as the Baptist had done at the river Jordan — by saying, 'be baptised … and ye shall receive the gift of the Holy Ghost.' (Acts 2: 38) The baptism by John took the one being baptised close to drowning. Immersed in the waters of the Jordan, freed of the dissolving waves of their own life, at the threshold of death they witnessed in a new dimension the advent of the deathless Life of the World. At the first Whitsun, John's prophecy was fulfilled: 'He that cometh after me … shall baptise you with the Holy Ghost and with fire.' (Matt. 3: 11) The rushing wind, the cloven tongues of flame on the heads of each apostle, Peter's words to the multitude (Acts 2: 1–41) — understood by all who listened regardless of being fettered to their own languages — in these things the Spirit God completed the manifestation of the Trinity, as Christmas had begun it.

Easter, the death and resurrection, is the manifestation of the Son God. It is wrong to compare Christ's death with any human, *individual* death. It was the death of a god — all our deaths, mankind's death — which took place on the cross. A drop of this Mystery of Golgotha, of crucifixion and resurrection, is interwoven with our individual deaths because the nervous system, which is the basis of our waking, perceiving, imagining consciousness, is always permeated by the powers of the Mystery of Golgotha. To begin with, it enters our consciousness through our becoming aware of being *accompanied* by death throughout our lives; by the knowledge that not only do we have to die at some time (the *memento mori* of old), but that death gnaws ceaselessly *within* our ordinary life. However, in future death will be felt to be less an enemy and more an accompanying friend, and in this presence will appear the new, the higher life, the life which overcame — and overcomes — death.

The signs of this life are the five wounds of Christ. During the forty days between Easter and Ascension, the Risen One appeared *with* the five wounds. They were inscribed, healed and star-like, in the resurrection body. Rudolf Steiner spoke of them as the five wounds which a fully incarnating ego such as the Christ ego would inflict on a mortal body.[52] The wounds were more a confirmation rather than a result of the nails and the lance. We ourselves do not carry the five wounds because our 'I' does not incarnate fully — it is the Resurrection Body which will allow the ego to incarnate fully. So the wounds, the fivefold star of death, the sign of the guilt of accumulated destiny, are still there on the body of the risen Christ, yet healed, truly star-like. They are the root and seed from which the new, guiltless life arises. Not only does death accompany us but also that which conquers death and bears the sign of the five stars.

After Whitsun comes Trinity which encompasses Christmas, the Father God; Easter, the Son God, and Whitsun, the Spirit God. We could also say the baptism by water at Epiphany is the Father God; the baptism by fire at Pentecost is the Spirit God, and Easter, when death fully permeates human existence and new life rises out of it, is the Son God.

BOTTON VILLAGE NEWS, 9 VI 1967

uriel: shades of warmth

The origin of the world was warmth. Through a process of densification the air element then emerged, but this was not all — in the condensing process a soul-like 'inner' and a matter-like 'outer' appeared. Matter cooled, and at the same time the unending variety of what we now call Creation evolved — plant-like forms on Old Sun; animal-like forms on Old Moon and, to begin with, human-like and crystalline rock forms on Earth. The soul, on the other hand, evolved in the course of the Old Sun, Old Moon and Earth stages towards a threefoldness of thinking, feeling and willing which was crowned by the Trinity from the time of the Mystery of Golgotha.

Today, warmth has many aspects. It is principally divided into soul warmth and physical warmth. To a large extent soul warmth is active — we permeate our thoughts, our love, our soul activities entirely with warmth. Physical warmth is in all the warmth (directly or indirectly) that we receive from the sun. This increases in summer as the entire earth is warmed as the arc of the sun grows longer and higher. In its archetypal nature, warmth always has two sides relating to the human being — a relaxing summer warmth can turn into a threatening thunderstorm. In the soul, love can coexist with a choleric outburst in which we selflessly pour out our compassion towards creation either with selfish possessiveness or with delightful insights which may arise as a result of our curiosity. The thunderstorm is physical, but its awe-inspiring manifestation may have something threatening or judgmental about it. Summer is the season in which the soul-nature and matter-nature aspects of warmth become mixed. In winter the matter side is cold, hard and dark, perhaps even frozen, while our soul tends to manifest warmth and light. The concept of the Trinity is the mediator between the Christmas-image and the summer-image. The words of John the Baptist: 'He must increase, but I must decrease' (John 3: 30) is spoken out of the primeval reality of warmth. Matter relies on warmth from outside to warm it through — in the last analysis this comes from the sun but it is devoid of morality. Since the Mystery of Golgotha, the soul side of warmth is the only source of warmth in the world, but it is morally active warmth. By active warmth I mean that out of insight, love, compassion and selflessness I pour my strength into those parts of the world that need my help. Christ is the Sun hero because He moves His dwelling from the Sun into each human soul. In the end we shall all be Sun heroes, and matter will then depend for its warming on us, just as the snow melted around St Seraphim.[53]

To return to the beginning, warmth is the origin of the world. The soul-side of warmth was a mirror of knowledge for whatever evolved out of the archetypal warmth. But in humanity it would always have been the same mirror; no differentiation among human beings would have been possible. The world event of the Fall tore this unified warmth asunder. As a result of the Fall, the universal ripening process led to people becoming more individual, more unique. The saying 'Your eyes will be opened' (Gen 3: 5) means that we will all see the same, but each of us wants something different when we see different things and people. Thank goodness not all men want to marry the same woman! The Fall divided warmth up between individuals. Morality became an affair of the single human soul, and hand-in-hand with this differentiation went the individualisation of wants that led to personal karma and reincarnations. What followed was that in the condensed, earthly regions life became increasingly independent of the gods and their realms, so much so that we often forget them and become materialists — materialists slain by the blindness caused by not recognising the gods. Our condensed existence between birth and death bears the imprint of the heavens in all its innumerable creations. This twofoldness of the world after the Fall not only had materialism as its final consequence, but in the earthly part of this twofold world the human 'I' was able to develop. The human 'I' not only enabled humanity to experience freedom, but also to exercise responsibility.

There is a mysterious relationship between the Mystery of Golgotha and the human I-principle. In those who were willing, the divine Son was able to unite with the human 'I', and thereby with the earth. In the course of the earth's evolution, increasingly the image of the Trinity will rise because in the last discourses Christ said 'You are my friends.' (John 15: 14) With these words we human beings are drawn more and more towards the cross and the resurrection. We ourselves have to die in life and rise again so that through this the Father and the Dove can appear. On our way from creature to creator, increasingly our own soul's threefoldness (our thinking, feeling and willing), will have to unite with the summer-image of the Trinity.

CAMPHILL CORRESPONDENCE, JULY 1991

from historical time to seasonal time

The events of the Mystery of Golgotha were gradually changed from historic facts which happened at a certain date or year, into seasonal festivals. From having been remembrance dates they became woven into the course of the year. So the birthday of John the Baptist shone out and gave its stamp to summer; the birthday of Jesus now stands for winter; Easter is spring and Whitsun the abundance of blossoms. At the Synod of Whitby in 664 AD when the Roman Church put an end to Celtic Christianity, the date of Easter was one of its two themes. The representatives of Celtic Christianity tried to keep it tied to the historical date, but the Roman Church insisted it should be the Sunday after the first full moon following the spring equinox![54] Even dates like the Adoration of the Kings and Ascension, although historical dates, are linked in our minds with the time of year in which they fall.

In the Gospel of St Mark, (Mark 6: 14–29) the story of the beheading of John is told in a remarkable fashion. After Herod says 'It is John whom I beheaded', a kind of insertion follows as if a window were opened on the imprisonment of John. It includes the scene of Herod's birthday with Herodias and Salome's dancing, and Salome carrying in the head of John on a charger. This is all told as if set in a different time-space from the rest of the gospel 'For Herod himself had sent forth and laid hold upon John'. Concrete facts, events and utterances are described through this window in much the same way that we would describe past events, facts of history. These events are concrete in the sense of our everyday world, as concrete as are the contents of the Fifth Gospel. We become aware that the rest of that gospel and the four gospels together, belong to a quite different time-space.

In the centuries before Christ, the experiences and concepts of history emerged very slowly. They reached the shores of the historic consciousness of the Occident mainly through Tacitus. This consciousness presupposes a very definite experience and understanding, namely that an event, or a person, is preceded by others and will be followed by others — a procession stretching from the infinite past into the infinite future. What we call 'concrete' is any insertion into this procession. We identify ourselves and our lives with the view through the window of time-space.

But the end of the Dark Age has arrived and our experience of 'concrete' will assume a different meaning. In the gospels, the raising of the youth of Nain (Luke 7: 11–17) is not 'preceded' by the healing of the centurion's servant. (Luke 7: 2–10) They are intertwined as in a wreath. The wreath of stars (the zodiac) has no beginning and no end, but it has composition and structure in itself. Through the window of the time-space of John's imprisonment and beheading we look upon the stages of history in the same way as the historic consciousness of the Occident had to understand history in the Dark Age.

From the beheading of John emerges the Feeding of the Five Thousand. (Matt. 14: 15–21, Mark 6: 32–44, Luke 9: 10–17, John 6: 5–14) The Light Age emerges out of the Occidental historic consciousness. The Washing of the Feet and the baptism by fire follow the baptism by John in the purifying waters of the Jordan.

BOTTON VILLAGE NEWS, 6 VIII 1965

on the origin of social ideas from beyond the threshold

Rudolf Steiner stressed repeatedly that real social ideas (obviously including those in a threefold social order) must originate from beyond the threshold. Why? Is not the concept of the threefold social organism a very terrestrial, and very reasonable, idea? I will try to describe how little it is an idea, and how much it is a series of phenomena which are understandable only in the light of the spiritual world.

The first of the historical events that gave life to the concepts of a threefold ordering of social conditions was in 1917 when the Memorandum was presented to Polzer-Hoditz,[55] secretary to the Emperor Karl of the Austro-Hungarian Empire. The conditions of the Austro-Hungarian Empire in the preceding 50–150 years had sparked these thoughts. It became clear, especially during the 1914–1918 war but even before it, that either the freedom of the spiritual sphere would have to be established (and after it a human middle sphere and an associative economic sphere), or nationalism in its different guises of would win the day. In hindsight, we can see clear reasons why the Austro-Hungarian Empire split up into separate nations — Hungary, Czechoslovakia, Romania, Yugoslavia, etc. — thereby feeding the later Bolshevist onslaught. But the threefold social organism had a more global aim (the chance opportunity to embody it in the Austro-Hungarian Empire being merely a prototype), namely to make human life on earth possible. In the West lay the future economic potential of humanity; in the East lay the heritage of an ancient, though not yet Christian, spirituality.

The Fall had many consequences, most of them still hidden from us, but one consequence was the Tower of Babel (Gen 11: 1–9) with the subsequent loss of a common language resulting in the split into nations. Christ had to come in order to reveal the human being to all peoples: Jews, Scythians, Romans, Gauls, etc. Today, the human being shines through the veils of the many kinds of nationalism. The ideal of nationalism and its political ethos of never interfering in the internal affairs of another nation does not strengthen the reality of humanity, or the various attempts to establish human rights. Nationalism is only justified in the spiritual-cultural sphere.

But we all share in equality. Human rights are as valid in Ecuador as in Austria. We all share in the trade of the economic sphere because production, circulation and consumption in all its variations are global facts. National boundaries are artificial: the nation-state and the three spheres exclude each other. The root of so much struggle and conflict lies in the non-awareness of the three spheres. The concept of nation is an old-fashioned leftover because the individual and his humanity is above national-cultural differences.

The individual, earthly person is above the three spheres. Human beings on earth between birth and death have East, West and Middle within their souls. Hence an American need not be especially economically gifted, or an Indian spiritually endowed. As states and the three spheres exclude each other so does human individualism and patriotism. Two thousand years ago it was the sign of St Paul's Christianity that he was all things to all people — an Athenian to the Athenians, an Ephesian to the Ephesians, etc. Today, we all have to be Pauls in this respect. But there was something else in Paul that is connected with our situation. Through suffering his three days in the existential abyss of blindness, he succeeded in transforming the most rigid, abiding Judaism into a Christian world experience. Our Christianity is like soaring high over any religion, permeating the world — its past, its content and its aims — far more intensely than other religions can.

A human being is only human in so far as he aims at development, not horizontally, but vertically. It is not enough for him to be going on from school to university or training college, and then later changing one job for another — merely going from youth to maturity, or from being a single person to becoming a parent. In order to become a human being, it is necessary to strive towards a spiritual existence.

Because the social organism consists of human beings, like them it must originate in the spirit, beyond the threshold. Today, the social organism should be more than an earthly arrangement within which human beings can live peacefully together, be fed, medically treated, etc., but be left to choose their own development individually, which means egoistically. A social organism can only do justice to human beings today if it has in itself something that is spiritually and humanly demanding. This means that its spiritual individualities are related to each other — in a threefold social organism people associate in the economic realm, deal with each other in the middle sphere, recognise each other in the spiritual sphere of freedom — but they relate to each other always as whole human beings, including their total body-soul-spirit existence.

The threefold social organism must be of spiritual origin because it reckons with the whole person, and that means with the human being as an ideal, not with the American, Chinese, Indian or anything else.

CAMPHILL CORRESPONDENCE, JUNE 1985

liberty — equality — fraternity

This battle cry of the so-called French Revolution is really the dawning of a longing for a new social dignity. In our time we are still in its dawn. The

French Revolution was by no means only French, nor was the battle cry a unique formulation, but the physical outbreak of this longing began in France. The longing, only then coming to maturity, was and is a genuine human one; the battle cry being its content. One reason for the bloody chaos in which the French Revolution 'ended' was that it threw the three concepts into one pot. In one respect, the social history of the 19th and 20th centuries is the history of these three concepts.

The anthroposophical idea of the threefold social order tries to differentiate within the spheres of an organism — liberty in the spiritual-cultural sphere, equality in the human sphere, fraternity in the economic sphere. No doubt the continuation of this idea (which had its prologue in 1919 and came to a provisional close in 1922) will be under different conditions if the understanding of these distinct delegations can spread.

Fraternity within the economic sphere makes it quite clear that a relationship must exist between producer and consumer regarding the price and quality of food, for example; between the farmer or gardener, the food processor and the consumers

Liberty belongs in the spiritual sphere. We can distinguish an opinion, a floating belief that this is true and that is not (often setting people of differing opinions at loggerheads), from an idea which is something that tries to be realised by a group of people, or through money, etc. The demand for freedom in the spiritual sphere is difficult to understand, especially in an anthroposophical social organism like ours. The older, well-versed anthroposophists can easily become spiritual dictators; the younger ones mere believers, no longer thinking for themselves. Others can be emotional, non-thinking revolutionaries possessing only one slice of reality. Spiritual freedom means educating yourself so that you reach this sphere within yourself. The human being becomes worthy and able to change his thinking when he has to live within the mantle of a threefold social organism.

Equality is not just a separate sphere — it is also the gate to the others. In essence, our time is the time of brotherhood, and we aspire to it from the simpler experience of equality. Brotherhood seems to be the magic influence of the threefold mantle towards the social world it tries to embrace and shape. Rudolf Steiner said that anthroposophy would develop among those who live within a threefold social organism.

Brotherhood is also the inclination towards the mantle. We are interested in our brother's or our sister's ideas, and with him or her we can enter into an association. We do not doubt that as a human being he or she is equal to all other human beings on earth. We have an immediate experience of their infinite value in the past and future of the world process. This experience — empathy is largely the dawning of it — is reduced or blotted out by politics and governments. In a dictatorship it is fear that does the blotting out. The moment that fear darkens the experience of another human being, empathy is extinguished.

In a democracy, feelings are more complicated because in a democracy there are two layers in politics. One is linked with voting — we are never sure whether a member of the government is speaking out of himself or as a member of a particular political party. The second layer is connected with international politics, the secret services and the higher echelons of the civil service — these do not change with each new government but are hidden from the ordinary mortal. Consciously or unconsciously, we all feel some guilt over the enormous stockpile of atomic weapons, the Third World economy, tensions in the Middle East, pollution, etc. This is not only moral guilt but also common sense guilt; a completely helpless guilt. Do government officials feel it too? Or do they feel politically self-righteous?

Strengthening the experiences of our eternal being will make empathy complete. The possibility of relating personally to every other lies in each one of us. Through anthroposophy, this possibility can widen out into equality, and from there to an awakening to the threefold social organism.

BOTTON MIRROR, 16 I 1988

the beheading of john the baptist & the feeding of the five thousand

We know that the twelvehood of the disciples arose through the spiritual being of John the Baptist. The first manifestation of this twelvehood was the Feeding of the Five Thousand described in all four gospels. (Matt. 14: 15–21, Mark 6: 37–44, Luke 9: 13–17, John 6: 5–14) This Feeding of the Five Thousand is a picture of the Christianity of our time. The five refers to our fifth post-Atlantean cultural epoch, and the thousands refers to the multitude fed from the hands of the disciples with the five barley loaves and two fishes.[56] The whole event is in reality a prophetic vision of the disciples. The supersensible image, as well as the event it points to, is due to John having been beheaded. As children of our time, for each one of us the day is 'far spent'. Each of us tries to live up to the saying "The Kingdom of Heaven is within you" and it shines ever more radiantly as the Communion from the hands of the twelvefold circle of the disciples continues. The hidden root of this event is that other scene two thousand years ago — Herod's birthday, Salome's dance and Herodias holding the platter with the head of John the Baptist. (Matt. 14: 1–12, Mark 6: 16–29)

We can imagine thousands of small flames growing steadier and brighter in the gathering dusk. We can also imagine that the brotherliness of our time is based on the 'You' becoming increasingly radiant. In our time there is a growing respect, tolerance and acknowledgement of the other person as a human being. Very often, of course, he is not allowed to be simply a human being because he has to be German, French or English; he has to be this or that in professional, industrial or civil service life, and to be a brother, father, etc., in private life. We are seldom allowed to be simply 'human beings'.

The tempestuous storm scene is like descending from a mountain, the ascent of which is Herod's birthday, Salome's dance and the beheading of John the Baptist. The snow-clad summit of the mountain, shrouded in clouds, makes room for the Feeding of the Five Thousand.

In Botton, even though status is unimportant, the rising waves of sympathy and antipathy, of aggression and cowardice, of habits, of family peculiarities and insecurities, threaten our community just as in the gospels the Feeding of the Five Thousand is followed by the mighty storm on the lake. The lake is stilled, however, by the appearance of Christ walking over its waters. 'And when they were come out of the ship straightway they knew him' (Mark 6: 54) 'and immediately the ship was at the land' (John 6: 21). In the wind and waves of our emotions we dream, but our Self is bound up with these emotions and unless Christ appears and releases us, we are their victim and at their mercy. Herodias married Herod; she had been married to Herod's brother Phillip before, and Salome was the daughter of that first marriage. John the Baptist's head on the platter becomes the image for the powers of the anti-Grail.

John's death by beheading is like the end of the path which began with the Fall, with Adam and Eve eating the fruit of knowledge — a path which resulted in such events as those on Herod's birthday. Through John's death, the darkness of the blind spot in mankind's vision was opened. Thus the Feeding of the Five Thousand could take place. It is a manifestation of the advent of Christ in the etheric world. Only through an imitation of John the Baptist in a kind of inner beheading, a sacrifice of our intellect but without losing what we have gained by humanity's fall into intellectuality, will we bathe in the abundance and shining glory of an etheric world ruled by Christ.

BOTTON VILLAGE NEWS, 24TH JULY 1970

~ toward michaelmas

moral intuition and the threefold social organism

The warmth of summer, the long, high arc of the sun, allows nature to reach her greatest expansion of form, colour, scent, sound and movement. There is infinite variety in flowering and fruiting plants; in the differing greens of bushes and trees; in insects and birds; in the many four-legged creatures. This might evoke the four kingdoms of nature — mineral, plant, animal and human being — in any thoughtful observer, and the question may arise: In what way is the human being more than just a part of nature? How does he differ from it and, from an anthroposophical viewpoint, how does he form the beginning of the tenth hierarchy?

Each of the kingdoms of nature includes the one below it and adds a further dimension to it. Plants are fixed in their place like the minerals, yet they have growth and life; animals live and grow but they also move and have sense-perceptions, and in addition to all these gifts and capacities, the human being is endowed with consciousness and morality in the widest sense. However, the human being is more than just another dimension over and above the animal because in his very being he *excludes himself* from the totality of nature and the cosmos. Stones, plants and animals are part of the 'wheel of life', the 'balance of nature' — plants are dependent on weather and stars, for example, and animals are bound by instinct to their cosmic and terrestrial surroundings and to the scent and movement of their prey. All three lower kingdoms are intrinsically linked in a seamless, mysterious totality. Only the human being is solitary, lonely, homeless, excluded. He is linked with others in karmic comradeship, but this does not, of itself, change his solitary condition.

It is morality that forces him to make continual decisions from his personal loneliness (although amid the comforts of life he is often unaware of it), and it also forces him to be homeless. All other creatures have homes, yet man is homeless because he is on the way to becoming a creator. He has added an enormous number of things to the natural creation by nature and cosmos. He stands midway between natural and man-made creation. As the active creator of this man-made creation he is lonely, but he is also free. Nature is passive, so even when the lion attacks the gazelle, it does so because it *must*. Natural creatures are dependent on their instincts, on prey, on water, on the stars, etc. Whether a human being wants to move or not depends on him alone. He can even extend the borders of his freedom to include life and death themselves, as, for example, in hunger strikes or suicide bombing missions.

Morality has two fields of play. One is very large and indefinite, akin to the whole of civilisation, the other is smaller, akin to culture. Morality is the *response* — not the reaction — to the needs of the surrounding world, and is fired to a greater or lesser extent by what Rudolf Steiner described as moral intuition.[57] It is a response which contains the *good* that is appropriate to the moment or situation, in the context of the physical world, soul world or spirit world. In this vast arena of nature and cosmos, humanity alone is the source and fount of the good within it. Although creation is natural and divine, is wise and enormously manifold, it is not 'good' as such, so man-made creation depends entirely on the use we make of it and how we act within it. This wellspring of the good must therefore be individual. Individuals can be good only as individuals (arrangements or institutions may, but can never be free). To what end? For the sake of mankind becoming the fountain of the good, the gods allowed the Fall which is the road to the 'I am', and thereby to selfishness. Karma is the education towards unselfishness but without losing the 'I am' — which is why karma and moral intuition are two interdependent realities.

Our age is strongly biased towards the good. But regarding knowledge, it is a very unclear, materialistic age. No wonder; it is the time of democracy and the welfare state which both try to achieve the good, not as something arising out of the individual, but as something corporate, something that avoids individual mistakes and tries to be on the safe side. This reduces people to numbers and loses sight of their spiritual essence and being. The state only *seems* to triumph in the sphere of the good because it achieves what individuals in the past were too weak to achieve alone. The problem today is how to rescue the good from the sphere of equality and install it in its rightful place — the sphere of freedom. In its organisation, the centralised state (be it communist or capitalist) ignores the uniqueness of each human being, and relies on outer arrangements to achieve the good. But arrangements issue from intellectual thoughts, and as soon as one group of people dictates to another, it paralyses the good in the individual to whom it dictates. It is quite obvious that as long as hospitals, welfare organisations, universities, colleges and schools are owned and run by the state, goodness is driven out of them (as evidenced by instances of the police or the army having to quash riots or strikes).

In thinking about any threefold social organism, we have to distinguish between what is simply appropriate for any human being — the welfare state has often merely adapted gross social and physical injustices of the past — and the network of moral intuitions which unites humanity in a mysterious and apocalyptic way. The reality of the threefold social organism should arise out of a just understanding of the cosmos and humanity.

DATE UNKNOWN

to have no time

We are excluded from the realm of *time*. We have our existence, we live and move, in space over which falls the shadow of time. We see this directly in plants — first the root appears in space, then the cotyledons, then stem and leaves, then the flower and finally the fruit with its seeds. What appears one after the other is obviously a single unit, a contemporaneous whole, and it is only owing to the conditions of space that it appears separated into parts bound together by the power of growth. It is the invisible archetypal plant. What appears in our thinking as the concept 'plant' contains all these parts. The invisible, archetypal human being is the eternal human being developing over many lives, just as the archetypal plant develops throughout a year. In the external world the 'parts' of the plant are connected through growth and decay. The seed is a quite visible thing in the decaying plant, but in the case of the ageing human being his seed, his karmic future, will only appear in future lives and so is still invisible.

The power of thinking and the power of growth seem to be connected with each other. Rudolf Steiner often described why, ideally, the child should go to school only after the powers of growing and forming have come to a preliminary end. Then the child can begin to think, and thus to learn. The human being is excluded from this world of life and growth because his ability to think, to have concepts — acquired first in school, later through the media, public opinion and ordinary social situations — erects a wall between life and the sense world. What is beyond the wall is only 'imaginable' (as also is anthroposophy). We can also say that our thoughts are the deadening shadow of what is alive beyond the wall, so the concept 'plant' is only a dead thought. But if our thoughts were to become alive, we would discover that they are part of the world beyond the wall.

The days of our life are lived in space: they are 'space' days. We have our memories — of being a child, of doing this or that in adulthood, meeting this or that person, etc., but the flow of time in which these events swim remains invisible to us, and is a dim experience at best. These 'space' days are divided into hours of work, eating, sleeping, etc. The thought that 'I have no time', or, 'The day has only 24 hours', turn these days into an arid stretch of duty. How can this aridity be permeated with life? How can 'having no time' be widened, or the shackles of 'no time' be undone?

The answer lies in being able to permeate our activity with *understanding experience*; to treat our work not as a chore which happens from time to time, but as something we have willed, and therefore understood and cherished through spiritual scientific enlightenment. In this way we will discover that our time could be divided far more efficiently; that there is more 'time' than we had imagined. The discovery that our lack of time is due to bad timing reaches a certain crescendo if we can share it with others, and they are usually grateful because their own timetable seems to leave them too little time as well. To have more time is valuable for society, not just for oneself.

The main thing is that our day is not divided into work and pleasure, or into things we like and things we do not like. Understanding our experiences enlivens any job and makes the timetable amazingly wide and unselfish. Liking or disliking part of a day tires and deadens us.

BOTTON VILLAGE NEWS, 31 VII 1987

the three highest senses are guarantors for the spirit

It is through the three highest senses, those of ego, thought and word,[58] that we recognise the *other human being* as an individual possessing self-consciousness, having the same capacity for thought that we ourselves have, and making sounds which constitute a word-bearing language. This recognition is as direct in our time as are our sensations of red, cold, loud, bitter, etc. with the slight difference that it takes no effort to perceive red but it does need effort to recognise the other as an ego-bearing person with a name, and to recognise thoughts as thoughts. But if we observe ourselves without bias or preconception, we find, perhaps to our astonishment, that these three experiences are direct ones and, also to our astonishment, that they are not contained in any other experience — we do not *see* that the other person is an ego-bearer with self-consciousness, just as we do not actually *hear* whether he speaks or merely makes noises. In other words, we do not perceive the difference with our 'material' senses. Rudolf Steiner's discovery that we have three sense-like abilities that enable us to *perceive* what lies behind material existence is of the greatest importance for the whole of anthroposophy.

People ask, 'Do you believe in reincarnation? How can you prove it?' Even without anthroposophy we can discover that we have many self-evident experiences which do not need proving. All our sense perceptions belong to these. We do not *prove* the redness of red, the saltiness of soup, etc. How do we 'prove' reincarnation? The 'proof' that somebody else is a person comes through our experience of the black of the pupil of their eyes and in meeting their gaze. In meeting this gaze we become aware that the black, apparent nothingness of the pupil actually contains many invisible qualities. Guided by anthroposophy we can learn to divine these qualities, they are the richly-embroidered patterns on the mantle of accumulated earth-lives. (Rudolf Steiner and anthroposophy itself insist that, in our time, we should never simply *believe*; we should take things as hypotheses and check them against our own *unbiased* experiences, and let those we cannot verify stand as question marks.) We can discover that we have many, many experiences that we normally fail to notice. They are blotted out by prejudice, by scientific theory, and so on. It is the same with the senses of word, thought and ego.

Our senses today seem to have two sides, each sense looking through its physical realm into a special place of the spiritual world and, at the same time, to the respective part of the physical world for which it was created. The completeness of the circle will become clearer only in the course of our future development. The initiates of the distant past experienced the physical world, as we now think and perceive it, as a 'higher world': what for us is the 'here and now' was for them a distant future. The words in the gospel, 'The light of the body is the eye' (Luke 11: 34) refers to our own distant future. We think we perceive the difference between physical and supersensible with the senses but it only seems so because of the consciousness we are living in now. As Goethe said, we seek a theory for the blue of the sky, but in fact this sky blue *is* already its theory.[59] If we look at a face, our sense of ego perceives that a person is present; if we listen to language our sense of word perceives words and if someone explains his thoughts to us we perceive thoughts. If we were imbued only with the senses of sight and hearing we would imagine that the understanding of ego, language and thought is merely a possible theory.

The apparent twofold function of the senses in our time has to do with their attachment to the astral body. We love to hear *music* (not just tones), and listen to an *eloquent* speaker; we love to look at a *beautiful* face. We use these and other senses in creating our emotions — scents involve the sense of smell in emotions. As long as the senses are servants of our emotions, all knowledge gained through them is subjective. The more selfless the senses become, the more they are detached from our emotions, from our astrality, the more they can be open spaces of the spiritual world sounding and shining in us.

SOURCE UNKNOWN, 8 V 1991

light-space — word-space

Although we are inserted into earthly existence through light, we can never see it — it is as if it always comes from behind us. We see the sun itself, the source of light, only as a white, yellow or orange disc so blinding that it is normally impossible to look directly at it. Our surroundings (the landscape and sky, our rooms, our bodies) are lit up brightly or dimly, and coloured objects appear. The colour attached to objects appears on their surface — our light space is a space of surfaces. Space is a continuously coloured whole from which our consciousness is banned.

Sounds and the spoken word fit into this surface-space, but the word itself does not. When words live in us silently, as in meditation, we become aware that a new space, a soul-space, is hollowed out within us, and although we can create it only when we are awake, it is beyond sleeping and waking. The light space belongs to our waking consciousness, so our emotions, thoughts, sense-impressions and memories are blotted out when we fall asleep. The use of our body also belongs to waking consciousness when the body and its parts (limbs, muscles, senses), obey us to a greater or lesser extent. But we are also fettered to it more than we imagine. Both our limitations and our abilities are due to the constitution of our body. This was not the case in the past, and it will be different again in the future, but in our age of the consciousness soul it has to be so. One of the evils of our time is that our bodies are thought of and understood as machines, and therefore we become blind to their human limitations and abilities.

The word-space hollowed out in us through meditation is not only inward, adding a new dimension to our soul, but we also feel it to be something quite impersonal. What we knew beforehand as personal — memories, thoughts, etc. — we recognise as belonging to our body. The word-space is not exactly impersonal, but is of a different soul-substance. That this can be so is because the word in meditation is silent and not spoken. This means that word and breath are at last separated. During meditation, the more the breath moves by itself to our periphery, the more the word can silently unfold and arise within us. Because we normally use only the spoken word, it is difficult for us to experience the soundless, the breath-less word. The spoken word has within it a certain aggressive force — the breath has a tendency to fly directly towards the one who is being addressed. The inner word is mild and has no attacking direction. It bears within its sounds not self-assertion, but listening.

The pupil in the centre of our eye is the negation of the light space. Its gaze is the revelation of the listening word. Like our pupils, the vestments and the altar are black in Lent.

BOTTON VILLAGE NEWS, 20 III 1964

light and space

Our eye is the only sense organ that we can close against incoming impressions. Moreover, there seems to be a connection between our waking state and open eyes, and our sleeping state and closed eyes. For this reason, our sense of sight is not merely one sense among several others — hearing, taste, smell or touch (not to mention the additional senses which Rudolf Steiner made us aware of) — but rather a kind of beacon that lights up and awakens our consciousness and which therefore, when extinguished as the lids close, induces sleep, or at least makes sleep possible. And just because it is a kind of super-sense allied more to our consciousness than our other senses are, it blurs the part which those other senses play.

Because of our experience and concept of space, it is usually very difficult to imagine pure sense impressions, and this is particularly true in the sense of sight. What do we know of space? There is, obviously, a connection between movement and space (not movement in the sense of flexion and extension of muscles, from inside, as it were, nor the movement we observe from outside, whether our own or others'), but the movement we perform in crossing the intervening space when walking from here to there, or when we raise a teacup from the table to our lips or lift our arm to take a book from the shelf. Certainly, we can observe our walking and lifting, but we come to the concept of space not through observation, but through our guided will. The will itself remains dark but its guiding intentions belong to our conscious thinking.

We can easily gain the mistaken impression that we see things in space — an error which is cleared up when we consider the experiences of blind people after a successful operation to restore their sight. The images we actually see are spaceless, are pure images. Only by moving, by exerting our will, are they placed in space. It is will and space which are linked, not sense-experience and space. Will shoots into our sense-images and therefore our sense-world seems to be spatial, especially our sight-world.

Yet the riddle of space is explained not only by our movements and the exertion of our will: it is also linked with the question of light. Strictly speaking, our eye does not give us the sense for perceiving light. It is the sense itself that allows us to see perceptible objects, colours and so on, since light is invisible. We infer its existence from the fact that the world becomes perceptible or disappears from sight. Space also becomes visible because of light, or so it seems, but in fact it is only lit up, made visible to us because, like light, space is something we cannot see, touch, taste, etc. What we have is the experience that it appears to us through the presence of light. Through the presence of the invisible light, invisible-space becomes illumined-space and it is into this that we are able to walk and to look.

The alliance between light and will resulting in the concept of space is of the greatest importance for us in the fifth post-Atlantean epoch because we have the overriding experience that our earthly life unfolds in space. Both light and will are beyond and outside our consciousness — only colours are visible; only thoughts are conscious. The union between light and dark resulting in space surrounds us with a sham security, hides the abyss between the sensible and the supersensible world, and thereby hides the Guardian of the Threshold.

BOTTON VILLAGE NEWS, 2 II 1968

psychoanalysis & the villages

A few years ago Karl König said that our Camphill villages have to do with the redemption of psychoanalysis and that the curative education in our schools has to do with the redemption of 'test-psychology', or what we simply call psychology today. Tonight we will try to unearth the roots of psychoanalysis — the teachings of Freud himself — but also what is taught in the schools of psychoanalysis and psychotherapy that have appeared since.

Although psychoanalysis and psychotherapy have gone through many transformations, they have their roots in the materialism of the 19th century. In that crude and abstract materialistic system, the human being (like his natural environment) was gradually reduced to a mass of atoms and molecules. Materialism — all-cognising and boundlessly optimistic — was out to discover the causes of our world, we had only to investigate the matter which constitutes our earth, our universe and man himself, and we would uncover the causes for everything that exists! Technological development seemed to prove it: electricity, railways, machinery of every description... The brain was known to be the cause of thinking, so it only remained to find the cause of everything else in our thoroughly knowable world!

One of those who stood against such beliefs was the German philosopher Friedrich Nietzsche.[60] Nietzsche's life (1843–1900) went through very distinct phases. In his early years he was professor of history and philology at the University of Basel, and he tried in his own way to understand the universe and human culture. The last eleven years of his life were spent in mental darkness, but in the years leading up to his madness he wrote several books all aiming in a similar direction. The middle span of his life between these two phases was spent observing the world. He confronted the desert of causality-bound materialism coolly, psychologically, and came to understand human actions and human attitudes as masks which hide what lies behind. He penetrated through the behaviour to its meaning. A stone thrown into a pond makes ripples: cause is followed by effect; what happens is determined (outwardly) by a past cause. But as Nietzsche saw it, a significant human action is determined (inwardly) by a future intention.

Nietzsche was one who prepared the way not only for anthroposophy but also for psychoanalysis since it was from Nietzsche's psychological observations that Freud developed his theory and method. He drew his image of the human being from Nietzsche's recognition of the meaningfulness of human behaviour. Freud saw the human being in his ordinary ego-consciousness as influenced from above by the 'super-ego', and from below by the 'id'. The super-ego was a father figure of authority, clothed in ideals and precepts of decent living; the id was a collection of drives and instincts focused in the Oedipus complex (the drive to murder one's father and marry one's mother) or Electra complex (the drive to murder one's mother and marry one's father). These drives imprinted themselves into ordinary ego-consciousness, into the day-soul, forcing the human being to express himself in words and actions along the lines indicated by Nietzsche's psychological conclusions. When this expression pointed towards neurosis it could be alleviated and healed by psychotherapy which allowed the content of the id to rise to the surface of day-soul consciousness. Such was Freud's view of the human being, prompting his particular form of therapy.

Rudolf Steiner brought a new view, and with it a new therapy. The human being was re-observed, re-experienced, re-cognised, and what now presented itself as therapy was no isolated individual treatment — the human being was seen as a threefold entity. This insight emerged in 1917 in an inconspicuous appendix to Rudolf Steiner's book, *The Riddles of the Soul*.[61] In it he revealed that the human soul's incarnation into the nerve/brain system, the rhythmic system and the metabolic system enables our thinking, feeling and willing to incarnate and develop its day-consciousness. Then, almost at the same time, Rudolf Steiner's concept of a threefold social organism made its appearance. A lecture given on 23 April 1919 called 'Esoteric Prelude to the Exoteric Treatment of Threefolding'[62] laid bare the three spheres of a truly human society — the cultural/spiritual sphere (which should rightly include all aspects of education), the sphere of human rights (the realm of justice and of politics) and the sphere of the economic life.

How is the threefoldness of the human being related to the threefoldness of the social organism?

'We can correctly compare the social organism with the human organism only if we think of the social organism as set up the other way round. And if the economic life is compared with the human nerve-sense system it will naturally follow that the political life will be compared with the rhythmic system. But the cultural-spiritual life on earth could be compared with the metabolic system because the laws according to which both act are similar. For the economic life evolves naturally from sources which have a similar significance for the social organism as the individual capacities brought with us at birth have for the human being. As the life of the individual depends upon those gifts, which he brings with him at birth, so does the economic life depend similarly for its primal requirements upon the gifts of nature. Primal necessities such as the soil, etc. are like the capacities with which a person is endowed at birth. The amount of coal or metals in the earth and the fruitfulness or otherwise of the soil are the gifts, the talents, so to speak, of the social organism.

Human productions of the spiritual life stand in the same relationship to the *social* organism as the metabolic system stands to the whole *human* organism and its functions. All we carry out in the form of art, science, technical ideas and so on, is the meat and drink of the social organism, its nourishment.'

Whereas the spiritual-cultural realm of the social organism, fed by the human being's free thinking, can be compared only with human metabolism which is fed by food, so the economic realm of the social organism, fashioned according to the mineral gifts of the earth, is dependent on the gifts of human invention — human art and science — and thus can be compared only with human thinking, with the individual spirit of man.

The human being — spirit, soul and body; thinking, feeling and willing; nervous system, rhythmic system and metabolic system — is enveloped by a threefold social organism *in reverse.* We think and move, act and live within a social organism that embraces and surrounds us 'the other way round'. And this is what makes us unable to comprehend the social organism with ordinary thinking. In essence, it is entirely different from us, although it consists of human beings. Karl König told us that the social organism is the Greater Guardian, and that we are enwrapped in it as by a kind of invisible, occult fact.[63] We know that when a human being sets out on the esoteric path, thinking, feeling and willing (which until then are interwoven as in the Mixed King in Goethe's Fairy Tale), begin to separate. But at the same time a 'reversal' takes place and we should orientate ourselves such that we learn to see this, too. That we think, feel and will in the way we do is due to the Fall. The gods planned our creation differently: they envisaged the human being steeped in everlasting innocence and glory. But we fell from that primeval glory into reverse. We can become whole again, we can right ourselves, only in a true social life which we can approach through the Being of Christ. Rudolf Steiner's threefold social organism is not a theory or a programme — it is a power, a power that manifests within society, a power by which a threefold social life *will* come about. Reversal means just that.

There is a verse by Schiller[64] which Rudolf Steiner often quoted:

Seekest thou the highest and greatest?
The Plant can teach it thee.
What *it* is, will-lessly,
Be thou, but purposefully.

So it is. Thus we can change again through esoteric training.

Through 19th century materialism the human being gained his freedom, freedom from anything outside himself. No longer was his fate to be determined by the gods. His rational intellect began to train itself out of its own power. Freud, among others, tried to reach an understanding of the human being. Essentially using his insight and cognition, they all tried to arrive at therapy, even going so far as attempting to revise the social order. The last hundred and fifty years have been burdened by the so-called social problem, yet what this problem is remains a question. I see it exemplified in an ordinary, everyday occurrence — when the so-called 'man in the street' meets the civil service, for example in the post office. (This scene could be translated into any society since capitalist countries are not essentially different in this respect from socialist ones). There is a common assumption that society cannot be organised without becoming impersonal and so when a person goes to buy a 25p stamp, the clerk in the post office hands it over without looking at him. He does the work he is paid to do and does not let subjective impressions enter into it because the personal and the objective must not be combined. The post office clerk typifies the inevitable tendency of any civil service, but more than that he typifies the problem of our materialistically-based society.

By contrast — and significantly — the Camphill Movement has *not* developed a civil service, although our numbers might now warrant it. Instead, it all hangs together miraculously in the free exchanges of any of our meetings, which is something the general experience of society in the 20th century has proved to be unworkable. In Camphill, we treat the social organism with respect and with regard for the mysterious threads that weave through it. Therefore our meetings are always more than business meetings. They take into account that when several people are gathered together something cleverer or greater than they are can speak: not that we understand this, but we come more and more to feel it.

The materialistic view of the human being — all that has culminated in psychotherapy — has presented an asocial science of man. Theories about the human being may seem to correspond with the truth but they have left out the mysterious, esoteric element in the social organism. We in the Camphill villages are beginning, dimly, to seek for it. We do not look upon our villagers as 'patients' who have to be 'treated' in a more human version of the mental hospital. Neither do we try to curb psychotic illnesses, for instance, with the widespread use of quick-fix tranquillisers. In our villages, what helps and heals is not that *they* are patients and *we* are staff, but that we and the handicapped together *share* a common social organism. In all our villages, wherever they may be in the world, we try to ensure that the social life is arranged in a threefold way and that the three spheres are in balance with each other. We try to make sure that these three spheres are a reality for each of us and that the king or leader of this threefold social organism is the totality of those who take part in these three spheres. In its wholeness, the organism is a congregation. Therefore, the king is not only the single 'I' but the Act of Consecration within each single 'I'. With our inwardly crowned egos we are members of these three spheres. We bring to them our whole selves, the dark as well as the light. But all that we bring is held together by the Service, or by our own ego insofar as it is able to take in the Service.

We cannot bring the fallen human being and the esoteric reality of the social organism together so readily, but nature presents it to us symbolically in the butterfly's relation to the flower, as Rudolf Steiner pointed out so poetically.[65] A butterfly is the blossom freed from the fetters of the earth, or a blossom is the butterfly shackled to the earth by gravity. Again, remember what Schiller said of the plant; that it is the human being in reverse, that it is completely innocent although it bears this innocence as an image. The goal is for the human being to become like the plant, except that for him innocence cannot be something static; he has to make the effort to become innocent in the social organism in which he may find himself.

The butterfly is a blossom that flies through the air, but it also belongs to the animal kingdom, having something resembling legs, a metabolism and a rhythmic system. In the lecture cited above, Rudolf Steiner tells us that the substance on the wings of a butterfly (be it a cabbage-white, purple emperor, or even a simple moth), is borne upwards through the atmosphere and carried around the earth, and up there it forms what he calls a butterfly corona. Just as the sun has an aura around it, so has the earth — an aura of the spiritualised matter of butterfly wings. This lights up, many-hued, and glistens out there in the cosmos, and when the gods look down to the earth they see it. But they see more; they see the light of this mantle of spiritualised matter shot through with warmth, with the warmth of all those birds that have died and been taken up by the warmth ether. Elsewhere, Rudolf Steiner spoke about the earth's mantle of warmth and said that it is the bearer of human karma.[66] It is here that human deeds and destiny can find their balance, and through human evolution the mantle itself becomes enriched.

With the coming of the reversal of thinking/nerve, feeling/rhythm and willing/metabolism, guilt re-emerges — the same guilt that began with the Fall. Something is needed to bridge the gap between the guilt of human beings and the innocence of the social organism. The butterfly sacrifices its substance into the earth's mantle and the human being must also give something up. The colour and life of the substance of the butterfly wing are a symbol for the human being of what should be given up, but perhaps they are more than a symbol. The butterfly corona is permeated by the warmth ether, which is the bearer of human karma, and the transition from guilty humanity to innocent social organism is very much a matter of karma.

In so far as it comes about, the innocent social organism can itself hasten this transition. It can work back on human ills with help and healing. What is *embraced* by this innocent social organism is right for us and brings health to our karmic relations. What makes for disturbance in karmic relations is what is done *outside* this organism, outside the social connections among human beings, as Rudolf Steiner said in his lectures on psychoanalysis.[67]

That is why I gave the example of the post office clerk who is concerned only with the 25p stamp and not with the customer. But it is not just the civil service which becomes objective and impersonal. What of psychotherapists themselves? What of the many doctors who try to treat our complex modern human ills? Human beings go to them as patients, as they go to the clerk in the post office as customers, and both patient and customer are served — objectively, impersonally — but this giving and receiving takes place outside the social organism. Karmic relations are disturbed by it and, more immediately, the customer or the patient leaves with his true need unsatisfied because he has been served impersonally. What was once personal has now become impersonal in our day. The personal has been denied when it should be integrated into the social organism. The customer does not merely want a 25p stamp, nor the patient a psychoanalytical unburdening. Each is seeking, unknowingly, for the social organism which alone can bring true healing.

The title of this lecture was perhaps a bit grand, but Karl König's remark so many years ago has continued to live with me, and there is no doubt that our Camphill villages are in some way connected with the redemption of psychoanalysis.

LECTURE, BOTTON VILLAGE, 20 VII 1967

[*Comment by Dr Thomas Weihs who was in the audience*]

I remember Dr König describing the threefold social organism as the Greater Guardian, but although I never forgot it, I did not understand it. It is now clear to me from Peter's description of the polarity between human threefoldness and the reversed threefoldness of the social organism in connection with the inner path.

The relationship between individual and society is *the* problem of our age. Western individualism prevents the development of social forms while communism sacrifices the individual to the social form. Neither has realised its own threefold structure. And I must confess that until tonight I, too, believed that this problem could only be *suffered*. Yet I think that tonight we have had a glimpse of the fact that it can be *lived with* and conquered.

We know that in striving towards our true spirituality we encounter the reversal of the threefoldness of our own soul. We can realise that our thinking attains to morality when it is reinforced by the powers of our will, and our will leads us to wisdom when it becomes permeated by our thoughts. We realise, too, that in this process we meet the promise of our unity with the spirit. Yet tonight we have understood something more. We have rightly seen the significance in the inmost striving of the individual soul. But hitherto we had seen this as significant only for the individual himself. Now we can begin to appreciate that what we approach here can be encountered in the glory of human society as well. *This is the Christ.* I believe this gives us a new connection to the whole substance and essence of the 'village impulse' in Camphill.

the social organism and the threefold human being

Rudolf Steiner's endeavours regarding the social organism were directed so as to show that it has a being of its own; that it is not just our relationship to one another as we are, but that it is an organism in its own right.

He described that our head, the region of our gifts and all that we brought with us from before birth and our past life, corresponds to the resources of different localities of the earth, each endowed with its gifts of coal, metals, stones, soil fertility and so on. Our consciousness pole corresponds in the social organism with the economy, with what originates and develops from these natural foundations — trade, producer-consumer associations, and so on. The sphere of the cultural or free spiritual life would correspond to human metabolism, to the life pole. The sphere of human equality lies in between, in our rhythmic system.

Compared to the human form, this social organism is inverted; it stands on its head. The head of the social organism is in the earth, in a definite area of the earth with its particular gifts. We human beings stand on earth with our metabolic organs pointing earthward relative to our head, but the metabolism and limbs of the social organism point heavenward. We are sustained by the earth locality that we inhabit, but the social organism is fed by our gifts. Thus far, we have been guided by Rudolf Steiner. It is now up to us to find out how this relates to our experiences, knowledge and conscience. What follows here is only a small part of this situation.

Because of its reality, it is important to grasp the interdependence between human beings and the social organism, which are two separate beings. We live and exist in the element of the social organism. Compared with human beings, the social organism and its three spheres is standing on its head (just as the plant roots correspond to the human head), and it is endowed with the same guiltless innocence that plants have. The element in which we live and exist, the social organism, is an element of innocence. Our relationship to others must first traverse this element before we can reach them. Meeting another human being is therefore meant to become a catharsis, a purification which transcends sympathy and antipathy. This realm of innocence will be achieved if we become conscious of the realm in which we meet one another — as a person or in one of the spheres of the social organism. Meeting the other one as a person is a complicated process, but it is the process which underlies our social life.

The threefold being of the individual and of the social organism should appear in its true light from the following examples. For a teacher, scientist, composer or painter it is a blessing if others take an interest in their ideas or work. We feel blessed if we find ourselves in a situation in which we have to discover how to do justice in an unbiased way to the other person. If someone sells me some cheese, on the one hand he fulfils a need of mine and, on the other, those who produce the cheese with him should do so in a co-operative way with a shared economic responsibility regarding the whole undertaking of cheese-making. We can never really separate our activities from the community of human beings within which they take place. My need for cheese; my being just or unjust to others; my teaching; my painting, etc., only makes sense within a social organism. The innocence comes in because we are used to saying, I eat, I love (or hate) others, I teach, as if the social relevance of our deeds is something merely added to our activity. But the social context will have to become an integral part of our activity and thereby the 'I' will be freed from the prison of its own ego. Thus the social life, with which we are constantly bound up, becomes the educator of the human being.

It is obvious that these are the three modes of relating to other people — considered not as single persons but regarding their activities within the social organism. Underlying these modes is selflessness. In our creative cultural activities each one of us is unique, an observer. In our humanity, each of us tries to do justice to the other. And in our economic producer-consumer relationships we are also involved as individuals. But if enthusiasm, admiration, delight and love do not enter the observing mode, we will fail in our intention. We will make that which we experience into an object and thereby miss it as a process, as the incarnation of an idea. An intuitive element must enter our thinking. Each of us has to bear his own cross, his own karma, and each one of us has to find the wind of freedom in his own biography, otherwise he will waste his life. But everyone is related to people; everyone is part of varying situations. The element of thematic composition, of inspiration, enters here so that justice is done to all these thematic threads. Selflessness will come into the economic life if our disciplined, objective thinking enters our will. Production will have to adjust itself to needs without interference by advertisements or politics. Human beings will have to purify their awareness of needs — catharsis, being on the road to imagination, enters the picture.

Only if the three modes appear in their single, independent identities will they emerge and evolve their inherent natures. The first realm of the social organism is the cultural-spiritual life — all the thought activity of the individual, even if used in the other two realms. The second realm is that of equality and of inter-human relationships. The third realm is economic activity and events — producing, consuming and trading. Money, in fact, is connected with all three realms. The activity and power of the State is meant to be restricted to the second realm only. But we can well see that the social organism is an independent organism only regarding fallen human nature. Regarding the human being and his archetypal resurrected nature it is not. Where the red roses on the black cross begin to flower, and through their inner, Christian efforts human beings regain their innocent Nathanic nature, the social organism becomes part of their being. Our endeavours to establish the threefoldness of the social organism are really efforts towards the Christianising of our existence. As long as this striving does not grow into the threefoldness of our human relationships, it must remain a refined egoism. There will come a time — and the innocent threefold social relationships is the dawn of this sunrise — when esoteric and social efforts will become one. Only when the social life becomes part of individual existence will Christ walk among human beings.

BOTTON VILLAGE NEWS, 25 II 1978

duty & responsibility

Until about the 15th century, no thoughts or feelings about duty disturbed the surface of the human soul. Before that a human being was more fixed in the place where he was born and into his profession: a nobleman was noble, a gardener could only garden, a craftsman behaved according to his guild, a housewife cared for her family and a monk led a religious life. Moreover, many right things happened as a matter of course. We did these things, but as we had no choice, there was no merit attached to them.

Now we are freer and therefore we can not only do our duty but also choose to withdraw from the obligations of our surroundings and be lazy. Duty along with its shadow, laziness, is a product of the age of the consciousness soul, and because of the polarisation of duty and laziness, we feel fulfilment of duty to be something good, and laziness to be something bad. While this may be true, in our time we should go a step further, for in the gospel it says, 'So likewise ye, *when ye shall have done all those things which are commanded you*, say, we are *un*profitable servants: we have done that which it was *our duty* to do.' (Luke 17: 10)

Responsibility is the sun against which the star of duty pales. At the beginning of the fifth post-Atlantean cultural epoch, mankind matured, developed individual thinking, and no longer obeyed those in authority in a child-like manner. Morality became a matter of being responsible for one's own decisions. Doing one's duty is a matter of course, but the taking of responsibility entails a certain freedom of decision, always and every day anew, and with it all the minor things which need to be done, not out of duty but because we choose to do them. This is only possible if we have developed a sense of morality. For the slave in ancient times, morality was almost non-existent because he had merely to execute someone else's orders. In the past, the difference between gentry and commoners consisted to some extent in the gentry having greater access to morality than the commoners. Today, *every* human being develops individual responsibility for their deeds.

Duty can easily become self-righteous while responsibility should be warm and light, yet inherent in it is the danger of a new form of egoism. Individual responsibility depends on our conviction that the thoughts we act out of are true. Because they are our *own* thoughts, they cannot but be imbued with a certain self-righteousness, so the actions originating from them are tinged with selfishness. Nowadays every human being is caught in this impasse — the impasse of modern Christian morality. The only solution is the extremely difficult exercise of what Rudolf Steiner calls 'selfless self-consciousness'.

BOTTON VILLAGE NEWS, 19 VIII 1960 & 16 III 1962

the song of the earth

The safe house of summer begins to crumble and the first cold and dark gusts of autumn wind start to blow through the cracks. When one season ends and another dawns, we experience their magnitude, the great majesty of their course. How pale and inappropriate are the memories of snowy blizzards, spring days, or the scents of early summer compared to the dense present, the 'now' which encompasses us. We cannot see beyond the engulfing season, either to past or future, as we remember an instance in early childhood.

But this magnitude of the seasons has something inhuman about it, like all things belonging to nature. There is an abyss between the human self and nature. We can have feelings about the seasons (as poems have shown since the earliest times), and they evoke various moods within the human soul, often sentimental, but they themselves are silent and majestic. In a religious and spiritual way, this chasm between human soul and the seasons is superseded by the seasonal prayers and colours of the Act of Consecration of Man. It is superseded in a different way in art, in which we can discern the generally human tendency of Christianity.

One of the greatest musical creations of our time is Gustav Mahler's 'The Song of the Earth', especially the last part *'Der Abschied'* ('Farewell'), which celebrates autumn. It is an autumn of life, the release of death, but its autumnal mood is permeated by compassion as seen in its archetypal form in the Parable of the Good Samaritan, (Luke 10: 30–37) which we read now when summer passes over into autumn.

The parables are quite different from illustrations, or a pictorial form of teaching. They seem to contain moral exhortations. But the exhortation is only their 'understandable' exterior. Morality is really a huge world and the parable is like a door opening into an interior as wide as the seasons, filled with living warmth. Works of art can unfurl the wings of the soul, so that at times we feel the nature life of the seasons permeated by this vista of moral warmth, as we find in the autumnal compassion of 'The Song of the Earth'.

The seasons are life, evoking then subduing growth; part of the life of the earth and of earthly beings. They seem to have moods, joyful and sad, but attached to these moods there must be a soul which expresses itself in the seasonal moods. It is our own soul, for the human soul is really as wide as the world; it only seems small and narrow because our consciousness is narrow. Therefore we project our narrow feelings of joy and sadness onto the seasons. Because the content of our soul is narrowed down, we can raise our head out of the waters of the soul, as it were, and have a dry, clear consciousness within. In this way we are able to think undisturbed.

Our inwardness is lifeless, yet with it we can 'understand' the parables, and human morality can start only in our lifeless inwardness. Hence we equate life with our external world; consciousness and morality with our inner, lifeless world. The parables contain life *and* consciousness, as the archetypal parable of the sower shows. (Matt. 13: 3–23, Mark 4: 3–20, Luke 8: 5–15) Parables comprise the whole world-width of the soul, and they reach into realms of the seasons where our consciousness and limited feelings do not.

The seasons have no moods. What is shown in the parables is only apparently human. In reality, it belongs to the part of our soul which permeates the seasons. But our 'I' is greater than the seasons. The time will come when the small cell of our consciousness will widen and we will become aware of our world-width. The moral warmth of the seasons will make us into kings and priests of the world. The darkness and frost of winter, the scents and flowers of summer, will then be within us, but this 'within' will be worldwide. Christ said 'I have overcome the world.' (John 16: 33) Through the deed of Christ we will become greater than the world, as Adam in Paradise was greater than the animals he had to name.

The parables are like seeds, full of sprouting and growing powers. Works of art, like 'The Song of the Earth' are schools in which we learn to live within the parables.

BOTTON VILLAGE NEWS, 11 IX 1964

democracy, karma & the third mystery drama

Once upon a time democracy was born out of an enthusiasm for the equality of all human beings within the community of mankind. But then it grew up and came to mean merely the balance of power, by means of voting, between political parties. It still clung to a pale hope that, despite reducing each voting person to a number, to a unit of '1', this balance of power would represent and produce equality. This is a notion of democracy which comes from the West and, in a world that is becoming ever more westernised, it has become a kind of sacred cow demanding silent acquiescence and instant obedience! When we hear that in a few months' time there will be free elections in this or that country, we may feel: 'All is well! They have found the way to solve all ills.'

But *real* democracy will *never* be achieved by reducing the human being to the figure '1' and then counting up the 1's. Consider this. You buy apples and together they make up a certain weight and you pay for that weight. Already there is something slightly untrue because each apple is a little different from the others. How much the more is each human being different, vastly different, from his fellows! However, in politics, it is believed that we can find the common denominator of all these differences, and that is where the fallacy creeps in. Human beings are indeed equal to one another but, unlike eggs or apples, each is equal to the other in his or her absolute uniqueness. There is only one layer in each human being that can be reduced to the figure '1'. If you confuse this layer with the others, or even with all layers, you are simply saying, 'The human being is an egg or an apple.'

A chasm yawns between our social and political life. Today's concept of democracy hinders us from thinking about our political life with realism or common sense. Although hamstrung by all manner of conventions and limiting conditions, our social life does have a certain amount of originality and can, occasionally, address the individual — if not outspokenly then at least in our experience. The chasm is due to the two things which cannot be reconciled: human beings reduced to a common denominator on the one hand and, on the other, the relationships we have, individually, with one another. Here in Botton, where we face the same dangers in our social forms as in society at large, we do not vote but we try to reach common ground in our various groups. If we are relatively successful, we should remember that Botton has a mere 320 inhabitants while Britain alone has 50 million.

A *new* social order (and here 'social' includes 'political'), can only be founded on a new relationship from human being to human being. We will have to accept each of our brothers and sisters in the world far more deeply and with his or her spiritual countenance, meaning irrespective of colour, official position or of opinions. Opinions give rise to sympathies and antipathies, and these cloud the reality of the other person since they have to do with *us* rather than with *him/her*. If in our time we can overcome sympathy and antipathy, and therefore foster quite unbiased relationships with *any* human being, it will be possible for each of us to imagine ourselves empathetically in, and as, the other person, and from that person's existence and constitution uncover the opinions with which he agrees or disagrees. We will then realise that the opinions of the other have the same value as our own. But since they are dependent on each person's constitution and existence their value is therefore doubtful. We must get beyond mere opinions and come to insights.

One more step lies hidden in the process of democracy. The first step was voting, the second was the depth of encounter between one human being and another. The third step concerns the karmic nature of these encounters.

In Rudolf Steiner's third mystery play *The Guardian of the Threshold*,[68] the main characters in their various ways all cross over the threshold. Strader, the brilliant inventor and engineer, who is led to spiritual science through his wife Theodora, on one of these occasions has to experience how Ahriman tries to make use of twelve people, in their deep unconsciousness, for his own aims. In a later scene Benedictus, all knowing, all-wise, questions Strader thus:

Benedictus: You surely know quite well why all these souls,
  displayed by Ahriman, drew near to you
  when he by force intruded in their destinies?
Strader: This, too, my pain made very clear to me.
  It showed how in an earthly life, long past,
  I was connected with an Order,
  which now has formed the Occult Brotherhood.
  It showed, too, my relationship to all
  those people who revealed their actual selves.
  And I could feel that Ahriman intends
  to use these ties which in our future lives
  must firmly bind their souls to mine.

They are twelve because, for Ahriman's purposes, they are stripped of their individuality and reduced merely to the fact that they are a countable, measurable twelve. He says twelve is enough, and the thirteenth is again like the first.

Living is ordered by numbers, which are countable. The number of years it takes for the sun to pass through the twelve constellations of the zodiac (a Platonic year), is the number of breaths we take in a single day,* and there are many other patterns we have not yet discovered. These numbers give shape to life, making it possible for order to appear on many levels, but they do not do so in isolation. It is Ahriman's aim that numbers *alone* should rule, stripped of karma, of bearing and of living individuality. In their as yet largely unconscious being, these twelve people in the play may 'belong' to Lucifer (five of them) or Ahriman (the other seven), but beyond 'belonging' they are individuals, composed of gifts, weaknesses and qualities in respect of their karma, which essentially means that they are *on the way*, potentially free. Ahriman says — and not even Strader can hear him although he has to watch and endure the whole process — that he has tried to appropriate seven for himself and give five to Lucifer, but in the long run he has never succeeded. Karma is the real enemy of Ahriman, and in the end it is the Lord of Karma who is stronger than he is.

The real task is to combine karma with democracy. In order to do so it is not necessary to be clairvoyant or to undertake karma exercises. Only one thing is necessary, and it is indicated in the Sermon on the Mount, 'Whoever shall compel thee to go a mile, go with him twain.' (Matt. 5: 41) You should feel your way into the impulses, deliberations and limitations of the other person. You should take on his karma while at the same time preserving your own. You must involve your own will (and not only your ideas) in helping him. You will thus lend him your strength.

The future of democracy lies hidden in these directions and this is why, in Camphill, our quest is to create 'community'. We may love to sit for hours in neighbourhood meetings, or let our urge for social life flow into long talks on the telephone, and 'waste' our time gossiping on the footpath or in the store. But behind all these masks is the reality we are genuinely searching for — the courage to widen our karma so that we can embrace the karma of the other person. Obviously we have not achieved much of this yet, but whatever we achieve in the smallest degree, here in the speck that is Botton, or in the

---

* 18 breaths per minute x 60 minutes x 24 hours = 25,920 breaths per day. Cf 12 zodiac signs x 30 degrees per sign x 72 years precession per degree = 25,920 years in each Platonic year, which is the time taken for the sun to rise again in the same constellation on the first day of spring.

various Camphill centres and in other such communities, will one day be powerful leaven for a democracy of humanity.

BOTTON VILLAGE NEWS, 27 I 1988

∼ michaelmas

the first scene of the fourth mystery drama

Michaelmas is the festival of the human being, but the human being in his reality as the image of God, and therefore in the threefoldness of will, emotions and the consciousness that makes freedom possible — the human being in body, soul and spirit. Perhaps in this light we may perhaps ask why, at Michaelmas this year, will the first scene of Rudolf Steiner's fourth mystery play, *The Soul's Awakening*,[69] be performed.

The content of this first scene revolves around two questions. Should we transform an old firm with its sawmill and very basic wood workshop so that it includes an art department and a kind of college for spiritual-scientific adult education? And if so, how? If this were to happen, the firm would become a threefold undertaking. The rough, physical woodwork would undergo aesthetic refinement, be lifted up into a diversity of artistically coloured and shaped objects — the physical would become ensouled. Finally, it would be clarified and enlightened by consciousness; by words, thoughts and concepts.

This problem persists throughout the whole play. It is the main character, Strader, who is meant to devise the technical ground plan on which the threefold structure of the firm should rise, but he dies before the problem can be solved. A further, fifth drama was originally intended but never written, ostensibly because the beginning of the First World War in 1914 made it impossible. However, when the war ended, the writing of the plays was not continued. Perhaps this was because the solution to the fourth mystery drama was attempted in a variety of other ways, with the founding of schools, farms, centres for curative education, clinics, etc., out of spiritual knowledge, in all of which a threefoldness was attempted to a greater or lesser degree.

From 1955 onwards one can certainly relate our villages — places for and with handicapped adults, and the fruits of anthroposophy — very directly to the fourth mystery play. Firstly, we have workshops. Then, we have artistic efforts of many kinds; choirs and music for services and festivals, eurythmy, acting, etc., as well as a great deal of humanity, love and care. Finally, we have a culturally diverse adult education programme. This is a threefold structure, economic, social and spiritual.

The workshops are also a mirror picture of our threefoldness. They would not be as human as they are if they were not part of a social threefoldness, if they were not permeated by the humanity, artistic effort and equality of the second sphere, and by the cultural and adult educational efforts of the third. Workshops play a special part in the social order. There is the products catalogue which not only advertises our wares but is also a survey of what we are able to provide for customers who want and need it. For those who actually work in the workshops, it is delightful to see a panorama of what is done, and also what is wanted by consumers across the world from Japan to America. The catalogue is a mighty window into the world. Trade opens the window, and the wind that blows in is neither Swiss nor English nor Japanese, but simply human. Ideally, all three spheres are permeated by religion and care for the land; by agriculture in the widest sense. But, condensed in the workshops, the economic sphere is the most real of all. Everything else we do tends towards the nature of an island, its style not quite in step with our time. This cannot be otherwise in any anthroposophical or Christian Community centre because these can only serve the future of mankind as 'islands', although they also cannot avoid the limiting qualities of islands, too.

Trade, as symbolised in the catalogue, is our salvation. The worst thing about islands is their self-righteousness, their egoism, and our cultural sphere and our lifestyle are not free of this. Being part of a threefold order, the workshops bear a sacrifice towards the future. In the world at large, workshops have grown into factories and have mostly lost the other two spheres. This is not the case in our own workshops because our products bear the imprint of having been worked on by people, and in that work justice has been done to their humanity. Something of the archetypal image of the human being goes into the world with our products. Trade, that open window, redeems the tendency to introspection.

Michael is the spirit of our time. His mission is nevertheless dependent on there being a recognition that the human being is threefold. Thus, the first scene of the fourth mystery play can be seen as relevant to Michaelmas.

BOTTON MIRROR, 9 IX 1988

michaelmas: kindling courage

In autumn we become aware of the ways in which the growth, colour and scent of summer are imbued with thought. In the profusion of leaves, blossoms and ripening seeds, as well as in the animation of animals, birds and insects, a tremendous variety of shaping, directing principles reveal themselves, and these might be compared with thoughts — not human but divine thoughts. In each plant, in each phenomenon, we may uncover a wealth of past evolutions, star constellations, geographical and geological peculiarities, if only we can disenchant them with our human thinking. The whole of creation waits to be 'thought' by us.

Summer is a glory for our senses. In autumn this glory wanes and all that had been built up for our senses to enjoy, decays. But the enormous edifice of thought in creation persists. Michaelmas is really the call to fill this edifice with our own fire so that through the warmth of our interest these thoughts may be brought to life and begin to relate to one another in a new way. That which had been an edifice filled with wisdom becomes something built of moral fire.

The old, original creation depended upon the thoughts of the gods. The new creation depends upon the dignity and glory of humanity. If we can take ourselves in hand, and come to recognise and understand our divine origin and purpose, we will enable a new society to arise out of a cultural world-autumn. Opposing this is much that surrounds us by way of human creation. The continual background music we experience and the enormous network of machinery invented, to a large extent for our own ease and convenience, exemplify the efforts of the devilish, Ahrimanic powers to lull us into the kind of resigned, torpid sleep that will hinder our will from rising into the reviving fire.

This lulling to sleep (experienced both by anthroposophists and non-anthroposophists alike), is made easier because that which works against the kindling of our individual fire is fear — fear of the reality of the spiritual world, fear of the Guardian of the Threshold. The Guardian of the Threshold not only shows us our personal imperfections; he actually is us, he is ourselves in our world reality. The human being is not merely a speck of dust on a larger speck of dust called the Earth, and thus of no consequence for the cosmos. In reality, the human being is an enormous being reaching from the Earth out to the stars and to beings beyond the stars. The fear of beholding ourselves in our cosmic greatness, the shame of being lulled to sleep and of having forgotten our cosmic origin and purpose, the awareness of having failed the gods in not kindling the reviving fire — all this is realised in the gaze of the Guardian, who is, really, our own self.

Courage is not only a virtue in the darkening autumn days. Courage is also the force which can recognise Christ as the One who can only be reached through lighting the fire in ourselves and between I and You — the One who is greater than all fear because He is greater than the world.

BOTTON VILLAGE NEWS, 30 IX 1966

sophia

Sophia is the Divine Wisdom. Rudolf Steiner often described how for the ancient Greeks — and even on into the Middle Ages — wisdom was an actual being.[70] Later, in the time of 'Philo-sophia', this being became hidden behind the divine splendour of ideas. The more human beings became able to think for themselves, the more this divine splendour of ideas was darkened, until all that remains today of Sophia's enlightening grace are shadowy, intellectual thoughts.

Anthroposophy can only appear in the form of these shadowy, intellectual thoughts at first. Our self-consciousness stems from our ability to think, and although limited by this shadowy, intellectual faculty, our ability to say 'I am' is owed to it in fact. Were this not so we would lose all sense of identity, which we are deeply afraid of. Our inability to feel connected to the spiritual world is mainly due to this fear, and fear of death is nothing else than the certainty that because we owe our modern consciousness to the body, after death it will be different and we wonder: 'When the body dies, will my 'I' not die too?'

All the variety of earthly knowledge, which today we call science, has one common denominator — its truths are all objective, cold, beyond comfort and ideals. Because they are truths which can be proven, they seem to force us to accept them, but the proof is biased. We can try to prove anthroposophical truths, but although possible the proof will not convince anyone, since behind all anthroposophical insight lies what is called in the Act of Consecration of Man the healing spirit. Only that which is helpful and healing and lifts us into a sphere of warmth and ideals is truth. It is neither invented nor subjective. Its objectivity shows itself, for instance, in the way we hang the picture of the Sistine Madonna by Raphael over the bed of an expectant mother. Art only

makes sense in this light, as Schiller says:[71]
> Only through the rosy dawn of beauty
> Can you penetrate into knowledge.

Anthroposophy is the wisdom that embodies the soul and spirit treasures which lie in humanity, but which are hidden within our 'I' consciousness. Anthroposophy inserts its findings into our intellectual consciousness, and Anthroposophia is the being of which anthroposophical thoughts are but the shadow. The divine, heavenly woman described in the twelfth chapter of the Apocalypse of St John is the true soul of the human being, Anthroposophia, standing on the moon, clothed with the sun and crowned with stars.

* * *

Since the 15th, 16th and 17th centuries, knowledge has become a tool for achieving technical progress. Since the last century, partly with the help of electricity, inventions have crowded in on us with ever increasing speed — jet aircraft, spaceships, tranquillisers, lasers, genetic engineering and Borglund's giant crops, to name but a few. Who would say that the achievements in medicine, biology and physics are not highly beneficial? Yet they will force humanity into the abyss because knowledge is *not only a tool*. Knowledge has a place in the build-up of the human being, but it is a very different way of knowing than the way in which schools, colleges and universities teach. It is not the inventions as such that will force humanity into the abyss, but the *way* of knowing. It prides itself on being the *only* way, but under the yoke of this kind of knowing the human being withers.

The difference between knowledge used merely as a tool and knowledge as a fundamental capacity of the human being can be seen in the part that human *will* plays in it. Today we suffer increasingly from the division of thinking and will. Now, at the beginning of the Light Age, this is enhanced because thinking, feeling and will have begun to separate and fall apart. Our thinking has led to many inventions but it avoids morality because our will is not involved. What does thinking without will mean? It means that we fail to become aware of the moral content of our sense impressions and so humanity is forced into the abyss of destruction and misery.

Our so-called objective science is the product of an intellect without morality; it is based on sense impressions only and avoids morality. If we look at an untidy room, or a plant in the process of metamorphosis — a process to which we, too, belong — or even if we look at a piece of mineral and in it confront the existential polarity of form and substance, initially our consciousness soul prompts us to look without thinking. It is only when we add moral judgement to our sense impressions that we recognise in a piece of physical matter, for example, the form-pole or the substance-pole that makes matter necessary. Here we may quote the German philosopher, Johann Gottlieb Fichte, who said that creation is formed-out duty. When answering the question, 'What is anthroposophy?' Rudolf Steiner said that creation is nothing other than formed-out duty. In fact, he said, it is 'duty, duty, duty.' Only when we add morality to our sense impressions can their inherent quality be restored and enlivened. In this way, we may develop a so-called 'sense-free thinking'.

When our thinking turns into devotion as, for instance, when we partake in the Act of Consecration of Man, and also when we silently speak the words of a meditation, we can have an experience of what sense-free thinking is. The so-called enlivening of our thinking can then be achieved. Morality-imbued sense perceptions and sense-free thinking are well known to us as trends in the everyday web of life.

The woman in the Book of Revelation who gives birth to a male child (Rev 12) is an image of the human soul struggling to forge the powers of the ego. Was she not forced to flee into the wilderness? By submitting to the yoke of 'knowledge-as-a tool', and allowing ourselves to be flooded with amoral sense impressions, we have gained the ability to say 'I' to ourselves. However, in the process we have lost our crowned, starlit soul. The 'I' we have gained may be a provisional one, but it will still enable, indeed require, us to become like St George and slay the dragon of 'tool-knowledge' and amoral sense impressions. Thus we will free the virgin (our soul) clothed and endowed by sun, moon and stars, gracing us and the world with her undying beauty. As the living, spiritually ensouled reality of old recedes in human thoughts, so our own living reality will arise and freedom will again become possible.

'The human being descended from the experience of the heavenly to that of earth on the paths of thinking. Thus he gained earthly consciousness. It is Michael's task to lead us with our earthly consciousness back whence we came, but by the paths of the *will*.'[72]

* * *

There was always an aura of mystery about the being of the Sophia, as though she were veiled, because she embodied something of the eternal in the human being, something not found in our earthly evolution. Over the course of time she has appeared in many guises — as the 'Mater Gloriosa' at the end of the second part of Goethe's *Faust*; as Dante's Beatrice; as Aleksander Blok's 'Verses About the Lady Beautiful',[73] but also as the Madonna with child and her forerunner, the goddess with the Jacchos child in the Eleusinian Mysteries; as Isis with the Horus child, and now as the New Isis because, as Rudolf Steiner tells us, the Egyptian culture is recapitulated in our time.

Inscribed beneath the old statues of Isis were the words, 'I am the All. I am the past, the present and the future. No mortal has yet lifted my veil.'[74] Sense impressions and thinking with an 'I am' consciousness were not always as they are now. People could not base their existence on today's 'I am' consciousness which separates human beings from one another. In ancient times, people felt like grapes in a cluster, or grains in an ear of corn, their dream-like security resting in their family, tribe, caste or nation. The glorious image of the Divine Sophia, clad in a splendour of colours of the sun, moon and stars, had no meaning for them.

The legend of the New Isis is represented by the sculpture of the Christ between Lucifer and Ahriman, which was carved by Rudolf Steiner for the first Goetheanum. Looking at it, the human being should, and would, have become aware that he oscillates between great and small things, light and dark, warm and cold, life and death, and between new, irresponsible, selfish departures and sedate, calcifying, sclerotic immobility. Christianity would then be seen as the balance between opposites, not good against evil.

By taking these thoughts into our thinking, feeling and willing and also into our senses, we would have made our 'I am' increasingly real, and in this way we would have become aware of the legend of the New Isis. She is the sleeping Isis with the cow-horns, and the Ahrimanic visitor, the new Typhon, at first seems to be the father of her child. She takes the child into the world where, overcome by the world's power, it falls into fourteen parts. With the aid of science, the new Typhon unites these again and is able to multiply the child fourteenfold. But in his real being the child returns to his mother who receives him from the hands of elemental beings. Through becoming aware of the Word in the sense of St John's Gospel, the paper crown that she had been wearing above the cow-horns turns into real gold.

This New Isis legend is told at greater length in the lecture given by Rudolf Steiner on 6th January 1918.[75] It highlights one of the threads in the story of our time. Underneath *this* Isis is written, 'I am the human being. I am the past, the present and the future. My veil every mortal should lift.' The human soul — the woman bearing the man-child, the New Isis — is asleep. It is deceived and hidden, and it thinks that Ahriman-Typhon is the father of Horus, the 'I am' child. While it makes possible the shadow of the 'I am' — and with it our freedom — intellectual, abstract thinking covers us and the world with a grey pall. The slumbering, unreal human soul wears a paper crown composed of endless printed pages — books, periodicals, newsletters, leaflets, agendas, minutes — the list is endless.

Regarding the pupil of Saïs, Novalis wrote about one of the statues of Isis:

> One person reached and lifted the veil of the Goddess of Saïs
> And what did he see but — wonder of wonders — himself![76]

Anthroposophia, the New Isis, the human soul, can only be the thousandfold variations of the human being. To say our soul is hers is wrong because, according to the legend, Typhon conceals that which we call our soul behind illusion and a grey haze. It is *our* soul but in *her* reality, and therefore it comprises all mankind.

BOTTON VILLAGE NEWS, 3 & 17 XI & 1 XII 1972

the silent stars above us

Leaving science for a moment with its proofs, its telescopes, spaceships and its authority in order to concentrate on what we can see and grasp with our common sense, we see around us rooms, towns, landscapes, etc., while underneath us is the firm ground and above us the sky, either the night lit with stars or the day illuminated by the sun. Our physical earthly existence is lived within our field of vision — the space in which we see objects is accessible to sight — and even the space encompassed by our senses of warmth, hearing and touch takes its lead and orientation from optical space. The stars are also within this field of vision, as if they are visible objects like trees or houses only very far away, but this is merely a preconceived idea.

We think that what we perceive and understand is the limit of our consciousness. Aided by instruments such as telescopes and microscopes, we have perfected our understanding and consciousness over the course of time, but we have not yet widened or enlarged it. When grasping the world with our unreflecting experience and consciousness, we cannot fail to see the outer world as twofold. In the light of day, on the one hand, there are earthly landscapes with natural environments and many man-made things. In the darkness of night, on the other hand, there are the innumerable stars spread out in the vault of heaven, loosely ordered in their mysterious constellations, moving precisely in their courses.

On older star maps the beings who were experienced around a particular constellation (Lion, Bull, Bear, Perseus, etc.) were drawn. The moon and planets which seem to wander against the backdrop of the fixed stars (Aldebaran, Sirius, Spica, etc.) have these beings in their names (Venus, Jupiter, Mercury, etc.).

In our time, this mysterious duality of the experience of earthly life has become drastically biased towards the Earth (with its dangers and opportunities), very much expanded by humanity's growing consciousness. The star-strewn night sky has receded into the pallid background that street lighting relegates it to, becoming either a backdrop to romantic fancy as with the poet Novalis or, since Copernicus' time, imprisoned in our astronomy as part of the world of modern science (meaning the stars are now as weighable, countable, and their distances as measurable, as anything else).

Set against this is our intuitive experience — unclouded by the popular scientific prejudices we are fed from school onwards — that the starlit night sky is the visible herald of an invisible world that gazes down upon us on the sunlit earth between birth and death, but which under normal circumstances we cannot see. We also sense that despite being reduced to shining points, the stars are more real than the great variety of objects which cover the surface of the earth. Nothing convinces us more easily that the stars are heralds than when they appear to be more real than our earthly surroundings. Living in the country where our upward gaze to the stars is unimpeded, we feel our security is tremendously enhanced compared to living in a town with its street lights. We discover that our insecurity hinges on our senses because fear intervenes when we cannot rely on one or other of them. The security we receive from the stars is of a very different order — the perishable and transitory permeates our ordinary surroundings, while the eternal and deathless belongs to the realm of the stars.

We human beings are both mortal and eternal. During the day we are free and during sleep we begin to reap the fruits of our freedom. We undergo (albeit unconsciously) the consequences of our actions under the gaze of the divine necessities, an involvement which only reaches its full reality after death in preparing a new earthly life. Sleeplessness is often only a symptom of the basic disharmony between sleeping and waking.

Through Rudolf Steiner we have learnt from spiritual science that the heavens are not somewhere far away, outside us. From the moment of the

Mystery of Golgotha on they are within us. The time is over when, like frightened or admiring children, we saw and experienced the divine beasts and beings in the stars. Now our adult consciousness reaches into the star worlds — we are all astronauts (but without leaving the earth), comrades of the stars, their rays and spheres, partaking in the darkness, the pain and the suffering of the earth.

BOTTON MIRROR, 22 II 1991

the fifth chapter of the book of revelation

Flowing through the fifth chapter of the Book of Revelation there is more of the essence and idealism of Botton and Camphill than might at first appear — but first, a short description. Before the throne of creation appears the Lamb, one of many images of the Christ being, who is able to open the seals, thereby gradually revealing the purpose and karma of the past, its sufferings and achievements. This is surrounded by the 'sounds of a new song'.

As described in the fourth chapter, the throne surrounded by the four beasts, the rainbow and the seven spirits, is an image of primeval creation becoming Nature. The twenty-four elders, the Lamb and the book express the human being within Nature in his emerging independence. The book anticipates this independence — its contents are revealed only when the Lamb opens the seals and the new song is heard. The human being as the crown of creation, unique in his spiritual goal and destination, steps onto the stage of Nature through the power of the Lamb. But if this uniqueness, this perfection of the individual were not followed by something else, it would end in pride and contempt for the other person, and would suffocate Christ. But the power of the Lamb does not end in the perfection of the individual; it expresses itself in the relationship of human beings, in the varieties of our social life. Today, we are still single, separate individuals, relating to and talking to each other; seeing, feeling, hating, loving each other from our isolated standpoints, enclosed within our monolithic fortresses.

A time will come when, like the beginning of the new creation, social life will be *music*. The old creation, the image of the throne, has come to an end. It has become rigid and repeats itself like an unending array of single, separate facts and forms. But it has become a safe sheath for the beginning of the new creation, the creation of the Christ-Word-endowed human being. This creation is a musical one: the old one was a plastic, sculptural one. A variety of single entities is followed by relationships, by intervals. In order that intervals, harmonies and melodies become possible, the single tone must be formed, definite and distinct. So, too, we must be individual persons before we can create the music of the social life, its melodies and harmonies.

The social life of the past was determined by a silent hierarchy. The social life of the future will be brotherly music, resounding from the earth into the heavens.

BOTTON VILLAGE NEWS, 13 V 1966

the book of revelation & the trinity

The colour and prayer of Trinity is the frame which embraces the Act of Consecration of Man. Of course it is interrupted by the colours and prayers of the other festivals in the cycle of the year which all last for some weeks — Advent, Christmas, Three Kings, Lent, Easter, Ascension, Whitsun, St John and Michaelmas. And since these festivals carry their own brilliance, we tend to feel a certain drabness about the colour and words of Trinity. It is like being back home again in our old familiar surroundings after a holiday. But that feeling disappears immediately we realise that underlying the time of Trinity is the Book of Revelation which concerns the Christianising of the human being and the Earth's further evolution.

The complex construction of the Book of Revelation is arranged round the Trinity like three huge mountains surrounded by foothills and smaller peaks. The Father appears in the image of the Throne, surrounded by the four apocalyptic beasts, the rainbow and the twenty-four elders. The Son appears in the image of the Lamb, the altar and the book. The Holy Spirit appears in the image of the Bride of the Lamb and the descending New Jerusalem. The human being — as creature — is accompanied by and permeated by the Son. Human beings transform the Earth into its future through the power of Christ by the Holy Spirit. The human being as creature was created by the flowing together of the powers of the divine Bull, Lion, Eagle and Angel-man; by the rainbow — the human soul — and subject to the aims of the different ages represented by the twenty-four elders. (Rev 4)

The human being is not only created as a child but also as a Son, himself becoming a creator. In chapter 5 the Lamb appears and the old creators sing a new song. There is also the heavenly book (which is really a forerunner of the Lamb), but none can open its seals. Only when the Lamb appears can the seals be opened. Despite being the Son of God, the Lamb appears as a new power in humanity. The human being himself opens the seals of the book of history and only insofar as he himself begins to understand the meaning and purpose of his history (about which innumerable books have been written), can he open the seals. The Lamb then appears again on a higher curve of the spiral (in chapter 7 verse 9), as the light of those who die, foreshadowing the New Jerusalem. Then in chapter 14, the Lord appears again in a third curve as Lord of the Harvest of the Earth, dissolved in sound, the voices singing a new song with the harps. The harvest of the Earth is the deeds of humanity. (Rudolf Steiner predicted that in the course of time music will become the most direct revelation of Christ.[77])

In chapter 10 the man swallows the book. The tenth chapter is the central crossing-point of the whole Book of Revelation (as is the raising of Lazarus in the eleventh chapter of the Gospel of John), the altar having appeared explicitly in chapter 8. It is silently present whenever the Lamb is mentioned; wherever the Son-sphere is touched.

And just as on the first Whit Sunday the fiery tongues descend as the first sign of the Holy Ghost (Acts 2: 3–4), so the Bride descends, clothed in fine linen, and the New Jerusalem appears, radiant with precious stones, pearls and gold. 'And the city had no need of the sun, neither of the moon to shine in it: for the glory of God did lighten it and the Lamb is the light thereof.' (Rev 22: 23)

These three themes underlie the Book of Revelation because this book is the inspiration of Christ Himself, through John.

BOTTON VILLAGE NEWS, 12 XI 1971

michael & the trinity

Through the incarnation of Christ, the Holy Trinity became a physical reality. Divine threefoldness, whether Hindu or Norse — Brahma, Vishnu, Shiva, or Odin, Vili, Ve[78] — is a precursor of the Christian Trinity. Only after Christ's life on earth could the naming, the christening, of a baby be done in the name of the Trinity. Christening leads the baby into the realm of Christ on earth, which is a realm fashioned by the Trinity.

But 'Trinity' entails spiritual, not materialistic, understanding and world experience. To see and comprehend the unity in what is threefold requires an understanding acceptance of invisible ideas and invisible beings. In this, the plant is the great friend and comforter of humanity with its threefoldness of root, stem and leaves, and blossom. Its modulation and metamorphosis guides human understanding into the trinitarian structure of the universe. Goethe was the herald of this trinitarian dawn.[79] We can see the threefoldness of the body (metabolic, rhythmic and nervous systems), of the soul forces (thinking, feeling and willing) or of the soul itself (sentient soul, mind soul and consciousness soul), and of the human being (body, soul and spirit). We also see Man surrounded by the three lower kingdoms of nature (mineral, plant and animal).

But the course of the seasons seems to be fourfold — spring, summer, autumn, winter; or growth, flowering, fruiting/decay, apparent death. The spirit powers take hold of matter and lead its growing accumulation to the point of greatest expansion. They submit the plant to a 'cooking' or heating process so that in autumn what was green and flowering is burnt to brown, yellow or orange. But the fruit and seed is ripe, hard and complete.

We can comprehend the course of the seasons in a *threefold* way only if we see the seed-forming process as being inserted into plant growth in a different dimension — recognising the course of the seasons as being essentially a flat backdrop which thus becomes three dimensional. Growth and flowering is very roughly from April to July; burnt-out decaying is August to November; death and silence is December to March — Father, Son and Spirit. Inserted into this is the seed. As part of the growing plant, the seed is still green. When growth comes to a stop and the plant flowers and bursts into colour and scent, the seed slowly matures. As the plant decays and burns up, the seed hardens and ripens. Finally, in the winter period, the seed drops, lies on the ground and is buried in the earth. Through seed-formation, the earth and the world of plants become one. Only in the unity of earth and plant do we see the threefoldness of the year distinctly. But, at the same time, we have to understand the seed as a pointer towards the Idea of the plant — not a material conglomeration of chemical compounds, but the point where the invisible Idea, the archetype, of this or that plant can incarnate.

To grasp the Trinity in earthly life entails spiritual, not materialistic, experience. The incarnation of a spiritual entity can only proceed in a threefold way. To be unable to behold the Trinity in earthly phenomena is to be drowned in substance, in matter. In trying to look up to Michael, the human being raises his consciousness above matter. It is not our nature but our consciousness that is ensnared by the dragon. By becoming *aware* of some of the dark inner or outer snares, we already begin to follow Michael's beckoning light.

BOTTON VILLAGE NEWS, 9 X 1964

michael: october — november thoughts

The descent of summer into autumn and on into winter is gradual and yet dramatic. There is the darkening green of August, then the brilliant colours of September and October and finally the bareness of November. This is the dying process in outer nature, in the sense world. But *inwardly* there is an activity, a sprouting, a forward-looking, light-filled and ever widening soul life which looks upon the gathering darkness outside with confidence: a confidence that this soul-light (what Rudolf Steiner calls 'the summer of the soul'), will rise sun-like at Christmas, at the time of greatest outer darkness. And this newly found soul-light in autumn will accompany us throughout the whole year. It allows us to look upon the outer events in our biography, particularly the dark times (which are our own karmic darknesses), with equanimity — even with hope and trust.

We can observe the autumn colours of the leaves and say these are due to the decreasing sap and life in the tree. But if we look with the strength of our newly-found soul-light at the waning outer life and light, we can also say that just because the outer colours have dimmed, *new* gold, green and blue — ever present, in fact, but hidden by outer life — can appear. Amid the darkness and barren emptiness of nature in November, the word-pictures of the Apocalypse are heard in the seasonal Bible readings — from the golden-white Son of Man to the New Jerusalem from which the gold, green and blue spring of a new heaven and earth arises in human souls. Then, at Christmas, the World-light shines in our soul, mildly yet mightily, so that we can be strong enough to create afresh a new world in the 'World-November' of the next year — the outer November which foreshadows the world's end, and the inner one, which foreshadows its new beginning in us.

Michael is the Archangel of autumn, but he is also the Spirit of our time. How can we think about this? The main evil of our time is the blindness that stems from a paralysis in our ability to think. If we were able to think deeply about everything around us, our veils of blindness would slowly lift and we would see and experience new things as our consciousness widened. The diminishing green of spring giving way to the colours of autumn would indicate not only the decrease of life, but also the emergence of new colours from a background of bareness, emptiness and nothingness, challenging us to be courageous and develop the ability to contemplate the images found in the Apocalypse.

Above all, ours is an autumnal time, a time of widening consciousness; a time of becoming aware of the colours that point to the Son of Man against this barren background. The creation in spring is the Creation of the Father God. The autumn colours, brilliant in the West, are the spring colours of a new creation, this time created by the Soul of Man, the Son of Man within the human soul, the Son God. Michael, the god of consciousness, widens creation through our activity and, as the countenance of Christ, points the way to the shining light of the spirit world, to a life won back from death.

BOTTON VILLAGE NEWS, 1 XI 1991

the perfect & the deathless

In the yearly darkening, decaying evening of autumn there is one memory of summer that surpasses all others — *the perfection of nature*. The perfect forms of leaves and blossoms, the well-ordered habits of animals — the patterns of their fur, the organisation in a beehive — all this is due to elemental activity in the rising part of the year. Decay and hibernation signify the waning part of the year.

In autumn, we can wander among the darkening decay but we can still admire the diversity of the leaves and the multicoloured flowers. Their scent is the first thing that goes (except for the untiring rose). None of the autumn flowers has much scent, or perhaps only a scent of autumn. They all have dark colours, while the colour of summer's symphony has the brightness of day. But, apart from their forms, there is something glorious about these colours, especially the *leaves* of bushes and trees. The botanists tell us this indicates the withdrawal of sap, which is perhaps only one side of the matter — that of decay, the evening of their lives, before eventually being blown off and trodden underfoot. But is there not another side connected with a triumphant future which appears only for a comparatively short time around Michaelmas? Are not these autumn colours in the leaves of quite a different order than the spring and summer colours in the blossoms?

When the trees first unfold their leaves in spring they appear to be green. However, with the sun shining through them, they appear a tender red, rose, purple or violet, until later on when spring turns to summer their density makes them appear green once more.

In following the guidance of Rudolf Steiner's *Calendar of the Soul*, this second, waning, half of the year confirms the triumph of the soul and the widening of its realm. Christmas is the climax of this period. During the summer half of the year we are pressed into an abundance of sense experiences. During the winter half, our soul awakens to its independent freedom.

But humanity is not dependent only on natural conditions. Throughout the whole year, whatever the season, there is something of summer and sense-greed in us, as well as something of freedom and self-consciousness — an independence from emotions and sense experiences — in us, too. Are not the colours on the autumn leaves parables of soul moods? In the cool of the autumn winds we can look at the leaves with detachment; they are outside ourselves, made harmless, as it were. But these autumn leaf colours are not just signs of our soul-moods, they are also promises of a future in which the world of nature and our inner, soul world will no longer be as separate as they are now. In old Lemuria 'our' feeling was still part of surrounding nature — volcanic eruptions, waterfalls, emotions of various kinds — were all one. Inward and outward separated from each other very slowly. The promise of autumn colour is the merging once more of nature and humanity, but it will be determined by the selfless human 'I' and will be permeated by thought.

Christian Rosenkreutz took the first step in the further Christian evolution of humanity. The freedom that we feel in autumn, the freedom we owe to Michael, is the freedom of a new spring, but a spring that is not a part of nature and the perfection created around us by the powers of the Father-world — it is a freedom which humanity can use only hesitatingly. It is a freedom that is not hemmed in by the perfection surrounding man but which makes illness and death part of human existence, while in perfect nature, malformation, illness and death are deviations from the norm. This new and humanised nature, this spring in autumn, was inaugurated by Christian Rosenkreutz. This spring is dependent on the imperfect freedom of human beings, but it means that new elemental beings can emerge in connection with this freedom. It is as if a light behind the advancing decay, a light appearing at certain moments, makes the colours sing in a deathless way.

Rudolf Steiner advised the Christian Community priests to read The Book of Revelation in November, for amongst all its terrors it contains the promise of a deathless future. (Rev 21: 4) The rich colours of autumn are its heralds.

BOTTON MIRROR, 12 X 1990

revolution & evolution

The French Revolution introduced something new into human history and development — *essential human equality* — and thereafter it became possible for human beings to relate to one another on equal terms. This had been prepared on America's revolutionary road to independence and in the various lodges of the 'Age of Reason', but it entered the flow of historic events in the so called French Revolution which was not, in fact, confined to France but became a widespread movement, tearing down the walls between social classes, between gentry, clergy and 'citizens'. A new ability arose in humanity — to recognise one another as human beings without the 'masks' of royalty, church-hierarchy, military rank, race or nation. We all still stand in the evolutionary current that began with the French Revolution but soon after its glorious beginning became drowned in cruelty, blindness and blood, and seemed to end with Napoleon.

The *equality* of human beings can only be recognised and affirmed if at the same time their uniqueness, their incomparable differences, are recognised with awe and love. To learn to know, and to love, the infinite uniqueness of every human being has only become possible in our time. The French Revolution was not able to do this. Only in our time are we allowed to know the reality of this uniqueness through sensing that each human being has many lives, bears his or her burden of destiny, and yet is free. Therefore it is only in our time that real equality is possible. And only in our time have we begun to learn about mankind's distant past, not just through the findings of archaeology and palaeontology, but through spiritual science — a past in which no solid matter existed. In this respect we can see Napoleon's discovery of the Egyptian Rosetta Stone as a symptom of history, because the result was that it then became possible to read the hieroglyphs and hence the main archaeological breakthroughs could follow.

In the far distant past, mankind received three gifts — uprightness, speech and thinking — three gifts which made both the uniqueness and equality of individuals possible.[80] These three gifts revolutionised and humanised Man as he was then. We see them today in miniature, so to speak, in the first years of the child, as the foundation of each human biography. The grace of the three gifts comes from above, from the heavenly worlds. The Being who was later born as Jesus united three times with the Son of God, with the pre-earthly Christ. Thus the human being became able to *stand* within a still dark nature; he became able to *speak*, to 'repeat creation' in his words and so communicate with others, and thirdly he became able to embrace god and creation with his *consciousness*, and thereby began to be independent of nature. These three gifts were the mighty antidote against the Fall, and thereby mankind was endowed with unselfish freedom. Standing upright, talking, and thinking — these are the basis of our equality as well as our uniqueness, and therefore they are the basis of our relationships with one another, the basis of our future brotherhood.

The failure of the French Revolution was the inability to understand that equality can only be achieved through individual and brotherly recognition of one another. The relationship of one to another is therefore of the greatest importance, for without effort in this direction any attempt towards a life that is socially just (whether on a smaller or larger scale), must founder. Policy arrangements and organisations are attempts to build walls to hem in chaos, but such walls become less and less appropriate for modern human beings. Human relationships are important because only through them can the individual become aware of his or her own value. It is a social process and therefore self-evaluation is always wrong.

Herein lies the mystery of a *congregation*. In it, and in each sacrament, is found the empty grave — the presence of the Risen One is discovered in the world as well as in the 'I' and in the 'You'. It is the congregation-forming element that makes possible the freedom of an unselfish 'I' and of brotherliness. The three gifts have returned. In childhood they enable us to become free; in adulthood they enable us to use that freedom to become human beings, and therefore brothers.

THE THRESHING FLOOR, VII/VIII 1989

observing & willing

We all possess the faculty of observation and can look with varying degrees of prejudice, understanding and empathy at the world of human beings and nature. This faculty in each of us leads to what we call individual personality — the loner — and just because each of us is a loner we can develop our own abilities. In former times, people were less individual, less segregated from each other. Family ties and bonds between people who spoke the same language were far stronger, and the difference between the content of one soul and another was much less important, less distinct. In fact, it was only after the Renaissance that pictures and books were *signed*.

Because the 'I am' was far less countenanced, people had fewer personal opinions and less conscience, so they were inspired more by the hierarchy to which they belonged: their church or king. We have gained our independence, our power of observation — and our loneliness — but we have lost our sense of allegiance. The Protestant reformer (Wycliffe, Luther or Hus) was someone who, in discovering his own conscience, became able to *judge*.

In our time, a further ability is added to observation, namely the ability to act out of what is observed, not out of abstract reasoning as the protesting reformers did. This action is not born of general ideals but from empathy with the observed; towards the need of the 'you'. As an example, in the Reformation people became aware that confessional 'indulgences' were used to pass money to Rome, and we can see how souls were fettered by this kind of usage. Today we can try to undo the fetters of one or other person to whom we are related by sharing our insight with them. We might hear a child crying in a slum area and become a member of a party that tries to eradicate slums. However, we might be so touched by the crying that we go to the child to find out why he is crying, and try to comfort him. We can delight in our ability to observe without doing anything as a result. In Botton there may be gossip about a physical or soul neighbour, but rarely do we hear about the qualifying good of that person on whom, after all, a certain amount of our responsibility hangs.

We slowly discover after decades that our ability to observe is given by the gods in our time so that we may act towards the observed. Our head is able, coolly and objectively, to observe and perform as many moral acts as we wish in our imagination. But *only our moral deeds make us valuable in world progress*. We had to become individuals separated from the world, enclosed in ourselves, but observation alone makes us hermits, silent loners in the world. Reacting and responding to the observed world with our moral deeds would transform us into the long-awaited messengers of a Christianised universe.

If in Botton we could use our observations for moral purposes and not for gossiping about others, we would sense the first breath of a Christian relationship to one another. Courage alone can turn the frog of gossip into the prince of morality.

BOTTON VILLAGE NEWS, 1 II 1986

will & social life

'Michael re-ascends the path that man followed in the course of his descent as he progressed through the successive stages of his spiritual development to arrive at the exercise of intelligence. But Michael will guide the will upward on the path by which wisdom travelled downward on its way to its final stage, intelligence.'

Rudolf Steiner[81]

The Archangel Michael preserves human freedom. Though his hand beckons and his gaze fills us with earnestness, it behoves *us* to employ our will. If he were to will *in* us, if he were to motivate us, he would diminish our freedom.

Weakness of will, the expectation that someone else will decide for us, is one of the great evils of our time. It is fed by two things: hierarchy and wages. Hierarchy lets us say that we are only doing what we are told to do — an example being the various Nazi officers at the Nürnberg Trials insisting that 'It was my superior who had responsibility.' Working for a wage tempts us to put our will only partially into our work, or to work solely for what the money can buy. We can easily see how little actual will goes into work such as this. Look at the almost universally poor craftsmanship we have come to expect nowadays from tea-drinking workmen playing transistor radios or a 'Walkman' to make life seem worthwhile, or even bearable. Anthroposophists are not immune to this. There is the danger of being so fascinated by Rudolf Steiner's ideas that they forget that it takes another part of their being, their individual will, to make ideas complete. Will is not only in what we *do*, it is also in our thinking. Our thoughts remain repetitive slogans, mere labels, unless our will moves them about, relating them to other thoughts and experiences. Only through our will can we make these thoughts our own, and incorporate them into our common sense.

In any social organisation, anthroposophical or otherwise, will is the foremost consideration. In the pioneering stage the things to be willed are in front of one's nose. When they have been achieved, it is much more difficult to know what to will next. The bigger and more differentiated the social organisation grows, the more difficult it becomes to exercise will, and we need much more of it to achieve anything at all. Resignation is a far easier option! For example, we can say that we cannot get beyond Mr X (as if he were a dictator), or that there is no platform to talk over this or that issue, or there is a lack of understanding in others; there is bias, pressure- or power-groups. We are surrounded by a growing wall of ghosts which, in reality, is nothing more than the counter-picture of one's own, insufficient will.

But this insufficiency is not really brought on by itself. The will to which Michael beckons is insufficient because the more differentiated the *social* organisation grows the more social must our will become. To begin with, in the pioneering stage, our will is not social. The will becomes social because in trying to bring our ideas to fruition we have to do justice to all the other individuals involved — we need to have understanding, not merely a blind enthusiasm for one another. The *will that becomes social* is the only antidote to hierarchy. Many communes withered away because despite being sure that they had to eradicate hierarchy, they ended up with chaos because the will of their members could not become a social will in any real way.

In turn, the only way to make the will social in our time is through Christianity and its understanding (in the language of *The Book of Revelation*) of 'to put on white garments'. The strengthening of the will for each other can only arise by turning to Christ. It is Christ's strength alone which strengthens our will. The stars of truth shine no less brightly, but if we are trying to become Christian we should try to approach them through and with those with whom we live.

In Advent we feel most keenly the insufficiency of our will, the gap between it and the demands of the outer world. The world of nature grows bare; colder and darker. There has to be so much more inner initiative at this time of year, yet we feel we are nothing and cannot fulfil the task for which the gods sent us into the world, and for which the world craves. And because the stars of truth shine with such glory now, a greater effort of *will* is needed to bring their light down to earth. But Michael cannot instigate that will — everything in the world process now depends on our own decision and responsibility. It is fatal to think that because we are anthroposophists essentially nothing can happen to us!

BOTTON VILLAGE NEWS, 26 XI 1977

~ ADVENT ~

BOTTON VILLAGE NEWS 1991

～ *a d v e n t*

a d v e n t & t h e c h r i s t i a n i s i n g o f k a r m a

Among the prophetic words of John the Baptist in the gospels are those in which he says that while he baptises with water, after him will come one mightier than he who will baptise with fire. In ancient times, purification of both body and soul by ablution was a necessary prerequisite for any attempt to gain entrance to the spiritual worlds, and John's baptism was that kind of purification.

The asceticism of the Middle Ages was an effort to purify and cleanse the soul by wounding and deadening the 'flesh'. Over the past 150 years there has been a great deal of charitable activity among Christians, coupled with a somewhat philistine morality. This can be seen as an attempt at 'justification by purity'. The human soul longs for purification, for union with the Divine life in which it was embedded before the Fall. But over the past few hundred years, certainty in the spiritual worlds became blurred and the innate religious longing for purification turned into Victorian charity. In the modern climate of atheistic technology, any longing for purification is felt to be nonsensical.

A new urge towards catharsis can arise only from insight into karma and reincarnation. Baptism by fire — purification through the flame of the eternal ego — entails the balancing of deeds from life to life. This is the cleansing by fire which can be compared to ablution by water. We ourselves are our own destiny; we ourselves are our one-sided insights and one-sided deeds, and we ourselves are allowed to suffer the balancing of this one-sidedness by the grace of repeated lives on earth. Purification no longer consists in the narrow, somewhat self-righteous longing to perfect oneself in *one* life, but rather in surrounding the cross of our destiny with roses in the course of *many* lives.

When the rainbow appeared over Noah's sacrificial offering (Gen 9: 13–14) in the purified air after the sinking of Atlantis, God made a covenant with Noah that there would be no more punishment and destruction! This is preceded by words about blood — blood in which lives our destiny: 'And surely the blood of your lives will I require ... for in the image of God made he the human being'. (Gen 9: 5–6) Individual biography began to dawn and individual destiny to evolve. Later, when Abraham met Melchisedek, priest of the most high God, and received bread and wine from him, (Gen 14: 18–20) the same pledging rainbow shone over their meeting. The glory and the mildness of Christ shines around both these scenes, and this promise is fulfilled in our own time only when the rainbow appears in our Advent prayer, preceding the light of Christmas. Christ has entered our blood and is related to the destiny and biography of each one of us, surrounding each of us with a rainbow. That which shone over Noah for the post-Atlantean races, and over Abraham for the Jewish people, now shines around each of us *individually*.

Christmas is an Earth festival which, in our time, can be celebrated only by individuals. The rainbow is the token of the karma that Christ took on. This karma is not about punishment and destruction, like the Flood and the fire raining on Sodom. It is the exact equivalent and atonement of the past, entailing repeated earth lives for its fulfilment. At the same time, it is so intricately woven into the events of humanity that it becomes beneficial for the surrounding world. This is the Christianising of destiny in the present time. The rainbow is its promising sign of hope.

BOTTON VILLAGE NEWS, 11 XII 1964

sacrifice & community

> Thus speaks within my being's depth
> Surging to revelation
> Mysteriously the World-Word:
> Imbue the aims of your work
> With my bright Spirit Light
> To offer up your Self through me.
>
> *Calendar of the Soul*, verse 36, (second week of Advent)

These Advent verses from the *Calendar of the Soul* seem to me to imply that a teacher, doctor, farmer, etc., working out of spiritual science, or indeed out of Christianity generally, must permeate him- or herself with the substance, and strength, of sacrifice. Christianity without sacrifice is no more than a shadow.

In the early days of the Camphill Movement, daily sacrifice was a very strong factor — but a conscious, joyous, natural sacrifice — and there were high expectations of it. It reached its peak sometime later in the guiding image of Iphigenia, the priestess of Artemis, and of Abraham's sacrifice of Isaac, (Gen 22: 1–14) leading to the story of the Golden Fleece, the purified golden outpouring of the astral body. It upheld our conviction, expressed in lectures by Rudolf Steiner on Iphigenia,[82] that any overt cultural stream must be accompanied by a hidden priestly stream, as the glorious outer culture of Greece was accompanied by the hidden piety represented by Iphigenia. Something of the inner piety of ancient Greece can be felt in the resigned modesty of their gravestone inscriptions. Nowadays, this virtue of sacrifice, which played such a prominent rôle in the past, has receded more into the depths of the soul and it is difficult to bring it out into the light of day and into the relationships of individuals with each other. For this same reason we often find it difficult to relate to one another spiritually, and to feel and think out of the substance of the Community.

Most people identify completely with their earthly life — they lament if something goes wrong and laugh if something succeeds, and their likes and dislikes follow rigid patterns, etc. But one of the efforts we are meant to make in modern times is not to become stuck, not to be so engrossed in the conditions of life that we are pitched headlong into joy or sorrow, greed or disgust. Rather, we are meant to relate to these conditions with a certain equanimity; to fulfil our duties and answer the needs of our surroundings equably or, seen from another angle, not to take our life as if it belonged exclusively to ourselves. We can then aspire to be useful citizens of the world, less hampered and biased by our own limitations or gifts; more flexible and responsive to the needs around us. Where is the sacrifice in that? It lies in sacrificing our possessions, our likes and dislikes, our gifts, our fear of shame — everything, in fact, to which we say 'I' or 'mine' in ordinary life. It is an act of deepest selfless selfhood and freedom because it is directly concerned with the inner world of our 'I' and nobody else can demand it of us.

This opens the way to fill our will, our deeds, with selfless love and, as Rudolf Steiner pointed out in the 'Michael Letters' of 1924,[83] only deeds done with love for the intentional object can serve Michael.

> 'Michael goes with love on his way through the world, with all the earnestness of his nature, attitude and action. Whoever attaches himself to Michael cultivates love in relation to the outer world. And love must be unfolded first of all in relation to the outer world, otherwise it becomes self-love. If this love in the spirit of Michael is there, then one's love of another being will shine back into one's own self. The self will be able to love without loving itself...'

Selfless love is an amazing — and rare — experience, and it is the *only* moral act that moves the world forward. But we really can love everything. That is why, especially in those early Camphill years, we all did what was *necessary* rather than what we had learnt or were gifted at, so that we should relate to earthly activities (housework, teaching, cooking, gardening or farming, etc.) without a personal or exclusive bias. If we were unable to love what was necessary we had not learnt the lesson that Camphill life was seeking to impart, namely to invest the totality of life around us with our 'I', and to permeate its earnestness with humour. Many situations cannot be tackled head-on by earnestness alone; only when tempered by humour is earnestness made bearable and real. Rudolf Steiner's sculpture of the Representative of Man includes the face of World Humour. Humour dissolves opinions and fanaticism and helps to prevent us taking ourselves too seriously.

In the Gospel of St Luke (18: 18–23) a young man is exhorted by Christ to give all his possessions to the poor and follow Him. Well, we may keep our possessions to a minimum, but in order to start upon the path towards becoming like the young man we must all sacrifice our karma to some extent, and not think we have to do everything and know everything. In the early years of community, the metaphor of the 'white shirt' signified our striving, karma-less being.

BOTTON VILLAGE NEWS, C. 23 XII 1988

thinking & the new christianity

'Then if any man shall say unto you, Lo, here is Christ, or there; believe it not.' (Matt. 24: 23) People will appear who call themselves Christ but are not, or who claim to be prophets but in reality are not. They will call up visions and work great wonders in order to lead human beings onto the wrong path, if possible also those in whom the higher being is already living. 'For as the lightning cometh out of the East and shineth even unto the West, so shall also the coming of the Son of Man be.' (Matt. 24: 27)

Ways into a spiritual world are offered increasingly today, Christian or not, and all have one thing in common — the rôle of thinking, or what is often called common sense, is subdued or silenced. The rôle of our widened awareness of the New Age seems to reveal forms and contents that purportedly lie beyond the limits of our *ordinary* consciousness and which we are asked simply to obey or believe in. The difference with anthroposophy, which also contains a multitude of revelations, is that we are exhorted again and again to take what we do not yet understand only as a hypothesis. If we do something out of mere belief, we do not reach it with our morality but simply obey someone else's morality, which is no way to the Christianity of our time. What we can penetrate with understanding or through experience we can be responsible for. And what is truly remarkable is just how much of Rudolf Steiner's revelations we *can* substantiate and underpin with our own thoughts and experiences. The guiding hand of spiritual science offers so much enlightenment that widens our earthly human and historic horizons inestimably!

The consciousness of our time is made of the stuff of thinking. We are thinking when we deliberate what tie we shall put on, or when we consider something philosophical, and we owe this thinking to our 'I' consciousness, our 'I am', which underlines all our conscious soul content and our physical actions. In the distant past, when our thinking was very different, our 'I am' consciousness was different, too. Nowadays, simply to believe or submit ourselves to a revelation can only be a kind of soul-suicide because the demands of belief paralyse our thinking and thus reduce the breadth of our 'I am'. If a revelation appears beyond the borders of our thinking consciousness but our understanding does not find a way towards it, we have no moral right to accept it.

In addition to this, in all his epistemological writings Rudolf Steiner describes how the world is divided in two in our human organism in that what our senses behold is outside us (including our body), while what we develop as thoughts and thinking lies inside. In Greek times, thoughts were experienced outside as well as inside, along with sense impressions, and an entirely different 'I am' consciousness accompanied them. The human 'I' and the world flowed into each other. Freedom and self-determination, alienation and Descartes' assertion that 'I think, therefore I am', would have been impossible at that time. History is the gradual unfolding of the Image of Man that is in every human being, and it can only be interpreted correctly by understanding it as stages in this development. And all of us are part of it in the course of our lives. A part of this unfolding is the place and value of thinking in the course of history. To deny the modern rôle of thinking and the 'I am' consciousness today is also to deny the rôle of history in the development of the human being, in the evolution of humanity.

The rôle of thinking — not in the sense of thinking about something but as a faculty of the soul as described, for instance, in the first of the six so-called Subsidiary Exercises[84] — is crucial in the whole challenge of today's Christianity and of human evolution in general. Christianity will only survive if it rises above mere feeling and enters that realm where conscience shines — where the 'I am' consciousness, responsibility, the understanding experience of Truth; in short, where the personal being of oneself resides. This 'I am' consciousness, this conviction of being a unique person, is developing only in our time. It began in the 15th, 16th and 17th centuries. The Renaissance was really a gigantic stage set for the rise of this person-being in each of us, and which is entirely owing to our ability to think.

The 'I am' consciousness is like a rock of light amidst the swirling phenomena of the modern world. Yet this rock of light has two flaws in its brilliance — Lucifer and Ahriman. In all the revelations that herald the New Age, only anthroposophy describes how there are two dehumanising powers. It is this insight that makes the new Christianity possible, the Christianity in which belief and faith are based on knowing. We can even go so far as to say that only a Christianity that recognises the powers of Lucifer and Ahriman is a Christianity of the Second Coming, a Christianity of the Light Age.

Moderation is the virtue of our time, and moderation is always a balance between too much and too little, between gluttony and asceticism. But in our time, *complete* goodness is impossible! Without the Ahrimanic powers, our food could not be broken down and we would be poisoned, and if our houses were not designed by architects who are inspired by Luciferic powers they would be strictly utilitarian (and thereby Ahrimanic), and we cannot buy anything without handling money, the condensed injustice of salaried work, etc. In order to channel the Light shining between these two darknesses, we should think or act for the sake of the object — for example, dress the wound for the sake of the wounded, not in order to assuage our own pity which the sight of the wound induces.

Make no mistake about it, we live in a dynamic age and we should have the corresponding confidence and courage! Such things as political parties, governments calling themselves democratic when voted in by a majority of 51% (ignoring the 49% left licking their wounds), wars like that in the Falkland Islands — all these become increasingly old-fashioned, a sclerotic crust under which lives a new, spring-like brotherly reality. The revolutionary power of this reality does not erect barricades or peddle arms, but it beats in hearts enlightened by knowledge, a knowledge which flows ever more surely from before birth. It is a reality felt by many, but mostly these feelings cannot yet be raised into thinking which is why the old thought-forms — wars, voting, politics, etc. — still persist. The Golden Fleece shines and moves between heart and head, manifesting the real New Age.

SOURCE & DATE UNKNOWN

the war of all against all

One of the statements of spiritual science which needs to be either clarified or simply believed is that the Lemurian and Atlantean epochs were destroyed by natural catastrophes — the first through fire, the second through water — and that our own, the post-Atlantean period, will perish through human conflict in the War of All against All.[85] On Lemuria and Atlantis, humanity was part of nature, a created being. Now, in post-Atlantean times, humanity is apparently already a creator being, although a selfish one.

In the past, the powers of the elements were very much stronger and also more unified, less separated, than today. At that time, humanity was much less individualised; it was part of the elements and so had no need to be clothed or sheltered in houses. We could imagine that fire was dominant in Lemurian times. Smaller or larger patches of earth-islands could preserve themselves in the midst of fire swamps and fire storms, as also could water-lagoons and air-clouds. The power of humanity must have roared in the fire. The wildness of humanity and the elements must have been permeated by a taming, individualising and separating feminine power which, by the end of Lemuria, exploded like a gigantic volcanic eruption, destroying the continent which lay between what is now Africa, India and Australia.

Humanity played a different rôle in Atlantis. The elements became less active and water dominated. The earth had a varying water content, and air and water in the form of mist and clouds still hid the sun, moon and stars. Human beings started to become independent with the beginnings of a bony skeleton, the appearance of uprightness and the rudiments of a soul. Over thousands of years, the world of the Atlanteans evolved from a sounding vessel of the Spirit into a silent diversified multitude, in which individuals gradually became able to speak. Originally, they possessed a boundless openness to the beings and events of the spiritual world. Later, the physical world became more accessible to the senses. Human memory transformed into an ability to think. Humanity seemed to be in the middle between the elements and what today we call the human sphere — science, philosophy, art, culture, technology and society.

The demise of Atlantis was through the element of water, but water that was motivated by an admixture of selfish, earthly human emotions, not just the wrath of the gods.

In the course of evolution it seems natural that the end of our epoch will be brought about by the actions of human beings. Physically, human beings are dwarfs compared with the power of the elements, but they are not dwarfs morally. With enough self-observation this fact is not difficult to discern. Just think how much in us is negative towards others, not to mention our materialistic blindness towards nature, the earth and the cosmos. Yet present-day ecological movements leave our *moral* deficiencies out of account. Pride, ambition, envy, jealousy, greed — often quite unconscious — tend to ruin any objectivity in our soul (it is different toward members of our family). The English saying 'familiarity breeds contempt' describes very aptly the danger of our sliding from positive to negative. Criticism entails a letting go, a falling into darkness and heaviness, especially when we grow older and identify ourselves with our body. Positivity always entails effort, rising to the light against heaviness. If it benefits others, humour is like the rising sun. It is remarkable that any positive appraisal of the other person seems to do them more justice; they seem to extend their abilities and become more available and useful within the social setting in which they are placed. Our surroundings seem to depend very much on how we look upon one another. It seems that if we meet each other with good will and positivity, then our higher faculties are called forth, while with criticism our timidity, fear, and cowardice towards the other call up feelings of worthlessness. At present this negative and positive (if sentimental) flotsam on the river of life is only in its infancy. In future it will increase immeasurably, as will our responsibility for the social organism within which we live.

In the War of All against All, the end of our age is inevitable. But this inevitability is given purpose through communities of goodwill in which a variety of human efforts — artistic, religious, economic, educational — will have to come together so as to create islands in the darkening river. In connection with each other, these islands will constitute the triumph of humanity leading into the future.

BOTTON VILLAGE NEWS, 24 IV 1992

 *references & endnotes*

⮑ *references & endnotes*

Note GA refers to the reference number in the *Gesamtausgabe* (Collected Works) of Rudolf Steiner.

The following anthroposophical publishers are abbreviated thus:
Anthroposophic Press, New York   AP (now SteinerBooks)
Floris Books, Edinburgh   FB
Rudolf Steiner Press, London   RSP

first year

1 Rudolf Steiner. *The Spiritual Beings in the Heavenly Bodies and in the Kingdoms of Nature.* GA136. Steiner Book Centre, Vancouver 1981 (See lecture 8.)

2 Rudolf Steiner. *Mystery of the Universe: The Human Being, Image of Creation.* GA201. RSP 2001 (See lectures 11, 16, 17 April & 15 May 1920.) See also: Rudolf Steiner. *From Beetroot to Buddhism.* GA353. RSP 1999 (See lecture 17 May 1924.)

3 Report of the Committee on Local Authority and Allied Personal Social Services. Frederick Seebohm (chair). HMSO 1968

4 Johann Gotlieb Fichte (1762—1814). Quotation may be from his 1804–05 lectures in Berlin, 'Outline of the Present Age', because in *The Riddles of Philosophy* Steiner says that Fichte reprimanded his age for its egotism in which everyone follows only the path prescribed by his lower desires.

5 Rudolf Steiner. *The Fifth Gospel.* GA148. RSP 1995 (See lecture 18 December 1913.)

6 Rudolf Steiner. *The Challenge of the Times.* GA186. AP 1941 (See lecture 1 December 1918.)

7 Rudolf Steiner. *From Jesus to Christ.* GA131. RSP 1973 (See lectures 7 & 13

October 1911.)
See also lecture: 'Faith, Love, Hope', 2 December 1911. In: Rudolf Steiner. *Love and its Meaning in the World.* GA130. AP 1998

8   Rudolf Steiner. *From Jesus to Christ.* op. cit. (See lecture 7 October 1911.)

9   Rudolf Steiner. *From Jesus to Christ.* op. cit.
See also lecture: 'Faith, Love, Hope'. op. cit.

10   Emil Bock. *The Three Years.* FB 1987 (See chapter 10, section 7.)

11   Rudolf Steiner. *The Gospel of St Mark.* GA139. AP 1986 (See lecture 23 September 1912.)

12   Rudolf Steiner. *The Fifth Gospel.* op. cit. (See lecture 2 October 1913.)

13   Rudolf Steiner. 'The Death of a God and its Fruits in Humanity.' 5 May 1912. In: *The Festivals and Their Meaning.* RSP 1981

14   Rudolf Steiner. *The True Nature of the Second Coming.* GA118. RSP 1961 (See lecture 25 January 1910.)
See also: Rudolf Steiner. *The Christ Impulse and the Development of Ego Consciousness.* GA116. AP 1976 (See lecture 16 August 1902.)
Rudolf Steiner. *Earthly and Cosmic Man.* Garber Communications, NY, 1986 (See lecture 20 May 1912.)

15   Rudolf Steiner. *Study of Man.* GA293. RSP 2004 [*The Foundations of Human Experience.* AP 1996] (See lectures of 23 & 28 August 1919.)

16   Rudolf Steiner. *The Festivals and their Meaning.* op. cit. (See lecture 17 May 1923.)

17   Rudolf Steiner. *The Reappearance of Christ in the Etheric.* GA183. AP 1983.

18   A number of books bring together Rudolf Steiner's work on the twelve senses. See for example:
Karl König. *A Living Physiology.* Camphill Books, Whitby 1999
Albert Soesman. *Our Twelve Senses.* Hawthorn Press, Stroud 1998
Gilbert Childs. *5+7=12 Senses. Rudolf Steiner's Contribution to the Psychology of Perception.* Fire Tree Press, Stroud 1996

19   Thomas J. Weihs. *Children in Need of Special Care.* (2nd ed. Revised A.M. & M.J. Hailey and N.M. Blitz.) Souvenir Press, London 2000

20 Rudolf Steiner. *The Gospel of St John and its Relation to the Other Gospels.* GA112. AP 1982 (See lecture 30 June 1909.)

21 Jonathan Swift. *Gulliver's Travels.* Penguin Books 1994
Padraic Colum. *The King of Ireland's Son.* FB 1978

22 Johann Wolfgang von Goethe. *The Metamorphosis of Plants.* Bio-Dynamic Literature, Rhode Island 1978

23 Jon Madsen. *The New Testament,* FB 1994

24 Rudolf Steiner. *The Challenge of the Times.* op. cit. (See lecture 1 December 1918.)

25 Rudolf Steiner. *Soul Economy and Waldorf Education.* GA303. AP 1986 (See lecture 1 January 1922.)

26 Henrik Ibsen. *Three Plays: Pillars of Society. A Doll's House. Ghosts.* Longman, Harlow 1995

27 Henrik Ibsen. *Hedda Gabbler.* Samuel French, London 1989

28 Rudolf Steiner. 'The Portal of Initiation'. In: *Four Mystery Dramas.* GA14. RSP 1982

29 Rudolf Steiner. 'The Guardian of the Threshold'. In: *Four Mystery Dramas.* op. cit. (See scene 9)

30 Reference is probably to: Rudolf Steiner. *Michaelmas and the Soul-Forces of Man.* GA223. AP 1982 (See lecture 1 October 1922.)

31 Rudolf Steiner. *Guidance in Esoteric Training.* GA42/245. RSP 1972
For a modern treatment of the auxiliary exercises see:
Florin Lowndes. *Enlivening the Chakra of the Heart.* RSP 1998

32 Johann Wolfgang von Goethe. *Wilhelm Meister.* John Calder, London 1981 (See 'Years of Travel', Books 1–3.)

33 Rudolf Steiner. *Karmic Relationships. Esoteric Studies.* Vol IV. GA238. RSP 1997 (See lecture 'The Last Address' 28 September 1924.)

34 Rudolf Steiner. *From Jesus to Christ.* op. cit. (See lectures 7 and 13 October 1911.
See also: Rudolf Steiner. 'Faith, Love, Hope'. op. cit.

35 Hans Christian Andersen. *Fairy Tales.* Oxford University Press, 1997

36 Rudolf Steiner. *Life between Death and Rebirth.* GA140. AP 1968 (See lecture 18 November 1912.)

37 Rudolf Steiner. *The Destinies of Individuals and of Nations.* GA157. RSP 1986 (See lectures 31 October & 28 November 1914.)
See also: Rudolf Steiner. *The Karma of Untruthfulness.* Vol. I. GA173. RSP 1988 (See lectures of 4–31 December 1916.)
Rudolf Steiner. *The Book of Revelation and the Work of the Priest.* GA346. RSP 1998. (See lecture 12 September 1924.)
T.H. Meyer. (ed.) *Light for the New Millennium.* Rudolf Steiner's Association with Helmuth and Eliza von Moltke. Letters, Documents and After-Death Communications. RSP 1997

38 Rudolf Steiner. *The Four Seasons and the Archangels.* GA229. RSP 1984

39 Rudolf Steiner. *The True Nature of the Second Coming.* op. cit. (See lecture 25 January 1910.)
Rudolf Steiner. *The Christ Impulse and Ego Consciousness.* op. cit. (See lecture 16 August 1902.)
Rudolf Steiner. *Earthly and Cosmic Man.* op. cit. (See 20 May 1912.)

40 Rudolf Steiner. *Michaelmas and the Soul-Forces of Man.* op. cit.

second year

1 Wolfram von Eschenbach. *Parzival: A Romance of the Middle Ages.* Vintage Books, NY 1961 (See Book XVI.)

2 Rudolf Steiner. *Calendar of the Soul.* RSP 1970 (NB. Various translations. Peter Roth used 'disenchanted' for 'conjured'.)

3 Rudolf Steiner. *World Economy.* GA340. RSP 1977 (See lecture 6 August 1922.)

4 Rudolf Steiner. *Anthroposophical Leading Thoughts.* GA26. RSP 1973 (See Leading Thought 142 and the essay of 4 January 1925.)

5 Johann Wolfgang von Goethe. *Faust.* (trans) George Madison Priest. Alfred A. Knopf, NY 1941 (Alternatively, Oxford University Press, 1969)

6 Rudolf Steiner. *The Philosophy of Freedom.* op. cit.

7 Margarita Woloschin. *Die Grüne Schlange.* Verlag Freies Geistesleben, Stuttgart 1982

8 Rudolf Steiner. *The Influence of Spiritual Beings Upon Man.* GA102. AP 1961 (See lecture 20 April 1908.)

9 Johann Valentin Andreae. *The Chymical Wedding of Christian Rosenkreutz Anno 1459.* Minerva Books, London.
See also: Paul M. Allen. *A Christian Rosenkreutz Anthology.* Garber Communications, NY 1996
Margaret Bennell & Isabel Wyatt. *A Commentary on the Chymical Wedding of Christian Rosenkreutz.* Temple Lodge, London 1989
Ehrenfried Pfeiffer. *The Chymical Wedding of Christian Rosenkreutz.* Mercury Press, NY 1947
Rudolf Steiner. *The Secret Stream. Christian Rosenkreutz and Rosicrucianism.* AP, 2000
Hans van der Stok. *Contemplations on the Chymical Wedding of Christian Rosenkreutz.* Camphill Press, Whitby 1981

10 Rudolf Steiner. *Calendar of the Soul.* RSP 1970

11 Rudolf Steiner. *The Philosophy of Freedom.* GA4. RSP 1999

12 Rudolf Steiner. *Harmony of the Creative Word.* GA230. RSP, London 2001 (See lecture 26 October 1923.)

13 Rudolf Steiner. *Building Stones for an Understanding of the Mystery of Golgotha.* GA175. RSP 1972 (See lecture 24 April 1917.)

14 Hermann Girke. *Franz Löffler. Ein Leben für Anthroposophie und heilende Erziehung im Zeitenschicksal.* Verlag am Goetheanum, Dornach 1995 (See p 71: a talk with Rudolf Steiner on 6 July 1924.)

15 Karl König. *Festival Plays.* Camphill Press, Whitby 1984

16 A.C. Harwood. (trans.) *Christmas Plays from Oberufer.* RSP 2007

17 Rudolf Steiner. *Love and its Meaning in the World.* GA130. AP 1998 (See lecture: 'Faith, Love, Hope', 2 December 1911.)

18 Rudolf Steiner. *The Gospel of St John.* GA103. AP 1973 (See 26 May 1908.)

19 Hermann Grimm (1828-1901). 'Das Leben Raffaels' (1872), 'Raphael als Weltmacht'. In: *Fragments*. Vol. II. See also: Rudolf Steiner. *The Gospel of St Mark*. op. cit. (See 17 September 1912.)

20 Rudolf Steiner. *The Gospel of St Mark*. op. cit. (See 22 September 1912.)

21 Johann Wolfgang von Goethe. *The Fairy Tale of the Green Snake and the Beautiful Lily*. (trans. Thomas Carlyle) FB 1979.

    See also: Paul Marshall Allen & Joan deRis Allen. *The Time is at Hand!* The Rosicrucian Nature of Goethe's Fairy Tale of the Green Snake and the Beautiful Lily and the Mystery Dramas of Rudolf Steiner. AP 1995

22 Rudolf Steiner. *Founding a Science of the Spirit*. GA95. RSP 2007 [Formerly *At the Gates of Spiritual Science*. RSP 1986] (See lecture 3 September 1906.)

23 Rudolf Steiner. *The Work of the Angels in Man's Astral Body*. GA182. In: *Angels. Selected Lectures*. RSP 1996 (See lecture 9 October 1918.)

24 See Rudolf Steiner. *The Fifth Gospel*. op. cit. (See lectures of 6 October & 18 December 1913)

25 Rudolf Steiner. *The Spiritual Hierarchies and the Physical World. Reality and Illusion*. GA110/132. AP 1996 (See lectures 7 & 14 November 1911.)

26 Additional material: Thomas Aquinas. *Summa Theologica*. Resources for Christian Living, USA 2000

27 Jean Jacques Rousseau. *Emile*. Penguin Books 1991

28 First version of the poem 'Patmos' is in the cycle *Vaterländische Gesänge* by Friedrich Hölderlin:

29 Rudolf Steiner. *The Driving Force of Spiritual Powers in World History*. GA222. Steiner Book Centre, Toronto 1972 (See lecture 23 March 1923.)

30 Carlo Pietzner. *Who was Kaspar Hauser?* FB 1983 (Contains the play '...and from the night, Kaspar')

31 Rudolf Steiner. *From Elephants to Einstein*. GA352. RSP 1998 (See lecture 2 February 1924.)

32 Rudolf Steiner. *The True Nature of the Second Coming*. op. cit. (See lecture 25 January 1910.)

Rudolf Steiner. *The Christ Impulse and Ego Consciousness*. GA116. AP 1976 (See lecture 16 August 1902.)
Rudolf Steiner. *Earthly and Cosmic Man*. op. cit. (See lecture 20 May 1912.)

33 Rudolf Steiner. *The Archangel Michael. His Mission and Ours*. GA194. AP 1994 (See lecture 21 November 1919.)
Rudolf Steiner. *Building Stones for an Understanding of the Mystery of Golgotha*. op. cit. (See lecture 27 March 1917.)

34 Rudolf Steiner. *Verses and Meditations*. (trans. George & Mary Adams.) RSP 1979 (See p. 97.)

35 Rudolf Steiner. *The Calendar of the Soul*. (trans. Ruth and Hans Pusch.) AP 1982

36 Rudolf Steiner. *The Destinies of Individuals and of Nations*. op. cit. (See lecture 16 March 1915.)

37 Rudolf Steiner. *The Four Seasons and the Archangels*. op. cit. (See lecture 12 October 1923.)

38 Rudolf Steiner. *Das Ewige in der Menschenseele. Unsterblichkeit und Freiheit*. GA67. Rudolf Steiner Verlag 1992 (See lecture 14 March 1918.)
Rudolf Steiner. *Die Ergänzung heutiger Wissenschaften durch Anthroposophie*. GA73. (See lecture 7 November 1917.)

39 Fritjof Capra. *The Tao of Physics. An Exploration of the Parallels between Modern Physics and Eastern Mysticism*. Harper Collins, London 1975

40 ibid. (p 301)

41 ibid. (p 292)

42 ibid. (pp 258–9)

43 Rudolf Steiner. *From Symptom to Reality in Modern History*. GA185. RSP 1976 (See lecture 26 October 1918.)

44 Rudolf Steiner. *Guidance in Esoteric Training*. op. cit.

45 Rudolf Steiner. 'The Portal of Initiation.' In: *Four Mystery Dramas*. op. cit.

46 Rudolf Steiner. *Man and the World of Stars. The Spiritual Communion of*

Mankind. GA326. AP 1982 (See lecture 17 December 1922.)

47 Johann Wolfgang von Goethe. *The Metamorphosis of Plants.* op. cit.
See also: Rudolf Steiner. *Goethe's World View.* GA6. Mercury Press, NY 1985
Rudolf Steiner. *Goethean Science.* GA1. Mercury Press, NY 1988
Adolf Portmann. *Essays in Philosophical Zoology.* Edwin Mellen Press, NY 1991

48 Peter Tradowsky. *Kaspar Hauser: The Struggle for the Spirit.* (trans. John M. Wood.) Temple Lodge, London 1997 (See pp 97–98.)

49 Rudolf Steiner. *The Destinies of Individuals and of Nations.* op. cit. (See lecture 16 March 1915.)

50 Rudolf Steiner. *Aspects of Human Evolution.* GA176. AP 1987. (See lecture 10 July 1917.)

51 For an English rendering of this verse see: Peter Tradowsky. *Kaspar Hauser: The Struggle for the Spirit.* op. cit.

52 Rudolf Steiner. *The Philosophy of Freedom.* op. cit.

53 Paul M. Allen. *A Christian Rosenkreutz Anthology.* op. cit.

54 Rudolf Steiner. *The Foundations of Human Experience.* op. cit. (See lecture 1 September 1919.)

55 Rudolf Steiner. *Eurythmy as Visible Speech.* GA279. Anastasi, Hereford 2005. (See lecture 7 July 1924.)

56 Rudolf Steiner. *Christ and the Spiritual World and the Search for the Holy Grail.* GA149 RSP 1963 (See lectures of 29–30 December 1913.)

57 Johann Wolfgang von Goethe. *The Fairy Tale of the Green Snake and the Beautiful Lily.* op. cit.

58 ibid.

59 Rudolf Steiner. *The Karma of Vocation.* GA172. AP 1984. (See lecture 5 November 1916.)

60 Rudolf Steiner. *Goethean Science.* op. cit. (See chapter 2 'How Goethe's Theory of Metamorphosis Arose'.)

61 Rudolf Steiner. *Goethe's World View.* op. cit. (See chapters 2 & 3 'Goethe's View on the Nature and Development of Living Beings: Metamorphosis' and 'The Contemplation of the World of Colors'.)

62 Quoted by Friedrich von Müller in a lecture 'Goethe in seiner praktischen Wirksamkeit' given at Academie gemeinnütziger Wissenschaften, Erfurth. 12 September 1832.

63 Rudolf Steiner. *World Economy.* op. cit.

64 Rudolf Steiner. *An Outline of Esoteric Science.* GA13. AP 1997
Rudolf Steiner. *Cosmic Memory.* GA11. AP 1987

65 Johann Wolfgang von Goethe. *Maximen und Reflexionen über Kunst.*

66 Friedrich Schiller: 'Die Künstler' (1789)

67 Rudolf Steiner. *Goethe's World View.* op. cit. (See section 1, 'Goethe's Place in the Development of Western Thought')

68 Johann Wolfgang von Goethe. *The Metamorphosis of Plants.* op. cit

69 Rudolf Steiner. *The Mission of the Individual Folk Souls.* GA121. RSP 2005 (See lecture 12 June 1910.)

70 Rudolf Steiner. *The Fifth Gospel.* op. cit.

71 Rudolf Steiner. *The Balance in the World and Man. Lucifer and Ahriman.* GA158. Steiner Book Centre, Vancouver 1977 op. cit.
Rudolf Steiner. *The Influences of Lucifer and Ahriman.* GA191/193. AP 1993 English edition contains five lectures of November 1919. op. cit.

72 Albert Camus. *The Outsider.* Penguin Books 1989

73 John Osborne. *Look Back in Anger.* Faber Books, London 1996

74 Rudolf Steiner. *The Archangel Michael: His Mission and Ours.* op. cit. (See lecture 21 November 1919.)

75 John Milton. *Paradise Lost.* Cambridge University Press, 1972–1976.

76 Friedrich Gottlieb Klopstock. 'Messiah'. An epic poem published between 1749–1773.

77 Rudolf Steiner. *The Archangel Michael. His Mission and Ours.* op. cit. (See

lecture 21 November 1919.)

78 George Orwell. *Nineteen Eighty-Four*. Penguin Books 1989

79 Hermann Broch. *The Guiltless*. Quartet Books, London 1990

80 Thomas Mann. *The Magic Mountain*. Mandarin, London 1996

81 Rudolf Steiner. *The Gospel of St Luke*. op. cit.

82 Rudolf Steiner. *The Spiritual Guidance of the Individual and Humanity*. GA15. AP 1992

83 Rudolf Steiner. *The Gospel of St Matthew*. GA123. RSP 1965

84 Rudolf Steiner. *The Occult Significance of the Bhagavad Gita*. GA146. AP 1968 (See lecture 5 June 1913.)

85 Johann Wolfgang von Goethe. *Italian Journey 1786–88*. Penguin Books 1970.

86 Johann Wolfgang von Goethe. *Faust*. op. cit. (See Pt. 2: 'Chorus Mysticus'.

87 Rudolf Steiner. *The Gospel of St Mark*. op. cit. (See lecture 23 September 1912.)

88 Rudolf Steiner. *The Spiritual Hierarchies and the Physical World. Reality and Illusion*. op. cit. (See lecture 31 October 1911.)

89 Jakob Wassermann. *Caspar Hauser: The Enigma of a Century*. FB 1983 (Alternatively, *Caspar Hauser. The Inertia of the Heart*. Penguin Books, 1992)

90 For the Rosicrucian motto see the following:
Rudolf Steiner. *The Inner Nature of Man and Our Life Between Death and Rebirth*. GA153. RSP 1994.
Rudolf Steiner. *The Mystery of the Trinity and the Mission of the Spirit*. GA214. AP 1991 (See lecture 30 July 1922.)
Rudolf Steiner. *The Evolution of Consciousness*. GA227. RSP 1991 (See lecture 27 August 1923.)
Rudolf Steiner. *The Christmas Conference for the Foundation of the General Anthroposophical Society 1923/1924*. AP 1990

91 Rudolf Steiner's comments on Kaspar Hauser are collected in:

Peter Tradowsky. *Kaspar Hauser: The Struggle for the Spirit.* Temple Lodge, London 1997
Terry Boardman. *Kaspar Hauser. Where did he come from?* Wynstones Press, Stourbridge 2006

92 Jakob Wassermann. *Mein Weg als Deutscher und Jude.* Deutsche Taschenbucher Verlag, 1967

third year

1 Rudolf Steiner. *The Gospel of St Luke.* op. cit. (See lecture 16 September 1909.)

2 Rudolf Steiner. *The Last Address.* op. cit.
Emil Bock. *Caesar and Apostles.* FB 1998. (See chap. 10.)

3 For identification of the name Hagar with the word 'stone', see Rudolf Steiner. *Deeper Secrets of Human Development in the Light of the Gospel of Matthew.* GA117. RSP 1957 (See lecture 23 November 1909.)

4 Antoine de Saint-Exupéry. *Wartime Writings 1939–1944.* Harcourt 1988 (See Letter to General X, June 1943)

5 Rudolf Steiner. *The Four Seasons and the Archangels.* op. cit.

6 Rudolf Steiner. *The Christ Impulse and the Development of Ego Consciousness.* op. cit. (See lectures 2 & 8 May 1910.)
See also: Rudolf Steiner. *Earthly and Cosmic Man.* op. cit. (See lecture 14 May 1912.)

7 Rudolf Steiner. *Love and its Meaning in the World.* op. cit. (See lecture 2 December 1911.)

8 Rudolf Steiner. *The Cycle of the Year as Breathing-Process of the Earth.* GA223. AP 1984 (See lecture 2 April 1923.)

9 Rudolf Steiner. *The Gospel of St Matthew.* op. cit. (See 6 September 1910.)

10 Rudolf Steiner. *The Occult Significance of the Bhagavad Gita.* op. cit. (See lecture 3 June 1913.)

11 Rudolf Steiner. *The Gospel of St Matthew.* op. cit. (See 7 September 1910.)

12 Rudolf Steiner. *Universe, Earth and Man.* GA105. RSP 1987 (See lecture 4 August 1908.)

13 Emil Bock. *The Childhood of Jesus.* FB 1997. (See chapter 11.)
David Ovason. *The Two Children.* Random House, London 2001 (See chapter 2.)

14 Rudolf Steiner. *Mystery of the Universe: The Human Being, Image of Creation.* op. cit. (See lecture 15 May 1920.)

15 Rudolf Steiner. *The Spiritual Hierarchies and the Physical World. Reality and Illusion.* op. cit. (See lecture 31 October 1911.)

16 This article appeared in: *Lebensformen in der sozialtherapeutischen Arbeit.* Freies Geistesleben, Stuttgart 1995 Trans. Margrit Metraux.

17 J.E. Zeylmans van Emmichoven. *Who Was Ita Wegman? A Documentation.* Mercury Press, Chestnut Ridge, NY. (See vol 1: 1876–1925.)

18 Karl König. *In Need of Special Understanding.* Camphill Press, Whitby 1986

19 Johann Wolfgang von Goethe. *The Fairy Tale of the Green Snake and the Beautiful Lily.* op. cit.

20 Schiller. *On the Aesthetic Education of Man in a Series of Letters.* Oxford University Press 1994

21 Rudolf Steiner. *A Western Approach to Reincarnation and Karma.* GA120/125/135/235. AP 1997 (See lecture 21 February 1912.)

22 Rudolf Steiner. *Anthroposophy and the Social Question.* GA34. Mercury Press, NY 1982.

23 ibid.

24 Rudolf Steiner. *A Western Approach to Reincarnation and Karma.* op. cit.

25 The 'Fairy Tale of Eros and Fable' is contained in: Novalis. *Henry von Ofterdingen.* Frederick Ungar, NY 1964
See also: Baruch Luke Urieli. *Eros and Fable: Novalis' Fairy Tale of Human and Earth Evolution.* Camphill Books, Whitby 1999. And: *The Novalis Fairy Tale: Human Encounter becomes Earth Evolution.* Camphill Books,

Whitby 2001

26 Rudolf Steiner. *Occult History*. GA126. RSP 1982 (See lecture 1 January 1911.)
Rudolf Steiner. *Earthly and Cosmic Man*. op. cit. (See lecture 2 May 1912.)

27 Rudolf Steiner. *Pre-Earthly Deeds of Christ*. GA152. Steiner Book Centre, Vancouver 1976 (Sec lecture 7 March 1914.)

28 *The legend of the Rood, with The three Maries and The death of Pilate, from the Cornish Miracle Plays*. F.E. Halliday (ed.) Duckworth, London 1955

29 Rudolf Steiner. *The Temple Legend*. GA93. RSP 1985 (See lectures 15, 22, & 29 May and 5 June 1905)
Rudolf Steiner. *The Christmas Thought and the Secret of the Ego*. GA165. Mercury Press, NY 1986 (See lecture 19 December 1915)

30 Emil Bock. *Kings and Prophets*. FB 1989 (See chapter 12: 'The Names of Solomon.')

31 Rudolf Steiner. *The Lord's Prayer*. GA96. RSP 2007

32 Rudolf Steiner. *The Gospel of St Mark*. op. cit. (See lecture 23 September 1912.)

33 Will and Ariel Durant. *The Story of Civilization VII: The Age of Reason Begins*. Simon and Schuster, NY 1961. (See pp 551–558.)

34 Paul M. Allen. *A Christian Rosenkreutz Anthology*. op. cit. lists the following: *Amphitheatre of Eternal Wisdom* (1609) by Heinrich Khunrath; *The Pleasure Garden of Chymistry* (1624) by Daniel Stolcius; *The Rosicrucian Brotherhood* (1629) by Robert Fludd; *The Parabola, a Golden Tractate* (c. 1630) by Hinricus Madathanus; *The Holy Mountain, a Rosicrucian Allegory* (1651) by Thomas Vaughan; *The Fame and Confession of the Fraternity of the Rose Cross* (1652) (trans.) Thomas Vaughan, and *The Hermetic Romance, The Chymical Wedding* (1690) (trans.) Ezechiel Foxcroft.

35 Rudolf Steiner. *Social and Political Science. An Introductory Reader*. GA24. RSP 2003

36 Rudolf Steiner. *Spiritual Science as a Foundation for Social Forms*. GA199. AP 1986

37 Sergei O. Prokofieff. *The Spiritual Origins of Eastern Europe and the Future Mysteries of the Holy Grail.* Temple Lodge, London 1993 (See section 2 of the Appendices.)

38 Rudolf Steiner. *The Earth as Being with Life, Soul and Spirit.* GA181. In: *The Golden Blade* 1971

39 Maxim Gorky. *Autobiography: Childhood. In the World. My Universities.* Citadel Press, USA 1973

40 Rudolf Steiner. *Goethe's Secret Revelation and the Riddle of Faust.* GA57. RSP 1932. (See lecture 24 October 1908)

41 C.P. Snow. *The Corridors of Power.* Penguin Books 1966

42 Rudolf Steiner. *Esoteric Christianity and the Mission of Christian Rosenkreutz.* GA130. RSP 2001 (See lecture 18 December 1912.)
Rudolf Steiner. *Between Death and Rebirth.* GA141. RSP 1975 (See lecture 22 December 1912.)
Rudolf Steiner. *Earthly and Cosmic Man.* Garber Communications, NY 1986 (See lecture 20 June 1912.)

43 Rudolf Steiner. *Man's Being, His Destiny and World Evolution.* GA226. AP 1966 (NB. This statement is not in the English translation.)
See: Rudolf Steiner. 'Self-Consciousness: The Spiritual Human Being'. Garber Communications, NY 1986 (See lecture 4 December 1921.)

44 Rudolf Steiner. *The Christmas Conference for the Foundation of the General Anthroposophical Society 1923/1924.* GA260. AP 1990

45 Rudolf Steiner. *The Mission of the Individual Folk Souls.* GA121. RSP 2005

46 Rudolf Steiner. *The Fifth Gospel.* op. cit.

47 References by Rudolf Steiner to all twelve colours seem only to appear in relation to the zodiac. See, for example, his *Entstehung und Entwicklung der Eurythmie* (pub. Rudolf Steiner Verlag, Dornach), in which Marie Steiner sketches the twelve colours.
See also: Rudolf Steiner. *Beleuchtungs und Kostümenangaben für die Laut-Eurythmie.* Band III. Rudolf Steiner Nachlaßverwaltung, Dornach 1982 (See pp 418–421.) And: Annemarie Dubach-Donath. *Entstehung der Laute in Makrokosmos.* Pt III. Philosophisch-Anthroposophischer Verlag am

Goetheanum 1974 (See pp 257–258.)
Margot Roessler. *From the Language of the Zodiac 1. The Sun-zodiac-experience.* Fiona Tweedale (trans). Coleg Elidyr, Llandovery.

48 Rudolf Steiner. *Verses and Meditations.* op. cit. (See p 117.) Dedicated by Rudolf Steiner to Edith Maryon in a book on the threefold social order, published in November 1920.

49 Rudolf Steiner. *The Tension Between East and West.* GA83. AP 1963 (See lecture 4 June 1922.)

50 Rudolf Steiner. *Knowledge of the Higher Worlds. How is it Achieved?* op. cit.

51 Rudolf Steiner. *The Archangel Michael. His Mission and Ours.* op. cit. (See lecture 21 November 1919.)
Rudolf Steiner. *Building Stones for an Understanding of the Mystery of Golgotha.* op. cit. (See lecture 27 March 1917.)

52 Rudolf Steiner. *The Gospel of St Mark.* op. cit. (See lecture 21 September 1912.)

53 Iulia de Beausobre. *Flame in the Snow: A Russian Legend.* Constable, London 1945

54 St Wilfrid's eloquence decided the issue in favour of Rome.
See Will Durant. *The Story of Civilization IV: The Age of Faith.* Simon and Schuster, NY 1950 (see p. 534)

55 Rudolf Steiner. *Social and Political Science. An Introductory Reader.* op. cit. (See pp 339–362.)
Rudolf Steiner. *Towards Social Renewal.* op. cit. (See Appendix: To the German People and the Civilized World.)

56 Rudolf Steiner. *The Gospel of St Matthew.* op. cit. (See lecture 10 September 1910.)

57 Rudolf Steiner. *The Philosophy of Freedom.* op. cit.

58 Karl König. *A Living Physiology.* op. cit.
Michael Luxford. (ed.) *The Higher Senses and the Seven Life Processes.* Camphill Books, Whitby 1996

59 Johann Wolfgang von Goethe. *Theory of Colours.* M.I.T. Press,

Massachusetts 1970

60 Karl König spoke of Nietzsche in his lecture on Kali Yuga (29th September 1959) and in lectures on 'The Life and Work of Rudolf Steiner'. (Whitsun 1963). Unpublished typescripts.
See also: Rudolf Steiner. *Friedrich Nietzsche — Fighter for Freedom*. Rudolf Steiner Publications, NY 1960

61 Rudolf Steiner. *Riddles of the Soul*. GA21. Mercury Press, NY 1997

62 Rudolf Steiner. 'Esoteric Prelude to the Exoteric Treatment of Three-folding'. Unpublished MS available from Rudolf Steiner Library, London. (See lecture 23 April 1919.)

63 Rudolf Steiner. *The Challenge of the Times*. op. cit. (See lecture 29 November 1918.)

64 Friedrich Schiller. 'Das Höchste' (1795) from the collection *Gedanken-gedichte*:

65 Rudolf Steiner. *Harmony of the Creative Word*. op. cit. (See lecture 26 October 1923.)

66 Rudolf Steiner. *Pastoral Medicine*. GA318. AP 1987 (See lecture 14 September 1924.)

67 Rudolf Steiner. *Freud, Jung and Spiritual Psychology*. GA178/143/205. AP 2001

68 Rudolf Steiner. 'The Guardian of the Threshold'. In: *Four Mystery Dramas*. op. cit. (See scene 9.)

69 Rudolf Steiner. 'The Soul's Awakening'. In: *Four Mystery Dramas*. op. cit. (cf. trans. by M. Burton & A. Locher. Temple Lodge, London.)

70 Rudolf Steiner. *The Christmas Conference for the Foundation of the General Anthroposophical Society 1923/1924*. op. cit. (See 25th December 1923.)
Rudolf Grosse. *The Living Being Anthroposophia*. Steiner Book Centre, Vancouver 1986
Sergei O. Prokofieff. *The Heavenly Being Sophia and the Being Anthropo-sophia*. Temple Lodge, London 1996
Robert Powell. *The Most Holy Trinisophia and the New Revelation of the*

Divine Feminine. AP 2000
Thomas Schipflinger. *Sophia-Maria: A Holistic Vision of Creation.* Samuel Weiser, Maine 1998

71 Friedrich Schiller. 'Die Künstler' (1789)

72 Rudolf Steiner: *Anthroposophical Leading Thoughts.* op. cit. (See no. 105, 'The Michael Mystery'.)

73 Alexander Blok. *Verses About the Beautiful Lady.* 1904.

74 Rudolf Steiner. *Ancient Myths.* GA180. RSP 1971 (See lecture 6 January 1918.)
See also: Plutarch's *De Iside et Osiride,* in which he refers to an inscription on a statue of Pallas Athene which he renders: 'I am everything which has and which is and which shall be, and there hath never been any who hath uncovered my veil.' Elsewhere he says that the Egyptians often called Isis by the name of Athene, which signifies, 'I have come from myself.' (Gerald Eedle in *Anthroposophical Quarterly,* Winter 1974.)

75 Rudolf Steiner. *The Search for the New Isis: The Divine Sophia.* GA202. Mercury Press, NY 1983
See also: Rudolf Steiner. *Ancient Myths and the New Isis Mystery.* GA180. AP 1994 (See lecture 24 December 1920.)

76 Novalis. *The Novices of Saïs.* (trans. Ralph Manheim.) Archipelago Books, NY 2005

77 Rudolf Steiner. *True and False Paths in Spiritual Investigation.* GA243. RSP 1969 (See lecture 22 August 1924.)

78 For Odin, Vili and Ve, see Kevin Crossley-Holland. *The Norse Myths.* Penguin Books 1982
See also: Rudolf Steiner. *The Mission of Folk-Souls.* op. cit.

79 Rudolf Steiner. *Goethe's World View.* op. cit.
Rudolf Steiner. *Goethean Science.* op. cit.

80 Rudolf Steiner. *Pre-Earthly Deeds of Christ.* op. cit.

81 Rudolf Steiner. *Anthroposophical Leading Thoughts.* GA26. RSP 1973 (See Leading Thought 106, 19 October 1924.)

82 Rudolf Steiner. *Wonders of the World, Ordeals of the Soul, Revelations of the Spirit.* GA129. RSP 1963 (See lecture 18 August 1911.)

83 Rudolf Steiner. *Anthroposophical Leading Thoughts.* op. cit. (See 23 November 1924.)

84 Rudolf Steiner. *Guidance in Esoteric Training.* op. cit.
    See also: Florin Lowndes. *Enlivening the Chakra of the Heart.* op. cit.

85 Rudolf Steiner. *The Apocalypse of St John.* GA104. RSP 1977 (See lecture 30 June 1908.)

acknowledgements

The encouragement given me throughout the long preparation of this book is just too broad for me to thank everyone individually. But the help of some people was crucial in bringing this project to fruition, and I would like to acknowledge my gratitude to them particularly.

Firstly, and pre-eminently, the greatest debt of gratitude must be to Ann Richmond, Peter's loyal secretary who took shorthand notes verbatim as he dictated often complex thoughts in his own, colourful language. She typed almost all his English articles and essays and prepared them for publication in both *Botton Mirror, Village News* and other periodicals. Without her selfless skill and dedication over many, many years, the raw material for this book might not have been available. My thanks also go to Lillian Stroud who typed every article onto a word processor; a major undertaking.

This book owes its conception to Vivian Griffiths who initiated the project by extracting Peter Roth's articles and essays from the *Botton Village News/ Mirror* archive stretching back to 1959. He and I have not only spent many hours gardening together (and numerous administrative meetings), we have also enjoyed long discussions on how to render Peter's thoughts — brilliantly conceived yet with a quaintly Austrian inflection — into the Queen's English.

Christof-Andreas Lindenberg knew Peter since the early days of Camphill in Scotland, and therefore I am very grateful for his biographical sketch. It provides a glimpse into the background of one of those unique individuals whose destiny was interwoven with the community endeavour that we know today as Camphill from its precarious advent in Vienna.

I am greatly indebted to the following friends for their invaluable editorial work. Christopher Kidman, who painstakingly edited over one third of the book between eurythmy lessons, choir rehearsals and other projects; Brian Rée, my former Botton Bookshop colleague, who made numerous corrections and offered many suggestions; Bob Clay who made perceptive amendments and improvements; Henning Hansmann who worked on the manuscript each day over the last few months of his life, and Maureen Ramsay (to whom Henning's uncompleted work was passed by his wife Sigrid), whose literary experience and knowledge of the Christian Community proved invaluable in editing the entire book.

My thanks also to Margrit Metraux and Anna Smith for their extensive translation work, and to Barbara Roos and Georg Schad for help with some German words and expressions.

I am grateful to Michael Luxford who interpreted many of Peter's obscure references, particularly those on Egypt, and gave editorial suggestions and moral support throughout. Also to Brian Dawes and Wanda Paluch who edited some of the scientific essays, and to Charles Lawrie who gave valuable advice and helped with some Steiner references. Johannes Surkamp gave his comments on European political history, and Dr David Gordon commented on psychoanalysis.

Thanks also to Gunhild Muschenheim, Information Officer for the Library of the Goethe Institute in London, who provided the sources of most quotations by Goethe, Hölderlin and Schelling, as well as biographical information on several personalities.

So many people gave me their time and advice on numerous occasions, but the following should be particularly thanked: Joan Allen, Friedwart Bock, Charles Bamford, Gerda Blok, Peter Button, Guy Cornish, Gilles Droulers, Russell Evans, Marianne Gorge, Hartmut von Jeetze, Hartmut Junge, Vivienne Klockner, Michel Marcadé, Cornelius Pietzner, Patricia Pohl, Roy Sadler, Sally Schad, Deborah Ravetz and Wolfram Wacker.

I could not have inserted Peter's essays on the Gospel readings without the help of Hans-Werner Schroeder's little booklet *The Gospel Readings in the Cycle of the Year*.*

Without the generosity of Botton Village and the Sheiling Community near Ringwood, I would have had no home from which to undertake this huge task. It has been my great privilege to live in them both for many years, and be helped by them when in need. For this I am more grateful than I can express.

Last, but by no means least, I would like to thank Dr Simon Roth who was at first reluctant to see his father's Austrian-Camphill-English made public in book form, but after reading a partially edited manuscript gave his wholehearted support and made further helpful suggestions. Finally, it should be noted that before his death Peter was fully aware of this project and gave it his blessing.

It has truly been a privilege and a joy to produce this book.

Wain Farrants

---

* Floris Books 1991

sources and permissions

I am grateful to the following for permission to include their original material in this volume:

The Cresset, published quarterly in the early days of Camphill in Aberdeen.

The Anthroposophical Society in Great Britain for permission to reprint articles from *Anthroposophical Quarterly* and *Anthroposophical Review*.

Botton Village News and *Botton Mirror*, all their editors (too numerous to remember), their contributors and loyal readers.

Camphill Correspondence, bi-monthly journal of the Camphill Movement.

The Threshing Floor, journal of the Movement for Religious Renewal.